INDIAN NATIONAL ARMY
A Documentary Study

INDIAN NATIONAL ARMY
A Documentary Study
(In 5 Volumes)

Volume-I

(1941-1942)

T.R. SAREEN

GYAN PUBLISHING HOUSE
NEW DELHI-110002

Indian National Army—A Documentary Study

Rs. 4500 (Set)

ISBN: 81-212-0833-5 (Set)
ISBN: 81-212-0844-0 (Vol. 1)

Published in 2004 in India by
Gyan Publishsing House
5, Ansari Road, Darya Ganj, New Delhi-110002
Phones : 23282060, 23261060, Fax : 011-23285914
E-mail : gyanbook@vsnl.com
Website : http://www.gyanbooks.com

Laser Typesetting at : Shree Vaishnavi Creations, Delhi
Printed at : Chawla Offset Press, Delhi

To

Raghav, Rachan and Sumeet

List of Documents

Appendix-I

Appendix-II

Appendix-III

Appendix-IV

General Introdution

The history of India's struggle for freedom was unique in the sense that it was conducted on two fronts, one inside the country which believed in non-violent means as propagated by Gandhiji, and the other through the efforts of Indian nationalists abroad, who wanted to wrest freedom from Britain by an armed revolution. In their bid to overthrow the British they sought help from many foreign powers. They joined hands with Germany during the First World War, and forged an alliance with international communism after the Russian Revolution for the same purpose. The objective was the same when they collaborated openly with Japan during World War II. Their alliance with Japan culminated in the formation of the Indian National Army (I.N.A).

No doubt, the INA itself was defeated alongwith Japan, but even in its defeat, as Nehru says, it became a symbol of India's fighting for independence. The very idea of an Indian army founded and commanded by an Indian of unquestionable patriotism was enough to evoke enthusiasm from an unarmed people long used to watching the display of British military might. The INA represented the last attempt of the Indian people to fight together for the liberation of a united India. Even Gandhiji, not a very sympathetic critic of the ideology of the INA, admitted that :

"Though the INA failed in their immediate objective they have a lot to their credit of which they might well be proud. The greatest of these was to gather together under one banner men from all the religions and races of India and to infuse in them the spirit of solidarity and oneness to the utter exclusion of all communal or parochial sentiment."[1]

The formation of the INA was neither abrupt nor entirely the handiwork of the Japanese. Indian revolutionary nationalists had been carrying on their anti-British propaganda from Japan even before the First World War. At that time Japan was an ally of England and could not therefore openly express sympathy for Indian nationalist aspirations, nevertheless, it unofficially supported and helped Indian revolutionaries instead of persecuting them to oblige Britain, as Siam and the U.S.A. had done. The anti-British activities of Barkatullah, Lala Lajpat Rai, Rash Behari Bose, H. L. Gupta, Kesho Ram Sabarwal and many others were not only tolerated but also given considerable encouragement by many Japanese leaders. Japanese politicians like Count Okuma, Inaki and Toyama Mitsuru, the hero of the Black Dragon Society, defended the Indians and impressed upon the Government of Japan that it should ignore the repeated British demand for the extradition of two important Indian revolutionaries, Rash Behari Bose and H.L. Gupta.

Even after the First World War, for a few years some Japanese leaders were still not very enthusiastic about the question of Indian freedom. As Matsumoto, former Attache in the Japanese embassy in London says, "the moderates in Japan were eager to maintain good relations with Britain and pleaded caution on the question of Japanese interference in Indian affairs; in view of British sentiments on the subject of Indians in Japan, the choice was between friendship with Britain and with a handful of Indian revolutionaries."[2]

The policy changed on the eve of World War II, when active cooperation began between the Indian nationalists and the Japanese. The credit for this cooperation in East Asia and for the initial formation of the INA goes to Sardar Pritam Singh, General Mohan Singh, Mohammad Akram and the Japanese intelligence officer, Major Iwaichi Fujiwara. The Indian groups in Japan under Rash Behari Bose, Anand Mohan Sahay and Raja Mahendra Pratap had been watching the deteriorating relations of Japan with Britain and the U.S.A. and hoped that Japan's success in the conflict might help the struggle for India's freedom. In fact, Rash Behari Bose had approached the Japanese Imperial General Headquarters for help in the event of War with Britain. His views on collaboration were listened to, but no promise was made. Independent of the Indian nationalists in Tokyo, however, the Japanese high command decided to encourage other Indian groups in East Asia.[3]

The Indian community in East Asia was quite strong numerically and economically and the Japanese were particularly interested in forging links with them. The Japanese had two basic aims in view while cultivating an alliance with the Indians. First, their cooperation was essential in the event of an Anglo-Japanese war, since neither the local population nor the Chinese could be trusted. Secondly, Indians could provide valuable information about the British Indian troops stationed on the Thai-Malaya border. The task of negotiating with Indian groups was assignend to Fujiwara and Colonel Tamura, the Japanese Military Attache at Bangkok, who used the assurance of all-out Japanese help to the cause of Indian independence in order to win over the Indian nationalist groups in Thailand and Malaya.

During the negotiations the idea of the formation of a volunteer force for the liberation of India from among the Indian prisoners of war was mooted. The idea was discussed between Pritam Singh, Baba Amar Singh, Major Fujiwara and Colonel Tamura, and some sort of agreement was reached even before the Pacific War. Sardar Pritam Singh and Baba Amar Singh, were former members of the Ghadr Party and had been operating in Thailand. They had formed an Independence League of India and were friendly with the Indian troops. Both parties came to an agreement to collaborate with each other. It was agreed that Pritam Singh's organisation would undertake certain activities as soon as war broke out between England and Japan; it would march with the Japanese army and carry out propaganda among Indian soldiers of the British army. In fact, the ground under the feet of British power was to be cut by shaking the loyalty of British Indian soldiers in Malaya; if possible they were to be won over and reemployed against the British.[4]

The Pacific War broke out in December 1941. Japan smashed her way to Java, Malaya and Burma right up to the eastern frontier of India. With the defeat of the British, the first batch of the Indian army units under Captain Mohan Singh surrendered to the Japanese. As arranged earlier, they were given most cordial treatment by Sardar Pritam Singh and Fujiwara Kikan— a liaison agency under Fujiwara. By his seeming sincerity, Fujiwara inspired Mohan Singh with the idea of liberating India with Japanese assistance. Mohan Singh pondered over the idea and its implications for several days and then, as if in a mystical revelation, grasped the significance of the suggestion and the urgency of his mission. He agreed to organise the Indian army units being abandoned by the British into a well-knit Indian National Army.[5] Initially, the idea of the formation of the INA was not, however, fully supported by the Japanese military administration in East Asia.

They reluctantly agreed to its formation but allotted it the limited role of controlling Indian prisoners of war and maintaining law and order in some territories under their occupation; they looked at it as a valuable instrument of propaganda or of local policing, rather than as an army of liberation.

Despite this attitude, Mohan Singh proceeded with the formation of the INA, especially after the fall of Singapore when the Japanese handed over to him nearly 45,000 personnel of the Indian army who had surrendered at a ceremony at Ferer Park.[6] Mohan Singh began the conversion of the soldiers of the Indian army into a nationalists army with one important advantage—both officers and soldiers of the British army were in a state of psychological shock and had lost confidence in the leadership of the British. Under Mohan Singh they felt secure and, when a new mission was proposed to them, their response was encouraging. In view of the heterogeneity of the Indian soldiers, it was not an easy task for Mohan Singh to turn them overnight into fighters for freedom, but it goes to his crecdit that he was able to bring about a semblance of unity among them. By the middle 1942, about 40,000 P.O.Ws in all had agreed to join the INA. There was an enthusiastic response for enlistment from Indian civilians also. Lectures were given to the volunteers on the political and economic problems of India, on the lives of the Indian national leaders and Indian efforts for achieving freedom. Men of different faiths were encouraged to live together and eat from the same kitchen and celebrated religious festivals jointly.[7] It was all inspired by the lofty ideals of unity, faith and sacrifice, and every soldier had taken a solemn pledge to sacrifice his all for the honour of India. A nationalist army was ready in the middle of 1942 to launch an attack on the British for the liberation of the Indian people.

At the same time, Rash Behari Bose, on account of his standing with the Japanese, took over the presidentship of the entire movement in East Asia. In coordinating the efforts for India's independence he called two conferences at Tokyo and Bangkok where resolutions were passed to organise the INA and invite Subhas Chandra Bose to East Asia from Germany to lead the movement. Mohan Singh was a man in a hurry and wanted to capitalize on the favourable conditions then prevailing in India. India was in the grip of the Quit India Movement; British military power in the region was at its lowest ebb; and an initiative by the INA might have dealt a serious blow to the British. But for their own reasons, the Japanese postponed the drive towards

India and their Indian nationalist allies started doubting their intentions. British propaganda also played its role and Mohan Singh began to believe that the Japanese wanted to use the Indians as their tools. These doubts led to a crisis towards the end of 1942, particularly because of the failure of Japanese liaison officers to understand the Indian point of view. The officers did not have a definite idea of Japanese policy towards India; consequently, they were unable to cooperate with the Indian nationalists to the satisfaction of the latter.[8]

In this dispute,Rash Behari Bose sided with the Japanese and dismissed Mohan Singh. But the Indian nationalist in East Asis realized that it was not possible to carry on the movement under the leadership of Rash Behari Bose who did not question the wayward policy of the Japanese as boldly as Mohan Singh did. The consequent crisis of leadership was resolved only with the arrival of Subhas Chandra Bose from Berlin; Rash Behari Bose, as a Japanese citizen, had failed to inspire confidence in his comrades.[9]

By the time Subhas Bose was allowed to land in East Asia the war situation had taken a new turn and Axis powers had suffered reverses at many places. Nevertheless, the conception of Indo-Japanese collaboration changed after Subhas assumed command of the INA. He possessed an indomitable will and great organisational ability. While Mohan Singh had thought only of strengthening the INA as a military machine, Subhas had a wider vision of mobilising the entire Indian manpower in East Asia into an irresistable army of liberation and of hurling it against the British in India. After he had been assured full support by the Japanese, he thoroughly re-organised the Indian Independence League and the Indian National Army; thereafter, he formed the Provisional Government of Free India and came to an agreement with the Japanese military authorities with regard to the role of the INA. Subhas convinced the Indians in East Asia of the sincerity of Japan and boosted their morale by dispelling their doubts about the ultimate victory of Indian nationalist forces. He made them realize that Japanese military assistance to the INA against the British was as necessary for the Japanese to ensure the security of their own co-prosperity sphere as it was for the achievemtent of India's independence.

After his arrival in Japan, Subhas met the Japanese premier, Tojo, on 10 June 1943, and again subsequently on 14 June. The latter was highly impressed by his patriotic zeal. Here was an ardent revolutionary whose whole life had been devoted to the cause of India's independence and whose thinking was very close to that of Japan. Naturally, Tojo had no hesitation in conceding his demand for unconditional help to the Indian independence movement. Two days after the meeting, Tojo declared in the Diet that Japan was determined to extend every possible assistance to the Indians to eliminate Anglo-Saxon domination in India and enable the country to achieve full independence. This statement came at a time when the war was not going well for Japan. But Subhas was optimistic; his patriotism and eagerness to liberate India made him oblivious to the changing reality of the war, and he was convinced of the ultimate victory of the Axis powers. The Japanese liaison agency, now known as Hikari Kikan, was placed under Yamamoto, who had known Subhas in Berlin.[10]

Subhas took over the leadership of the movement on 4 July 1943 from Rash Behari Bose and was overwhelmed by the reception he received, He told his audience that he was 'absolutely sure' of their victory, but reminded them that considerable effort and sacrifice were required to achieve the goal. With his magnetic personality and fine oratory, Subhas soon created among his associates an acute awareness of their duty towards their country. Sahay recalls that under Subhas' leadership the officers of the INA regained their self-confidence and the civilian population realized that they had found a leader in whom they could place their trust unreservedly. The Indian merchants all over East Asia began contributing to the Azad Hind Fund and young men started pouring into enroll themselves as volunteers in the INA. The INA was galvanized into life and was publicized openly as 'India's Army of Liberation'; Subhas' fiery speeches inspired it with patriotism and a sense of sacrifice, and he outlined a twofold task for it : 'With the force of arms and at the cost of your blood you will have to win liberty. Then when India is free, you will have to organise the permanent army of free India whose task will be to preserve our liberty for all time'. He further emphasized the need for aid from the Axis powers as, in his view, there was 'nothing wrong if we accept their sympathy or even their help, should we need it'. At the same time, he wanted the Indians in East Asia not to depend entirely on foreign aid and to achieve independence by themselves.[11]

Though Subhas had taken over what Lahiri describes as a'made to order' movement but by putting his body and soul in the task he was able to expand it. His single-minded devotion to the cause of Indian independence did not fail to impress even those Japanese army officers who were still doubtful about his credentials. Both Mohan Singh and Subhas were very conscious of the need to bring about harmony among the different religious groups in the INA and Indian society in East Asia. They achieved remarkable success in bringing the Sikhs, the Muslims and the Hindus into a common brotherhood. But whereas Mohan Singh had conceived of the INA only as a military movement, Subhas widened its scope so as to make it the vanguard of a people's movement in South-East Asia and to raise it into a national campaign for freedom.[12]

Subhas was keen to set up a Provisional Government of Azad Hind and to fully reinforce the INA —of course, with the consent and help of the Japanese government. The Hikari Kikan was hostile to the plan, which was likely to affect its power and importance adversely, but Subhas could visualize that, if the Azad Hind Government was recognized by Tokyo, the INA would have to be recognized as an allied army of an allied government—a goal for which Indians had been striving since 1942. He hoped that the Azad Hind Government would ultimately replace the British government when India became free, but he knew that at that early stage the Provisional Government had symbolic rather than real value. As he explained, it was not 'like a normal peace-time government' and its objective was to conduct the final war against the British and their allies in India. The announcement of the setting up of the Provisional Government of Free India was made by him on 21 October in Singapore[13]. The next day the Provisional Government declared war on Britain.

From the day the Provisional Government was formed, the INA had a will, a purpose and a mission; it was now to fight out India's last war of independence, with the new war cry 'On to Delhi'. The reaction of officials of the Government of India to Subhas' slogan, 'On to Delhi', was mixed. They were no doubt perturbed by developments in East Asia, but had grave doubts about prospects for the movement. A British report on Subhas' activities ridiculed him, suggesting that during his tour of the southern regions under Japanese occupation he had announced his intention of flinging his allegedly well-equipped Indian National Army across the India-Burma frontier before the end of 1943 no less than five times. To deflate the movement, the British presented Subhas as a traitor and spoke of the INA with disdain. Nevertheless, the Commander-in-Chief of the British forces in a secret despatch to the Secretary of State for India was constrained to report that Bose should not be dismissed as 'a mere loquacious tool of the Japanese', for his influence on Indians, both in India and abroad—if not actually on the Indian soldiers—was a factor to be reckoned with.[14] An official analysis of Subhas' position at this time further stated rightly that 'Bose has now finally burned his boats with us by virtue of his association with Germany and Japan, his political future being entirely dependent upon the continued military success of the Japanese and the paralysis of British rule in India by internal revolt.' British officials, however, were convinced that the internal revolt was not possible since public morale and internal security was fairly steady. They believed that his chances of whipping up a major revolt would appear to be small. Had he arrived in East Asia last August or even during Gandhi's fast his prospects would have been much better': naturally Bose's efforts to send agents to precipitate an internal revolution in India were not very successful.[15]

Subhas, however, hoped that the INA would have a tremendous psychological impact on the Indian people and would spark off a revolution inside the country once it stood on Indian soil. Mohan Singh was never given any indication about the role which the INA was to play by the Japanese in their march towards India, but Bose was determined that it should play a significant one in ousting the British, with or without the Japanese army. He believed that strategy rather than military strength would defeat the British. As the Supreme Commander of the INA, he knew that an outright victory against the superior British and American forces was impossible, but he firmly held that armed activity near the borders of India would provoke Indians to rise against the British. Bose's success in making an effective appeal to the patriotism of Indian officers and his powerful leadership, together with the liberty given to unwilling men and officers to leave the INA if they so desired, seemed to have changed the character of the army into a real, revolutionary force. Subhas reorganised the entire structure of the Army. The Directorate of Military Bureau was converted into the headquarters of the Supreme Command. Bhosle was appointed the Chief of Staff. Each unit of the INA was placed under a Divisional Commander. Intensive military training was imparted to them by officers, and Bose himself took a keen interest in raising morale. He revised the pay of the INA ranks, reviewed it straining at every opportunity, improved its rations and made every effort to bind the officers in true commradeship. Lectures were arranged for the soldiers from time to time so that they could understand the significance of the purpose for which the Army had been organised. The lectures were published by the Indian Independence League and distributed among the ranks.

Before the INA could develop into an independent and strong force, it was necessary for Subhas to settle the question of its relationship with the Japanese army. The Anglo-American block had spread word that the INA was a puppet army raised and equipped by the Japanese to serve their own ends. This impression had to be obliterated from the minds of INA soldiers before they could be expected to play their rightful role in the war of India's liberation. Besides British propaganda, even some Japanese army commanders thought that the INA was fit only for intelligence work and could not be relied on in actual fighting. For instance, Field Marshal Count Terauchi,Commander of the Southern Expeditionary Force, told Subhas that in the event of the Japanese advance towards India, the main burdan of fighting would be borne by the Japanese army and the INA would be utilized for propaganda and purpose. This role was not acceptable to Subhas and other INA commanders. The soldiers of the INA, too, did not consider this role adequate. Mohan Singh had raised his voice against the Japanese attitude and been ousted, but Bose was a stalwart, both physically and figuratively, and commanded the respect of the Japanese. He frankly told the Japanese that the only role acceptable to the INA during their advance towards India was that of the vanguard, Indian freedom had to be won by Indians, for the freedom secured through Japanese sacrifice would be worse that slavery. He declared that 'the first drop of bloodshed on Indian soil should be that of a soldier of the INA.[16]

Though Count Terauchi's reaction was not very favourable, the Japanese Chief of Army Staff, General Sugiyama, promised that in the impending Imphal campaign the INA would rank as an allied army under Japanese operational command.After these negotiations, Bose decided to move his headquarters to Rangoon in the first week of 1944, for he thought that Burma was to become the springboard for an attack on India. As the Supreme Commander of the INA, he saw to it that intensive training was given to the soldiers and he took a keen personal interest in each and every soldier. In view of the small size of the INA, it was decided to train the troops in guerilla warfare; they were to be lightly equipped for mobility and penetrate enemy lines. Japanese officers gave INA units guerilla training, including in musketry, bayonet fighting and camouflage work.

Towards the end of 1943, the Allies decided to start a counter-attack against the Japanese. To check this the Commander of the Japanese Southern Army was sounded on 7 January 1944 that 'in order to strengthen the defence of Burma, the G.O.C. Southern Army is to attack the enemy when the conditions become favourable and occupy and consolidate the Imphal area and the strategically important regions in North-east India.'[17]

With the Imphal operation just around the corner, Subhas had a very crucial meeting to discuss joint operations with General Mutuguchi at Maymyo, where a ceremonial photograph was taken. According to an eyewitness, after the photograph session, Bose, smiling from behind his spectacles, said to the General while going into the house. 'This is the first time. I am being photographed with Your Excellency. I hope our next photograph will be at Imphal before long'. The interpreter communicated this to General Mutuguchi, who replied: 'Please wait for about fifty days. I shall fulfil your desire'. Both Bose and Mutuguchi were very optimistic about the outcome of the campaign and the latter believed sincerely that the Imphal campaign would reverse the whole course of Japan's deteriorating war situation everywhere.[18]

The main strategy of the Japanese was to push their defence line from the Chindwin river to a more strategic place in the Indo-Burma frontier mountains in order to capture the Imphal and Kohima areas, which were the main base of the Anglo-American forces, and thus to forestall their design to attack and recapture Burma. To achieve this, the main operations were to be directed towards two sections, namely, the Arakan hills and Imphal. In these operations, the Japanese agreed to align three regiments of the INA with three of their own divisions,—the 15th, 31st and 33rd—comprising more than 100,000 soldiers. Two hundred soldiers of the INA were attached to each of the advancing Japanese units. These soldiers were divided into four groups, with different functions. The first group was to carry on front-line propaganda among British Indian troops; the intelligence group was to collect relevant information; the reserve group was to look after those Indian soldiers expected to surrender to the INA—Japanese forces; and the administrative group was to look after the area occupied by the Japanese army while advancing towards India.[19] As a matter of fact, the strategic planning of the Imphal campaign had a limited objective for both the Japanese and the INA. It was to provide the Japanese with a sure base for the defence of Burma, and for the INA a springboard for a country-wide revolution to oust the British.

The Arakan attack was launched by the 55th Division under Lieutenant-General Hanaya on 4 February 1944; the INA unit of the Bahadur Group under Major L.S. Mishra and the second unit of Subhas Brigade under Major P.S. Raturi were attached to the Japanese division. In the Arakan sector, everything initially went in accordance with the Japanese plan after the offensive commenced in February; but soon it met with tough resistance. The Japanese 55th Division, ignoring tough British opposition, took hold of Taung Bazar and trapped the 7th Division of the British Indian army. The attack was very sudden and, as Hugh Toye says, to a great extent its success was due to 'the reconnaissance and subversion of an Indian outpost position by Major L S. Mishra the INA Commander in Arakan'.[20]

The British too praised the work of the INA contingent under L.S. Mishra on the Arakan front. They admitted that, in the initial stage, the INA propaganda was able to persuade many Indian soldiers to desert the British Indian army and be subsequently absorbed in the Bahadur Group. But the INA failed to create really large-scale confusion among the Indian troops and to win them over to the Japanese.[21]

The main Imphal campaign was carried out by three Japanese divisions to which were attached two INA battalions. One battalion was to help the Japanese check the advance of the West African Division in Arakan, and the other to take charge of the Haka-Falam Sector. On 10 February 1944, Lieutenant-Colonel Shah Nawaz Khan, who was commanding the 2nd and 3rd battalions of the INA, was given orders to carry out an offensive on the Haka-Falam front, while Colonel M. Z. Kiani, Commander of the No. 1 INA Division, was asked to set up his divisional headquarters at Chamal on 17 April 1944.

The Japanese advance in the Imphal-Kohima area had been very swift. However, their initial success was met with stiff resistance from the British, who were able to keep up an almost continuous stream of air supplies. Soon the INA was fighting in eight different sectors of the Burma-India border, in the plains of Imphal and in the neighbourhood of Kohima. A detachment of the INA under Colonel S.A. Malik and Captain Itosa of the 33rd Division penetrated into Indian territory and planted the Indian tricolour at Moirang in Manipur on 14 April 1944. The swift Japanese advance in the Tiddim Bihsenpur sector brought some Indian prisoners of war into the orbit of Malik contingent, and they were sent back on sabotage work. Malik achieved tremendous success and, after establishing his base in Indian territory, he even organised a local Manipuri spy ring; besides, a number of captured British soldiers joined the INA voluntarily. The INA soldiers also established their headquarters at Moirang in the house of a local Manipuri sympathizer, Hemaru Thambalyuo Singh.[22]

The other two battalions of the Subhas Brigade under Shah Nawaz proceeded towards Haka-Falam in the Chin Hills. The Japanese considered it important to hold these two strategic points to protect their lines of communication. Shah Nawaz established his base at Myitha Haka on 24 February 1944 and took over charge of the defence of Haka on 3 April from the Japanese. His men successfully patrolled areas around Falam. In May a part of the 2nd battalion raided the British patrol base at Klang, about 20 miles west of Haka.

The INA and Japanese forces wanted to stop a British offensive before it could materialize or gather adequate strength, and operations had been taken up simultaneously in both the sectors, The INA was halted within three miles of Imphal because it lacked air support while the enemy, in a desperate last-minute stand, poured reinforcements into Imphal by air. Lord Mountbatten, the British Commander, was to defend Imphal at all costs. In the defensive battle he adopted a strategy which proved successful. He subsequently recorded that: 'The Japanese High Command played into our hands by staging an all-out offensive. It was most fortunate that at this stage the enemy should choose to fight us on our own ground near our own base, in the only areas where our existing lines of communication could adequately support us in a large-scale campaign, and when our áir bases were sufficiently near the front to enable our supply to be undertaken.'[23] With the onset of the monsoon, the position became desperate for the INA and orders for withdrawal were given. INA soldiers had to walk hundreds of miles without a morsel of food over days on end. With the hills shrouded in mist and the tract either washed away or under ankle-deep mud because of incessant rain, it was difficult even to retreat. During the few months of fierce warfare, INA soldiers had given ample proof of their fighting qualities and courage. They coped successfully with the numerically superior and better equipped enemy forces, and gave them a crushing defeat on various fronts. But they were not destined to accomplish their mission. The postponement of the operation was made public by Subhas in a special order in which he said the INA would 'launch a mighty offensive against our enemies once again' as soon as preparations for it were complete. But the postponement of the campaign was a prelude to the final catastrophe.

The failure of the Imphal campaign was attributed to many causes by participants in it. Count Terauchi ascribes the defeat to the Japanese lack of preparedness in getting supplies to the front and 'to the underestimation of the enemy's capacity of supply by air'. The British propagated the idea that the Japanese made the 'fatal mistake' of supposing that, as soon as India was invaded, there would be a nationalist revolution which would completely neutralize British and American military strength in India, thereby 'leaving the field open for Bose's puppet forces to fight for India'.[24]

But at the same time the Army Headquarters in India admitted in a secret dispatch that the results of the Japanese offensive might have been disastrous for the British had they been able to establish 'a solid foothold in the area' and finally in India; and that 'the conquest of even a single Indian State by the Japanese would have widespread repercussions upon morale and politics', as 'the plain of Imphal was a prize whose capture by the Japanese might have altered the whole course of the war in Eastern and Southern Asia and influenced deeply the history of India and China'.[25]

The exploits of the INA have been glorified by many of its members, but perhaps Fujiwara's assessement of the INA is the most balanced, though he admitted at the time of writing that it should not be taken as 'a positive or accurate judgement'. 'As a revolutionary army', he writes, 'its morale was high as it was quite well organised; but the standard of its tactics, training and leadership was low', and 'it lacked in particular offensive strength and tenacity'. Fujiwara observes that the INA lacked in technical training and mountain warfare skills, and had no experience in the construction of fortifications; it could not absorb the disappointment of reverses and suffered from psychological setbacks which forced it to go on the defensive. But he concedes that its revolutionary spirit, organisation and discipline—which were generated first by General Mohan Singh and nurtured by Subhas Bose, and which were the very foundation of the INA—were maintained by the officers and men of the INA.[26]

The strength of the INA lay in its devotion to the cause of India's independence. The thought of winning a piece of their homeland back from the enemy was uppermost in its mind and almost all INA soldiers went wild with joy when they crossed into India. Some even got down on their knees and kissed the earth. Two Japanese war correspondents who had accompanied the INA forces have given the following account of the occasion: 'We were deeply moved when we saw the Indian soldiers bursting out with joy when they had the first glance of the mountains and rivers of their beloved motherland .... The cries of Jai Hind, Jai Hind, rent the sky and reverberated in the enemy camp through dense jungles on the borderline.'[27]

Despite defeat, Subhas was not willing to give up the fight for the liberation of India: 'the roads to Delhi are many and Delhi remains our goal. The Azad Hind Fauj will fight to the last man and to the last round', he told the Indians after reaching Bangkok. He continued his propaganda, and when the Gandhi-Jinnah meeting was scheduled to be held in the summer of 1944 he urged Indians not to believe that a settlement between the Congress and the Muslim League could lead to independence.

After the Japanese surrender on 15 August 1945, Subhas was allowed to proceed on his journey in a plane provided by General Terauchi. The plane crashed and Bose's death was announced to the world on 23 August. His tragic death and the surrender of the Indian National Army at Singapore marked the end of a vibrant chapter in India's struggle for freedom from abroad. The British attempt to denigrade INA officers by putting them on trial for treason towards the end of 1945 was doomed to failure as the subsequent events proved.

The British, both in England and India, were understandably hostile to its members—particulary in the officer corps. Their antipathy towards the INA ranged from tolerance born out of necessity, to bitterness. Wavell the viceroy, himself had a very low opinion of the INA men 'who were for the most part the weaklings and softlings of the prisoners of war in Malaya'.[28] While there was a difference between the War and the Home Departments as regards the prosecution of the INA, they were one in their opinion that no INA personnel would be reinstated in the army.

At a meeting in August 1945 it became apparent that there were two extreme points of view on the question of policy towards the INA. One was that members of the INA had committed a most serious offence and should all be punished with the penalty that the law provided. The other was that the INA men were not pro-Japanese, that their sole object was to achieve freedom of India, and, since India was being promised freedom in the near future, there was no valid reason to take a serious view of what they had done. Wavell was undecided, as it was not known whether Subhas was still alive or dead. He wrote to the Secretory of State on 20 August about the difficulties involved in handling the INA as 'this was the first occasion in which an anti-British politician had acquired a hold over a substantial number of men in the Indian Army and the consequences were quite incalculable. Many of the INA men obviously had a great regard for Bose and he might yet become a national hero'. He wanted the Cabinet to consider Subhas' case carefully and observed that it would be a good thing if he was disposed of without heing sent back to India.

For the authorities in India, Bose's death no doubt solved difficult problem of dealing with him, but 'his patriotism and achievements, even though from the wrong side of the fence', in their view was 'likely to hold an important place in the nationalist mind', and his case was bound up with the future of the captured members of the INA. This assessment of the military intelligence was not altogether wrong. In June 1945, when the captured INA prisoners were being harassed in Burma, Bose echoed the feelings of all Indians when he declared that public opinion might not be strong enough in India to achieve independence, but it would certainly stop the prosecution of the INA prisoners. And this was exactly what happened. The government had no alternative but to initiate the prosecution under mounting pressure from the army, but it decided to prosecute only a limited number of INA members. The Viceroy categrically ruled out 'harsh measures against the INA as a whole', as it 'would undoubtedly be wounding to the majority of Indian opinion.' Taking a middle line, he proposed to 'punish only the leaders', while others 'were to be treated with clemency'. The lenient policy was advocated by the Viceroy in view of popular sympathy for the INA and the knowledge that, even if their conviction was 'secured, which is doubtful, pressure for remission of sentence would be great and the convicted persons would certainly be released by the Congress Government if they came into power'[30]. In a communique it was announced that all INA prisoners were to be discharged and no pensions to be given to them under the code of conduct rules. The communique further clarified that 'there can be no question of re-employing in the Indian Army anyone who has violated the soldier's code and betrayed his companions'. Another communique on 28 August 1945 stated that it was 'necessary to take some disciplinary action either by discharge from the army or by trials by court martial' against those who were alleged to have committed 'particularly heinous crimes'. The idea of a wholesale prosecution was given up and it was decided to proceed against chosen INA personnel; but even then the British could not expect the approval of the Indian masses and political parties. Already, the public was hailing INA members as heroes. The Congress passed a resolution in September which said that it would be a tragedy if INA members' were punished for the offence of having laboured, however mistakenly, for the freedom of India'.

Three INA officers were chosen for the first court martial. They were Shah Nawaz, G.S. Dhillon, and P. K. Sahgal. The opening of the trials on 5 November 1945 brought into focus the inadvisibility of the policy of the government. There were unprecedented riots all over the country, and seldom had there been a subject that had 'attracted so much public interest' as these trials. The general line of defence was the INA men were motivated by patriotism and, therefore, should not be punished at all.

From the Indian point of view, the success of the trials was thanks to popular support and the able defence put up by Bhulabhai Desai. Desai argued that the INA was an organised force of a properly constituted government which the accused had joined as true patriots; therefore, they had every legal right to fight on behalf of the government they supported. Bhulabhai Desai carried on his defence for more than ten hours spread over two days. The burden of his defence was that the case before the court was not a personal case, that 'the honour and the law of the Indian National Army were on trial before the court'. His testimony exploded the myth spread by the British that Indians had joined the INA to escape inhuman torture at the hands of the Japanese, or to safeguard their lives. He forcefully asserted the right of a subject people to wage war for its liberation and contended that the prisoners of war had voluntarily organised themselves into the INA, which was the army of the Provisional Government of Free India. Hence, the charges levelled against them did not come under the purview of the Indian Army Act.[31]

Despite the convincing arguments of the defence counsel, the three officers were found guilty of waging war against the King and were sentenced to transportation for life; their arrears of pay and allowances were forfeited. Though under pressure, the C-in-C later remitted the heavier part of the punishment, namely, the sentences of transportation for life.

There were different opinions about the outcome of the trials and their impact on the Indian political scene. From the Indian point of view, they dealt a 'deadly blow to British prestige, canalizing the mass fervour into the fight for freedom'. On the other hand, British diehards thought that 'by conceding the demand for leniency the Government of India weakend the clan of the army'. Sir Francis Tuker, the most senior British officer in the Indian army wrote that the trial had tended to erode the discipline of the Indian army by lightly punishing those who had 'cashiered' themselves from the army and turned against it.[32] A British Parliamentary delegation which came to India in the beginning of 1946 to study the situation reported back that the effect of the INA trials had been very severe but varied markedly with different elements in the army. The old, long service class, such as V.C.Os, was deeply offended that 'the INA have not been treated with the full rigour of the law, but the younger generation are impressed by the political aspect'. Nevertheless, it concluded that the army could still be 'relied on to do its duty except in th event of civil war in which case its loyalty would inevitably be divided among the combatants'. But soon the government realized that the army's troops were 'the only stable element in the country' which could be relied upon for maintaining peace and order in any eventuality'. In fact, the INA trials had completely shaken discipline in the Indian army and soldiers were now more nationalist in their outlook than before.[33]

The year 1946 opened with widespread strikes in the Royal Air Force. This was followed by the revolt of the navy in various parts of the country. Commenting on the indiscipline and strikes in the army and air force, the Chief of General Staff was informed by the G.O.C. Eastern Command that the widespread disturbaces were meant to persuade Indian troops that their future lay in throwing in their lot with the Congress, which was effectively the ruler of India, rather than with the British. The navy report also revealed that the revolt, besides creating disturbances amongt the naval forces at Karachi and Bombay, had created dissatisfaction in the lower formations of various overseas commands of the Royal Air Force and had introduced the word 'strike' for the first time in the history of the services. The report further admitted that the political campaign for freedom had reached 'a crescendo' and that the INA affair was violently exploited to incite Indians still serving in the army. The report revealed that the deeds of the INA had heightened the political consciousness of the armed forces, and that it was no longer possible to rely on Indian troops.[34] All this made it quite apparent to authorities that they could no longer rely on Indian army to rule India and it was decided to grant independence to India on 15 August 1947.

Though defeated on the battlefield, the INA achieved a tremendous victory in India. Its own glory was shortlived, but it hastened the process of the liquidation of the British Empire. After Independence, the INA heroes became what Ganpullay calls 'back numbers' for the only fault of having agreed to fight militarily for the freedom of their country. They drifted into different fields and could not become a part of the Indian army—the role which Subhas had envisaged for them. Wavell noted this change after he had a talk with Jawaharlal Nehru in May 1946 and wrote to the Secretary of State for India: "I think, from what he said, that Congress has begun to realize that the INA is not entirely a creditable asset'. In order to make the erstwhile INA soldiers less effective, Nehru suggested to the Viceroy that some employment opportunities should be provided to 'keep them out of the hands of the more extreme elements' However they were not to be taken back in the army, for the C-in-C had warned that, 'if after the formation of the National Government, the political parties sought to reinstate INA personnel in the Army, that would have a serious effect on Army morale and he himself would resign rather than agree to it'.[35] Wavell conveyed these sentiments of the C-in-C to Nehru, who was still toying with the idea of employing INA personnel, made it very clear that there was no question of re-instatement of INA personnel in the army so long as British power remained. Even the question of their employment in the police was categorically rejected. Nehru yielded to the above threats.

Notes and References

1. *Harijan*, 14 April 1946.
2. South-East Asia Translation and Interrogation Centre, *Historical and Intelligence Bulletin* No. 241, Historical Section, Ministry of Defence, New Delhi (hereafter referred to as SEATIC Bulletin).
3. SEATIC *Bulletin* No. 234. This *Bulletin* is very important as it contains a detailed account of the activities of Fujiwara Kikan and the INA based on the interogation of Fujiwara in 1946 at Singapore.
4. *Ibid.*
5. 'How the INA was Born' by General Mohan Singh, *Bombay Chronicle*, 8 Dec. 1946.

6. For a detailed study of the subject, see T. R. Sareen, *Japan and the Indian National Army* (New Delhi, 1986). This article is based on the above book.
7. Mohan Singh, *A Soldier's Contribution to Indian National Independence* (New Delhi 1974), pp. 82-83.
8. Indian Independence League Papers, F. No. 453, NAI, New Delhi.
9. T. R. Sareen, *op.cit.*, p. 106.
10. Memoirs of Colonel Yamamoto, available in the history of the freedom movement records, NAI.
11. Arun, *Testament of Subhas Bose* (Delhi, 1946), p. 39.
12. Military Department, F. No. L/WS/2/45, IOLR, London.
13. See details about the formation of the Provisional Government of Azad Hind and its policy in S. A. Ayer, *Unto Him A Witness* (Bombay, 1951) pp. 180-90.
14. F. No. 601/7553/H (Historical Section).
15. Mil. Dept. F. No. L/WS/1/1576 (IOLR).
16. Shah Nawaz, *My Memoirs of INA and its Netaji* (Delhi, 1945), p. 75.
17. F. No. 601/7775/ H. (Historical Section).
18. Joshiro Takagi, *Imphal* (Tokyo 1963). The book is in Japanese, and only extracts already translated into English have been used.
19. Memoirs of Lt. Gen. Saburo Isodo, Head of the Hikari Kikan (English translation used).
20. Hugh Toye, *The Springing Tiger* (Delhi, 1962), p. 115.
21. General Headquarters, India, *The Japanese Campaign in Arakan* (Simla 1944).
22. See INA Martyrs' Memorial Number published from Moirang.
23. Quoted in Biseshwar Prasad (ed.), *History of the Indian Armed Forces in the Second World War* (Delhi, 1966) p. 159.
24. F. No. 355/INA (Historical Section).
25. F. No. 601/7398/H. (Historical Section).
26. SEATIC bulletin No. 240 (Historical Section).
27. Quoted in Ba Maw, *Breakthrough in Burma* (London, 1968) p. 354-55.
28. F. No. R/3/1/330, IOL.
29. Wavell to Pethick-Lawrence, 20 Aug. 1945 in Nicholas Mansergh (ed.), *The Transfer of Power 1942-47*, Vol. vi, p. 107.
30. Memorandum by the Secretary of State for India, 24 October, 1945; *Ibid.*, pp. 382-3.
31. See INA Defence by Bhulabhai Desai as reproduced in Motiram (ed.), *Two Historic Trials in the Red Fort* (Delhi, 1946).
32. Francis Tucker, *While Memory Serves* (London, 1950), p. 53.
33. See Report of the R.I.N. Commission of Inquiry, F. No. 601/7968/H (Historical Section).
34. See Note on Wavell's interview with Jawaharlal Nehru, 2 May 1946 in Nicholas Mansergh (ed.), *The Transfar of Power 1942-47*, Vol. VII (London 1978) pp. 394-95.

Introduction to Vol. I

During their struggle against the British, Indian nationalists sought help from many foreign powers. The nature of foreign assistance varied from time to time and was determined by the relationship of the assisting country with Britain. In the present documentary study it is intended to trace the links between the Indian nationalists and Japan during the Second World War and how their collaboration resulted in the formation of the Indian Independence League (IIL) and the Indian National Army (INA). Though the interest of the Japanese in the activities of Indian nationalists' fighting from abroad began during the First World War, yet the alliance took concrete shape only after the Second World War.

The credit for putting the Indian Independence movement in East Asia on a sound footing and for the initial formation of INA goes to Sardar Pritam Singh, General Mohan Singh and Major Fujiwara. As head of the Japanese Intelligence agency, Fujiwara appreciated the demand put forward by Indian nationalists on the eve of the Pacific War for the formation of an Indian Voluntary Army from amongst the civilians and the Prisoners of War of the British Indian Army. Fujiwara inspired Mohan Singh after the defeat of the British in Malaya in 1941 with the idea of liberating India with Japanese assistance and thus the INA was born.

By the middle of 1942, IIL had been properly organised and INA had taken shape as a well-disciplined military unit under General Mohan Singh. But it was soon apparent to the Indian patriots that the Japanese wanted to utilise this army as an instrument of propaganda rather than an army of liberation. General Mohan Singh was irritated at the indifferent Japanese policy. He was a man in hurry and wanted to capitalise on the favourable situation then prevailing in India. At that point of time India was in the grip of the Quit India Movement, the British military power in the region was at its lowest ebb, and an initiative by the INA might have given a serious blow to the British. But for their own reasons, the Japanese postponed the drive towards India and their Indian nationalist allies started doubting their intentions. The British propaganda also played its role and General

Mohan Singh began to believe that Japanese wanted to use Indians as their tools. These doubts led to a crisis of confidence towards the end of 1942.

In this dispute Rash Behari Bose sided with the Japanese and dismissed General Mohan Singh. But Indian nationalists in East Asia soon realised that it was not possible to carry on Indian struggle for liberation under the leadership of Rash Behari Bose who did not question the wayward policy of the Japanese as boldly as Mohan Singh did. The consequent crisis of leadership was fortunately resolved with the arrival of a dynamic leader, Subhash Chandra Bose from Berlin.

The documents included in this first volume cover the period from December, 1941, when Indian nationalists joined hands with the Japanese military authorities till December, 1942, when General Mohan Singh, who had organised the INA was dismissed and imprisoned by the Japanese.

Curiously enough, even after more than fifty years some of the official records regarding Indian National Army are not open for consultation in India as well as abroad. Despite archival restrictions, a vast amount of material is available both official and non-official in various institutions and archives of India, Thailand, Malaysia, Singapore, Japan, England and the U.S.A. A few good works have also been written by some historians and others having links with the INA., these are General Mohan Singh, 'Soldier's Contribution to Indian Independence', Fujiwara, 'F. Kikan', S.A. Ayer, 'Unto Him a Witness', C. Lebra, 'Jungle Alliance', K.K. Ghosh. 'The Indian National Army', and Hugh Toye, 'The Springing Tiger'. But still a comprehensive and objective history of the Indian National Army based on original sources is yet to be written and this can be done only if all the documents are made available to the scholars.

The publication of documents on any topic can be the outcome of selection. This is an inevitable result of vast range of records available on the subject. The hitherto unpublished documents included in these volumes were collected from India Office Library and Records, Public Records Office, Imperial War Museum London, National Archives of India, and Historial section of the Ministry of Defence, Government of India and other repositories in South East Asia and Japan. The principal categories of documents are the reports of the Army Department or War Office, speeches, statements and memoirs of the participants and the interrogation reports of some of the prominent members of the I.N.A. As far as possible the documents have been arranged chronologically though some overlapping is bound to be there. For example, British report on the Fujiwara Kikan was compiled after the war, but has been placed amongst the documents of the year 1942 as it throws a good deal of light on the events of that period. Similarly an interrogation report of Major Fujiwara, who played an important role in the formation of the INA alongwith the report of Mohan Singh have included in this volume. These reports were compiled after the war, but deal with this crucial period and contain information not available any where else. These reports may be read with the memoirs of Fujiwara which he prepared in 1959 for the Foreign Ministry of Japan. The relevant extracts form this memorandum which was written in Japanese have been translated into English and are included here with he hope that these will clarify many points mentioned in the earlier documents. These are given in the Appendix alongwith the statement of N.S. Gill, which throws a great deal of light on the Japanese Policy towards I.N.A.

The emergence of the INA after the defeat of the British Indian Army was viewed with grave concern by the authorities in India and England Eleborate security measures were taken by the Indian Army and they carried on propaganda against the INA. At the same time the Director of the Military Intelligence (D.M.1) was keen to have information about the intentions of the INA, their leaders and the nature of threat they were likely to pose for India. For getting the information they employed large number of loyal agents. On the basis of the information received the D.M.I. was submitting reports with his comments. The reports prepared by D.M.I. have been included in these volumes. The study of these reports show as to how well informed the British were about the activities of the INA, and their collaboration with Japan and how they kept the Indian public in the dark about the very existence of the INA. The documents about the British policy included here also show as how much they were worried by the activities of Subhas Chandra Bose and the INA.

In this selection, the original documents have been reproduced as closely as possible. In rare cases punctuation have been added and spelling mistakes rectified. Where possible short explanatory notes have been given. The documents in this volume mainly deal with the circumstances leading to the formation of the I.N.A. and I.I.L. proceedings of the Tokyo and the Bangkok conferences, clash between Rash Behari Bose and Mohan Singh on the one hand and between Japanese on the other hand and the crisis which led to the arrest of Mohan Singh.

The documentas presented here are by no means exhaustive, they merely indicate to the research students the nature of the materials available on the subject and may prove to be halpful to them to understand the working of Indian nationalism under Bose as compared to Gandhi. However, it will be necessary for the students to verify the official reports with the private memoirs included in these volumes.

During the course of my studies of the I.N.A., I had the opportunity to meet many persons who were closely connected with Bose and the I.N.A. They were kind enough to either place at my disposal the documents which they had in their possession or their memoirs which they had written, but did not publish. I have included some of them in these volumes. I am extremely thankful to them especially A.M. Sahay, Shah Nawaz Khan, General Mohan Singh, Hugh Toye, S.A. Ayer , Capt. L.C. Talwar and many others for their kind help.

For the compliation of these five volumes. I received assistance from many organizations and individuals in India and abroad. Though it is difficult to mention them individually, but I would like to place on record my gratitude to them. Without their help it was not possible to compile these columes.

Volume one was completed when I was a Senior Fellow of he Indian Council of Historical Research for a period of one year. I am thankful to the Council for their assistance and especially to prof. S. Settar, who was then the Chairman. He encouraged me to complete this work even though the council did not extend the Fellowship after one year.

I will be failing in my duty if I do not place my appreciation of help which I have received from time to time from the staff of the Historical Section of the Ministry of Defense. They have been very cooperative and allowed me to consult the I.N.A. papers when these were in their custody. To consult these papers, I got the special permission through the efforts of Dr. D.C. Verma, for which I am grateful to him. I am equally thankful to the staff of the National Archives fo India, Assam State Archives Dispur, Guwahati U.S. National Archives, Maryland, India office Library and Records, Public Record Office London National Archives, Singapore, Malaysia and Thailand, for their assistance from time to time.

I have no words to thank the members of the I.N.A. Relief and Enquiry Committee. I have visited their office often at Darya Ganj for the last more than thirty years. They were very helpful and even provided me with the full set of the documents which were presented to the court as exhibits at the time of the trial of the I.N.A officers in 1945. The relevant documents from this collection have been included in these volumes.

Last but no the least, I am obliged to Dr. S.R. Bakshi and my wife Dr. Anuradha their for their friendly assistance and advice in the preparation of these volumes. It is hoped that these documents may prove useful to the students and teachers.

T. R. Sareen

New Delhi : 6.10.2003

1

Appeal from Sardar Pritam Singh, Sikh Missionary, to Indian Soldiers in Malaya Asking them not to Fight for the British in the War[1]

5 December, 1941

Dear Indian Soldiers in Malaya and Burma : We advise you to follow the programme of the Indian National Congress under the direct leadership of our great Saint Mahatma Gandhi and the programme instructed by our Indian patriots abroad. The programme for you is that you should never obey the orders of your English Commanders when they would order to attack Thailand. Thailand is connected with India through religion of Lord Buddha, Culture and Sanskrit literature. Therefore, Thailand is a brother country to India. So you should not fight this in any case. And you should never fight Japan, Germany or any other country who is enemy of British, because all such countries are our indirect friends. So to come to the conclusion, you should never help England in this war. If English loose this war there would be ample chance for India's freedom. Some deceiving English propagandists would cheat you and the writer has heard that English dogs bark before innocent Indians to show that they (English) are saving India from Germany, Japan or some other enemy countries of England who want to govern India. But it is wrong. No country has ever done any wrong to India, except these English pirates and thieves in disguise of democratic devils—as they call themselves. Congress and patriotic Indian like Independent League of India prohibit you in helping English.

---

1. Indian National Army papers, File No. 295. I had consulted these papers when these were in the custody of Ministry of Defence. These have now been transferred to the National Archives of India. (In future referred to as I.N.A. Papers.) Copy of this appeal in original hand-written is reproduced in K.S. Giani, *Indian Independence Movement in East Asia*, Lahore, 1947.

2

Speech of Pritam Singh on the Occasion of the Opening of Independence League of India in Bangkok Requesting Indians to Refrain from Helping the British War Efforts[1]

9 December, 1941

The whole of Japanese nation unanimously in a single voice taken a pledge to take her fate for the fulfilment of her incomprehensible spiritual aim of liberating the whole of Asia from the British yoke. We welcome this God given opportunity that Indians have been waiting for since 1904. By the grace of God we are starting on a non-stop voyage to reach India's goal of complete independence. The members of the Independence League[2] of India either in India or abroad firmly believe that all the Independence movements started by the patriotic Indians in India or outside can only prosper when they receive worldwide sympathy and solid help, alongwith their heroic struggles against the British.

In the past, Indian national leaders repeatedly urged the British to reconsider to abandon their blood-sucking policy towards India for which the English never cared the least. British Jingoism is corrigible now. The day of decision has now come when the God's curse in inflicted upon the British for their wicked and treacherous deeds.

England is gasping for breath on the verge of death, having tasted the result of her incendiary declaration of war against Germany, and now she has to face indestructable armed forces of Japan.

1. I.N.A. Papers; File No. 295.
2. Independent League of India was a secret organisation in Thailand founded by Sardar Pritam Singh. On the eve of the Pacific war and after the landing of the Japanese forces in Thailand, its existence was announced on 9th Decembe, 1941 and its branches were opened in various cities of South Thailand as they were overrun by the Japanese Army. League collaborated with the Japanese.

Nations in the world have stood up in increasing members, declaring England as the common enemy of Humanity and this combined power, still increasing in number, directly and indirectly help the achievement of Indian freedom. The liberation of India would also emancipate the whole of Asia from British imperialistic suppression and rule, and emancipated Asiatic countries would not then be called the colonies of any empire. Thus would the Asiatics would no more be the black coolies of the White Anglo-Saxon.

Every attempt made by the Indians to achieve freedom of India has always been called "a revolt" by the English, perhaps because other nations were not in a position, under the circumstances then prevailing to openly sympathise towards it. From now on we wish and surely hope that all the freedom loving nations in this world whole-heartedly and openly sympathise with Indian patriotic movements and would officially recognise the Indian people's legitimate right of complete Independence of India.

We appeal to all our Indian, brethren wherever they are, to refrain from helping the British war efforts, and to stand up together to attain the glorious Indian freedom. All Indians should fight to eliminate the Anglo-Saxon from the whole Asia whatever energetic endeavours and sacrifices they have to make.

Immortal Prophets and Martyrs of India call upon you to serve your Motherland Bharata.

3

Copy of an Important Notice by the Japanese Forces on Entering Thailand Assuring Indians to Carry on their Business Peacefully[1]

10 December, 1941

Every Indian in Thailand is hereby informed on the behalf of the Commander-in-Chief of the Japanese troops, Bangkok :–

1. That the Indians should carry on their business as usual. I assure them that no interference will be made in their work, etc. by the Japanese troops. But if any body, inspite of so much assurance, will try to escape from this country or spread false rumours or raise objections, will be considered as an enemy and will be liable to be punished. Remember the following four things in mind :—
   (a) Perform your business peacefully.
   (b) Don't spread false rumours.
   (c) Don't escape from Thailand.
   (d) Love the Japanese and respect them, in order that the Japanese should love you in return.
2. If any one who will fail to comply with the above four advice will be considered as an enemy and will be punished.
3. We Azad Hind League, guarantee your safety.

By the order of Commander-in-Chief
Japanese troops.

---

1. I.N.A. Papers; File No. 9.

4

Aims and Objects of Azad Hind Sang formed by Pritam Singh with Japanese Help after the Pacific War[1]

21 December, 1941

Minor details regarding the formation of the Azad Hind Sang or Azad Bharat Sabha in Bangkok as given by persons interrogated here, are slightly conflicting, as is to be expected, but the account given here is the nearest to the truth obtainable at present.

Its objectives were :—

(a) Close collaboration with the Japanese.

(b) The supplying of volunteers for subversive role on Malaya and Burma Fronts.

(c) Propaganda and broadcasting to stir up anti-British feeling.

Its lending members who had been operating secretly for two or three months prior to the arrival of the Japanese in Bangkok were as follows :–

(1) Giani Pritam Singh[2]

(2) Baba Amar Singh

(3) Master Bhagwan Singh

(4) Amar Singh Suchdev

(5) Seva Singh

---

1. I.N.A. Papers F. No. 384.
2. Sardar Pritam Singh (1910-1942). Son of S. Maiya Singh, belonged to a noble Sikh family of Lyallpur district. After matriculation joined Lyallpur Agricultural College and Sikh Missionary College. On request from Sikh Missionary Society, Bangkok, was sent on April 11, 1933 to act as a priest in Thailand. Was associated with Raja Mahendra Pratap and Baba Amar Singh. Even before the Pacific War was in league with the Japanese and had full faith in Japan, negotiated for help with Major Fujiwara for the liberation of India. Was instrumental in the formation of Indian National Army and the Independence League of India. Died in plane crash in March, 1942 while going to attend the Tokyo Conference.

(6) Labh Singh Matta
(7) Kishan Singh Sethi
(8) Raj Singh Kalra
(9) Master Kartar Singh

The Sang was sponsored and financed by the Japanese, including Major General Tamura, Lt. Ito/s.c military attaches and Major Fujiwara, who is believed to have been working as an employee of the Tamura Koma Shoten a Japanese firm in Bangkok.

On 9th Dec. 41, the formation of the Sang was made public, its H.Q. was established in the house of Ram Singh Kalra in Tung Maha Mek Rd. near the Bangkok Wireless station, Serial No. 7 above assisted by :–

(10) Ishar Singh Daler
(11) Jaswant Singh Sethi
(12) Kundan Singh

Went round Bangkok distributing registering persons as members. The following were probably its earliest recruits:–

(13) Tarlochan Singh
(14) Nandan Farsi
(15) Dunia Shukul
(16) Sadhur San Ahuja
(17) Ram Surat Chobe
(18) Gopal Singh
(19) Harnam Singh
(20) Gurbax Singh
(21) Keshar Singh
(22) Anurudh Shukla
(23) Peshawari Lal
(24) Ganga Singh
(25) Indar Singh
(26) Autar Singh (Narulla)
(27) Mehal Singh
(28) Narain Singh (Narulla)
(29) Gurbax Singh (Chawla)
(30) Ishar Singh (Narulla)
(31) Amar Singh
(32) Babu Changur Singh
(33) Lal Singh (Padre)
(34) Amarnath Suchdev
(35) Dr. Onkar Singh
(36) Master Karnail Singh

(37) Naranjan Singh
(38) Mehal Singh
(39) Amar Das (Champi)
(40) M.A. Shastari
(41) Lal Singh
(42) Harbans Singh
(43) Sardara Singh (Golati)
(44) Sukhu Bhagat
(45) Arjan Das
(46) Puran Singh
(47) Narain Singh Shagufta

Subsequently 80 per cent of the Indian population of Bangkok was persuaded to register as members.

The more prominent leaders of this Sang, were semi-educated and lacking in personality and capability, who, knowing of the impending arrival of the Japanese forces, had decided to be the first to collaborate, with a view to enhancing their own personal position and venting their anti-British feelings. Due to this, and it's being Japanese controlled and considered to be a purely Sikh organisation, the Sang quickly fell into disfavour of thinking Indians of a more true nationalistic outlook, including the D.N. Das and Swami Satyananda Puri.

On the departure of Giani Pritam Singh to Malaya, D.N. Das and his following commenced organising the Indian National Council. This led to friction which continued until the amalgamation of the two parties in April 1942. This amalgamation was mainly brought about by the work of (Lt. Col.) Naranjan Singh (Gill) and (Major) Mahabir Singh (Dhillon).

Activities of the Sang

The main activities of the Sang are as follows :–

(a) Recruiting and organising of Giani Pritam Singh's Malaya party.
(b) Publication on 9 Dec. 1941 of leaflet, and arrest of 50 Indians attempting to leave Thailand on 16 Dec. 1941.
(c) Baba Amar Singh's Mission to Saigon to spread the movement (accompanied by Serial No. 21 on 11 Dec. 1941).
(d) Major Minami's "Burma Party".
(e) Organisation of volunteer group, total about 50, including members of Giani and Minani parties and a few others.
(f) Organising broadcast and propaganda section consisting of Serial Nos. 2, 3, 6, 7, 9, 11, 20, 38, 39, 40.
(g) Subversion of 4,000 I.A. officers and men who actually came

over to the Japanese (figures taken from Seva Ram's report, and subsequently the formation of Mohan Singh's I.N.A.[3]

(h) The formation by Feb. 1942 of I.I.L. Branches at :–

Alor Star	
Sungei Pattani	Kuala Lumpur
Kulim	Kajang
Taiping	Klang
Kuala Kangsar	Negri Sambilan Seramban
Ipoh	Malacca
	Penang
	Singapore

whose membership totalled about 150,000.

It is apparent that the Japanese themselves realized that the Sang though it was initially of great importance, was not, truly representative of the Indian people in Bangkok and shortly after their arrival in Bangkok they called for the formation of an Indian National Council to represent the Indian community.

The Azad Hind Sang, inspite of its leaders, met with unexpected success.

---

3. This refers to the anticipation of Sardar Pritam Singh that the British forces would be defeated in Malaya. After having come in contact with the soldiers of the British Indian Army before the War, he expected to form a voluntary Army from amongst them who would surrender. Having this in mind, Pritam Singh insisted for this provision in the agreement with Fujiwara. Pritam Singh was keen to train this army for the liberation of India.

5

Captain Mohan Singh to Major Fujiwara Iwaichi Conveying the Willingness of Indian Prisoners of War to Join Hands with Japanese Forces and to Form Indian National Army to Fight the British[1]

31 December, 1941

Reference your notes and Memoranda handed over to us on 30th and 31st December 1941.[2]

We have thoroughly studied all points and in principle we agree with them. Certain minor modifications and suggestions are placed before you for your consideration.

1. Our modified Views as Regards Cooperation with Indian National Army

We consider it a point of great honour for us to accept kind, valuable and reverable leadership Mr. S.C. Bose and his party in Berlin. We all know that he is an extremist who believes in revolutions and radical changes. People in India are most anxiously waiting for any movement started by Mr. Bose and they are ready to support him. He is extremely popular amongst all freedom loving Indians, even his political enemies have great respect and regard for him. His photos can been seen in practically in every house in India. In most cases people worship him like a god. He is a leader whose very name will stir up a great revolution

1. *Ibid.*
2. The memorandum could not be traced. Hugh Toye thinks that these papers were destroyed. On the basis of the original copy of this letter which the British discovered from the papers of M.Z. Kiani, they were sure that it was written by General Mohan Singh and Mohammad Akram. The text of the letter does not give the name of the person who wrote the letter but it was addressed to Fujiwara Kikan.

amongst Indian masses, which will have strong reaction in the Indian Army. It will cause a split in the Indian National Congress circle and the majority of the Congress will join Mr. Bose. We, members of the Indian National Army are prepared to shed every drop of our blood for Bose. His very name puts new life into us.

We sincerely appreciate the Japanese Government's efforts to cooperate with Mr. S.C. Bose. We further request that the Japanese Government may kindly use all its political influence to get Mr. S.C. Bose's support and leadership for such a great movement. If the Japanese Government is successful in it, then in our opinion half the battle in India is won. The day Mr. S.C. Bose's name comes before us we promise that if it suits our purpose we will openly condemn the Indian National Congress.

We appreciate very valuable work done by Mr. Pritam Singh in Malaya. We have great respect and regard for him and will do our best to enhance his influence and prestige. We are willing to cooperate with him with great pleasure.

2. We request that as far as Co-Prosperity Sphere is concerned the Japanese Government may very kindly discuss it directly with Mr. S.C. Bose. We will be most willing to agree to any decision mutually agreed upon by the Japanese Government and Mr. S.C. Bose. We only went to see for our information details and description of Co-Prosperity.

3. Participation of Indian National Army[3] in Malaya and Burma

It is true that the Army which is not prepared to fight in the front line is not worth its name. We do not want to be disinterested and passive observers of the Japanese operation. We also realise that we will not be able to show our face to the world if Indians do no play any active part in freeing their motherland. On the other hand it will be an honour to the Indian National Army to fight side by side with the glorious and world-famed Japanese army. We request that before sending the Indian National Army to the front line the following point should be considered.

3. Pritam Singh had in mind the formation of the Indian Voluntary Army. During the discussion, Fujiwara suggested that the Army thus formed may be known as "Volunteers for Indian Freedom:" but Mohan Singh suggestion that it should be called the Indian National Army was gladly accepted by all. For the first time, the name was mentioned in this letter to Fujiwara of 31st December, 1941 from Mohan Singh.

(a) The present Indian National Army consists of men belonging to twenty different regiments coming from different parts of India. It is in fact a very strange mixture. In several cases they speak different languages. To train them under new leaders and under new ideas to fight against the army from which they have come requires some time.

(b) It is also essential that when the Indian National Army is used for the first time it should set a very good example of its bravery and fighting spirit. It should enter the battlefield most modernly armed and equipped. As it is going to fight side by side with the Japanese Army, it is requested that it should be armed and equipped and trained in the same manner. It is just a foundation today, we hope in the near future it is going to be a very big Army. Putting it in the frontline with inferior equipment is sending it to be butchered as was done by the English. This will set a bad example and morale will be lost.

(c) If the Indian National Army is used in Malaya we must not forget that in several cases our men will be fighting against their own units. In certain cases they have got their real brothers and other near relations serving in their own and other units in Malaya. To prepare our men to fight against all this again requires time.

(d) We should also remember that the Indian Army consists of soldiers who have once thrown their arms away on the battlefield. The soldier who lays down his arms in battle may be :

   (i) Timid and thus frightened to fight.

   (ii) Discontented and thus not willing to fight.

   (iii) Exhausted by continuous troubles and hardships which he has undergone since he has come to this country. He might have made up his mind to do no more fighting.

   (iv) In certain cases he is just separated from his unit by force of circumstances otherwise he would be fighting for his regiment. To build up the morale and fighting of such soldiers requires selected leaders and stern discipline.

(e) The present strength of the Indian National Army is very small. For its reinforcement and further extension it is entirely dependent on the Indian Army and the Indian in India. Therefore, it is essential that the Chief theatre where this army should be used should be India where it will attract several

Indians to join and enlarge it.

Considering all those points we request the first time the Indian National Army is used in the front line should not be in Malaya but Burma or better still in India. This will give us some time to prepare. We do not want to set any bad example.

4. As far as the leadership of the Indian National Army is concerned all the officers attending the conference held at Alor Star on the morning of 31st December raised a strong unanimous objection to the words in Malaya', and they requested that' in Malaya may very kindly be deleted from that sentence.

6

British Assessment of the Role Played by Fujiwara Volunteers in the Surrender of British Forces at Singapore[1]

15, February, 1942

The Fujiwara Kikan volunteers were the Indian Army soldiers, who immediately or very shortly after surrendered to the Japanese in Malaya in Dec. 1941 and early Jan. 1942, rallied to the cause of Mohan Singh. For the remainder of the campaign up to the capitulation on 15 Feb. 1942, they worked in cooperation with the Japanese and against their erstwhile brothers-in-arms, thus becoming the initial recruits for what later became a fully organised and actively militant anti-British Organisation–the I.N.A.

Following their occupation of Thailand in 1941, the Japanese military authorities contacted the members of the Indian Congress Party, Bangkok, and were successful in enlisting their support to organise subversive activity amongst Indian troops during the impending campaign in Malaya.

This work was in charge of a Japanese Intelligence Officer, Major Fujiwara. His functions appear to have been almost entirely administrative; he spoke no English, and was always assisted by an interpreter.

On the Indian side the lead was taken by Sikhs, notably one Giani Pritam Singh, who established an office in Haadyai in southern Thailand close to the Malaya border, and on the outbreak of hostilities followed in the wake of the advancing Japanese forces.

It is clear that the subversion of Indian troops was a carefully thought-out and integral part of the Japanese plan of campaign. In the first few days of the war, surrender leaflets were dropped by plane, and

1. Combined Services Detailed Interrogation Centre Report No. 31 (C.S.D.I.C.). The above note was prepared in August, 1945, but since it covers the period from December 1941, it has been uncluded here.

the fall of Penang within ten days of the outbreak of war was ascribed by Baba Amar Singh to the excellent work done by the Fifth Column.

The campaign proceeded favourably for the Japanese from the start, and prisoners were not long in coming in. Amongst the early surrenders were :–

8 Dec.	1941	Sub. Allah Ditta Khan
11 Dec.	1941	Capt. Patnaik[2]
11 Dec.	1941	Jem. Puransing Khawas
15 Dec.	1941	Capt. Mohan Singh
15 Dec.	1941	Capt. Mohd. Akram
15 Dec.	1941	Jem. Sadhu Singh

The facts appear to be these :–

(a) The opinion of the Sub Maj. of 1/14 Punjab (a Dogra, and after the collapse of the first I.N.A. a non-volunteer) is that in his on Mohan Singh was conscientious and efficient, and enjoyed the trust alike of his CO, his fellow-officers anu his men. His conduct during the campaign up to the time of his surrender is stated to have been above reproach, and he was in the company of his CO, Lt. Col. Fitzgerald at the time of surrender.

(b) Another report has it that Mohan Singh and Mohd. Akram used frequently to boast of the manner in which they had surrendered to the Japanese.

On this much graver issue, the available information is as follows :–

(c) One informant has stated that at an unspecified date previous to the outbreak of war, a number of responsible ICOs including Lt. Col. Gill 19 Hybad and Mohan Singh were sent on an espionage mission to Thailand. While performing this duty, they came into contact with Giani Pritam Singh and other Indian revolutionaries, with whom they made an agreement to divulge to the Japanese information of a military and security value with a view to the overthrow of British power. They also agreed to carry out propaganda work among Indian soldiers.

(d) In this connection, it is interesting to note the statement of (another soldier) that when 1/14 Punjab was at Tg Pao near Jitra in Sept. 1941, Mohan Singh went on one month's leave, from which he was recalled after twenty days, and that on his return, the relations between Mohan

2. Capt. Patnaik belonged to the Medical Unit in the British Army. He was amongst the first batch of Indian soldiers who surrendered to the Japanese. Shah Nawaz records that the Japanese tried to pursuade him to form a nucleous of a voluntary army, but he refused. See Shah Nawaz : *My memories of I.N.A. and Netaji, Delhi 1946, p. 15.*

Singh and the other officers of the on became somewhat strained.

(e) A further statement is to the effect that as early as Oct. 1941 he knew that Baba Amar Singh and other Sikh revolutionaries were active in Thailand.

(f) On the other hand, Major M.S. Dhillon, RIASC, who was closely connected with Gill and Mohan Singh considered that liaison between those officers and the Japanese was unlikely.

(g) In further refutation of the suggestion of collusion between Mohan Singh and the Japanese is a reported conversation between (another witness) and Mohan Singh, in which the latter mentioned–but was himself clearly not privy or accessory to a probable agreement between the Fujiwara Kiken and Giani Pritam Singh.

(h) Finally, it appears that some initial pressure had to be brought by the Japanese on Mohan Singh and Mohd. Akram before they agreed to engage in Fifth column work.

From the date given above, the following meagre conclusions appear consistent :–

(a) While there is little doubt that India officers were fully aware previous to the outbreak of war of the activities of Japanese-sponsored anti-British elements, there is no positive evidence that Mohan Singh or any other Indian officer had contact before capture with calls of disaffection in Thailand or Malaya.

(b) Despite the strong pro-Sikh bias of the first I.N.A., and the suspicious circumstances of the meeting early in the campaign of Mohan Singh and Giani Pritam Singh, it is considered, in view of his strongly nationalist sympathies which became immediately evident, that while Mohan Singh was probably ripe for subornation, his encounter with Giani Pritam Singh was purely fortuitous, and not the result of a previous arrangement.

After capture near Jitra about 15 Dec. 1941, Mohan Singh was taken to Alor Star, where about ten days later he appears to have yielded to the mingled threats, blandishments, and promises of position and prestige offered by Giani Pritam Singh and Fujiwara. For the next fortnight his movements are somewhat obscure, but he appears to have been employed in preparations for the reception of PW in Alor Star and Ipoh. No contact on infiltration work was done at the time, and the PW were employed solely on fatigue duties.

This was a period of consolidation and organisation. In the words of Major Fujiwara "The foundation of the I.N.A. was laid at Jitra, Alor Star and Ipoh".

It is clear, however, that knowledge of the subversive activities of Mohan Singh must have been bruited abroad even amongst soldiers still fighting on the British side before the end of 1941. In this connection the incident may be noted of Sep. Ghulam Mohd, 5/2 Punjab ("Salooni"– possibly a "quick release") who after inadvertently wandering into the Japanese lines about 26 Dec. 1941 rejoined his unit, five days later started a whispering campaign about the kind treatment shown by the Japanese to PW, and about a mysterious Sikh "General", who was fighting alongside the Japanese. This story magnified and distorted, would spread quickly through the on and beyond, and must have tended to undermine the morale of the sepoys.

In the first few days of 1942, Mohan Singh moved his HQ from Jitra to Ipoh, and sent out parties to organise the collection of stragglers and wounded. These parties were unarmed, and at this stage do not appear to have been engaged in shouting or other frontline work, but were kept at some distance in the rear, with instructions to shepherd PW into the camp at Ipoh, where they were informed, "all arrangements had been made by Capt. Mohan Singh". Following the battle of Slim River on 7 Jan. 1942, when three boes of Indian infantry were dispersed in confusion, 2/4,000 PW were rounded up, and immediately subjected to intensive propaganda by Mohan Singh and his henchmen. This propaganda was almost completely successful, and the majority of the PW readily agreed to transfer their allegiance to the Japanese side.

It was at this time that the plan was first made of sending organised contact parties of PW to accompany the Japanese, not only to round up stragglers and wounded, but, if necessary, fight against the British forces.

When volunteers were asked for from among the PW in Ipoh, the response is reported to have been at first half-hearted, but after further explanation and persuasion, some hundreds stepped forward. As the Japanese wished for a party of approximately only 200, some selection was necessary. On the method adopted, some informants maintain that, so far as the rank and file were concerned, men were quickly detailed in a haphazard fashion. In view of the extreme dull-witt of some recovered 'F' volunteers, there is reason to believe that this may be the case. Others state, however that the VCOs appointed to lead the party, and others present at the time, picked out those who by their intelligence, keenness, and physical fitness would be most suitable for this work.

After being selected, the volunteers were given white armbands with a latter 'F', and told that if challenged by Japanese troops they were to announce that they belonged to the 'Fujiwara Kikan'.[3] Opinions differ as to whether they were issued with arms at this stage.

Their tasks were :–

(1) To collect stragglers and wounded and indoctrinate them with anti-British propaganda, and where opportunity offered, to send them back to their units as "quick-release agents".

(2) By infiltration into the British lines and mingling with Indian troops to spread alarm and despondency, disaffection and confusion, and by thus undermining morale to induce desertions.

(3) To assist the Japanese in all respects, if necessary by fighting, and to give them information of operational value.

About 21 Jan. 1941, the 180 volunteers who had been selected in Ipoh under command of Sub Allah Ditta, 22 Mtn Regt, (who had just been given the rank of 'captain') and accompanied by Mohan Singh and some Japanese, moved to Kuala Lumpur, where a further call for volunteers to make the number up to 200 brought an immediate response. In Kuala Lumpur, further propaganda lectures were given. About 23 Jan. 1942 a conference, attended by the senior Indian officers and a few Japanese, was held, at which final orders were given.

After final arrangement had been made, the party left Kuala Lumpur about 25 Jan. 1942 and proceeded via Malacca to Muar, where they rounded up about 600 PW, mainly of 219 Jat and 5118 R Garh Rif who were immediately set to collect stragglers, rations and imn.

About 29 Jan. 1942, leaving he freshly-captured PW behind, the Fujiwara Kikan, taking with them a lorry-load of arms, proceeded to Batu Pahat, where the arms were distributed and everyone was given money. In preparation for the final assault on Singapore Island, practice was carried out in combined operations, and the party was for the first time divided into sections as follows (numbers are approximate) :–

	Officers			Strength
No.	Sub	Allah Ditta	22 Mtn Regt	
	Jem	Puransingh Khwas	2/1 Gr	18
No. 1 Sec	Jem	Pritam Singh	R Bombay S & M	39

3. An organisation known as "Fujiwara Kikan" was formed after the Pacific War. In Japanese, Kikan means liaison agency-the Japanese called their agencies after the men who led them. This organisation in its initial stages had both Indian and Japanese members and were issued bands with letter "F" which stood for "Fujiwara, Friendship and Freedom". It served as a liaison agency between the I.I.L./I.N.A. and Japanese Military authorities in South East Asia.

			(Sikhs)	
No. 2 Sec	Jem	Sujjan Singh	1/14 Punjab (Dogras)	42
No. 3 Sec	Hav	Hukam Singh	4/19 Hybad (Jats and Kumaonis)	28
No. 4 Sec	Jem	Fazal Dad	5/14 Punjab (mainly Gurkhas)	38
No. 5 Sec	Jem	Fateh Khan	5/14 Punjab (Gurkhas, PMs and Pathans)	45
No. 6 Sec	Jem	Dilmansing Thapa	2/1 GR (Gurkhas)	19
				229

Two Japanese officers accompanied the party, and one or two Japanese soldiers were attached to each section.

On 6 Feb. 1942 the Fujiwara Kikan moved from Batu Pahat to Kota Tinggi opposite the eastern end of Singapore Island.

On 9 Feb. 1942, No. 4 Sec. under Jem Fazal Dad was attached to assist in the service of the guns of a Japanese army unit, with which they remained up to the time of surrender.

In the meantime, the remaining sections and HQ Sec crossed Johore Strait to Pulau Ubin on 10 and 11 Feb 1942, where for the next few days they did general fatigue duties for the Japanese.

On 12 Feb 1,942, HQ Sec and Nos. 1, 2, 3 and 5 Secs were sent on an infiltration mission via Johora Bahru to Singapore, while No. 5 Sec on the night 13/14 Feb. 1942 crossed by country boat to Singapore Island at Tampinos Bahru, where on 14 Feb. 1942, they were successful in raising the Japanese flag.

By this time the situation on Singapore Island had so far deteriorated that the members of the Fujiwara Kikan were enabled easily to mingle with units still fighting, and so effect large-scale surrenders. Owing to the extreme caution and unwillingness on the part of recovered PW, to account for this part of their experiences, little is known of this confused period, but from information supplied by recovered members of the Fujiwara Kikan itself, as well as the suspicious circumstances of some surrenders it is clear that the success of the Fujiwara Kikan among the demoralised and dispirited Indian troops must have been considerable.

With the fall of Singapore, the history of the 'F' given volunteers as an independent unit ends. At the Ferrer Park meeting on 17 Feb. 1942, the 'F' volunteers were seen strutting about displaying their armbands; for a few months they enjoyed a privileged position as members of Mohan Singh's bodyguard at Moun't Pleasant; and with the inauguration of the I.N.A. in Sep. 1942 they became merged in Nehru Bde. Some later rose to high rank in the I.N.A. while others quickly sank back into obscurity; following the collapse of Mohan Singh some became non-volunteers.

The degree of responsibility that can be attached to the Fujiwara Kikan for the defeat of British army in Malaya cannot yet be decided. In contrast to the very fully documented data in existence about Ram Sarup's party which left Kuala Lumpur for Burma shortly after the departure of the Fujiwara Kikan, the information about the later party is meagre. Emphasis has inevitably tended to fall on the later feats of the I.N.A. and until recently the Fujiwara Kikan has been neglected.

The Fujiwara Kikan undoubtedly played a very large part in weakening the morale of Indian troops in Malaya, and it is around this body of traitors that the ignoble traditions of the I.N.A. developed. But there are still gaps in our knowledge.

In particular information on the following topics is very scanty :–

(1) The detailed movements of Mohan Singh.

(2) The conduct of Suh Allah Ditta Khan, 22 Mtn. Regt. (The first active JIFC and the comd. of the Fujiwara Kikan in the field) between his desertion and his meeting with Mohan Singh.

(3) The surrenders on Singapore Island for which the Fujiwara Kikan were directly responsible.

7

Japanese Premier General Tojo's Address before the Diet on the Fall of Singapore Exhorting Indians to Get Rid of the Ruthless Despotism of the British[1]

16 February, 1942

As already announced by the Imperial Headquarters, the Imperial forces have occupied Singapore yesterday, February 15th.

The Army and Navy authorities will make their report concerning the circumstances of the actual fighting. However, I am glad to state my views and conviction at this opportunity.

At the outset of the War, following the issuance of the gracious Imperial Rescrip[2] our forces immediately crushed the main body of the American-British Defeat; and in 18 days they brought Hongkong to submission; in 26 days they occupied Manila, and in 70 days they brought about the fall of Singapore. Thus the important bases of the United States and Britain for their encroachment on East Asia for many years past have all fallen into the hands of the Imperial Forces. Such strategic points as Borneo, Celebes and New Britain have also been occupied by our forces, and moreover the main body of the Dutch East Indies fleet has been annihilated. The Imperial Army and Navy are now carrying out operations in a vast area, on a scale unparalleled in the history of mankind.

These brilliant victories are solely due to the august virtue of His Majesty the Emperor under which the officers and men of the Emperial forces are bravely and energetically carrying on their campaign. To the

---

1. I.N.A. Papers. F. No. 294. This speech is also reproduced in the publication. Our Freedom and Japan brought out by Indian Independence, league Headquarters in 1943 from Bangkok.
2. This refers to the Imperial Rescript issued by the Japanese Emperor on 8 December 1941 declaring war on United States and Britain.

spirits of those who have offered their lives for the defence of the empire, without concern for their homes and their own lives, to those officers and men who are sick or wounded in remote strange lands, to those who are strenuosly fighting on Land, sea, and in the air by defying extraordinarily difficulties and dangers, and to those fellow-countrymen who have sent their husbands, sons, and brothers to the front enabling the latter to exert themselves without worry and who are looking after their homes or helping them and are doing their best in the service behind the guns by enduring all difficulties - to all of the them I wish to render my profound appreciation.

As I have already stated on various occasions, the object of the War of Greater East Asia has its origin in the great ideal which inspired the founding of our Empire. It aims at securely establishing a new order of co-existent and co-prosperity on ethical principles, with our Empire as its nucleus, by making each country and people in Greater East Asia have their proper place. It is completly different in its essential character from the attitude of the United States and Britain toward East Asia.

Singapore and other strategic points, which have hitherto been the bases of the United States and Britain for the invasion and domination of East Asia, are resurrecting with boundless hope and glory as bases for the construction of the New Order and defence for the peoples. Malay Peninsula are already starting on the road for such new construction with steady strides.

On this epochal occasion I wish to reiterate once more the real intentions of Japan to the peoples and countries concerned.

The Imperial forces are steadily carrying out offensive operations in the region of Burma also with its strategic points falling one after another into their hands. But the true intention of Japan in marching into Burma is to crush British military bases as well as to cut off the route for American and British aid to the Chiang-kai-shek regime. It is farthest from the thought of Japan to regard the Burmese people as her enemy. Therefore, if the Burmese people take full cognizance of the actual situation of Britain, which has exposed its utter inability, and offer to co-operative with Japan by shaking off many years past. Japan will gladly extend them its positive cooperation for the establisment of Burma for the Burmese, the long-cherished aspiration of the Burmese people.

It is a golden opportunity for India having, as it does several thousand years of history and splended cultural tradition, to rid herself of the ruthless despotism of Britain and participate in the construction of the Greater East Asia Co-prosperity sphere. Japan expects that India will restore its proper status as India for the Indians and it will not stint herself in extending assistance to the patriotic effort of the Indians. Should India fail to awaken to her mission forgetting her history and tradition, and continue as before to be beguiled by the British cajolery and manipulation and act at their beck and call. I cannot but fear that an opportunity for the renaissance of the Indian people would be forever lost.

8

Proceedings of Joint Conference of Representatives of Indian Independence League, Malaya and Thailand Regarding the Policy to be Adopted for Collaboration with Japanese for the Liberation of India at the Forthcoming Tokyo Conference[1]

9 March, 1942

Present : The following gentlemen were present.

The Indian Independence League, Malaya.

1. Shri N. Raghavan.
2. Shri B.K. Das.
3. Shri Suchca Singh.
4. Shri K.A.N. Iyer...
5. Dr. Majumdar...

From Singpore

6. Shri S.C. Goho.
7. Shri K.P.K. Menon...

Indian Independence League, Thailand.

8. Sardar Pritam Singh.
9. Sardar Amar Singh.
10. Dr. Onkar Singh.

Indian National Council, Thailand :

11. Swami Satyanand Puri,

Indian National Army.

---

1. Indian Independence league papers collected by the History of Freedom unit F. No. 45/3. Now deposited with the National Archives of India, New Delhi. (In future referred to as I.I.L. papers). See also. K.S. Giani. op. cit. pp. 33-40. The above collection is very important to understand the early activities of the Indian National Army and Indian Independence League in South East Asia.

12. Captain Mohan Singh.
13. Captain Mohamad Akram.

Indian Prisoners of war.

14. Lieut. Col. N.Z. Gill.
15. Major M.L. Kiani.

Mr. Otagura attended the meeting as observer.

Shri N. Raghavan presided and requested Major Fujiwara to open the Conference. Major Fujiwara expressed very great pleasure at having had the opportunity of meeting the representatives of the Indian Independence League of Thailand and Malaya. The meeting was of particular significance in that it was being held in the citadel of British Imperialism in Asia, namely Singapore. He wished the conference every success and earnestly hoped that their endeavours to liberate India would be crowned with success. He regrets that he could not remain longer with them owing to other engagements. Shri Raghavan thanked Major Fujiwara for his very encouraging words. Major Fujiwara then left the meeting.

The Chairman then requested Sardar Pritam Singh to address the meeting. Sardar Pritam Singh explained how the Indian Independence League was formed in Thailand at Bangkok and then thanked the Indians in Malaya for their ready cooperation in having organised branches of the League in all centres of Malaya.

The Chairman proposed a resolution appreciating the patriotic work of Sardar Pritam Singh and thanking him on behalf of the Indian community in Malaya for his selfless work in the cause of the liberation of their motherland. The resolution was acclaimed unanimously by the conference.

The Chairman then pointed out that two points were to be considered by the conference.

1. Whether the present time is the proper occasion for the Indians in Far East to take action for the attainment of Indian Independence.
2. If this is the proper occasion, how should We proceed towards the attainment of our goal.

Captain Mohan Singh said that he got into contact with Sardar Pritam Singh at a place near Jitra on 15th December, 1941 and learned about the Indian Independence League. Subsequently he met Major Fujiwara, and after that he had been in constant touch with them. At first he was doubtful of the Major's purpose, but now he was fully convinced of his sincerity in desiring to assist in the liberation of India from British control. The situation that all of them had visualised to that time was completely changed with the fall of Singapore. They did not expect to find in

Singapore such a very large number of Indian soldiers, nearly 50,000. The total strength of the Indian Army now in Malaya was near, 60,000. To feed them, to equip them and to look after their other requirements would be a big problem, and the Indian Independence League must give immediate consideration to it.

Lieut. Col. Gill spoke about the 50,000 Indian prisoners of war at Singapore and wished to know what was to become of them.

Swami Satyananda Puri explained the formation and objects of his organisation, the Indian National Council of Thailand. The objects were mainly, (1) to work in cooperation with the political activities in India, (2) to win the sympathy of the Indian National Congress, (3) to secure all India leader as President of the organisation. Explain the third object, he told the meeting that Pandit Jawaharlal Nehru was reported to have stated that Indians residing outside India could not interfere in Indian politics and that those who do so could be considered as traitors. This organisation was therefore afraid that it might by treated as a body of Quislings in the pay of the Japanese. Unless all possibilities of such a stigma were removed, nothing could be achieved. He therefore suggested that contact should be established with Sri Subhas Chandra Bose and that he be requested to lead us. Swami Satyanand Puri said that he had sent a Telegram to Shri Bose from Bangkok on 2nd February 1942 to that effect and had received a reply over the radio agreeing to accept the Presidentship of the Indian organisation in the Far East working for Indian Independence.

Shri S.C. Goho requested Sardar Pritam Singh to explain to the conference the purpose of the proposed delegation to Tokyo.

The Sardar said that the delegation was proposed to meet in an informal conference at Tokyo, to discuss the problem of Indian representatives and to negotiate with Japanese authorities terms of cooperation with Japan for achieving the independence of India.

Lieut. Col. Gill stressed the importance of carrying out effective propaganda in India to prepare the necessary atmosphere so that the Indian army overseas would receive the willing cooperation and help of all Indians when it should match into India. The Indian army had been till now fighting under certain pledges. Before they can break those pledges, they should be convinced that their former pledges were, really in keeping with the honour and self respect of free Indians, and that breaking them they would not be doing anything unsoldierly or dishonourable. For that too propaganda among them was essential.

Sardar Pritam Singh said that some propaganda was being carried on in the troops and that more would be done on that line.

Shri K.P.K. Menon discoursed at length on the Policy followed by the Indian National Congress till now. Two years ago the Working Committee of the Congress asserted complete independence as the goal of India. In the past the Congress had followed two methods both without success. It had first tried to appeal to the good sense and democratic sentiments of the British to grant freedom to the Indians. Later on, on the outbreak of the present war, Mahatma Gandhi started the 'No war campaign' which, however, did not ask the country to desist from helping in the war efforts by positively refusing men, money and material for the prosecution of the war. The result has been a "watchful inactivity" on the part of the Congress. There was a third course remaining, viz. the application of force. India was not prepared for that, but now that Japan was willing to offer us help, we should accept it. Efficient and effective propaganda should also be carried on both inside and outside India.

Shri S.C. Goho spoke on the necessity of creating in India confidence in the intentions of Japan regarding India.

Swami Satyananda Puri suggested that Japan should make a declaration assuring Indian Independence. He mentioned that he had heard over the radio that the Working Committee of the Congress had removed on 13th January, 1942 "non-violence" from the creed of the Congress.

Shri Sucha Singh stressed the necessity of immediate action as delay would be detrimental to the cause. India was ready for action.

Lieut. Col. Gill agreed with Shri Sucha Singh. He said that if the British were to know of the intentions of the overseas Indians, they may remove the Indian units from India to the Middle East and replace them with British units. Moreover, delay would make the strength of the British in India greater as they would be able to produce more ammunition and war materials. Hence delay would be suicidal to the cause.

Summary of conclusions reached at the conference.

1. This is the time when all Indians in Asia should unite for Indian freedom.
2. We believe that the psychological moment has come to strike for Indian freedom.
3. The first thing to do is to carry on propaganda within and outside India among the military forces and civilians.
4. Shri Subhash Chandra Bose should be requested to come to Tokyo and accept the leadership.

The meeting was adjourned till 1.30 A.M. Tokyo time. Tuesday, 10th March.

A Joint Conference of representatives of the Indian Independence League of Malaya and Thailand was held on Tuesday, 10th March, 1942.

Here follows the summary of the conclusions arrived at the conference.

1. Preferably with, otherwise without, the approval of Indian National Congress, we decide to act, if we shall be convinced that the action that we are going to take will be in the best interest of India.
2. We decide to work for the liberation of India with the assistance and support of the Nippon Government.
3. Propaganda and infiltration is to be carried out by each and every means. Details are to be left to an expert Committee.
4. The Tokyo conference is to be attended by Shri N. Raghavan, Shri K.A.N. Ayer, Shri S.C. Goho and Shri K.P.K. Menon as representatives from Malaya and Sardar Pritam Singh and Swami Satyananda Puri as representatives from Thailand.
   The delegat from the Indian army will be decided later on.
5. The delegation can at this stage (at The Tokyo conference) commit themselves to not more than inducing the Indian National Leaders to the view that may be adopted by the delegates at the Conference.
6. A resolution for placing Indian Prisoners of War in Singapore on the same footing as the Indian National Army unanimously, passed, to be forwarded to Major Fujiwara and any one else he may suggest.
   The Conference was adjourned since die.

9

Proceedings of Tokyo Conference which Decided the basis of Indo-Japanese Cooperation during the War for the Overthrow of the British in India; Indicate the Role of Indian National Army in its Fight for India's Liberation

28 March, 1942

The Indian Independence conference was held under the Chairmanship of Mr. Rash Behari Bose, at Sanna Hotel, Tokyo, Japan from Saturday, the 28th March, 1942 to Monday the 30th March, 1942 at which the following representatives were present[1] :

1.	Mr Rash Behari Bose.	2.	Mr. H. Raghavan
3.	Mr. K.P.K. Menon	4.	Mr. S.C. Goho
5.	Mr. Mohan Singh	6.	Mr. N.S. Gill
7.	Mr. G.M. Khan	8.	Mr. M.R. Mullick
9.	Mr. Osman, Hari Singh	10.	Mr. Piara Singh
11.	Mr. D.S. Deshpande	12.	Mr. A.M. Nair
13.	Mr. C. Lingham	14.	Mr. B.D. Gupta
15.	Mr. S.N. Sen	16.	Mr. L.R. Miglani
17.	Mr. Rajah Sherman	18.	Mr. K.V. Narain.

First day, Saturday the 28th March, 1942

Mr. Rash Behari Bose Chairman, opened the conference at 2 p.m. with the welcome address to all the delegates and other gentlemen and requested their whole-hearted cooperation in the attainment of the common object, viz. the complete Independence of India.

1. Foreign department, File No. 313-X/1942., National Archive of India (NAI). General Tojo, sent a message to the delagates expressing the intentions of Japan towards India and its desire to go ahead with its mission of destruction of the Anglo-Saxon powers. For the text of the message see K.S. Gyani, *op. cit.* p. 45.

At the outset the Chairman expressed heartfelt condolence on the demise of four colleagues, namely Mr. Pritam Singh, and Swami Satyanand Puri. Mr. K.A.N. Ayer and Mr. Mohammed Akram from Malaya who were to attend this conference and who met with a fatal air accident while on their way to Tokyo.

All stood up and offered profound prayer in silence for the repose of the souls of departed patriots.

The conference resolved to send letters of condolence to the bereaved families and Mr. Raghavan kindly undertook the responsibility of conveying the letters.

Resolved

1. (a) That this conference is shocked and grieved at the news of the air disaster in which four Indians representative viz. Messrs. Ayer and Mohammed Akram from Malaya and Mr. Pritam Singh and Swami Satyanand Puri[2] from Thailand who were travelling to Tokyo lost their lives and while expressing its deep sense of sorrow, place on record the great loss to the movement and the Indian generally caused by their untimely deaths.

   (b) That the copy of this resolution be sent with the condolence of this conference to the members of the bereaved families.

That this conference sends its sincerest condolence and sympathies to the members of the bereaved families of Mr. Otogora and six other Japanese gentlemen who lost their lives while travelling by the same plane to Tokyo.

At this Colonel Iwagoru, who attended representing the Government of Japan, kindly gave an adress of Welcome to the members of the conference. On behalf of the Imperial Government of Japan he expressed whole-hearted support to this conference in its noble efforts to achieve independence of India.

---

2. Satyanand Puri-(1902-1941) was a professor of Oriental philosophy at Calcutta University before he left for Thailand in 1932. On the recommendation of Rabindra Nath Tagore. His real name was Prafulla Kumar Sen. He founded the Thai-Bharata Cultural Lodge to foster close cultural relations between Thailand and India. Was President of Indian National Council formed in December, 1941 after the outbreak of war. Was not impressed by the Japanese support of Indian Independence. While going to Tokyo in March, 1942 died in the plane crash, alonghwith Sardar Pritam Singh and others. Swami had a deep suspicion about the Japanese intentions, but in order to protect the Indian Community in Thailand, he agreed to cooperate with the Japanese.

See Appendix "A".

Mr. Raghavan on behalf of the conference thanked suitably Colonel Iwagoru and through him the Imperial Japanese Government and the Japanese people for their kind encouragement.

Agenda No. 1

Attitude of the Indian regarding this war was taken up and the following resolution was read and unanimously passed.

Whereas we believe that this war of Greater East Asia is sure to destroy British influence and power in Asia, and whereas we believe that this golden opportunity for the realisation of India National Goal which is nothing but complete Independence and whereas depending upon the self-conscious effects of various Asiatic nations, a new Asia is sure to rise as a result of this war, we hereby resolve that we must join hands with Japan in accordance with the decreed policy of the Imperial Japanese Government, made through premier General Tojo on the occasion of the fall of Singapore.

Organisation

(a) Formation of local branches of leagues, for the duration of war, President to be elected by Committee from at the meeting of the representatives of the Place. Vacancy on the Committee to filled by the majority votes of the Committee.

President, not removable without the vote of the three-fourths of the members of the Committee.

(b) Central. The president of the various local bodies together with the representatives of the Indian Army in East Asia, which representatives shall not exceed the total number representatives who will lay down the general policy of action and elect a COUNCIL OF ACTION consisting of the President and for staff members, of whom at least two shall be from the military.

The council of action shall be responsible for the working cut the general policy and in such working out they shall appoint departmental officers of the purpose of administration.

Department Civils

(a) Foreign Department or liaison department
(b) Finance Department
(c) Legal Department
(d) Propaganda Department
(e) Relief Department

(g) Civil Volunteers Department

Indian National Army Headquarters Military

(a) War Department

(b) Recruiting Department

(c) Military Intelligence and Military Police Department

(d) Prisoners of War Department.

1. It is resolved that, if in the discretion of the Council of Action it is feasible to summon a meeting of the representatives and take their advice on matter of the general policy the Council shall do so.

2. It is resolved that, before taking any military action against India, (including Ceylon) contrary to the wishes, policy or opinion of the Indian National Congress, the Council of Action shall first get the approval of the Committee of the representatives and act as directed.

3. We request that military action against India will be taken only by the Indian National Army and under the command of Indians. Together with such military, naval and air cooperation and assistance as may be requested from the Japanese Authorities by the Council of Action.

Requests to the Imperial Japanese Government

1. It is resolved that, in further clarification of the attitude of Japan towards India, the Imperial Japanese Government be requested to make formal declaration to the effect.

(a) That Japan is willing and ready to give all possible help to India to sever its connection from British Empire to attain complete Independence.

(b) That on such severance of India from the British Empire Japan would recognise the full sovereignty of India on attaining Independence.

(c) The absolute independence of India would be guaranteed by the Imperial Japanese Government.

(d) That the Imperial Japanese Government of Japan would exercise its influence with other powers and induce them to recognise the Independence and sovereignty of India.

(e) That the framing of the future constitution of India will be left entirely to the representative of the people of India.

2. It was also resolved to request the Imperial Japanese Government to render such financial help for the successful carrying out of our object as may be required from the time to time on the distinct understanding that such help is to be treated as a loan to be repaid to Japan by the National Government of Independent India, when it comes into being.

3. To give all facilities for propaganda, Travel transport

communications, within the area under the control of the Imperial Japanese Government, in the manner and to the extent requested by the council of action and also all facilities to come into contact with the National Leaders, the workers, and organisations in India.

4. To clarify the position of Indian troops now under control in occupied territories.

5. To recognise and facilitate the use of the present National flag of India in all territories under Imperial Government of Japan.

6. To consult in all matters of administration affecting the Indian Community the Indian Independence Leagues of the respective places and places where there are no league recognised leaders of community approved by the league branch nearest to such place.

(a) This conference resolves that in order to obtain full support and cooperation of Indians in various parts of Greater East Asia, a fuller meeting of Indian representative should be called at Rangoon or any other suitable place at the earliest opportunity and that M Rash Behari Bose is hereby authorised to take the necessary step to give effects to the various decisions made by the conference pending their ratification at the later conference as stated above.

(b) This conference hereby appoints Mr. Rash Behari Bose as interim president of the Council of Action.

(c) Resolved that next conference shall be held before the 1st of June, 1942 possible and in any case not later than 1st of July, 1942, and interim president shall make necessary arrangements.

(d) Resolved that next Conference besides the Presidents and/or Representative of various Indian Independence League as hereinafter limited (in person or by proxy) and military representatives of Indian Army in East Asia, in all the members attending this conference should be invited to attend.

(e) The Conference to ratify the decisions herein shall be held at Bangkok in the 3rd week of May 1942, and representative and/or presidents not exceeding the number indicated herein below may attend the said conference.

Japan	8	Hong Kong	8	Thailand	9
Changhai	8	Macao and Manila	2	Indochina	5
Malaya	20	Burma	20	East India	8
				(Java, Sumatra, Borneo, Celebes)	

Total : 90

Representatives of the Indian Army in East Asia will also attend as previously agreed to (Under Agenda III. (b).

General

That this is Committed to a definite policy of the closest cooperation with Japan and it shall on electing an official definition of the term "Greater East Asia Co-prosperity sphere" and its application endeavour by every possible means at the command of this movement :–

1. To persuade Independent India to be a member of the sphere on a footing of equality with Japan.

2. To confer on Japan the most favoured National treatment on a reciprocal basis.

(A) This conference place on record its profound gratitude to the Imperial Government of Japan, for their active sympathy in the cause of Indian Independence and expresses its thanks for their generous hospitality and for the ample facilities provided for the successful termination of this conference.

(B) This conference put on record its profound thanks to Mr. Rash Behari Bose who by fact patience and generality as Chairman contributed not a little to the success of this conference.

(C) While they individually find themselves in perfect agreement with the decisions of this conference, the members of the good-will mission of Malaya hereby make they do not commi Indian in Malaya to the decisions of this conference but will try their best to induce them to the views of this conference. Mr. Osman's[3] suggestions on education and other matters contained in Appendix B, attached hereto are noted for action at the opportune time.

Appendix 'A'

"It is my great pleasure to greet you at this conference which would mark new birth of "India for the Indian". To day your dual ideology of

---

3. *Baba Hari Singh Allas Osman Khan*
An old member of the Ghadr Party, had played a prominent role in the Indo-German conspiracy to smuggle arms and ammunition in India during hte first World War. He lived in hiding after the War under alias Osman Khan in Indonesia and worked for a number of years with Emil Helffrich. He went to Shanghai in 1930 and was associated with the Japanese Naval authorities. Worked under Commander Hidoka of the China Intelligence Section. On the eve of the War, tried to establish contacts with the other Indian revolution aries in East Asia. With the help of the Japanese sent two persons to Thailand to inform Baba Amar Singh to contact Japanese Military Attache for help to start armed struggle against the British. Played an active role at Tokyo Conference. Went to Andamans in 1942 to start a branch of Indian Independence League. Had an implicit faith in Japanese sincerity.

"Independence of India" and India for the Indians over which you have been most concerned is going to realised before long because it is my belief that outbreak of the war has created an opportunity which is most favourable for its realisation. If you lose this golden opportunity by being crowardly lazy or too much involved in mutual antagonism, you and your descendants would remain slaves for nobody know how long. The objective world situation is rapidly changing. It is your mission to prepare fully and immediately so as to adjust your slaves for the fast changing times and liberate India from the British yoke. We the Japanese are prepared to give the spiritual and material aid to your revolutionary task without any compensation or condition. It is needless to say that the common enemy British will employ every means, such as the deceit, bribery, "Divide and rule policy and threats. On these points we must be very cautious. "Heaven helps those who helps themselves". Indian Independence cannot be sought from anybody, for less from India's enemy England, from whom you can only except oppression. India's able leaders must make good use of the surroundings international conditions, in order to lessen the amount of sacrifices involved. In her part what Japan expects from India that she should do away with all the retardings ideas of religious and class antagonisms and the various revalries between political and military ways of Independence, that she should realise that the realisation of Indian Independence in itself is a great revolution to be led to success only on the strength of her leader's firm determination and of the fiery patriotism of all the Indian and that realising that one action is superior to hundreds of arguments she should make use of conditions surrounding her and advance for the attainment of independence. And we wish to assist her in their ambition of India, and that we will not hesitate to extend and any help to the Indians in their fight and that without any ulterior motives.

Please take your own time and engage yourselves in calm deliberation so that you may arrive to a plan of action which may be beneficial on all parts for future India as well as East Asia. This is my request to you all, and it comes from the bottom of heart.

Appendix 'B'

1. Specific instructions should be given to any troops attacking India to refrain themselves and to stop others from destroying places of worship belonging to the various religious bodies in order to avoid any sort of friction liable to be caused by such sabotage acts.

2. As soon as possible the property of the Indian Government and other rich Indians considered pro-British including the Indian princes should be placed under the joint control and custody of the occupying Indian troops to avoid embezzlement or looting etc.; so that on expiration the war the Indian Government may be in the position to cover up the expense.

3. In all kinds of Government affairs, external or internal the Indian Religious leaders should not be consulted and their membership should never be taken in various state councils.

4. Compulsory education, irrespective of male and female sect, should be started as soon as possible on realisation of the independence of India.

5. Various societies opened in different cities found not in favour of achieving complete Independence of India and not cooperating with the main body, should be dissolved as soon as possible.

6. Able and patriotic volunteers should be enlisted from every part of East Asia including Shanghai, Honking, Java, Sumatra, etc. so that they can enjoy equal privileges in order that they also partake in serving their motherland.

7. All Indian Nationals, irrespective of their financial standing class or religion, should be treated on an equal footing in the matter of state affairs.

8. In war time just as women in all countries of the world are allowed to take full share in rendering their best service for the freedom of their respective countries, similarly Indian women are also anxious to fulfil their duties, in every possible way for the freedom of our country. But in the British region, the women of India have not been given the same power and freedom which men have so far, as a result of which women in India have not been allowed to take part in Government affairs. In order to rise them to the same standard of freedom as the men we should allow them the discretion of taking active part in serving our motherland even against the wishes of their parents, husbands and other relatives supposed to be Pro-British. Military training should be considered as compulsory part of education.

10

Interrogation Report of Major Fujiwara; Explains the Circumstances Leading to the Formation of Indian National Army; How he Inspired Capt. Mohan Singh to take Charge of Indian Prisoners of War; gives Credit to Sardar Pritam Singh for his Patriotism; Comments on difficulties faced by him in Dealing with Japanese High Command for an Independent Status for Indian National Army (Extract)[1]

Fujiwara[2] in April 1941 was told to concentrate on American Affairs as he might be sent to America. However, owing to general deterioration in relation between Japan and America he was unable to go. It was not until August 1941 that he began to study Indian Affairs.

Before he left for Siam he was told to work as Assistant to the Military Attache Col. Tamura. He was to control and support members of the Indian Independence movement. Fujiwara requested Gen. Okamoto head of No. 2 section to choose someone more suitable for the job than himself. He pointed out that he had no experience of work of this kind

---

1. South-East Asia Translation and Interrogation Centre. Bulletin No. 234. This report may be read alongwith the memorandum-compiled by Fujiwara at Appendix III.
2. Fujiwara (1907-1986)
Born in 1907 in Hygo. After graduation in 1927, he entered Military Academy, Tokyo and joined the staff college in 1935 . Became a staff offier in 1938. At the time of his posting in Siam, he was promoted as Major-Rated by the British as being of doubtful reliability, still was considered as a clever staff office with plenty of initiative; was popularly called the midwife of Indian National Army; was associated with its rise and fall; was head of Fujiwara Kikan till 1942. After the war became a Lieut. General in Japanese Self-defence Force. After retirement was head of the Fujiwara Asian Research Institute in Tokyo.

and knew nothing India. Besides he could not speak either English or Hindi or any other language spoken in Southern Asia. His objections was overruled and he was told that he would receive instructions from Col. Tamura who was experienced in this type of work.

According to reports from the Military Attache in Bangkok, the Indian Independence League which had its headquarters at Bangkok and which had branches in Shanghai, Hongkong and Siam had contacted the Japanese Military Attache about June 1941 in order to obtain help from the Japanese Government against the British and to develop Indo-Japanese collaboration. The Military Attache had sent in optimistic reports of the size and power of the Indian Independence Movement but these had been belied by report from Col. Ichida[3] then stationed in India who reported that the political parties in India especially the Congress was not favourably inclined, despaired Japan. The Congress party according to Col. Ichida strongly condemned Japanese aggression in China and upholding its principles of non-violence did not welcome assistance from the Asian countries. In Ichida's opinion, therefore little cooperation from the India was to be expected. No links were established with the Congress party.

Further there was no prominent Indian resident in Japan who could be used as a leader of these movements. In fact the Japanese were afraid that some of the Indian residents in Japan might be British agents. A certain Mahender Partap had visited Col. Odeki in Imperial H.Q. in 1941 about the publication of a Hindustani Newspaper in Japan but the Japanese were not impressed.

For these reasons, the Japanese had to pin their hopes for Indo-Japanese cooperation on the I.I.L. in Bangkok. However, the Japanese were hamphered by their lack of experts on Indian Affairs. Takaoka Daisuke, a member of the Diet and Kimura Nikki a professor at the University of Ceylon and one or two others wrote books attempting to explain India to the Japanese but Fujiwara did not think that these publications had been particularly effective. Among the Military Generals Sugiyama and Imamura, Lt. Gen. Hono, Ando, Kuroda and others had been stationed in India during the reign of Taisho 1912-26 when they were junior officers. But at that time there was no question[7] of war between Britain and Japan and they had take no advantage of their opportunities. Col. Toshima who had previously been Military Attache in India was in

---

3. Col. Ichida was Japanese Consul. General in India.

Brazil in December 1941 and Col. Ichida was at that time interested in D.I.A. Neither was therefore available to give their expert advice.

In Bangkok, Col. Tamura realised that Fujiwara had no experience of the work he was requested to do, nor had he training in languages. Tamura, therefore instructed him to stay in Bangkok in order to get acquainted with the life and situation in the Southern Area.

In the middle of October 1941, Tamura introduced Fujiwara to the I.I. League. According to Tamura's introductory explanation it was a secret organisation working for the Indian Independence which had first approached him in the summer of 1941. It had its headquarters in Bangkok and its principle figure were Amar Singh and Pritam Singh. Amar Singh was too old for successful work and the real power was Pritam Singh. Tamura considered that collaboration with these people was the only way of making progress on the Indian question. Col. Tamura therefore asked Pritam Singh to meet Fujiwara. The first meeting was devoted to mere introductions. Fujiwara met and talked to Pritam on about three occasions. One occasion he was accompanied by Amar Singh. As interpreter Fujiwara used Ohtaguro who had been a teacher in the Japanese Elementary School in Singapore.

At first the discussion was about political condition in India and the current state of affairs in the independence movement. Fujiwara listened to Pritam Singh and formed his general impression of his personality. From these conversation Fujiwara obtained the following impressions :–

(1) Both Amar Singh and Pritam Singh were ardent and zealious enthusiasts for Indian Independence, who had no ulterior motive.

(2) I.I.L. had no connection with the Congress and although they appeared to have some members in Hong kong, Shanghai and Southern Siam they did not have as powerful an organisation as the General staff had expected.

(3) The I.I.L. did not have friendly relations with the other Indian parties in Bangkok (Swami, Das).

(4) The I.I.L. did not appear to have any organised branches in Malaya and Burma.

(5) Pritam Singh had a great respect for Subhash Chandra Bose.

Towards the end of November or the beginning of December information reached Tamura that there was little chance of compromise in Washington and war between Japan and Britain and America was inevitable.

On instructions from Tamura, Fujiwara drafted an agreement which was approved by Tamura for the Japanese and by Amar Singh[4] for the

Indians. The Agreement was reported to the Japanese Southern Area Army Headquarters. Pritam Singh became much more active when he heard of the likelihood of war. The Agreement was briefly as follows :

(i) The final objective was stated to be the establishment of peace in Greater East Asia by cooperation between two equal and free nations– Japan and India.

(ii) The I.I.L. was to prosecute a campaign against Britain to secure complete independence of India from the British yoke. For this purpose, Japan pledged herself to give all possible aid and guaranteed that she had no ambition in India whether political, economic, cultural, religious or otherwise.

(iii) The I.I.L. was to pursue the following policy as soon as the war started.

(A) The I.I.L. would advance with the Japanese Army into Southern Siam and later into Malaya where they would expand the I.I.L. and encourage anti-British feeling. At the same time, they were to promote cooperation between Indian residents and the Japanese.

(B) The I.I.L. was to organise a voluntary army who would fight for Indian Independence. This Army was to be staffed by Indian Army officers and men and from local Indian volunteers. (This article was suggested by Pritam Singh who considered that an invasion of India by Japanese forces alone would be misunderstood and would not be welcomed in India. He wanted Indians to take part in her own liberation).

(iv) The Japanese Army was to show its support for the Indian Independence by a friendly attitude towards Indians in the areas that they occupied and conciliatory treatment was to be accorded to Indian Prisoners of War.

---

4. *Baba Amar Singh 1883-*
A great Indian revolutionary, son of Wariam Singh, a Jat Sikh of Ludhiana was born in 1883. Went to Siam in 1903 served as a surveyor on the Northern Siamese railway under the Germans. During the war came in contact witht he Ghadrites. Was convicted in the Mandalay conspiracy case and sentencted to death, which was later converted to life imprisonment. After serving 20 years in Rangoon, was released in 1937. Went back to Thailand in early 1940 to pursue his aim of outing the British. Contacted his old Comrades in Bangkok, Shanghai, Singapore and Burma. Worked closely with Pritam Singh in the Indian Independence League. joined the Japanese on the eve of the Pacific War and was instrumental in signing an agreement with Lt. Col. Tamura, the Japanese Military attache in Bangkok.

(v) The I.I.L. was to extend its organisations to all areas in the South-East-Asia in the wake of operation. The Japanese guaranteed full support.

(vi) Thc I.I.L. undertook to prosecute a vigorous propaganda campaign in all occupied areas as well as in India proper. On their part the Japanese undertook to allow the I.I.L. to use all Japanese propaganda organs including Tokyo (Tokyo broadcast were not clearly received at that time. But Berlin broadcast by Bose were thought to have made a profound impression in India).

(vii) Details were to be discussed by local H.Q. and minor problems dealt with as they arose.[5]

Fujiwara pointed out that the Sikh elements predominated in the movement at that time. He felt that there would be little possibility of major developments of the I.I.L., unless it could embrass all Indians of whatever caste, race or religion. Pritam Singh agreed.

Information that war would start within a few days was received on 4 December 1941 and Fujiwara was then appointed the staff of the Southern Area Army. At the same time Col. Tamura was told that Indian affairs in Siam and Malaya would henchforth be the responsibility of the C-in-C Southern Area simultaneously Southern Army placed all matters pertaining to Malaya directly under the Commander of 25th Army. As a result the Tamura-Pritam Singh Agreement was referred to 25th Army. On 6 December, a signal was received stating that war would begin on 9 December and Fujiwara contacted Pritam Singh to make preparation to move South. They left Bangkok for Singora on 10 December by Air. Pritam Singh was accompanied by 21 Associates and Fujiwara by Captain Tsuchimchi and 2 Lt. Yonemura who had been working in the military Attache's office in Bangkok since November 1941. On arrival in Singora, Fujiwara reported to H.Q. 25 Army and met the G.O.C. Chief of Staff. Fujiwara acquainted himself with the plan of operations and with dispositions of Japanese forces. At the same time he received orders to form the Fujiwara Kikan whose duties were :

5. No authentic copy of this agreement could be traced in the records available in India or U.K. Fujiwara's version of the agreement as given in his Memoirs F. Kikam is quite different from the one he has given during the interrogation. Another Japanese Government publication *Subash Chandra Bose and Japan* mentions that in the agreement the Japanese Government agreed to put Pritam Singh's organisation in touch with Subhas in Berlin. But on this point, Fujiwara is silent. A copy of hte agreement was sent to the Imperial General Headquarters at Tokyo and the Southern Army Headquarters at Saigon for information and approval. It is not known as to whether, this was approved by the Japanese authorities.

(a) To carry out the policy laid down in the Tamura-Pritam Singh Agreement (emphasis was placed on support of the I.I.L.).
(b) To send out Liaison officers with each column to secure proper treatment for India P.W. and Indian residents in the area occupied. They were to prevent friction between the Japanese Army and Indian everywhere.
(c) To rescue and protect the Sultans and if possible to support pro-Japanese propaganda among the Chinese and the Malayas.
(d) To report all cases of misbehaviour of Japanese towards the local population.
(e) To ensure secrecy regarding the plans and movements of the Japanese army when they were cooperating with the I.I.L.

Army H.Q. ordered all operational units to cooperate with the Fujiwara Kikan in all measures adopted by the Kikan so long as they did not impede operations.

The officers of the Kikan could not speak either English or Hindustani. It was, therefore all the more necessary to carry out the promises they had made and to show their friendliness by deeds if not by words. With this aim they had to support the locals even in disputes with the Japanese officers and men even though their inclination might be against such action. They had to be careful to show that they considered the Indians the equals of Japanese and had to avoid any suggestion of patronising. As these principles had been very carefully installed into the minds of all members of the Kikan, they were able to command the "affectionate respect and trust of the Indian prisoners". No unfortunate incidents occurred between December 1941 and April 1942.

Plan for Assisting the I.I.M.

(i) Establishment of Branch of I.I.L. at Alor Stor. After the successful outcome of the engagement at Jitra Kikan HQ and I.I.H.Q. were transferred to Alor Stor on 12th December 1941. Arriving at Alor Stor the I.I.L. at once convened a meeting of Indian locals. Pritam Singh spoke on the principles of Indian Independence Movement. He received a very enthusiastic welcome and opened a branch there. At the same time the Indians who had fled from their homes gradually returned.

(ii) Arrival of Mohan Singh. On the afternoon of 13th December the I.I.L. reported that there was a battalion of Indian troops located some 25 miles east of Alor Stor, who intended to surrender owing to their large casualities. Also their escape route was cut. The Commander of the battalion was an English Lt. Col. Fitzpatrik and all the other officers and men were Indians. Early in the morning of 14 December Major Fujiwara and Pritam Singh accompanied by interpreter Otagura set out unarmed to contact the battalion. Following the advise of some Indian locals they stopped on the way in a rubber estate and established contact with the British Commander by means of local inhabitants. While carrying out the surrender negotiations, they had a breakfast with the British Commander. The negotiations were carried on in a friendly spirit and they immediately left for the Battalion position where arrangements for surrender were made. Captain Mohan Singh was the senior Company Commander. The Battalion handed over all their weapons in a well disciplined manner. Afterwards Pritam Singh established friendly relations with the Indian officers. Immediately after they had returned to Alor Stor the British Commander was sent to Japanese Army HQ.

*(iii) D*iscussion with Mohan Singh for about a week after the surrender of the Battalion. Major Fujiwara discussed matters with Captain Mohan Singh explaining to him the Emperor's desire for the emancipation of the subject peoples. Captain Mohan Singh expressed his earnest wish to see India independent. He understood the principles of I.I.L. movement and agreed with them in general terms, but stressed the importance of forming a volunteery Army. It was first necessary to instill the idea of independence into the minds of the officers and men of the Battalion. Major Fujiwara agreed with Mohan Singh in this particular and stressed the importance of active enthusiasm. It was left to Mohan Singh to instill these concepts into the minds of the Indian officers and men without undue haste.

(iv) Mohan Singh criticism of Japanese Policy. On 19th December the Kikan moved to Sungei Patni and thereafter to Taiping. Captain Mohan Singh had a number of conversation with Pritam Singh and in conversation pointed out to Fujiwara that the Indians disproved of Japanese aggressive policy in China and Manchuria and of their method of colonisation in Korea and Formosa. Fujiwara promised, however, that the principles of Tamura–Pritam Singh agreement would be upheld in every respect as regards India and that Japan had no imperialist intention in the Southern Area. Mohan Singh expressed confidence in Bose as a leader and considered that there would be more chances of success for the movement if he could be brought to take charge.

(v) Interview with Yamastita on 17 December Pritam Singh, Mohan Singh and other officers visited Japanese 25 Army H.Q. in Alor Stor and met General Yamastita. Yamastita gave the interview in order to show

personally his support for the movement, his respect for their patriotism and to promise all possible assistance through Fujiwara. The I.I.L. advanced to Sungei Patani on 19 December from there to Penang and by the end of the December 1941, it had advanced to Taiping. Ipoh was reached in the beginning of January 1942. The I.I.L. held meetings everywhere, they always received an enthusiastic welcome as at Alor Stor. Branches were established at each place. Fujiwara accompanied Pritam Singh. Raghavan and Menon who were both influential persons were contacted in Penang.

As a result of the activities of the I.I.L. local Indians became reconciled to the Japanese Army and many sepoys who had deserted after the battle of Jitra after discarding their uniform and arms began to come to the Indian Barracks at Alor Stor and Sungei Patani. Towards the end of December, Mohan Singh who was suffering from his 39th bout of Malaria visited Fujiwara in Alor Stor and announced that he had made the following decisions.

(A) With the assistance of the Japanese, the Indians would set up an Independence Movement.
(B) An Indian National Army would be organised at once.
(C) The I.N.A. should be clearly connected with the I.I.L. for the time being.
(D) Mohan Singh should be responsible for the guidance of Indian P.W.
(E) The Japanese Army should accord friendly treatment to Indian P.W.
(F) Those who wished to participate in the I.N.A. should be enrolled under the command of Captain Mohan Singh.
(G) The I.N.A. should be recognised as an ally of the Japanese Army.

These discussions were conveyed to the Army Commander who agreed and stressed that the way to success for the movement was close cooperation between I.N.A. and I.I.L.

In the above conversation Mohan Singh added that though he had taken some time to reach these decisions, his determination was incontrovertible as it was in accordance with the feelings of the Indian officers and men in Sungei Patani and Alor Star. Fujiwara expressed his respect for these decisions and promised all possible support for the I.N.A. but he emphasised the need for close cooperation between I.N.A. and I.I.L.

Fujiwara's Impression of Mohan Singh

Fujiwara formed the impression from the time he met him at Alor

Stor that Captain Mohan Singh was an ardent and strong willed patriot who was very careful in the way he came to a decision. He was considerate to his subordinates and was sincerely respected by them.

On 3 January 1942, the Kikan and the I.I.L. moved to Ipoh. I.N.A. H.Q. followed and the I.I.L. opened another branch at Ipoh. In accordance with the wishes of Mohan Singh the Indian Army prisoners from Penang were concentrated in Ipoh. Here there were no Japanese guards and activities were unrestricted. In the Camp, the Liaison officers of the Fujiwara/Kikan lived, worked and charged there pleasures with the Kikan troops. In Ipoh, at the request of the I.N.A. and I.I.L. pamphlets for use among Indian soldiers and civilians were produced. These were entrusted by the Fujiwara Kikan to Japanese Air units for distribution.

The I.I.L. and H.Q. of Fujiwara Kikan moved to Kaula Lumpur on 15 January. They remained there till 12 February. As the Japanese Army progressed I.I.L. opened branches in Kuala Lumpur. Sere-mben, Malacca, Maur, Johore and other large and small cities occupied in the day to day advance. They held discussions and cooperated mutually with influential Indians in each place. They assisted Indians in difficulties and protected Indian deserts and stagglers. With the influence of volunteers, it was clear that the influence was spreading throughout Malaya. The I.I.L. reported all cases of illegal requisitioning of goods from Indians to the Fujiwara Kikan who took steps to remedy grievances. Any other reasons for Indian discontact with the Japanese Army were also reported to Fujiwara Kikan for action. As a result of these measures, local confidence in the Fujiwara Kikan increased.

Activities of the I.N.A.

I.N.A. H.Q. moved to Kuala Lumpur in the middle of January. Mohan Singh in collaboration with Fujiwara Kikan made many effort to improve the quarters and supplies for some 2,000 Indian P.W. interned in Kuala Lumpur and Maur. In addition he collected volunteers for the I.N.A. and made preparations for organising the force. A certain amount of training was carried on.

After the battles of Jitra, Salim and Maur Indian's deserted in large number and took to the jungle. It was realised that much of the arms and equipment thrown aside by these man was going into the hands of the Communists.

With the unexpected speedy progress of the operations it was anticipated that the British Indian Army would retire to Sumatra and Java without putting up a strong resistance in Singapore. Recognising this fact, Mohan Singh realised the need for immediately increasing the number of volunteers for the I.N.A. Therefore, he chose out a number of able men and sent them to the front to carry out pro-I.N.A. propaganda. According to Fujiwara there were about 200 members of the I.N.A. at the time of the capture of Singapore. He was unable to give any details of their activities during the attack on Singapore, but some 1500 Indian desertee and stragglers were rounded up by their efforts.

The surrender of the British force was signed on 15 February 42 and on 16 February Fujiwara was made responsible for all Indian P.W. Fujiwara prepared a speech to deliver to all Indian P.W. This speech was approved by the Chief of Staff who also agreed to do his best to provide quarters and supplies for Indian P.W. Fujiwara took charge of some 45,000 P.W. at Ferer Park from British Staff officer Hunt. Immediately afterwards Fujiwara delivered his speech on 17 February 1942 followed by Pritam Singh and Mohan Singh.

The I.N.A. and Kikan worked day in and day out to house, feed and supply the tens of thousands of Indian soldiers spread throughout Malaya peninsula and in Singapore. Japanese guards and Indian camps were withdrawn and autonomous control established.

As in other places over Malaya mass meetings were held in Singapore. After negotiations with the Japanese Army freedom of association, freedom of speech and permission to hoist the Congress flag were agreed to. On 1 March 1942, Southern Army informed 25 Army that the staff department was arranging a meeting of representatives Indians in Tokyo to discuss measures for the establishment of Indian Independence. Ten representatives from Siam and Malaya were required Fujiwara and Col. Iwaguro were ordered to accompany these representatives and Fujiwara was warned that, Col. Iwaguro would replace him as O.C. Fujiwara explained this project to the I.N.A. and I.I.L. and conference was held at the house of Mr. Goho. The following representatives were nominated.

I.I.L. Raghavan, Menon, Aiyer, Goho, Swami Satyanand Puri, Pritam Singh.

I.N.A. Lt. Gill, Mohan Singh and Captain Akram.

The party left Singapore on 10 March, 1942.

The first aircraft arrived safely but the second aircraft had an accident owing to bad weather and all were killed.[6]

While in Saigon, Fujiwara was officially informed that Col. Iwaguro

---

6. Those who died in the plane accident were Swami Satyanand Puri, Pritam Singh, K.A. N-Ayer and Mohammad Akram.fdf

would be taking over from him and that he would return to Southern Army H.O. after he had reported to Imperial H.Q.

As a result Fujiwara did not take part in the conversation which took place in the Sano Hotel. Fujiwara returned to Singapore on 15 April. While in Tokyo, Fujiwara reported to the Chief of the General Staff to the chief of No. 2. Section and to the Head of the 8 Departments. In his report, he emphasised the following points.

(a) The Indians flatly refused to allow the Independence Movement to be used to further Japanese Imperialist ambitions and would not allow the I.I.L. or the I.N.A. to be used as puppets. Such method would not receive support from inside India.

(b) The I.I.M. should be based on the support of the masses and on public opinion. No success for the I.N.A. could be expected without enthusiastic backing. As a result it was essential that there should be close cooperation betwee the I.I.L. and the I.N.A.

(c) All Indians of every party in the I.I.M. aimed at complete independence with democratic constitution like that of Britain. They did not generally sympathise with Axis plans and aspirations and resented interference or coercion. In supporting Indian Independence, Japan had to acknowledge these facts and had to be careful not to attempt to force upon I.I.L. and I.N.A. Japanese principles and methods. Condensation from others was deeply resented by the Indians.

(d) Indian opinion disliked Japanese aggression policy in Manchunia, Formosa, Korea and China. In order to gain the approval of Indian opinion it would be necessary to review Japanese policy in these spheres in relation to the new conditions. Further unless Japanese respect for liberty and equality was proved by their actions in the liberated countries of South East Asia, i.e., by respecting the independence of Siam and Burma, no success could be expected.

(e) It was desirable that the support of the parties within India be obtained for the movement and especially the support of the Congress party. For this purpose the I.N.A. and I.I.L. should confirm as near as possible to the policy of the Congress party.

(f) The basis of Japanese in supporting the Indian Independence Movement should be the creation of a united state which stood above difference of religion and caste. All action at encouraging such differences should be avoided. However, the Japanese should allow the movement to develop in its own way.

(g) Indians in Southern Area had a great respect for Subhash Bose, then in Berlin. To clarify these points Japan should make a clear statement of her fundamental attitude towards India and should take measures to prove her support of the I.I.M. All promises should be kept and they should sincerely be encouraged a spontaneous Indian movement for Indian Independence without ultior intentions. The Iwagura Kikan should be regarded primarily as a liaison unit. About 10 April Fujiwara arrived back in Singapore where he dissolved the Kikan and retired to Supreme H.Q. in Saigon arriving there by the end of April.

Fujiwara was much impressed by the passionate expressions of gratitude of members of the I.I.L. and I.N.A. and Indian P.W. when he bade farewell. Fujiwara was pleased to recollect that there had not been a single instance of unfriendly relations between the Indians and the Kikan during the period he was in charge, i.e., during the first stages of organisation.

11

Additional Information on the Events Leading to the Formation of the Indian National Army as given by Major Fujiwara during the subsequent Interrogation (Extract)[1]

Before going on to deal with the negotiations between Giani Pritam Singh and Fujiwara, a description of the state of political feeling amongst Indians in Bangkok will not be out of place.

2. Though Fujiwara, is himself unable to give many details about the pre-war Indian Independence movement in Bangkok, it now is possible to reconstruct from other sources, the part played by renegade Indians, who, in the hope of securing the freedom of their country from one power, were prepared to make themselves subservient to another. In Bangkok the whole Indian Independence movement under Japanese auspices throughout South East Asia originated. And, as by 1945 this movement was to have flourishing branches in all countries occupied by the Japanese, and in the I.N.A., under the dynamic leadership of S.C. Bose, was to weld itself into a fighting body which might have seriously prejudiced the Allied military effort in Burma and Malaya, some details of its early history are relevant and of more than academic interest.

3. While dealing with the inception of the Indian Independence Movement in Bangkok, it is a point of historical interest to note that it was in that city also that the diehards of the I.N.A. (belonging to S.C. Bose's entourage and to 'X' Regiment) took refuge in 1945 following the collapse of the Japanese forces in Burma.

4. The pre-war Indian community in Bangkok, comprising mainly petty traders dependent on the support of the British Legation and Consulate in the furtherance of their business interests, were not generally

1. F. No. 250/I.N.A. papers. The interrogation took place in 1946, but the events described cover this early period. As such the report is included here.

speaking, politically-minded. The "Indian Association of Thailand", a body functioning, under the aegis of HM Legation for common social and commercial interests, but excluding matters relating to religion or politics, and whose chief office-bearers were some of the senior members of the business community, had been in existence since 1928.

5. In 1940, a change was noticeable however, first by the election to the committee of the Association of some younger and more radically-minded members and by the foundation of Nov. 1940 of the "Thai Bharat Cultural Lodge". The leading spirits in this enterprise were : –

(1) Swami Satyananda Puri, a Hindu of good education and culture, something of an ascetic and visionary, and with strong political and nationalist leanings.

(2) Deb Nath Das, an Indian domiciled in Tokyo, whence he came with the avowed intention of organising anti-British activities.

6. The "Thai Bharat Cultural Lodge", apart from its ostensible object indicated by its title, was a body whose subversive trend was sufficiently indicated by the hoisting of the Congress flag at its inaugural meeting.

7. After this somewhat provocative and challenging ceremony of initiation, little was heard of the "Thai Bharat Cultural Lodge" during the next twelve months, a sate of affairs which can be accounted for :–

(1) By the return of Deb Nath Das to Japan, while Swami Satyananda Puri, his lieutenant, being more of scholar than politician, shared a vaning interest in the Lodge's political activities.

(2) By the coercive measures taken by HM Legation in collaboration which he Government of India to penalise Indians participating in anti-British activities.

8. During this uneasy period, two other personalities made their appearance, the first of these was Giani Pritam Singh, formerly a Sikh missionary, "whose conversation and aspect was always in religious tones and terms and gestures", and grand fatherly Baba Amar Singh, who we fears imprisonment for his part in the Mandalay conspiracy had served only to strengthen his implacable hatred for the British, and who, on the termination of his sentence, had managed to escape from India by evading the passport authorities and had established himself in the Sikh Gurudwara in Bangkok.

9. These two Sikhs do not, however, appear, if one source is to be believe, to have had complete mutual understanding, as is apparent by a visit paid to HM Consul General in the autumn of 1941 by one Lal Singh, an emissary from Baba Amar Singh, denouncing the treasonable activities

of Giani Pritam Singh. Shortly after, Baba Amar Singh, either knowing or appreciating that the zero hour for the Far East was at hand, and so probably desirous of lying low until he saw how the tide of war would go, removed himself to northern Thailand, while the reappearance of Deb Nath Das in Hongkong in Oct./Nov. 1941, was a further indication of the probable course of events.

10. In connection with the activities of Deb Nath Das and Swami Satyananda Puri, Fujiwara has stated that Col. Tamura told him that Deb Nath Das and Puri had called at the Japanese Embassy to sound the Japanese on their views on the Indian question. But as Col. Tamura had already committed himself to cooperating with Giani Pritam Singh, he told Swamy Satyananda Puri and Deb Nath Das to make up their differences with Giani Pritam Singh, as the Japanese did not intend to give support to any one Indian faction at the expense of the other. (If this information supplied by Fujiwara of Swami Satyananda Puri having approached the Japanese, is correct, Swami Satyananda Puri was much more than the visionary and other worldly ascetic which he has some times been thought to be).

11. Another account, of some interest, but as yet not confirmed from any source, is given by Civ. Kartar Singh in CSDIC (I) 'V' Sec. Repb. F/308 Page 7 and 'V' Sec. Intelligence Rept. No. 2 dated 23 Jan. 46.[2] This is to the effect that some time before the war, the Japanese brought to Bangkok two members of the San Francisco "Ghadar Party" from their Shanghai office. These men were :–

1. Kartar Singh Guami, who later went to Burma.
2. Harnam Singh Dhillon, who later went to Penang.

The following were also privy to the presence of these men in Bangkok :–

1. Amar Singh Sachdev (CSDIC (I) 'V' Sec. Rept. VK/11)[1]
2. Ishan Singh Sethi who was connected with the Immigration Dept. and stood guarantee for Kartar Singh Qaumi and Harnam Singh Dhillon ('V' Sec. Rept. F/277)
3. Master Bhagwan Singh CSDIC (I) 'V' Sec. Rept. F/278.

Kartar Singh further states that "Amar Singh Sachdev knew the Japanese schemes for going to war against the Allies and the Japanese,

2. These reports have not been reproduced, but can be consulted amongst the I.N.A. papers now deposited with the National Archives of India.

took him into their confidence and he was feeding fat on Japanese money".

Note : OC 'V' Sec. considers that these allegations made by Kartar Singh against Amar Singh Sachdev are somewhat exaggerated due to personal animosity. It is however, felt that there is at least a sub-stream of truth in them. They are not however confirmed by Fujiwara.

29. In considering the general political temper and atmosphere in Bangkok previous to the war, it is interesting to notice that Major Niranjan Singh Gill (B1190) who was sent on a secret mission to Thailand in Nov. 1941 to find out the attitude of Indians, has stated that, apart from Giani Pritam Singh and Chanda Singh (the notorious Osmanite), the community, mainly being merchants, showed but little interest in politics. (CSDIC (I) 2 Sec. Rept. 1096 para 4 on B1190).

Meeting between Giani Pritam Singh and Fujiwara

30. Fujiwara states that he had little contact with Indians prior to going to Bangkok, and that his knowledge of India was limited to what he had read in two books. He himself cannot understand why he was allotted this post, for he could speak neither English nor any Indian language. He thinks, however, that the probable reasons were two in number :–

1. He was the only officer of the General Staff who could be spared to be sent to Col. Tamura.

2. The CGS had selected him as a young officer, full of enthusiasm and ambition, and anxious to distinguish himself in some particular line.

31. On arrival in Bangkok in Oct. 1941, Fujiwara was welcomed by Col. Tamura, who told him to take a few days local leave to acclimatize himself, and to accustom himself to his new surroundings. There did not appear to be any urgency. He was told to take things easy, and that it would be useful to learn English. (Fujiwara states that, as his appointment was in the "I" Bch. and not in "Ips"–the members of which Bch always jealously guarded their secrets–he had no direct knowledge of the Japanese premeditated attack in Dec. 1941).

32. On settling down to work, Fujiwara was told by Col. Tamura that he (Tamura) had been approached by Giani Pritam Singh with a request for Japanese assistance in the cause of India's freedom.

33. It was only at the beginning of Dec. 1941, when the international situation began to take a more serious turn, that Fujiwara had four meetings with Giani Pritam Singh, who claimed that he had fellow-workers

in Singora and Haadyai in Thailand, and in Canton, Hong Kong, Shangai and even in New York. He has not however been successful, on account of the efficiency of the British security net, in making contact with any anti-British agents in Malaya, and added that it was impossible to get in touch with Indian military personnel, or to obtain information that would be operationally useful to the Japanese, owing to the frequent changes of station made by British units in Malaya.

34. The following points raised by Giani Pritam Singh were discussed :–

1. Relations between India and Japan should be on an egalitarian basis, i.e., India should not be in the same status as Manchuria and Korea. Indians in Malaya should not be militarised as the Chinese had been.
2. Giani Pritam Singh expressed no faith in the Gandhian doctrine of non-violence, asserting that Indian Independence could only be won by force of arms. He therefore sought Japanese cooperation to this end, in arms and equipment, with the proviso that the Indians should be allowed to raise and organise their own army of volunteers.
3. A representative Indian who could unite all classes should be invited to come to the Far East and the name of S.C. Bose was suggested.
4. Contact with Indians in Japan.

35. Comments on the above : (a) The issue of equality of status between Japan and India, and of the right to raise an army free from Japanese interference, thus raised (and expressed in terms (1) and (2) above) at the first meeting between Giani Pritam Singh and Fujiwara, was to lead to the dissolution of the first I.N.A., to cause friction between S.C. Bose and the Japanese, and was never fully resolved during the whole period of the Japanese inspired Indian Independence Movement. The failure of agreement on these issues from start to finish, is in itself sufficient evidence of the vain hopes of success which can be entertained by an Independence Movement, sponsored by and subservient to a major power, which is itself been on a military of aggrandizement and dominion.

It is of some significance to the future course of events to note that, in their first conversations with Fujiwara, both Giani Pritam Singh and Mohan Singh suggested the name of S. C. Bose as a leader of the Indian

Independence Movement. (Sec. Rept. 1007 para 37).

36. Fujiwara, submitted a name on his discussions with Giani Pritam Singh to Col. Tamura who forwarded it to Southern Area Army HQ in Saigon and to Imperial HQ in Tokyo. Fujiwara states that, as he had no idea how the attack would develop, and as he had not exactly made up his mind how he was to utilize the Indians in Malaya, This memo did not make any suggestions of a definite or detailed nature. The only other Indian with whom Fujiwara had a meeting in Bangkok before the outbreak of hostilities was Baba Amar Singh, an old man, but full of fire and violently anti-British.

37. About 5 Dec. 41, Fujiwara was appointed a Staff Officer on Southern Area Army HQ and was ordered to be prepared to report to Singapore (Southern Thailand) as staff officer (Propaganda) to .. 25 Army under Gen YAMASHITA.[3] His immediate superior was .. SUZUKI, Chief of Staff of 25 Army.

The Printing of Leaflets

38. The account so far given has indicated that, while the Indian community in Bangkok, being mainly interested in the success of their business enterprises, was not politically-minded, there were potential sources of disaffection which would be ready to seize an opportunity of striking at British power. It has further been indicated that one man (Giani Pritam Singh) had taken steps prejudicial to British interests by establishing clandestine contact with the Japanese, with a view to cooperating with them, and rallying the Indian populace to their side on the outbreak of hostilities.

39. On 7 Dec. 1941, Fujiwara told Giani Pritam Singh to await development and be ready to move. No sooner had the bloodless occupations of Bangkok had taken place on the night of 7/8 Dec. 41, then the well-laid plans of Giani Pritam Singh were immediately put into operation.

40. S.M. Ghosh reports (see CSDIC (I) 'V' Sec. Rept. F/293) that on calling at the office of the "Thai Bharat Cultural Lodge" on the afternoon of 8 Dec 1941, he was informed by Swami Satyananda Puri that he (Swami) had refused a request by Giani Pritam Singh for the use of the Lodge's cyclostyle machine to print surrender leaflets intended for distribution among Indian soldiers in Malaya.

3. General Yamashita Tomoyuki, after conquering Singapore, was transferred to a new post is Mancharia in July, 1942. After the defeat of Japan, he was tried and was executed in 1946.

41. On 9 Dec. 1941, Giani Pritam Singh, accompanied by Master Bhagwan Singh, again visited the "Thai Bharat Cultural Lodge" with the same request, but Deb Nath Das, who was in the office at the time, vehemently protested. That evening, Swami Satyananda Puri and Deb Nath Das were sent for by the Japanese Legation, where they were asked and again refused, to allow Giani Pritam Singh to use the cyclostyle machine for the desired purpose. On the following day, at the instance of Giani Pritam Singh, Master Bhagwan Singh, Baba Amar Singh and others, leaflets in Urdu, Gurmukhi, English and Hindustani (presumably printed at some locality other than the Thai Bharat Cultural Lodge) were distributed throughout Bangkok.

42. (1) While the distribution of leaflets amongst Indian tps, particularly in the early stages of the Malyan campaign, has been reported on numerous occasions, this is the first account which has been given of the planned treachery of Giani Pritam Singh in arranging to have them printed.

(2) From the apparent haste with which these leaflets were printed, support is given to the contention of Fujiwara that, while both he and his Indian collaborator had their plans well-made in advance, neither Fujiwara, far less Giani Pritam Singh, was privy to the detailed plans of the Japanese High Command. On the other hand, copies are in existence of letters prepared for distribution to Indian soldiers as early as Sept. 1941, which clearly show that Giani Pritam Singh had given thought long before the outbreak of war to the question of spreading disaffection among Indian tps.

(3) The reported attitude of Deb Nath Das is hard to follow. This man had lived in Japan before the war, and had a part in the founding of the "Thai Bharat Cultural Lodge", but detailed information about his movements in 1940 and 1941 is not available at CSDIC (I). If the account given by S.M. Ghosh of the objection raised by Deb Nath Das and Swami Satyananda Puri to the printing of leaflets on the cyclostyle machine of the "Thai Bharat Cultural Lodge" is correct, there are no grounds for the suspicion (aroused by the journey made by Deb Nath Das from Tokyo to Bangkok to take part in its foundation) that the "Thai Bharat Cultural Lodge" was sponsored and financed by the Japanese.

(4) If then, Deb Nath Das was not a dupe of the Japanese at this stage, it is felt that his state of mind was probably similar to that of Swami Satyananda Puri (and of Capt. Mohan Singh on his first meeting with Fujiwara and Giani Pritam Singh) which is interpreted as one of initial suspicion and distrust of the sincerity of Japanese motives towards India.

suspicion and distrust of the sincerity of Japanese motives towards India. That Swami Satyananda Puri very soon adopted a more trustful attitude to the Japanese is evidence by his acceptance of the office of representative Indian in Bangkok on 13 Dec. 1941.

(5) Civ. Kartar Singh states that the leaflets for distribution to Indian tps were mainly the work of Master Bhagwan Singh who arranged for them to be lithographed at Phit Buri. ('V' Sec. Rept. F/308 para 4 on Kartar Singh). As in 'V' Sec. Rept. F/362 on Master Bhagwan Singh there is no mention of such lithography having been done, and as counter-allegations are made by Bhagwan Singh against Kartar Singh, it is thought that there may be some personal ill-feeling between these two men.

Organisation of Giani Pritam Singh's Party and the Move to Malaya

43. On the same day (9 Dec. 1941) on which he made overtures to the Thai Bharat Cultural Lodge for cooperation in the printing of leaflets, Giani Pritam Singh held a meeting and organised the Azad Hind Sang, which was directly under the control of the Japanese. The only Mohammedan who attended this meeting was a maulvi, and the members were mostly Sikhs.

44. After waiting for word of the success of the Japanese landings in Malaya, Fujiwara, who had been standing by the Bangkok since he had his appointment to 25 Army HQ, flew from Bangkok to Singora in Southern Thailand on 10 or 12 Dec. 1941. He was accompanied by Giani Pritam Singh and three other Indians whose names he does not know, but who appeared to be of minor importance. (Their names are given in CSDIC (I) 'V' Sec Information Rept No. 2. dated 23 Jan. 46).

45. From Singora, the party proceeded via Haadyai to Alor Stor in Northern Malaya, where, by 14 Dec 1941, Fujiwara had established his HQ, and with the help of Giani Pritam Singh, had held the first meetings to organise a local branch of the I.I.L.

46. In Haadyai, in Southern Thailand, armbands were obtained for issue to Giani Pritam Singh and the Indians of his party, in order that they might be identified by Japanese soldiers. Fujiwara states that the 'F' on these armbands stood for 'Fujiwara, Friendship, Freedom'.

47. On 15 Dec. 1941, Mohan Singh was captured, Fujiwara has been unable to add to the detailed account given in 'S' Sec Rept 1007 on the circumstances of this surrender. It should be noted that the accounts given by both Fujiwara and Mohan Singh agree in the following

(1) That the initial suggestion for forming the I.N.A. came from Fujiwara and Giani Pritam Singh, and that Mohan Singh was at first hesitant about taking this decisive step.

(2) That having given the matter some thought (which he had ample opportunity of doing, as he lay on a sick bed for almost a week during this period) Mohan Singh, who was in Alor Star and Sungei Patani between his capture on 15 Dec 1941 and the end of that month, made a journey to Taiping with the specific purpose of freely offering his services to Fujiwara on New Year's Day, 1942.

48. Fujiwara agrees with the account given in 'S' Sec Rept 1007, paras 26 and 33, on the rivalry that existed between Mohan Singh and Giani Pritam Singh. The latter, having initiated the Independence Movement, would have liked to be regarded by the Japanese as the leader and to have Mohan Singh under his Comd. Giani Pritam Singh's idea was that the I.I.L. should be the executive body with the I.N.A. as its army and under its Comd. Mohan Singh, on the other hand, wished to be quite independent of the I.I.L.

49. Fujiwara's own attitude was that (to use his own imagery) he regarded Mohan Singh and Giani Pritam Singh as two wheels of an engine, and that he could not give power and prominence to one at the expense of the other. For this reason, Fujiwara considered it advisable to keep before the eyes of his two puppets the name of S.C. Bose (whom both men had individually named as the Indian who could best unite all factions). Fujiwara's main war was by diplomacy and conciliation to enlist the complete support of both men.

Giani Pritam Singh's Party

50. In his progress with Fujiwara in the wake of the advancing Japanese Army, Giani Pritam Singh had in the meantime by no means been inactive. In each town, as it was occupied by the Japanese, Fujiwara and Giani Pritam Singh delivered lectures on the sincerity of Japanese intentions towards India and on the necessity of avoiding panic. I.I.L. badges were issued to Indians civilians and their names were registered as members of the body. As they continued south, Giani Pritam Singh found that, as so many local volunteers were enlisted in the towns through which they passed, the recruiting party which he had brought from Thailand and outlived its usefulness, so that, at their own request, the majority returned to Bangkok in the latter part of January, 42. (Sec. 'V' Sec. Inf Rept No. 3 which confirms this).

51. Fujiwara states that, once he had appreciated the merits of Giani Pritam Singh and Mohan Singh, he left to them the organization of Indian civilians and Indian Army PW respectively. Fujiwara also points out that, as he was throughout the whole campaign primarily a staff officer under Gen. Suzuki on Army HQ, he had many other duties to attend to, and delegated much of his work to his two Indian assistants.

The 200 Volunteers or "Fujiwara Volunteers"

52. Fujiwara states that the Japanese welcomed the scheme of forming a party of Indian soldiers who would advance on Singapore alongside the Japanese, for in this way they could have confidence that the PW, who had fallen into their hands, and the civilian population, lulled into a submissive frame of mind by the specious promises of Japanese "protection" and of participation in the "co-prosperity sphere", were amicably disposed towards their new masters. The Japanese had been afraid that Indian soldiers, whose units had been defeated in battle, would adopt civilian disguise and cause havoc behind the lines. Fujiwara claims that no Fifth Column or intelligences work was done by the 200 party, who were used as a collecting agency for defeated and scattered Indian tps.

53. Fujiwara states that the party of 200 volunteers were armed for self-protection, but that these arms were never used, or were certainly never intended to be used, as offensive weapons. Fujiwara has no recollection of Sub Allah Ditta, 22 Mtn Bty nor of the incident referred to in 'S' See Repts 833 para 22, and 1007 para 58, where Fujiwara is stated to have given his watch to Allah Ditta.

Notes :– (1) The above account, combined with the evidence accumulated from many sources and confirmed by 'S' Sec Repts on Mohan Singh and Allah Ditta, lends weight to the general conclusion that the main duty of the party of 200 was the collection and organisation of stragglers.

(2) Fujiwara has confirmed the statement of Mohan Singh (see 'S' Sec Rept 1007 para 54) that he (Fujiwara) was unwilling to hand over rifles to Allah Ditta's party until Mohan Singh had personally assumed full responsibility for anything that might happen.

(3) It is felt that the aura of infamy and glory that has grown up around the treacherous, yet in the end petty achievements of this party of renegades, is largely a

product of rumour and exaggerated accounts of heroism. Allah Ditta himself records an instance of how, after the fall of Singapore, in order to increase his prestige in the I.N.A., he kept silent when some vingtorious, but entirely fictitious account was being given of his assistance in directing the fire of a Japanese part 36). It should in this connection be noted that Sub Allah Ditta himself states the 200 volunteers were selected on the basis of whet her they could swim since he imagined the party would have to swim from Johore Bahru to Singapore Island.

The Fujiwara Kikan

54. When questioned on the organisation bearing his name, Fujiwara stated that in reality it was not a Kikan in the same sense as the Twakuid of Hikari Kikan, but that it was merely a name given to himself and his small party of assistants. These assistants reported for two main purposes, as interpreters and to assist in the requisitioning of rations and supplies of the I.N.A.

These associates were :–

Interpreters

2/Lt. Kunizuka	(English)
Cpl Otaguro	”
Cpl Ishikawa	(Hindustani)

Administrative Assistants

Capt. Tsuchimochi	2 i/c. Dispatched to Burma Area Army HQ in Feb. 42, for the purpose of furthering the Indian Independence Movement and forming an I.N.A. in Burma (This was Ram Sarup's party)
Lt. Segawa	
” Yamaguchi	
” Nakamiya	
” Yonemura	

Civilians used in Singapore :–

Suzuki
Masubuchi
OTA
Hashimoto

Kitamura

ITO – Last seen in Bishenpur.

55. Regarding the Japanese members of his staff, Fujiwara stated that the four officers were all graduates of the Nakano School (a School of advanced "T" training) and had all come from Tokyo on this special assignment. None of them had any experience of India. The only other member of the party of whom Fujiwara has only information was Otaguro, who had been educated in a Japanese School in Singapore, and come to Bangkok just before the outbreak of war.

56. The Japanese attack on Malaya from Thailand was made in three columns in each of which Fujiwara allotted numbers of his party as follows :

(1) Fujiwara himself was attached to 25 Army HQ which formed the right flank of the Japanese thrust. With Fujiwara was Giani Pritam Singh, Otaguro and other Japanese and Indians. The advanced element of 25 Army was 5 Div., to which was attached Lt. Nakamiya with two Indians.

(2) One Regt. of 5 Div., to which were attached 2/Lt. Yonemura and a few Indians for contact work, was allotted the central sector.

(3) On the left flank, where 1 Regd of 18 Div advanced via Kota Bharu, was 2/Lt. Segawa and 2 Indians.

Notes :– (a) While there is much information on the party operating with Fujiwara, little is known about the parties under Yonemura and Segawa.

(b) Confirmation of the information in the last three paragraphs will be found in a note on the Fujiwara Kikan, based on an interrogation of Capt. Kunizuka by Field Security Service HQ, Singapore. (Their FS/A/2 to Singapore Security Bureau, copy to 'S' Sec. CSDIC (I) dated 19 Mar. 46 refers).

(1) To establish local branches of the I.I.L.

(2) Organise Indian PW into Camps. Only members of the Fujiwara Kikan were to have jurisdiction over Indian PW (i.e., any such PW captured by Japanese units were to be handed over to the Fujiwara Kikan).

The Surrender of Singapore and Fujiwara's Return to Tokyo

58. Fujiwara states that Mohan Singh and he remained at Kuala Lumpur until a few days before the fall of Singapore. (This is confirmed by Mohan Singh) Fujiwara has no new information to add on the events in Singapore at the time of the capitulation and immediately after. In Mar. 42, he accompanied the Indian delegates by plane to the Tokyo Conference, which he himself did not attend as he was granted leave, on

Conference, which he himself did not attend as he was granted leave, on the termination of which he returned to his post of Staff Officer (Intelligence) at Southern Army HQ. He was succeeded in his post, as Staff Officer i/c Indian affairs by Col. (later Maj. Gen.) Iwaguro who had also accompanied the party of Indians to Tokyo. Iwaguro had no previous contact with Indian affairs, but held an important appointment in the Ministry of War, where he was head of the "Adjutant Section" From the date of his return to Tokyo, Fujiwara's active connection with Indians and Indian affairs ceased.

Note :– Fujiwara has stated that the welcome which was given to Japanese tps by Indians in Malaya during the victorious advance down the Malaya peninsula far exceeded the expectations of the Japanese. The degree of importance which, from the time of the Tokyo Conference, the Japanese attached to the puppet Indian Independence Movement is seen in the appointment of an officer higher in rank than Fujiwara to take charge of Indian affairs, i.e. Col. Iwaguro.

Ram Sarup's Party and Captain Tsuchimochi

59. Asked whether the idea of sending a party of Indians to Burma had originated with the Indians themselves (i.e., Mohan Singh or Giani Pritam Singh) Fujiwara stated that in Dec. 1941 or Jan. 1942 a signal was received by him from HQ Southern Regions, ordering that, in view of the success of the Fujiwara Kikan in the Malayan operations, Fujiwara himself should go to Burma and organise a similar movement amongst Indians in order to facilitate the operations of 15 Army. Fujiwara, however, was instrumental in arranging for Capt. Tsuchimochi, his 2 i/c to be sent in his place.

60. Early in 1943, while Fujiwara was working as an 'I' officer on Count Terauchi's staff in HQ Southern Regions in Saigon, he was ordered to go to Singapore to try to help Col. Iwaguro to smooth over the trouble that had arisen in Singapore due to the collapse of the I.N.A. On arrival in Singapore he addressed a meeting of Indian officers "whom he looked upon and still looks upon as his good friends". In this speech Fujiwara spoke to the following effect : "Mohan Singh as a great friend of mine for whose opinions I have every respect. I am anxious that the I.N.A., which I started as a baby and reared up, should not collapse." He further exhorted them not to give us the struggle for the Independence of India, an honourable cause for which the I.N.A. had been called into being.

61. Commenting on this speech and on his relations with Mohan Singh, Fujiwara stated that while he was in charge of Indian affairs,

Mohan Singh and he had always remained on friendly terms. He liked Mohan Singh for his honesty, straightforwardness and boldness. They lived together like friends, and it was seldom that any doubts arose in Mohan Singh's mind. But after his return to Tokyo in Mar 1942, the friendly atmosphere, which, fostered by Fujiwara's diplomatic handling of Mohan Singh, had existed between the Japanese and the Indians, changed. Filing up doubts as to the sincerity of the Japanese began to assail Mohan Singh. At the time he went to Singapore in early 43 on his mission of reconciliation, Fujiwara had desired with all his heart that a understanding could have been come to between the Japanese and the Indians: but all his pleadings and persuasions were in vain.

Some Comments by Fujiwara on his Relations with Indians and on the Indian Independence Movement

62. Fujiwara states that during the short time he was i/c Indian affairs, he was adversely criticised by his fellow Japanese officers for being too friendly to Indians, and the opinion was even expressed that he was more of an Indian than a Japanese. Fujiwara indicated that he himself was sincere in his attitude towards Indians, and that more than once he adopted an attitude that was sympathetic to the Indians but was opposed to that held by the Japanese High Command. Fujiwara's opinion is that the I.N.A. would have been much more successful if it had been left to Indians themselves, in the same fashion that he left detailed administration to Giani Pritam Singh and Mohan Singh, and he further considers that if he had been retained i/c Indian affairs after Mar 1942, he should have done better than Iwaguro.

63. Fujiwara has little direct information of Indians after his departure to Tokyo in Mar 1942. From his observation of the I.N.A. on the Imphal front, he was given it as his opinion that the defeat of the Japanese in the Burma campaign was in no way due to the lack of fighing spirit on the part of the I.N.A.

64. Asked whether in his opinion, the I.N.A. was a purely propaganda army or if the Japanese considered it had a co-combatant status, Fujiwara maintained that it was definitely regarded as a combatant force, and that it was regarded as having an offensive role. As an example of this, he cited the stage of the Imphal operations at the end of June 1944, when elements of the I.N.A. details not known by Fujiwara were covering a position on both flanks of a Japanese unit astride the Palel-Mawle road, with the object of holding the Allied advance on Malwe, and so covering the withdrawal of Japanese 15 and receive from Kohima and Ukhrul.

(Fujiwara was able immediately to cite this example of the use of the I.N.A., as he had used to as tactical example when he had been an instructor at the Army War College).

65. It should be noted, however, that the Japanese do not appear to have committed the I.N.A. to battle until a definitely defensive stage of the campaign had been reached. When the Japanese offensive thrust towards Imphal and Kohima was in progress in the early months of 1944, the I.N.A. was kept in the rear. Fujiwara can remember the names of only Shah Nawaz, Malik and Kiani of the I.N.A. comds in Burma, but can give no information about their personalities or achievements.

66. Fujiwara denies completely the story that when Maj. Niranjan Singh Gill (RI190)[4] was staying in the Oriental Hotel, Bangkok at the time of his secret journey to Thailand to find out the degree of anti-British feeling amongst Indians, he (Fujiwara) was living in the next room.

67. He also denies the story recorded in CSDIC (I) 'V' Sec V/298 on Jagat Singh Dhillon of his having given a revolver to Harnam Singh Dhillon, as a token of esteem for his (Dhillon) having shot a British officer PW.

Hikari Kikan[5]

68. Fujiwara has no direct information on the Hikari Kikan, nor of its relations to the I.N.A. He states, however, that each of the three Japanese Div. (15, 31, 33) in Burma had a Hikari Kikan representative, who reported to Hikari Kikan HQ. The Hikari Kikan had liaison direct with 15 Army HQ, and with the I.N.A. He represented the chain of command thus :–

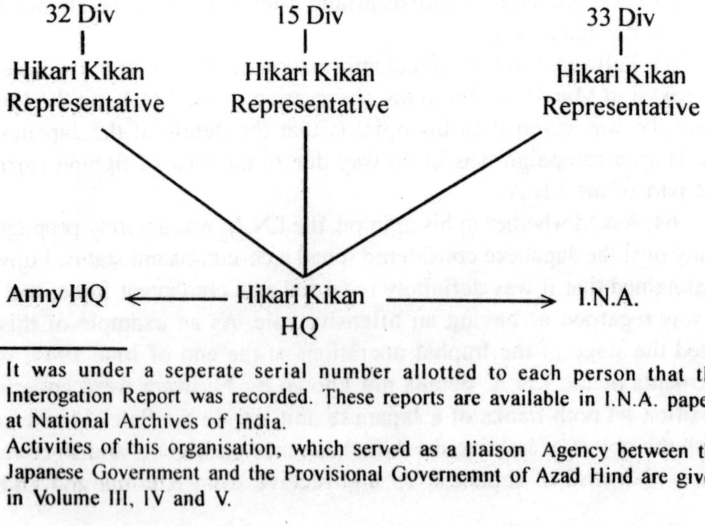

4. It was under a seperate serial number allotted to each person that the Interogation Report was recorded. These reports are available in I.N.A. papers at National Archives of India.

5. Activities of this organisation, which served as a liaison Agency between the Japanese Government and the Provisional Governemnt of Azad Hind are given in Volume III, IV and V.

Difficulties Experienced by the Japanese in Organizing the I.I.L. and I.N.A. in Malaya

69. Fujiwara has summed up the difficulties experienced by the Japanese in organising the I.I.L. and I.N.A. in Malaya as follows :–

(1) Mohan Singh's doubts as to Japan's sincerity in aiding India's fight for freedom.

(2) Lack of knowledge of Indian customs and religions by Japanese soldiers, and their generally insulting attitude towards Indians. The lack of military courtesies (saluting) by both Indian and Japanese. Illtreatment by the Kempei Tai.

(3) The failure of the Japanese to regard the I.N.A. as a wholly independent army.

(4) Members of the I.I.L. attempting to further their own interests through the formation of the I.I.L. and I.N.A.

Later War Experiences of Fujiwara

70. The movements of Fujiwara after his visit to Singapore early in 1943 are given in brief.

Apr. 43	Reported to HQ 15 Army in Rangoon, and participated in the Imphal operations as Staff Officer.
Aug. 44	Promoted Lt. Col.
Sep. 44	Became Staff Officer (Operations) 15 Army HQ.
Dec. 44	Received orders to return for posting to the Army War College as an instructor. Owing to scarcity of shipping was unable to proceed at once.
Feb. 45	Arrived in Japan and took up his appointment at the Army War College.
Apr. 45	Became Senior Staff Officer, 2 Area Army in Japan.
Jan. 45	Appointed Staff Officer, 57 Army in Southern Kyushu.

Conclusion

71. Fujiwara has confirmed but has not materially added to the considerable body of information now available on the Japanese-sponsored Indian Independence Movement, particularly in the crucial period between Oct 1941 and Mar 1942. From the information which he has supplied, the gravamen of the indictment, on the charge of collaborating with the Japanese even before the outbreak of hostilities,

must be levelled against a few malcontents in Bangkok.

72. There is no doubt that the latent nationalism amongst Indian in East Asia would have made the development of an Indian Independence Movement inevitable. But without the initial assistance of Giani Pritam Singh, Mohan Singh and a few more arch-renegades, the movement would never have assumed the proportions that it did.

12

Japanese Premier Tojo's Speech Regarding Military Activities in India for Helping the India Nationalists

4 April, 1942

Imperial Forces have previously occupied Rangoon, which is an important point in Burma, and the Andaman Islands, a strategically important point in the Eastern part of the Indian Ocean and a place of exile for Indian Independence Patriots. And now, advancing further, it has been arranged to strike a decisive blow against the British military power and military establishment in India.

In this way the firm determination of the Imperial Government to chastise America and Britain is being steadily realized.

If India should remain as previously under British military control it is unavoidable that Indian will suffer considerable war damage through the Imperial Government's attack to exterminate Britain.

From the outset the Imperial Government's intention has not been to regard India's four hundred million people as enemies. Towards the Indian people who would suffer war calamities in this event there is genuine sympathy.

The real intention of the Imperial Government is clear from statements in my speech of March 10th, in the Imperial Diet. That way I indicated my firm conviction that this was a golden opportunity for Indians to exert all their strength to create "India for the Indians" and to establish India's original form.

This coming autumn British power in India will be crushed. I hope again that India's leaders will avoid incurring pointless war havoc, misled by the soft talk of England, under whose control India's four hundred million people have been, and that, seizing this heaven-sent opportunity, they will break asunder England's yoke of many years and advance in the realisation of "India for the Indians."

1. File No. 254; I.N.A. Papers.

13

N. Raghavan's Views about the Japanese Policy Towards India's Independence

5 May, 1942

1. Declaring his fixed determination to fight for the freedom of his country from the Anglo-Saxon bondage with the help of friendly power, namely; Nippon, Mr. N. Raghavan, President of India Independence League, Penang, who attended the conference of the Indian Independence League has just returned from Tokyo.

2. In an interview granted to me at his residence yesterday, Mr. Raghavan was full of confidence that the sacred mission of Japan in driving British and Americans out of Asia would be successfully completed.

3. Mr. Raghavan said that he would like to appeal to all his countrymen not to miss opportunity of taking up arms. If need be, to fight for their own freedom in particular and to help the Nipponese Forces in fighting for the freedom of all Asiatic races in general.

4. When questioned about his stay in Tokyo, Mr. Raghavan was full of praise for the Japanese people and officials and said that when he was in Japan he had found Japanese people exceedingly polite, in fact he said, the grater the person, the more humble he appeared to be. He further told me that he had visited many cities in Japan and Formosa during his brief stay there, he had delivered some 70 to 80 speeches and he was much taken by the kindliness and very friendly disposition of the people. One thing which struck him most forcibly, he said, was that although it was war time, there was no blackout in Japan and life there appeared quite normal. As a matter of fact, the atmosphere there was one of the quiet confidence.

---

1. *Penang Daily News*, 5 May, 1942.

5. The people appeared very determined in help their Government to prosecute the Greater East Asia War to successful conclusion at all cost.

6. Referring to the unfortunate fatal plane crash in which four of his comrades, who were also proceeding to Tokyo were killed, Mr. Raghavan expressed his profound sorrow.

7. In reply to my question regarding the service held in Tokyo in memory of the dead, Mr. Raghavan said that in Tokyo, a most touching ceremony was held when prayers were offered for the response of the souls of these unfortunate representatives. He added that he was told that the ceremony was one of the greatest ever held in Japan.

8. Mr. Raghavan informed me that the families of the deceased had been compensated both by the Government and by the Air-plane company each of whom had given $ 10,000, thereby making a total of $ 20,000 to each of the deceased family.

9. On behalf of the Indian Independence League of Malaya. Mr. Raghavan said that he was glad to be able to offer a gift of $ 10,000 to the family if Japanese interpreter, Mr. Ottaguro who was in the ill-fated plane at the time of the accident and who had also lost his life.

10. It will be recalled that Mr. Raghavan left Penang to attend the Conference of the Indian Independence League in Tokyo towards the end of March. He said that he arrived there at the time when the cherry trees were in full blossom and they presented to the visitors most magnificent sight which they would remember for a very long time.

11. Mr. Raghavan was asked his opinion about the destruction of cherry trees in Washington by the Americans, he said that when he heard of revolting Americans action in cutting down these trees in Washington, he felt terribly ashamed that a Democratic Power like America, which had always boasted of its civilization, could have stupped to such a base and unspeakably mean action.

12. When in Tokyo, he added he and his comrades had met His Excellency Prime Minister Mr. Hideki Tojo who had promised them that Japan would assist India to fight to her full Independence.

12. In reply to my question again Mr. Raghavan said that His Excellency Prime Minister Mr. Hideki Tojo was very kind and polite to them. He added that unlike the British imperialism, there was no such thing as colour prejudice or colour bar in Japan.

13. On being asked whether he had any opportunity of listening in to the Penang Broadcasting Station, Mr. Raghavan said that he had the opportunity to listen in while in Tokyo and Saigon, where he stopped on his return journey. He said the reception was very good indeed.

14

Report by Lieut - M.M. Pillai and Lieut. V. Radhakrishnan, who Escaped from Singapore after its Fall; gives Detailed Information to the British about the Collaboration between Soldiers of the Indian Army and the Japanese

7 May, 1942

After the surrender of Singapore I was interned at Bidadari P.O.W. Camp until 1st May, 1942 when I was transferred to the Sapper Camp at Tyersall Park. Through intermediaries I was able to contact Lieut. Radhakrishnan, who was living in McNair road in his bungalow, as the Volunteers had been disbanded and not interned and plans were laid for our escape into India. These plans, however, were upset by my transfer to Tyersall Park Camp from which escape was difficult. Fortunately, Captain Mohan Singh issued orders that all Indian officers should meet him in person on 7th May at Bidadari Camp, and with that as an excuse I left for Bidadari Camp which I reached at midday on the 6th. Having reported my arrival there Captain Natarajan, M.C., I.M.S., and myself slipped out that night and surreptitiously made our way to R's bungalow where we spent the night.

When Lieut. Pillai came to visit me four days before the fall of Singapore, it struck me that he would make an excellent companion in the event of our attempting to escape should Singapore surrender. With this in mind I spent all my time after its fall collecting information which would help us on our way to India, and at the same time I visited all the P.O.W. Camps in an attempt to contact P. Eventually P. contacted me and we made plans for the escape. My first task was to raise funds. This I did by selling most of my possessions. On the evening of 6th May P.

1 Fortnightly Intelligence report Far Eastern Bureau. Ministry of Defence Archives, Liaison Office, the Netherlands. The information provided by them to the British was of great help.The British got information from many other agents.

and Capt. N. arrived at my bungalow. Our combined funds amounted to $ 600 and I had also managed to obtain, under false name, membership cards of the Indian Independence League. The money we had was barely enough for two people. It was even less sufficient for three. We bought cigars and tinned provisions like butter, jam, horlicks, tins of milk, etc., from a friend's shop and took the night train to Penang.

Buying tickets was an ordeal. The Japanese soldiers beat the passengers with a cane whilst buying tickets, and no tickets were issued unless money was given in Japanese currency notes in their various denominations. Their Commander-in-Chief issued a proclamation to the effect that all currencies were valid in Malaya! I bought the tickets and narrowly escaped the Japanese birch, an unfortunate Chinese girl next to me getting it on her thigh. The station was quite dark and there were some I.N.A. Sikhs on watch for P.O.W. escaping from the Island. We huddled ourselves into a goods carriage and lay in a dark corner.

Our dress was a dhoti, a long shirt and a Gandhi cap, all in Khaddar (home spun Indian cloth usually associated with the symbolic dress of a Congress volunteer), and a long towel which could either be tied like a turban round the head or left to hang from the shoulders. Incidentally, this is also the standard dress worn by Chetties Agents. Chetties are usually money lenders.

The train arrived at Bukit Mertajam on the afternoon of the 9th going very slowly over the Johore causeway at even less than walking pace. The bridges that had been blown up had been improvised by the Japanese and the train service was running. At the bridge near Kuala Lumpur one engine had capsized and we saw the capsized engine. The Japanese get over this difficulty by attaching the engine to the back of the train at the station before the bridge and pushing the carriages slowly over the bridge. Then when a carriage is well over the bridge another engine is hooked to this carriage, the old engine is disconnected and the train then starts. Pretty smart! we could not see very much of the route as we had to spend two nights in an overcrowded carriage which was very stuffy. We got down at Bukit Mertajan. To cover this distance by walking would have taken us at least a month as it is a journey of 500 miles.

We crossed to Penang by ferry which is still working, but controlled by the Japanese. At Prai our luggage was examined. We hid most of our money in our clothes as we had been told that we would not be allowed more than one hundred dollars each. We kept this amount in our purses and after rough handling by the Japanese examiners we were able to get out and reach a friend Ramakrishna Iyer in Beach Road.

We told Mr. Ramakrishna Iyer of our plans as we knew he could help us. He was the proprietor of the Malayan Corporation, a small firm of importers and exporters. He is a graduate, a Brahmin from Coimbatore; South India. He told us that it was possible to enter Siam with a passport of three month's validity. So the next morning we went to the Japanese passport office, which is housed in the previous government building in Beach Street, and gave our photographs in the typical dress of Chetties. We had to bribe the clerk, a Chinese, to have it done quickly and to tell the Japanese officer that we were bonafide merchants and thus avoid enquiries. Even the Japanese officer's peon had to be bribed. We gave as our address a bombed house in Market Street so as not to get our friend into trouble. The passports were ready the next morning. They cost us only 25 cents (about 6 annas) each, but we had to pay $ 5 each to the clerk and $ 2 each to the peon and $ 5 each for our passport photographs.

We then toured the town to see what state it was in. The jetty and parts of Chulia and Market Streets were bombed into ruins. Food was not very expensive and the Japanese had issued an order that it was not to be exported from the Island. Rice could be had and also such things as onions and potatoes, which we had not seen at Singapore, could be had at a price. Prices for clothing were very high. The trams were running and we heard that the hill railway would soon be in order. The water and electricity supplies were working. On the whole Penang was normal and it looked less like a battered city than any other in Malaya. Our messing was arranged by our friend in a hotel and cost us all $ 30.

On the afternoon of the 13th we left for the frontier Badang Bosar by train. On this route there was more destruction to be seen. The bridges were very crudely repaired and we saw some damaged aeroplanes at the Alor Star aerodrome. We reached Padang Besar on the same night. We slept there the night and the next morning, after rough handling by Japanese officers and soldiers and some Siamese, we jumped into a goods train with open vans bound for Siam. About 50 Japanese soldiers travelled on this train. On the wayside stations we saw a few Japanese soldiers standing and looking at the train and some were walking along the railway track in full kit.

We reached Haad Yai about 1000 hours. In a train opposite us, bound for the Malayan frontier, there were a few Indian Businessmen–Tamils. They asked us if we had Siamese passports and on our replying the negative told us to get in touch with a Mr. Mathu and a Mr. Velayudham

Pillai. We could get a passport of about a month's validity for about if we bribed Mr. Velayudham to stand security for us.

During this conversation, one of the emigration officers came and questioned us about our passports. We showed the Japanese one and he told us to follow him to the emigration office for further instructions. In the office we found a Siamese officer who spoke good English. He told us to get a surety for a temporary passport or we would have to return to Malaya.

We left our bags in the office and went in search of the two people we had been told to get in touch with. We found Mr. Muthu and the man who had advised us on the train. They told us to get photographs so we went to a Chinese shop opposite and were photographed. It cost us 8 ticals each (dollars and ticals are now at par) and they were ready at 2 p.m. Mr. Velayudham then appeared. He said he was glad to meet businessmen new to Siam, that he was willing to help us, but that we must not take part in any politics and that we must be back at Haad Yai by the end of a month. He undertook to stand surety for us for the sum of 800 ticals and explained that he only did this sort of thing for gentlemen he knew would not forget him. After exchange of information about businessmen in Malaya he took us to the passport office and stood surety for us. He appeared to be much respected by the government as the officers showed him deference. We paid him $ 60 with which he seemed to extraordinarily pleased. He gave us the following information about Siam which was collaborated the more northward we travelled :–

(1) The Japanese currency notes were discounted, the further north one went but British currency notes were accepted and very welcome. In and about Bangkok people only offer 70 per cent of its value for a Japanese note.

(2) The Japanese were building a powerful aerodrome and extending the one at Sungei Patani and one midway between Haad Yai and Sungei Patani. There were a number of Japanese troops at Haad Yai and they were monopolising the Siamese railways for the transit of their troops and material. They were preparing secret landing grounds for their planes near Yaad Yai.

(3) There was a good deal of talk of the Japanese having asked for the incorporation of the whole of Siam above Malaya to a line connecting Rahnong and Chumpon on the north. The reason advanced by the Japanese was that this would make it Japanese territory from Singapore to Victoria Point. The Siamese prime minister had refused his request. The Siamese were enraged and talking about war between Siam and Japan.

(4) The Japanese told the prime minister that they would incorporate the Southern Shan States with Siam in their new order in East Asia, after the defeat of the British. They would also persuade Marshal Petain to surrender to Siama slice of territory on the northern bend of the Mekong River. The Siamese were not willing to accede as they were of the opinion that the people of the Shan States would be willing to join with Siam in any case. It was therefore unacceptable as a reward from Japan to Siam. As to the Indo-Chinese territory, the Siamese were suspicious as they considered that the Japanese were merely trying to increase dissension between Indo-China and Siam. They presumed the Japanese must think them fools as this change would only increase the length of Siam's frontier with China and thus Japanese could transfer some of the burden of fighting the Chinese to Siam.

(5) The Siamese had asked for the incorporation of the whole of the region south of the town of Moulmein up to the tip of Victoria Point with Siam. The Japanese would not do this as it was essential to safeguard this vital region against possible British sea attacks and the Siamese navy would be unable to do this. In this event the whole of the Archipelago would be lost to the Japanese as well as the Nicobar and Andaman Island.

(6) On the outbreak of hostilities on 8th December, 1941, the Siamese troops fought the Japanese well near, Haad Yai even though they were outnumbered and outclassed by superior weapons. The Japanese casualties were over 200 and when the order ceasefire came from their prime minister the Siamese troops were furious and so were their commanders, who had the disadvantage of never knowing their orders till the last minute.

(7) Most of the Siamese were pro-British and particularly pro-American, but they were unable to express their feelings. There were spies everywhere from Russia, Germany and Japan, and even the prime minister's own spies as he was in fear of assassination.

(8) From the 1st April an order was issued that all men and women were to wear European dress. This led to a shoe shortage, so the order was modified and women did not have to wear shoes. Thus we saw the strange spectacle of women in gowns, skirts, hats but going bare-footed.

(9) There was a food shortage in the country.

(10) The Japanese had been ordered not to molest Siamese women. But cases occurred causing much ill feeling.

Haad Yai looks like a half built town where work has suddenly ceased. Railway stations in Siam had the English names blacked out. Very few of the Siamese would talk English and even the English time tables and information for travellers were not to be seen.

In the hotel where we stayed we found a few Sikhs talking late into the night drinking and shouting revolutionary slogans. There were more prostitutes than anyone else in this town. It has the semblance of an occupied town.

The next morning Captain Natarajan's fever was better so we left for Tap Tiang or Trang on the west coast to stay with a Mr. Muthia–a Chettiar. He was very helpful. He gave us the following information about Siam :–

(1) The richest Indian in the whole of Siam is a Sikh by the name of Bishambar Singh. There is no town without a branch of this man's shop. It is estimated that about a third of the houses in Bangkok belong to him. He was behind the financing of the I.N.A. and the propaganda on behalf of Indians overseas.

(2) The brain of the movement was Swami Satyanand Puri. He was in great repute as a scholar, and the Japanese made him the first Indian Consul of free India in Bangkok. He has since been killed in a plane crash.

(3) The Siamese Government intended arresting all Indians as British subjects on the outbreak of hostilities. All escaped internment by the action of Bhishambar Singh who subjected to the Siamese. Government surety freeing the rest of the Indians.

(4) There were not many restrictions on Indians whom the average Siamese regards with affection. Many kept their radio sets and were listening to our broadcasts. The Japanese influence was indirect and through pressure on the Government.

(5) There were continuous troop movements all over the country.

(6) There was a rumour that there were high staff officers of the German army in Siam.

(7) There was a proposal to snift the capital from Bangkok either down south or up north to Ayuthia.

(8) A lack of patent medicines in the country caused an influx of some clever limitations such as aspirin, etc.

After a day's rest on account of Captain Natarajan's illness we left Trang on the 17th by train reaching Chumpon that night. This to is on the east coast of Siam almost in line with Victoria Point.

That night was spent in a hotel and the next day we took a bus on our way to Renong. About 5 miles out of Chumpon we came to a big battalion H.Q. where we were told to alight. The Siamese National Anthem was played are a sentry told us to stand to attention and salute their flag. Our bags were examined and the bus moved on. There was an escaped Chinese from Penang travelling in this bus, who cor.. to his nervousness of the position of the Chinese in Siam.

We travelled about 30 miles by bus to the Pak Chan estuary where we got into a motor boat run by the Siamese Government. It was about 10 a.m. and after sailing for about three hours we touched a small village where we stopped for a meal. After the meal we continued the journey by boat arriving at Pak Nam at about 5 p.m. that evening. As the tide was low we had to wait for a canoe or sampan to take us up the backwater about 3 miles, to Ranong. The night was spent at a hotel and on the following morning we asked some Pathans the best route to take for Burma. The Pathans, so my information went, had a colony round the region of the Isthmus of Kra. Living in a Buddhist country, and being fanatical Moslems themselves, they were not over friendly with the natives and their loyalty to the British Government could not be questioned. They advised us not to attempt the journey as the jungles were full of Siamese and Burmese dacoits and the monsoon had commenced.

In a tea shop we met Abu Bakar Kaka, a Moslem from Malabar, who offered to take us to a Japanese official where we could obtain a passport to enable us to cross into Burma at Victoria Point. The official in question, when we got there, reminded us of a pocket edition of Mephistopheles, an old man of about 70, reputed to have been the brains behind the Japanese infiltration round Victoria Point. We concocted a story to enable us to procure passes giving us an unmolested passage to Moulmein. He was impressed with our story but said that he could not have passports ready until 23rd of May as he had to send rations to the Japanese troops in Sumatra and look after the 5 ships that were bringing Australian and Dutch P.O.W. from Malaya and Java. These troops were to be employed as a labour corps for making a road from Victoria Point to Mergui, cleaning up bombed houses, in towns like Tavoy, repairing bridges and existing roads. We realised that these four days were for checking up on us. However nothing could be done about it.

On the 23rd we obtained our passes and took a car to Pak Nam. Here we took a boat to Victoria Point arriving where about 4 p.m. in the evening. Before embarking we handed in our Siamese passports at the emigration office at Pak Nam and had them endorsed to the effect that we were leaving the country before the end of the month as this would release Mr. V. Pillai from all responsibility.

Whilst in a provision shop at Victoria Point an Australian sergeant came for stores. The prices were high but the shopkeeper was pro-Ally and he was allowed to take Rs. 15 worth of goods free, and was told to tell his friends that they could do the same. The Australian informed us that by tipping the Japanese sentry 20 cents a time he was allowed out. He gave his name as Eric Merrill and said he came from Perth. There had been talk amongst the P.O.W. of escaping but it was head that this was too risky as it meant almost certain death.

That evening, with the aid of the shopkeeper, we were able to catch the Japanese boat to Mergui. On account of a squall and fog we were forced to anchor off an island for the night of the 24th after only doing about 10 miles. We sailed early next morning with the weather continuing to be rough but not so foggy and on our way we say two aerodromes, a wireless station and a few Japanese soldiers.

A fellow traveller, whom we suspected of being a Japanese spy, informed us that Mr. Knife, D.C. at Victoria Point, was a prisoner at Bangkok. He was a Thakin officer so we asked him how the Thakins had obtained their arms and training. He replied that they had secret associations all over Burma, with members in the Government services. A party of Thakins had been trained in Japan and led the Japanese troops when encircling the British. Their weapons were obtained from secret German and Japanese sources.

We reached Mergui on the 25th at 5 p.m. after a rough voyage of about 200 miles. We stayed at a hotel, but Captain Natarajan stayed with some relatives who were indiscreet in their talk and people came to know something of us. We therefore decided to leave by bus, but as none was going till 2nd June we set off by foot. We set out early in the morning of 31st May, and after crossing a river at noon we reached a village on a rubber estate, 28 miles up the Tavoy road, that night. The headman of the village was very hospitable and gave us food and beds. Here we met a Bengali postmaster who told that the Japs had come to the estate a fortnight back and informed the coolies that they would receive work. The Burmese coolies, however, were working on the estate under instructions from the Thakins. He added that he had had a telephone message from the Japanese military at Mergui asking him to be on the lockout for 4 escaped Australian P.O.W.

The next morning we left and reached Palaw the same day. The town was under the Thakins though there were many Japanese troops in the vicinity. Petrol was difficult to obtain although the Burmese had hidden large quantities from the Japanese. A gallon could be illicitly obtained for about R. 10/-. The Thakins were forcibly recruiting young boys in the neighbourhood and training them as troops.

The next night we reached Palauk. Ploughing was going on, rains were said to be normal, and the place presented a green and fertile appearance.

We reached Pe on the 3rd June, Chaungwabin on the 4th, and late on the 5th we arrived at Tavoy. The next morning we toured the town and found it completely gutted. The electric supply, however, was functioning. The tin smelting company's shops were not working. Trade between Rangoon and Tavoy was functioning by means of country boats. The Japanese at Tavoy are living in the school building.

On the road to Tavoy many bridges had been destroyed by the retreating British and near Mandao the Japanese were rebuilding one. There were about 100 Japanese here presumably engaged on this work. It was near here that we saw 5 or 6 lorry loads of Dutch prisoners moving up with another lorry of Japanese.

We left Tavoy on the 7th by bus, having obtained tickets through the aid of a Bengali Doctor we met there, and arrived at Ye the same evening. Here we were befriended by a Raman Chettiar who put us up and arranged for a bullock cart and boat to take us as far as a place called Ilamaing which we reached on the 8th forenoon. There is a train service from here to Moulemein, of which we availed ourselves reaching the town on the 9th at sunset. We were accompanied by Raman Chettiar's son. He was of great help to us as he could read, write and talk fluent Burmese. On the route we found telegraph lines cut, wires pulled down, pole uprooted, looted stations and many similar acts of vandalism. The salt factory on this route was not working, and many stray Japanese soldiers were to be seen.

At Moulmein we stayed with Messrs the Bank of Chettinad Ltd. under the hospitality of Mr. Muthukumar. Our journey had now lasted a month, we were worn out through walking, a bullock cart ride, a boat journey, bus journey, etc. but we wanted to push one so we decided to start off again the next morning.

We found some parts of Moulmein badly damaged, but the city itself was comparatively untouched. High prices existed and people were fed up with the Thakin authorities; the Japanese were expected to take over the administration on the 10th.

We crossed over by ferry to Martaban. The engine of the paddle boat was in a bad way, the steam leaking giving us a mild steam bath. The Japanese were running this boat and the charge was two annas per man. The boat was overcrowded and it took us half an hour to cross.

At Martaban we caught the train. People were packed in like sardines. Here telegraph wires were down and bridges blown up but the Japanese were doing a lot of repairing. We came to some station and the train stopped. From here there were buses running to Pegu by stages but we had to walk as we had no money. We walked 5 miles and rested at a place called Nimphale. We heard that people coming from Rangoon had mentioned fighting between the Karins and Burmese.

Next morning we left for Kyaikte, by foot (22 miles) reaching it at moon. The railway bridge was broken but we were able to cross to the other side by a road bridge in the town, where there were Japanese troops. En route we found a goods train going to Moplin and travelled by it as far as Kyai Katha where we were fed by a South Indian Mohamedan fisherman who sent us along in a boat with a party of Indian merchants bound for Rangoon. The night was spent at Mewa, and after breakfast next morning we left for Pegu 12 miles away. Here we parted company with the Rangoon merchants and continued on foot, but we sent Captain Natarajan by bus, as he was enable to walk, and asked him to try and raise money and information for our journey north. Our rendezvous was the Bank of Chettinad Ltd., in Rangoon.

In Pegu we heard that the Japanese had taken over the administration from the Thakins whom they did not trust. We heard that a Thakin had murdered a Japanese officer and as a reprisal measure many Thakins were executed. The Japanese were favouring the other communities in contrast to the Burmese, and were trying to restore the city to some sort of normal life. The railway station was damaged, but trains were going at a slow speed to Rangoon and Mandalay. It was possible to get free tickets to these places, but too many enquiries made this idea unhealthy. We therefore abandoned the idea of going to Mandalay and set off on foot the next day for Rangoon. Hlegu was reached that evening and owing to the poor condition of our feet a Chetty took pity on us and arranged for our transport by Japanese lorries driven by Tamils, with the result that we were able to reach Rangoon on the afternoon of the next day–the 14th.

We met Natarajan at the Chettinad Bank and found that he had got involved with some pro-Japanese Indians who seemed to know far too much about us. They had suggested to Natarajan either that he join a party of fifth columnists who were scheduled to infiltrate into India through Manipur in July or else stay in Rangoon and practise as a doctor. We told Natarajan that he must straighten things out for himself as we were going on to Prome where he could catch us up. This we did and reached Prome on 17th having been lucky enough to get shoved into a train at Rangoon.

Whilst at Prome we heard that Akyab was being heavily bombed by the British. We saw the Japanese burning corpses in Prome at night with kerosene. These corpses came by lorries from the direction of Akyab.

We were now faced with the prospect of alternative routes; the Akyab route through the Taungup Pass, up the Irrawaddy past Monywa, Kalewa and Kalemo, upto Homalin and then by the Tamu road to Manipur, or through Mandalay and then north into northern Assam. The informative obtained made us decide the Akyab route impassable due to thick undergrowth, leeches, wild animals, absence of villages, many mountain streams and 160 miles of uninhabited territory. We eventually decided on the Kalewa route either through Kalemyo or via the Tamu Road. In the meantime Natarajan arrived and as he was set on the Akyab route we decided to part company. In addition to this he was ill and needed rest before resuming the journey.

Eventually, after 12 days stay, we left Prome by boat for Pakokku on the 29th June. On our way we touched Thayetmyo, Magwe, Minbu, Yenangyaung, and then on the evening of 5th July rascals of the Burma Independence Army siezed our boat, ordered us out and made the Burman boatman carry 50 of these Thakin soldiers free of charge to Pakokku as well as supply them with rice.

We took refuge in a Chetty's house at Salle. He tried to persuade us to stay with him, but we told him of a brother lying sick at Monywa whom we must reach at all costs. We eventually left Salle on the 9th July and walked to Chauk and from thence to Singu a distance of about 20 miles. The next morning we came to Nyau, 4 miles north of Pagan. We eventually reached Pakkoku on the afternoon of the 12th.

Leaving Pakkoku we walked to Yesagyo on the 13th, and Mauk on the 14th. The next morning we crossed the Chindwin and arrived at Chaungoo on the afternoon of the 16th. After resting here we continued to Monywa which we reached on the 17th.

We met three Manipurians coming from Mandalay. They had Japanese passes and were going to Manipur. They appeared to be fifth columnists. One of them, Guna Singh, spoke English and had been in the Burma Railways. They told us we could get passes from the Japanese to go by their motor boats (the ones of the Irrawaddy Flottilla Co. run by the Chittagong Mohamedan Serangs under Japanese orders) to Kalewa. We went to the Japanese to try for these passes. We were successful in obtaining these passes by spinning a yarn about a sick brother. On the

22nd July we left Monywa in one of these boats which contained about 50 Japanese troops amongst which were about 6 of their engineering corps. We did some translation work for them from one of the Brown and Sharpe Machine Shop manuals. We starved the first day, got some rice the second day, cleaned their vessel and arrived at Kalewa at about 5 p.m. on the 25th.

The whole town was deserted with the exception of some Japanese troops and a few Indian coolies impressed by the Japanese. We remained at Kalewa 4 days, after which we set out by foot on the last stage of our journey. At the 5th milestone of the Kalemyo road we were helped of two Japanese soldiers to cross a deep nala by boat. They bought our sweaters for Rs. 2. Later we had to cross another river and several mountain streams where the bridges had all been destroyed. We were providential stopped by a Burmese boy asking us not to take the Tamu road as Indians were killed by the Burmese on that road. In fact–we were on the wrong road. We then returned to a village called Indian Guji where we received hospitality. We had to wait here till the 2nd August before we were able to take a boat across the river. We eventually entered Kalemyo at about midday on the same day. It was wonderful to see a sign board saying Tiddim 66 miles and Falam 72. We chose the Tiddim route as it was shorter. We were so excited we ran although we had to climb some 2000 feet in 5 miles. After 11 miles we reached Stockade No. 3 of our outpost. Here we were made welcome and interviewed and sent on our way to Falam where we made our report. We reached Aijal on the 18th, Silchar on the 20th and arrived at Calcutta on the 23rd, and on the 26th August we reported at G.H.Q. New Delhi. Thus ends our narrative. We had travelled 1000 miles by foot, 1000 miles by boat, and 1000 miles by goods train. We had also journeyed by bullock cart, on tops of buses, motor boats, canoes, sampans, mules and ponies, but it was not a bad journey. Our chief consolation that we came through with information that has proved to be valuable. We are grateful to the men who helped and guided us and thank God for bringing us through safely.

APPENDIX "A"

Conditions in P.O.W. Camps–Singapore

(Report by Lt. M.M. Pillai and Lt. V. Radhakrishnan who escaped 7-5-42

A. Changi Civil — 1. This was one of the most modern prisons built in reinforced concrete at a cost of a million dollars, with provisions for armed sentries, and is almost like a fortress making escape virtually impossible with the sea opposite guarded by the Japanese.

2. All the British troops in captivity are kept here with the European personnel of the Volunteers and the P.W.D. engineers who were all commissioned into the volunteers a week before the surrender.

3. A certain part of the prison is earmarked for the civilian prisoners (European). Heads of Government departments, chiefs of commercial firms, firms of a semi-Government or a semi-military nature are all here. Lady Shenton Thomas, he Governor's wife, is allowed to stay with her husband who is here too.

4. **Guards** consisted of about one battalion of Japanese troops, which also included some I.N.A. personnel.

5 (a) **Health** generally bad. Dysentry, typhoid and cholera rife. This is partly due to the lack of proper medical aid owing to the shortage of medicines which had been taken away by the Japanese, and to the scarcity of medical personnel who, being Indians, were taken away from their units. This resulted in the deaths of several European soldiers.

(b) Japanese doctors supervise the hospital scrutinising prescriptions and medicines.

(c) Visitors are allowed in the hospital on permission being previously obtained from the Japanese doctor there, or through the recommendation of Japanese in the town.

(d) Wives of prisoners lying sick in the hospital may succeed in getting permission to visit their husbands during their stay in the hospital. This facility, however, is academic as firstly, there are very few Europeans that have their wives on the island, and secondly it is difficult to make the contact as information about the patients is hard to obtain. Thirdly, permission is not come by easily. The Bishop of Singapore is allowed to visit sick prisoners in the hospital twice a week, of which one of sit is a Sunday. He is free and acts as a channel in so far as contacts are concerned.

6 (a) **Food**. For the first few days food was scarce and poor, later two meals of rice and dhal were received a day with occasional meat, fish, cigarettes and small quantities of rolled flour, but no vegetables or sugar. Salt is plentiful.

(b) Six months of provisions existed in the prison and barracks which was unknown to the Japanese but was known to some Indians, and would eventually become common knowledge. These provisions were being used to supplement the meagre scale of rations.

(c) Food could be bought when on working parties, but this was forbidden.

7. **Treatment.** All officers below field rank were treated as O.Rs forced to work, some of whom were seen driving M.T. for the Japanese about the Island. Hard work was carried out all day in the sun with no amusements or any form of relaxation. From personal contacts I saw that during the three months of captivity they had become very emaciated and many of them looked thin and lean, with even the bones of the chest visible.

8. **Pay**. No Indians received pay, the assumption is, therefore, that the British did not either.

9. **Escapes**. Four P.W. attempted to escape which resulted in one being shot and the others being recaptured after shooting a Japanese sentry. This led to increased vigilance on the part of the authorities.

10. **Clothing**. Many were seen working in the sun almost naked except for a pair of ragged shorts.

11. **Communications**. Up to the time we left we had very reliable information that there was no communication with the outside world by way of letters or radio. Contact could be established with men on working parties.

12. **Morale**. Very high in spite of all their privations. They were cheerful and evinced an interest in news and had great faith. Never was I impressed by these people as when I saw them in their privation.

1. Seletar faces the mainland of Johore, is slightly north-east and about fourteen miles from the centre of the town.

2. The Australian P.O.W. are kept here. The general and current report is that the Australians preferred to remain apart from the British and Indians. The Japanese were only too willing to concede to this request, as it was to their advantage to foster and promote dissensions among the white prisoners. How far this report is based on fact I do not know, but it is widely believed and from personal knowledge, and the behaviour of individual Australian prisoners, I suspect there is truth in the report.

3 (a) **Health**. Generally worse than that of the British prisoners, and also due to the lack of medical equipment and the poor food received. This has resulted in several deaths.

(b) There are practically no visitors because firstly, the locality is far from the town and there are no means of transport, and secondly, the Australians being new to the Island have very few friends. Permission to visit it appears, in theory, to be easy, but in actual fact I had not heard of anybody having visited them, except for a Catholic missionary and the Bishop of Lahore.

4. **Food** and **Pay** similar to paras. 6 and 8 of A above.

5. **Treatment** similar to para 7 of A above with the addition that after May some 3,000 P.O.W. were drafted into Burma to Victoria Point, Mergui and Taboy where they were employed on works of reconstruction.

6. **Escapes**. None was heard of, but escape should be easy as there was no wire at the time that we left. Once outside the camp, however, everything would be against an escaper, not even a friendly pro-British inhabitant would dare to help knowing the penalty.

7. **Clothing** and **Communications** similar to paras 10 and 11 of A above.

8. **Morale** low whilst discipline was very bad.

1. This camp is wired and moted. The main part of the Indian P.O.W. is kept here. Bidadari is the cemetry on the road to Paya Lobar and is midway between Changi on the east and the town on the west. There was a regular bus service to the town and back when we left.

2. **Health**. Similar to para. 5 of A with the exception of the medical personnel, no shortage of whom exist.

3. **Food, Treatment** and **Pay** similar to paras. 6, 7 and 8 of A.

4. **Escapes**. The barbed wire having been put up by the P.O.W. themselves is not well done, and escape is therefore fairly easy. Escaping for I.O.Rs is extremely easy from working parties as no guards are provided and are even often unescorted from the camp to the place of work. Officers are kept as hostages with the Japanese inspectors of work and have to be responsible for the numbers of the party, but when a man is missing no report is made of this and it is left for the Japanese to discover this fact for themselves later in the camp with the result that no one can be blamed.

5. **Clothing**. In the main this is similar to para. 10 of A.

6. **Communications**. Contact with the camp was easy, in addition to which receiving sets were kept hidden.

7. **Morale**. Poor.

1. This is near to 10th milestone on the Bukit Timah road–the arterial road between Singapore and the mainland. The camp is a little off the main road, is not very well guarded and escape from here is rather easy.

2. 80 per cent of the I.N.A. are here, and in particular all senior Indian officers with Japanese sympathies; also all hospital and army postal personnel.

3. All other conditions are similar to C above with the exception of radios none of which exist and morale in particular is very bad.

1. This is a camp for Sappers three thousand of

whom were here, and is just beyond the Botanical Gardens which is some distance from the town but close to the European residential areas of Tanglin and Orchard roads.

2. Conditions are similar to C with the exception of (a) morale which is high and the troops are resisting enemy propaganda to join the I.N.A., (b) radio receiving sets are hidden in the camp and P.O.W. regularly listen to the B.B.C. and A.I.R., and (c) escape from here is not easy on account of barbed wire fencing and will become even more difficult when the I.N.A. are posted as sentries.

1. This camp is near the aerodrome and was formed about mid-April to hold about 2,000 prisoners of war (Indian).

2. It is fenced with barbed wire and like all other camps is in the process of being moated.

3. All other conditions are similar to C with the exception of radio sets none of which exists.

1. This is near Alexandra hospital and was formed about mid-March to hold about 2,000 Indian P.O.W.

2. All other conditions similar to C except that there are no radios.

15

British Assessment of the Japanese Policy Towards India after the Outbreak of the Pacific War[1]

12 May, 1942

On the outbreak of the war with Japan on December 8th, 1941, all the British officials and their families were interned in British Embassy and thereby cut off from all communication with the outside world, the only source of information available to them being the daily newspapers, which were allowed into the Embassy by the Japanese authorities.

Judging from these daily newspapers, one is inclined to believe that the activities of the Indians in Japan and the aim of the so-called War of Greater East Asia were on the following lines :–

First and foremost the real aims and meaning of the "Co-prosperity sphere" and the War of Greater Asia became clear, in as much as they clearly included in the influence of this Sphere not only the countries of the Far East, but also Burma, India and Australia. Further more, there was a possibility of including in this Co-property sphere, it the opportunity arose, the remaining countries of Asia.

One is also inclined to believe that Japan's policy, in reality, is based on the idea of racial grouping, i.e., West versus East, but at present efforts are being made to cover up this policy of racial and colour rivalry, yet however, much Japan denies this policy, it seems that racial and colour rivalry will be the natural sequence of the War of Greater East Asia if Japan is successful. India at the outset of the war and even prior to their successes in Malaya and elsewhere, Japan openly showed her interest in India and premier General Tojo publicly announced that the Indians should take this opportunity and revolt in order to drive the British out of India, thereby gaining for themselves their Independence.

1. Foreign Department F. No. 313-x/1942 National Archives of India, New Delhi (NAI)

This, in fact, seemed to be Japan's trump card, and according to the tone of the newspapers a revolt on the part of the Indians was a certainty, an impression which was no doubt gained from the opinions and the influence of the two Boses, i.e., Rash Behari Bose and Subhas Chandra Bose of the Revolutionary Party in India, now in Berlin.

It must be a great shock to Japan that no Indian leaders have so far made any pro-Japanese statements and that Indians have not revolted in the expected manner : furthermore, it must be very painful for her to realise that Congress and the Muslim League, however much they may offer as regards the future constitution of India, appear, as far as can be gathered here, to have come to some understanding with the British for the defence of India, If India is threatened by some outside Power.

Right from the start of the War, Rash Behari Bose, who was mistakenly considered to be a spent force, showed his true colours and came out into the open, proving that he had been in close touch with the Japanese authorities in the movement to drive out the British from India. He took over the leadership of the newly formed Indian Independence League, with A.M. Sahay as his assistant, while at the same time Subhas Chandra Bose assumed the leadership of the League in Europe with the same object, i.e., the overthrow of the British in India. One is obliged to think that Japan seriously believed in these two Boses and their followers and therefore in their miscalculation as regards Indias revolt. Even after the so-called failure of Sir Stafford Cripps mission, Japan began to fear that the Indians, far from revolting to help Japan against the Allies, will in the near future be likely to make the war a national causes, unite among themselves and support the allies against the Axis in general and Japan in particular. This attitude of India and its political leaders seems to have not only disappointed Japan but also to have assured her because it must have upset her plans. According to the tune the newspapers, she has now changed her attitude to India. At first it was war "India for the Indians" with the Indian themselves gaining their own independence and thereby forming a separate unit outside the co-prosperity sphere. But later a different tone, and very threatening one was adopted on a which was pursued unit the Bangkok Conference in June," first, if the Indian political parties and their leaders do not realise and appreciate the real aim of Japan and do not cooperate with her in driving the British out of India, then Japanese for Indian's sake must invade India and drive out the British herself, so that India may occupy her rightful place in the greater East Asia Co-prosperity Sphere under the benevolent guidance of Japan.

This change of policy was followed up by Japan's attack on Trincommule, Calcutta, Madras and Visakhapatnam in April, 1942. At that time she was still hoping that her success in Malaya and the capture of Singapore would make the Indian rise in revolt, but once more disappointed. After the occupation of Burma, the newspapers again displayed a hostile attitude towards Indians asking the Indian soldiers that if they did not revolt or if they allowed the British to used any Indian naval bases or the British Army to remain India, the Japanese could advance on India to crush the British. This was followed up by Air-raids in areas on Imphal and Mahalapur.

One has the feeling, that the Japan was posed to attack India and that this is the reason why she is making these futile excuses. However, one wonders what her next move will be, will she attack Australia, India or Chungking, first? Or all together? And will the impending monsoon, which may hold her up until October, give her time to prepare for major operation.

One must admit, that in the light of their past successes the Japanese have proved that they have every thing worked out in minute detail, and that neither the impossible country nor the difficult climate have caused any hitch in their operations, which seem so far to have been successful.

Since the occupation of Burma by the Japanese, the newspapers have started to print articles on the topography, geology and climatic conditions of India, and at the same time have been making such of the alleged speeches and writings of Gandhi in his Harijan newspaper, in which the demands, that the British shall clear out of India, all of which is no doubt propaganda for home consumption.

The following extract from newspaper article shows perhaps the Japanese line of thought or even the course of their future action :–

"The Imperial Japanese forces, which have driven out British influences from Asia, have brought India under their domination. The complete elimination of Britain from India must be the logical conclusion of the execution of the policy of fighting the war of greater East Asia to finish, etc. etc".

16

Ko Ishii, Japanese Ambassador, in Bangkok, to Vishitre Vadakarn, Deputy Minister of Foreign Affairs, Requesting him to Extend Support to the Indian Independence League to Carry on their Activities Freely in Thailand[1]

28 May, 1942

Dear Nai V. Vichitr,

In confirmation of our conversation of yesterday, I hereby wish to state that the Japanese Government is prepared to support the Indian people to establish "India for Indian People", and in this connection I wish to ask your Government to work jointly with us in the following ways :

1. The Thai Government is to cooperate with the Japanese Government with sincere sympathy to help positively the movement of the Indian people in their endeavour to get rid of British fetters and to establish "India for Indian People."
2. The Thai Government is to give facilities to the political movement of the Indian people in Thailand to a reasonable extent. As the Indian people desire to open a meeting of the representatives of all Indian people in East Asia in the middle of June at Bangkok, the Thai Government is to give the necessary permission for such meeting to be held at their request. The Thai Government is further to recognize that the central office of this political movement is to be set in Bangkok, and will consequently give facilities of travelling and dwelling to those Indian people connected with the said meeting.
3. The Thai Government is to give enough protection to the Indian people in their activities in cultural and economical life. I also wish to assure your Excellency that this movement will prove harmless to your country, and to that, the Japanese Government will pay its most serious attention to avoid any discrepancies that may have arisen.

---

1. File No. 401, I.N.A. Papers.

17

Japanese Premier's Message congratulating Indian Independence League for holding Bangkok Conference

15 June, 1942

It is with the greatest of pleasure that I send you my heartiest congratulations on the occasion of the convention of the Indian Independence Conference in Thailand, our ally, on the initiative of the leaders of the 2 million Indians living in Asia to create a new epoch in the movement for Indian independence.

Since the outbreak of the Greater East Asia War more than half a year has elapsed. During this period the British defences in Asia for Placating India has practically been wiped out by the gallant Imperial forces and a golden opportunity to realize the long cherished aspiration of Indian independence has come.

At this juncture if the leaders of the 2 million Indians in Asia in calling this conference respond to Japan's true desire for the Indians to create India for the Indians, Japan is quite prepared to give her unstineted support as it has been announced from time to time, and I might add that the Axis Powers are ready to cooperate in according their full support.

Britain, which is meeting with defeats in Asia, Europe, Africa and in all theatres of war, is facing an extremely miserable state of affairs which she brought on herself by her own mis-doing. She is now demanding great sacrifices of India through her usual crafty way of threat and supplication. However, the far sighted and able patriotic Indian leaders wisely realizing the heavenily bestowed destiny of India, and fully cognizant of the world affairs, are determinably resisting Britain, a fact which I want to express my deepest respect.

1. File No. 401, I.N.A. Papers. For the message from Thai Prime Minister P. Pibulsonggram, see *Bangkok Chronicle,* 15 June 1842.

Though the construction of India for the Indians constitutes my most sincere desire, India still remains British territory and military establishments, as well as military forces, are being daily strengthened. Japan is firmly determined decisively to destroy Britain and she will be competed to take action so long as British military strength remain in India. In order to rescue India from war disaster it is necessary that Britain should give up her ambitions in India or India herself must sever her relations with Britain on her own initiative.

Fortunately, as I believe the present conference represents the general public opinion of the Indian people of the East, I pledge that Japan is fully prepared to support the independence movement.

In congratulating most earnestly the success of the present conference I hope sincerely that the Indian people will fully understand Japan's true intentions and with the people both inside and outside of India working in close cooperation to achieve its cherished hope of independence.

18

Speech of the Italian Minister Signor Guido Crolla at the Bangkok supporting Indian Independence[1]

15 June, 1942

"It is indeed a source of deep gratification for me to attend the opening session of this Conference which, thanks to Thailand's hospitality, gathers here to-day the Representatives of the various Indian movements in the Far East.

The bonds between India and Italy date far back in history. They were existing even before the Roman Empire, which was a great attempt of unifying western and eastern cultures. In the Middle Ages the daring exploit of an Italian, Marco Polo, brought the two worlds closer again, while the Republics of Venice and Genea were intensifying their trade with India through the Mediterranean.

In more recent times Indian culture found and still finds in Italy many scholars and admirers and the Italian youth is taught in school has to appreciate the contribution given by India to the history of humanity.

The Italian people who have for no long hardly struggled to recover their unity and independence cannot but offer sympathy and understanding towards the suffering and aspirations of the Indian People.

Italy's interest for the cause of Indian independence is deeply rooted in the past. Indian exiles have always found in Italy a most cordial welcome and hospitality.

This particular sympathy, which is spontaneous, lively and disinterested has rootly found expression in the institution of a society in Rome called "The Friends of India", where Indian patriots of undaunted faith and sincerity, such as Iqbal Schedal, are working for the cause of Indian liberty followed by the friendly and unanimous encouragement of

1. *Ibid.* The text of message is also reproduced in Giani, *op. cit.* p. 74.

the Italian public opinion. "The Friends of India" wish to create as closer connections as possible between cognate associations existing in Germany, Japan and Thailand with a view to attaining the final aim through a better and greater co-ordination of their respective efforts.

The enduring passion of the Indian People is approaching its decisive moment.

The war which the Tripartite Powers are victoriously waging against India's secular oppressor is destined to create a new order in contrast with the old one ruled by Anglo-Saxon selfishness and abuse.

Within the frame of such a New Order the Indian People after having shaken the British yoke, shall, as a free Nation, find the place which their high civil and cultural traditions entitle them to.

Italy, Germany and Japan have no territorial ambitions in India. Their support is therefore all the more disinterested and their friendship all the more sincere.

The Representatives of Free India gathered in Bangkok to-day are confronted with the highly responsible task of shaping the future destiny of their own Country in accordance with the wishes and the interest of the Indian People.

In union with Germany and Japan, Italy is wishing this conference the best success."

19

Dr. E. Wendler, the German Minister's Speech at Bangkok Conference Promising Help for the Liberation of India[1]

16 June, 1942

It is especially gratifying to me as German Minister in Bangkok to be able to accept the invitation to attend the opening session of this Conference at which prominent representatives of the Indian people will deliberate as to the means of shape and safeguard the future of India in accordance with the wishes of the Indian people. I need hardly emphasize that Germany takes a lively interest in these questions as was also stressed a short time ago by the fact that the German Chancellor received at his headquarters the well-known champion of the Indian independence idea, Subhas Chandra Bose. The world war raging today will spell the end of the dominion of the British and Americans who have ever subjugated and used for their own purposes the peoples in their power. The nations allied to each other by the Tripartite Pact, Germany, Italy and Japan, will see to a just New Order, terminating Anglo-American tutelage over the rest of the world. Thus also the possibility arises for the Indian people, after nearly two centuries of subjugation by the British, a subjugation which has cost India so much misery and suffering, to shape the future destiny of their country according to their will.

The German people have shown the greatest sympathy towards the people of India. The outstanding cultural achievements of India during the course of her long history dating back-thousands of years, have always been the source of special interest in Germany. Germany was also the first country in Europe in which the great values in the spheres of Indian philosophy and poetry were fully appreciated. It is therefore self-evident that the German people, notwithstanding the

1. *Ibid.*

which they find themselves involved, even at the present time follow with much sympathy the significant happenings in India and, together with the peoples of Italy and Japan, show the greatest interest in the fight for freedom of the Indian people.

The Great Powers of the Tripartite Pact, Germany, Italy and Japan, are all the more in a position to raise their voices as sincere friends of the Indian people since they have no territorial interests whatsoever in India.

They have but one desire : that India and her people, in free self-determination, be heading for a better future and develop to a level corresponding to the riches of the Indian soil and the great gifts of its inhabitants.

20

Address of Rash Behari Bose at the Bangkok Conference Expressing Faith in Japan for the Liberation of India and Asking the People to Cooperate in the Struggle[1]

16 June, 1942

The creation of a Free, Happy and United India-an India which the Poet visualised and the superman is creating. The burden is ours. We have to carry it. The success is assured, once we put faith in India.

We are grateful to those who have been showering on us sympathy and encouragement in helping us carry this burden. The spontaneous sympathy from far and near-will ever remain as a treasure. We thank every one of you.

" Bande Matarm. Inqlab Zindabad, Azad Hind Zindabad ! "

Mr. Rash Behari Bose was then formally elected President. He delivered the following Presidential Address :-

" Your Excellencies, Friends and Compatriots!

" Allow me to express my sincere thanks for the great honour you have done me by calling upon me to occupy this chair and guide the deliberations of this historic conference. While greatly appreciating this expression of love and affection for me, I am not unaware of the fact that along with this honour you have placed on my shoulders a great responsibility by electing me the President of this Conference. However, if I have obeyed your command and taken this chair in spite of my knowledge of the intricacies of the problems that will come before this conference, I have been prompted to do so by my great faith in your spirit of co-operation and your sincere desire to put your heads together and to come to useful decisions without wasting much of your time on unnecessary discussions and arguments. I am sure I can count upon your unreserved help and

1. I.I.L. Papers F No. 45/3.

cooperation in successfully conducting the business of the conference.

" As I stand here, my thought goes to the unfortunate air accident, last March, that claimed the lives of our four valuable comrades-Swami Satyananda Puri and Gyani Pritam Singhji of Bangkok, and Captain Akram and Mr. Nilakanda Iyer of Malaya, while they were flying to Tokyo to attend our Indian Independence Conference.

" We can well realise the great loss to our cause at such an important period of our struggle and we all feel it very deeply. However, brethren, let us take it as inevitable and pray for the peace of their souls. In our grim final struggle against British Imperialism, we shall have to offer great sacrifices. Many of us will have to lay down our lives before the world can see India free. It can be well said that these four comrades have given us the lead, of which our compatriots in Thailand and Malaya can be well proud of.

" During and since 1837, when we first revolted against British Imperialism in India, hundreds of thousands of our most respected and beloved compatriots have laid down their lives in their efforts to free our Motherland. We cannot forget the fact that they have nourished the seeds of Swaraj with their blood and it is the result of their supreme sacrifices that we are to-day so near our goal and can hope with confidence to achieve independence in the near future. World knows only a part of the long list of those Indian victims of British Imperialism. Let us pay respects to the memory of those numberless known and unknown comrades. Placed as we are to-day, we can do very little beyond that. But the time is fast approaching when in very city and town in India, we shall find a worthy monument erected in their memory and we Indians will pay homage to them and look upon them with pride.

" Our homage is also due to those respected leaders and workers as well as the organisations that have in various ways made untiring efforts since 1857 to liberate our country from bondage. Their list is in no way small and in no way their contributions were negligible. Let us pay our respects to that greatest living Indian Mahatma Gandhi, who, with his magic wand, roused the Indian masses from the centuries-long slumber and has created self-confidence in them. We can have no doubt that when the new and true history of India will be written, Mahatma Gandhi's name will have to be mentioned as the Saviour of India.

" I do not want to take Your time by going into the details regarding India's struggle for freedom since 1857. Suffice it to say that although the failure of our revolt of 1857 was a great blow to the nation and although a general depression had overwhelmed the country, our efforts to overthrow

British rule never ceased. Under the circumstances prevailing in those days, the activities had to be carried on underground and within a limited scope; and whenever there was an opportunity, a revolt was attempted. After minor preparatory stages our first effort on a large scale was made when the war of 1914-1918 started. Our workers were active everywhere. The Indian army was prepared to join the revolt. A part of the Indian army had actually revolted rather prematurely. We thought we were going to succeed. Unfortunately we did not meet with success on that occasion. Thousands of our compatriots had to pay the highest price of patriotism. Thousands were sent to the Andamans and Mandalay and hundreds of them still remain rotting in prisons and concentration camps.

" During that war of 1914-1918 the British had been partially successful in receiving India's co-operation by telling lies and making false promises. Our people were misled by the fine phraseologies of the shred British diplomats. They promised us freedom after the war, as they are doing even during the present war. But soon after the conclusion of that war, it was realised that the British not only did not mean to keep their promises but definitely wanted to take away even that shadow of civil liberty that the Indians were having in pre-war days. When they protested against that, the response from the British side was in terms of bombs, bullets and machine-guns. Needless to mention that the tragedy of the Jallianwala Bagh of Amritsar in April, 1919, is still fresh in the memory of every one of us and the wound has not yet healed. It really cannot be healed until and unless we have completely destroyed the power that was responsible for the great humiliation of our people.

Every tragedy, however, has a lesson and so had the tragedy of Jallianwala Bagh. The blood of more than one thousand of those innocent martyrs, that included even our women and children, could not go without significant results. The great upheaval that swept India from one corner to the other, and the great movement of Non-Cooperation and Civil Disobedience that has been carried on by the Indian National Congress since 1919 and that has wonderfully organised the masses of India for political struggle, were undoubtedly the direct result of the massacre at Jallianwala Bagh.

" We all must bow our heads in reverence and be greatful to those brothers and sisters who by giving their lives at Jallianwala Bagh have created a new life in India. As we know to-day, millions and millions in India are prepared and determined to suffer and sacrifice their all for the cause of their motherland. When in 1939 the war in Europe started, Britain once again began to indulge in jugglery of words in order to secure Indian cooperation and help. But to the great delight of us all, to this very day the nationalist leaders in India have refused to be misled and have continued to resist all British efforts to drag India into war. Our respect goes to Mahatma Gandhi for the most admirable way, he has led the nation clear of all dangers of being entangled in this war.

" With this background in India, the Greater East Asia War was declared on the 8th December, 1941. No matter in which part of the world he or she might be living, whatever might be his or her attitude towards Japan, I refuse to believe that there was a true Indian patriot who was not extremely delighted and gratified in his heart of hearts when the great news of the declaration of War by Japan against the Anglo-American races reached his or her ears. I refuse to believe there is any true Indian patriot, whatever be his or her career or conviction, who might not have rejoiced, as from day to day, the mighty Imperial forces of Japan on land and sea and in e air went on administering crushing blows against their imperialism in Asia, and the British Imperialist bases in these parts began to totter one after the other like houses of cards. For is there a man whose eyes I cannot withhold joyous tears when he sees before his eyes the power of the greatest enemy of humanity and peace, the greatest aggressor of centuries being destroyed ? Those of us, who were destined to five and work in Japan, had particular reasons to be overjoyed at these most welcome happenings.

"We have been working in Japan for decades so that we can see Japan in a position to stand by the oppressed Asiatics and to liberate Asia. We were anxiously awaiting the day when Japan would fully realise the great significance of creating a free and united Asia and would feel convinced that it was in the interest of Japan herself, as also for the rest of Asia if not for the world as a whole, that the octopus grip of the Anglo-Saxon Imperialism in the East must be destroyed root and branch. We all were fully convinced that Japan alone was in the position to take the honour. Thus when on the morning of the most auspicious day, the day of the Enlightenment of Lord Buddha, we heard the most auspicious news of Japan's declaration of war against our common enemy, we felt that our mission in Japan was fulfilled. We felt convinced that India's freedom was assured. Being in Japan for decades, I knew well that Japan was not in the habit of talking and debating unnecessary and meaningless things. I knew well that she was not in the habit of taking any serious step unless she had fully washed her strength and was convinced of her success. I therefore did not share the views of those who thought that due to her continued military activities in China, she was too exhausted to challenge the mighty Anglo-Saxon, or the so called ABCD combined forces. I was one of those who had not the slightest doubt that the war in China was a prelude to the real war against Powers who were actually responsible for the continued fratricidal conflict between China and Japan. Happenings on the international chess board during the past more than ten years have been suggesting that such a worldwide conflict was inevitable. It was also apparent that the question of Indian freedom could be successfully solved only when Japan rose in arms against British Imperialism.

" Now that Japan and Thailand have taken up arms against our common foe, the joint efforts of our worthy allies ensure the doom of the British Empire and our complete victory is assured.

" These effective efforts on different fronts to destroy our common enemy, bring us a reminder regarding our own duties and responsibilities in this common effort for our common cause. We must ask ourselves what we have done and what we are going to do to contribute to this great cause. Only praising Japan, Germany and Italy will not entitle us to the position for which we are craving. We must contribute our mite and must make the greatest sacrifice we can make. Then alone can we command the respect and consideration of our worthy allies and then alone we can claim a place worthy of a great nation like ours in future international assembly.

Realising this very important fact, and our duty towards our motherland at this most important juncture, we in Tokyo promptly met on the 8th of December, 1941 at the Rainbow Grill and decided upon a programme of action. My Compatriots formed a committee and asked me to lead the movement and I gladly agreed to abide by their decision. We at first undertook to consolidate Indian opinion in East Asia in favour of a definite fight from without. Meetings were held in different centres of Japan and resolutions were passed emphasising the solidarity of our compatriots, the great need of declaring Independence of India by destroying British Imperialism, and expressing confidence in our work.

On the 26th December, 1941, for the first time in the history of Indians in Japan, a Conference of nearly fifty representatives of the Indian residents in Kobe, Osaka, Yokohama and Tokyo-all the four cities, where Indians reside-was held at the Railway Hotel at Tokyo to consider the problems. A resolution was passed calling upon the Indians to realise the gravity of the situation and the danger ahead of India. The resolution read as follows:-

"Whereas the continued defeat of the British and their allies in Europe and Africa has sealed the fate of the British Imperialism in Europe.

Whereas the most decisive destruction of British sea and land forces by Japan in the East has given a death-blow to the power and prestige of British Imperialism in Asia.

Whereas the war is fast approaching the shores and borders of India, the British stronghold, Axis powers may be obliged to invade India in order to destroy the main source of British fighting strength.

Whereas such an invasion will bring unimaginable and extremely unusual hardships, miseries and sufferings to millions of innocent and helpless Indians in cities, towns and villages, and

Whereas the only way to avoid this most unhappy situation is .to declare complete independence of India from British rule and to cut off all possible connections with British Imperialism in every possible way immediately;

The Indian Nationals residing in Japan assembled in this Conference, most seriously and earnestly appeal to the Indian National Congress and the people of India to immediately declare Independence and to capture all power from the British in India and to take immediate effective steps to stop each and every source of Indian aid to British Imperialist War and to declare on behalf of the people that India has no desire whatsoever to be involve I in this conflict and has never been willing to help Britain.Our representatives were sent to Shanghai and on 26th of January this year, a huge gathering of the Indian residents of Shanghai was held in Young Men's Association hall when similar resolutions as passed in Tokyo were very enthusiastically passel and our movement was given unanimous support.

In the meantime we established contact with the military and civil high commands in Japan and began to impress upon them the necessity of helping India in her struggle for freedom for the very achievement of the great object for which Japan had declared war against British and America. We made it clear to them that so long as British Imperialism in India continued, Japan could not expect a final victory in this war. At last: we succeeded in prevailing upon them and General Tojo, the Prime Minister of Japan, openly declare before the Imperial Diet that his Government was prepared to help the Indians in our efforts to free our country from the long bondage. In his declaration before the Imperial Diet on the fall of Singapore he said :-

"It is a golden opportunity for India, having, as it does, several thousand years of history and splendid cultural tradition, to rid herself of the ruthless despotism of Britain and participate in the construction of the Greater East Asia Co-Prosperity Sphere. Japan expects that India will restore its proper status of India for the Indians and it will not stint herself in extending assistance to the Patriotic efforts of the Indians. Should India fail to awaken to her mission forgetting her history and tradition, and continue as before to be beguiled by the British cajolery and manipulation and act at their beck and call I cannot but fear that an opportunity for the renaissance of the Indian people would be forever lost."

The declaration offered us great encouragement and we felt convinced, that India could safely hope to be free before the East Asia War comes to an end. Counting upon the promises of General Tojo, we established our headquarters at Sanno Hotel and started our activities and preparations in right earnest. We decided that a Conference of the representatives of Indian organisations in various parts of East Asia should be held for exchanging views regarding our future move. With the help of the military authorities things were conveniently arranged and the representatives of our compatriots residing in Malaya, Honkong and Shanghai along with us of Tokyo, sat in conference for three days and arrived at certain decisions and framed the preliminary constitution for the working an l progress of our movement. Those friends from abroad, who participated in Tokyo Conference, had occasion to come in contact with responsible members of the Japanese Army in Tokyo and to know more and more about the standing of our movement, Discussion at the Tokyo Conference were varied and we did our best to lay dowa a solid foundation upon which we could base our plan of action in future. We all know that the Conference in Tokyo was held at a time when things were less settled than they are today. Friends from East Indies were not present. We were deprived of the valuable help and advices of our friends in Thailand due to the unfortunate accident. Burma and Andamans were still in the hands of our enemies. We, therefore, were unable to come to a decision that could be claimed to be representative of the views of our compatriots in East Asia as a whole. We, therefore, decided to hold a larger and most representative Conference at a later date when the decisions taken at Tokyo were to be ratified. This Assembly in which we are participating, to-day is the result of that decision.

"The responsibility to convene this Conference was placed upon my shoulders and I was asked to hold it in this city. I am sorry that the Conference was delayed by a couple of weeks. We expected to arrive here earlier but due to extraordinary period, through which we are passing things could not be always done as expected and we have to adjust our selves according to circumstances.

" I know I have exhausted your patience by chronologizing the events and activities during the last more than six months. But, it was necessary to acquaint you with what has happened and how we have proceeded, before we sit down to business and put our heads together to knock out far reaching decisions.

"Friends, we all realise the gravity of the situation and also the fact that we are passing through the most important period of India's history. I don't want speeches. We had enough of that during the last more than five decades. We really cannot afford to waste our time on meaningless talks and arguments. Those who want to really serve the motherland cannot have much time to talk. If we go on talking without coming to any concrete decision, time will not wait for us and we shall be left only to shed tears at our past folly, and it will be too late to mend things. I know there are knotty problems that will come before you for discussions and will need your most careful consideration. I know you will have to do a lot of thinking and face a lot of doubts from within, before you can decide. But, if you have come with grim determination to thrash out a positive, concrete, and actually useful plan, you will be able to come to quick decisions. Let us all fully realise our responsibilities towards our land of birth and let us realise well, that our down-trodden country cannot afford to lose this golden opportunity that comes only once in centuries. Our brothers and sisters have in hundreds of thousands laid down their lives and have suffered and sacrificed for more than a century so that our country may be once again free. Let us rise to the occasion and carry their efforts to success so that the souls of martyrs in Heaven may find peace and be pleased. Let us rise and act so that the great preparations that Mahatma Gandhi has made during the last more than two decades, may bear fruit and our children in future may think of us with pride and respect as the members of a free nation.

"I know many of you have come with doubts and suspicious regarding the ultimate fate of our country as the result of our activities. I assure you that I can well appreciate your feelings of uncertainty and Your desire for security and yet I believe they are based on false promises. Having bitterest experiences of Imperialist exploitations for centuries, we have begun to doubt even our goad friends and if we insist on this attitude, the world will go on and we shall be left behind to regret our indecision.

"I want to sound a note of warning here. Our enemies have always been successful in keeping us divided and creating false impressions in our -minds on such occasions. On many occasions in the past, we have missed opportunities to free our country by being victims of lying British propaganda. I can only hope that we shall not repeat our folly. Our doubts and suspicions are to a great extent the results of shrewd and well-thought plans of our enemies to sabotage our efforts. Those of us who have intelligence enough and who are not blind to facts and happenings can see the way clearly.

"We should feel thankful to the Governments of Japan, Germany Thailand and Italy for their most friendly attitude they have been showing towards our cause. We must be particularly thankful to Japan for the most encouraging and hopeful definite promise of help in our sacred cause Let us not forget the words of Pandit Jawaharlal Nehru when he said :-

Success often comes to those who dare and act, it seldom goes to cowards.

"I make an earnest appeal to you all friends to see that when you conclude your session, you have a most practical and workable plan of action for India's freedom so that we can start our work right after the Conference and march ahead. We are fortunate enough to have the most valuable help of our Indian Army at our disposal. They deserve our great respect for the great service they have already rendered to our cause by refusing to serve the enemies of India. But their greater service is still awaiting our decision. No one can doubt the bravery of our soldiers in a righteous fight for a righteous cause. Our sympathy goes to the families and friends of those Indian soldiers who have, erroneously believing that they have been fighting for a right cause, lost their lives in Europe and Asia. They have been misled by the same propaganda of lies by Britain that is responsible for the unfounded suspicion in the minds of so many of us. I bow my head to the bravery of our soldiers and we should have no doubt that with their wholehearted support we are going to win our final fight against British Imperialism. Let us stand shoulder to shoulder and let us march hand in hand to success. Let us remember we have one indivisible Nation India one enemy England one goal complete Independence.

Bande Matram

21

Japanese Assessment of the Bangkok Conference[1]

18 June, 1942

A plenary session of Indian Independence League was held at the royal theatre in Bangkok on Monday, by over 100 Indian delegates from Tokyo, Shanghai, Hong kong, Malaya, Shonan Island, Borneo, Java, the Philippines and other places. There were also present, besides Mr. Teiji Tsubokami, the Japanese Ambassador to Thailand, the German and Italian Ministers, and these diplomats spoke in ardent support of the Indian Independence movement. It is certainly very significant that such a meeting was held at Bangkok in East Asia at a time when the position of Britain in East Asia has been completely undermined in the sequel to the development of the War of Greater East Asia and British Domination of India is on the brink of collapse.

The Indian Independence League has decided to establish its headquarters at Bangkok and to develop the Indian Independence movement vigorously through close collaboration with all its branches in East Asia. One prominent feature of the League is that it represents a Union to which men of all political factions and religious faiths are afflicted. It is indeed unprecedented in the history of the Indian Independence movement that a unified front has been formed by Indians irrespective of party and religious distinctions. That such a big Union has been brought into existence argues that the Indian Independence movement has a new and big advance.

The belief obtained among many people for a long time that India lacked internal unity was an unnatural state of affairs brought about by the policy of causing dissensions, which was consistently pursued by Britain. The British authorities attempted to paralyse the Indian Independence movement by diverting the attention of the Indian populace

1. *Japan Times and Advertiser*, 18 June 1942.

from political to religious problems. They deliberately misrepresented the Indian national movement for the acquisition of independence and freedom as a movement launched and carried on by a certain religious sect for the expansion of its influence, and accordingly brought pressure to bear on it in the specious name of protecting the minority rights.

Whereas, in Europe, the mention of majority or minority elements implies racial antagonism, it is not so in India, where it refers exclusively to religions. Although the Indian people embrace different religious faiths, they are of the same racially. If, therefore, there does exist a conflict of interests among the Indians, it is imply of a character either regional or religious antagonism. As a matter of fact, subsequently of World War No. 1, things in India have been moving in the direction of the formation of a united front among all classes for the vigorous pursuit of the independence movement in the face of all kinds of interference offered by the British authorities and, now a big Union of Indians in East Asia has finally been organised through the formation of the Indian Independence League. One noteworthy fact in connection with the Bangkok Congress is that Japan and other Axis Powers caused their Ambassador and ministers to attend the meeting and give words of support and encouragement. This fact demonstrates that the Indian Independence movement has the support of Japan, German and Italy. In the course of his message of congratulation to the congress. General Hideki Tojo, the Premier stated that "I take delight in being able to say that I have convinced myself that the present congress is an embodiment of Indian opinion in East Asia". He further declared that I swear to the Congress that the Japanese Empire is prepared to back the movement for Independence for India which is the aim of the present Congress that the Japanese Empire is prepared to back the movement for Independence for India which is the aim of the present Congress. By enlisting the support of the Axis Powers the Indian Independence movement has assumed world wide dimensions. India is no longer an isolated entity. It is a country which is working strenuously for the overthrow of British imperialism through close collaboration with the Axis Powers who are devoted to the establishment of a new world order. Britain who failed in the negotiations with India conducted recently through Sir Stamford Craps has now dispatched the Duke of Gloucester to India in order to placate the discontented, but his present visit is exciting no interest among the Indian people. This is quite proper and as it should be, for the Indian people who rejected Sir Stafford Cripps' proposals in their entirety are not looking for any present whatever, from Britain. In fact, the compromise plan produced by Sir Stafford embodied the maximum of the "concessions" which imperialist Britain could make to India. Judging both from the trends of internal conditions in India, the independence of India is irresistible. The leaders of the Indian independence movement are unanimous in demanding the withdrawal of the British forces from India and the severance of all connection with Britain. We feel confident that after the present Bangkok Congress, the Indian independence movement will go forward nakedly under unified leadership and we consequently look forward with high expectations to the success of this movement.

22

Mohan Singh's Appeal at the Close of the Bangkok Conference Requesting Indians to Prepare Themselves for Long and Hard Fight Against the British; thanks Japanese for their Support[1]

19 June, 1942

At the closing session of the Indian Independence conference, Captain Mohan Singh said : I am delighted that during my short sojourn in Bangkok I am again privileged to speak to you. The first time I was ordered to do so by the President but this time it is my own desire to talk to you.

Since the day of my arrival I had been looking forward for an opportunity to speak to you heart to heart. Listen patiently, I want to talk to you non-stop unless you signal me that what I say is no longer required and time for action has arrived. I except you all Hindus, Muslims, Sikhs—High or low—old or young to march together hand in hand. We will obey our heart's desire. Believe me, our hearts will not deceive us. Is there any better guide in this world than sympathy, truthfulness, love and unity, which I tell you, will take us along the right path.

The stone-hearted are those who are not moved. I say you are made up of the strongest steel. You shall not be beaten and shall be attracted to the liberty's magnetic pole. Aren't you feeling that force of attraction to day, if not I say you and your hearts are rusty. Burnish the rust and prepare the surface for the magnetic attraction–In short strengthen the will of sacrifice, Brethren, Behold! The world is undergoing stupendous change.

Look! Your next door neighbour is in the struggle. You cannot go on sitting dumb-founded. We must always bear in mind the example of

1. Papers of General Mohan Singh. See also I.I.L. Papers F. No 45/3.

the great Eastern Nation Japan. What a small country it was. But in a short time–I should say in the twinkling of an eye it has performed a miracle. The vicious encirclement by ABCD Nations has not only been broken but completely destroyed. So much so that the enemy in its run had no time to turn round and see what was happening behind.

Hundreds of aeroplanes, thousands of guns, hundreds of thousands of machineguns, rifles, motorcars and lorries and incalculable amount of ammunition have been left behind. Hundreds of huge dumps of ration, stores and other essential war materials in ship leads were made over to the Imperial Govt. of Japan. But the most important item of the war machine–millions of trained officers and men handed over were intact.

Funny enough! that Churchill—the mischief monger of the world, is still not ashamed of his eye-wash activities. Ladies and Gentlemen! I am not telling you fables. I have seen all this myself. This unparallel example of valour and sacrifice of the Nippon soldiers has annihilated the pride of the two big Nations. The world, you all know, is wonder-struck at this miracle.

The creation of the Almighty God is in transformation, Earth and heaven are changing and the whole map of the world has changed. Nations and the order of the world has changed. Those who were behind have gone for ahead of the mark. Those who considered themselves forward of everyone and were proud of thier empires are one the verge of extinction.

True! All this has happened but whither are we Indians. Are there any signs of change in us? I emphatically say, No. No signs of change at all. What is there lacking in us? I say sense of realisation of self-sacrifice and patriotism. Are we dead? No! We are in a state of slumber. This of course must end now. The time has come that we got rid of this evil disease.

I ask you, Brothers, what should we do to bring about the awakening. Do you want the scene of Bhagat Singh's crucification reported in front of you? Do you want our sacred temples at Nankana Sahib flooded with human blood and see the burning of people alive? Do you want your countrymen to repeat the scenes of bloodshed in the streets of Peshawar? Say, do you want a Japanese soldier to come in front of you and cut open his heart and show the anatomy of love and sacrifice. I do not understand what actually is wanted. We must transform ourselves. We have to undergo the treatment alone by ourselves and the very treatment is also in our own hands.

It astonishes me when I compare ourselves with other countries. Take for example Thailand, I say, the country of God and his blessed people. There is nothing to disunite them. No religious strife. They are proud Thais. Their culture ressembles Indian culture. To them platform of liberty is totally different from other things. There is only one faith—one understanding—oneness as Thais, say to live as brothers.

I am sure every small town in this country has an association of Thais, where every Thais, irrespective of what class or creed he belongs to, has the right to be a member. On the other hand isn't it lamentable that our weaknesses, yet urk in us even in this country where we breathe free air. Why isn't there an institution of Indians instead of smaller sectional clubs. I call this derogatory on the part of the Indian brothers of this town.

Religion is truth and as such is the force of humanity. A lover of religion is a worshipper of God. It does not matter what creed or faith he fellows and such a man is justice seeker and beloved by all. Temples, Mosques and Gurdwaras, I say all the places of worship are sacred to lovers of God.

But we Indians trapped in the British treachery have always disrespected the faith and religion of others. Have forgotten the truth. Have engrossed ourselves into ill-will. Have forgotten the Creator. I say, if I were to stand at one corner of India and shout at the top of my voice that God is this and God is that, I can assure you not one would listen to me.

Probably a few might call me a fool. But if I were to speak against Guru Gobind Singh, Lord Krishna or Prophet Mohammed, then what my fate would be, I am sure, you can visualize. It is terrible that there should be bloodshed on the names of those whom God sent as religious leaders than that on the name of very God. The worst part of it is that if a word is said against Guru Gobind Singh, a Sikh would get enraged and be prepared to shed his blood.

If anything is said against Prophet Mohammed then only a Muslim would consider it an insult. Mind you, both of them have been the leaders of human-beings. Why should we then dishonour them? Remember God is one and indivisible and as such same for all. Why should we get angry and despise our own people? If you pass an insulting remark about any town of a free Nation, then the whole nation will fight for its honour. But alas! India has been chewed into bits by foreign domination, yet none of us would feel it.

If Hindu Brothers come to know that Mohammedans have slaughtered a cow, then who can check the anger of Hindus. The whole community will be prepared to sacrifice itself. If Mohammedan Brothers come to know that a pig is being killed in the vicinity, the whole Mohammedan community would be ready for shedding blood. But we do not realise that on this triffling matter of killing animals millions of our brave soldiers have been slaughtered. I say the whole country has been butchered.

If a Hindu slaughters a pig, a Mohammedan slaughters a cow, we often shed our blood but never feel ashamed to this when notorious Englishman gets these animals killed and eats them. What a fate? We Indians cook and serve with our own hands dishes on the table of Englishman. Believe me this happens every day and night in India. You can always see this being done in Army Officers' Messes and Hotels.

We never realise how we are cutting each other's throat and yet never kill that person who is responsible in slaughtering our Indians, cows and pigs. Our religious faiths and the strength of the Nation has been disrupted so much that we are divided, sub-divided and redivided again into chips by the English.

A Mohammedan would be called an Infidel if he offered respects to a Sikh brother in Sikh words and style. A Sikh would be cursed by his community if he saluted and respected a Mohammedan brother in the Muslim words and style. A Hindu for similar offences would be removed from.his community. But have you ever realised that day and night you wish not only to the English but amongst yourselves Good Morning, Good Evening and Good Night, in totally foreign language and culture. Our children instead of calling the parents in our beautiful Indian languages shout in foreign language as Daddy and Mummy. We never feel sorry at this but would strangle the child's throat if the expression is in a Muslim way or Hindu way.

(a) Religions do not teach us hatred and division. Why do we fight? I say it is criminal to despics God's made man.

(b) Religions do not teach slavery. Why are we slaves? It is no fault of religion to live as slaves. We must be free or die in the struggle for liberty. A coward and a slave have no place and right to live in this world. Now is the time to rejuvenate ourselves. Yesterday's slaves are to-day's free men. We can amend the wrongs. I felt it as my duty that I should give you this as a warning signal and I have done it. Now that time is gone that if you are slapped on the right check. you should offer the left.

The right of right is obtained and retained by might. Fifty years ago, Japan sent to Europe books on Philosophy, law and order but the English did not understand. Later on Japan sent to them samples of toys, cloth and crockery but they did not see and listen. Eventually Japan picked up sword and defeated Russia just on the gospel of to live and let live. This, Gentlemen, opened the eyes of the world. European powers recognised Japan as a first rate Eastern Power. The tumultuous world has always been as such. Might is right.

In the struggle for existence the oppressed must overthrow the oppressor and must live. Today the whole is a battlefield. Clouds of tyranny and injustice are hanging over India. But remember when war is over justice is bound to prevail. If we are to live in this world in peace and justice, now is the time that we must gird up our loins and uproot the enemy from the sacred soil of India. Do not forgot that we have no desire to become the laughing stock of the world.

It would be no use to weep over the split milk when the time is gone. It is not the question of the present 400 millions, it is a question of the coming thousands of thousands generations of sons and daughters of India. Sacrifice and unity are our chariots to ride over the battlefield to fight and regain the ground of honour and glory. You have got the heart. Put the feet in stirrups and reins of confidence in the hands of Providence. We shall be victorious.

23

Resolutions Passed by the Bangkok Conference Confirming the Collaboration of Indians in East Asia with the Japanese for Overthrow of the Western Powers, Spells out the Demand for Expansion of Indian National Army[1]

20 June, 1942

The Bangkok Conference, held under the auspices of the I.I.L. of Greater East Asia and the Chairmanship of Rash Behari Bose, opened at the Silapakorn Theatre at 0900 hrs. on 15 June 1942 and lasted till 23rd June. Indian leaders at that time estimated that there were two million Indians in the "East Asia Co-prosperity Sphere".

Delegates came from Burma, Malaya, Thailand, China, French, Indo-china, East Indies and the Philippines. They totalled about 100 civilian delegates and 50 military.

The main objects were :–

1. To co-ordinate the movement for Indian Independence, which had already stated but lacked uniformity and cohesion, in those territories of East Asia, which had fallen under Japanese control.
2. To clarify the position regarding their inclusion in the "East Asia Co-prosperity Sphere".
3. To determine the purposes for which the I.N.A. should be used.
4. To decide what assistance could be expected from the Japanese without committing to Post-war Japanese domination.

The Japanese gave every assistance in this Conference and ordered

1. Indian Independence league papers F. No. 45/3. These papers were consulted when these were with the History of Freedom movement unit. These papers have now been transfered to the National Archivs of India. In future referred as I.I.L. Papers 45/3 For the text of the speeches at this conference by A.M. Sahey, Raghvan, and Gill, see Gaini, *op. cit, pp. 74-75.*

the Thai Government to do likewise. The conference passed the following resolutions :–

1. Whereas it is the objective of the war of Greater East Asia to destroy British Imperialism in Asia; and

Whereas it gives an opportunity for India to realise the goal of complete independence; and

Whereas it is the belief of this Conference that a new and regenerated Asia of Free Nations is certain to arise as a result of this said war :

This Conference expresses its sincere gratification at the war policy of Japan and convey to the Imperials Government its best wishes for the continued success of the Imperial Japanese Armed Forces.

2. This Conference conveys to all the powers fighting against British Imperialism its sincere congratulations and prays that their efforts may meet with complete success.

3. This Conference places on record its sense of deep admiration for the most determined manner in which the Nationalist Leaders at home have been trying to refuse to be drawn into this war on the side of the British and their Allies, and for the frank and definite demand for the withdrawal of the British from India. In the opinion of this Conference, unless the British withdraw from India and the Allied Forces cease to make use of India as a base for war operations and war preparations unimaginable and innumerable sufferings will be the lot of the people of India.

4. Resolved that a Movement for achieving complete and immediate independence of India be sponsored by this Conference.

Object

5. This Conference endorses the view of the Tokyo Conference held in March 1942 that the complete Independence of India free from any foreign control, domination or interference of whatever nature shall be the object of this Movement, and is emphatically of opinion that the time has arrived to take necessary steps for the attainment of that object.

Guiding Principles

6. Resolved that the Indian Independence Movement sponsored by this Conference shall be guided by the principles indicated below :

(a) That unity, faith, sacrifice, shall be the motto of the Indian Independence Movement.

(b) That India be considered as one, and indivisible.

(c) That all activities of this Movement be on a national basis, and not on a sectional, communal or religious basis.

(d) That in view of the fact that the Indian National Congress is the only political organisation which could claim to represent the real interests of the people of India, and as such to be acknowledged the only body representing India, this Conference is of the opinion that the programme and plan of action of this Movement must be so guided, controlled and directed as to bring them in line with the aims and intentions of the Indian National Congress.

(e) That the framing of the future constitution of India be only by the representatives of the people of India.

(f) That a joint Axis policy favourable towards India will be advantageous to India.

(g) That the sympathy, cooperation and support of Japan is invaluable in securing the object of this Movement, namely the Independence of India.

7. Resolved that an organisation be started for carrying on the Indian Independence Movement and that it shall be known as the Indian Independence League.

8. Resolved that the Indian Independence League shall immediately proceed to raise an Army called the Indian National Army from among the Indian soldiers (combatants and non-combatants) and such civilians as may hereafter be recruited for military service in the cause of Indian Independence.

Constitution

9. This Conference adopts the following Constitution for the Indian Independence League organisation.

(i) The Indian Independence League shall consist of :
- (a) A Council of Action,
- (b) A Committee of Representatives,
- (c) Territorial Branch, and
- (d) Local Branches.

(ii) (a) Local branches of the Indian Independence League may be formed only at a public meeting of Indians in any locality who shall elect a Committee and a President.

(b) Vacancy of such Committee or in the Office of the President may be filled up by the Committee.

(c) All Indians above the age of eighteen shall be entitled to be members of such Branch on compliance with the rules of the Branch.

(d) No such Branch shall be recognised as a Branch unless the Territorial Committee as constituted hereinafter accords and continues to accords to such Branch due recognition, provided however that all Branches of the Indian Independence League now in existence and recognised in the various territories mentioned in article (vi) hereof shall until otherwise decided upon be recognised by this Movement.

(iii) Representatives elected by the Committee of Local Branches in each territory shall form a Territorial Committee, and the Territorial Committee shall make such rules as it may consider necessary for the effective working of the Movement within the territory.

(iv) The Territorial Committee in each territory shall guide, supervise and control the work of the Movement within its territory and shall also elect representatives as constituted hereinafter.

(v) Territorial Committees and Committees of Local Branches under them shall have power to make rules not inconsistent with the rules by the Committee of Representatives or in case of Local Branches by the Territorial Committees.

(vi) (a) A Committee of Representatives shall be constituted by civilian representatives selected by the Territorial Committees in the territories herein below set out and by representa tives selected by the Indian National Army.

Japan and Manchukuo	4
Philippines	2
Thailand	6
Malaya	14
Burma	21
Borneo and Celebes	1
Hongkong, Canton and Macao	2
Other parts of China, including Shanghai	2
Indo-China	1
Java	2
Sumatra	1
Andamans	1
	57
Indian National Army	33
	90

(b) The Council of Action shall be at liberty to include in the above list of territories any other territory and fix the number of representatives from such territory to the Committee of Representatives, providing in that event for increase in the representatives from the Indian National Army, equal to two-thirds of the number fixed for such territory.

(vii) Every member of the Committee of Representatives shall sign the Oath of Secrecy in the prescribed form before he takes his seat on the Committee.

(viii) The Committee of Representatives shall be responsible for the general policy and programme of the Indian Independence Movement and its decision shall in every case be final and binding on each and every member of this Movement.

(ix) The Committee of Representatives shall have power to alter, amend or rescind any previous decisions made by it, including any decision arrived at in this Conference.

(x) No meeting of the Committee of Representatives shall be valid unless two-thirds in number of the Members of the Committee are present (either in person or by proxy).

(xi) A Council of Action consisting of a President and four (4) members, of whom at least one half shall be from the Indian National Army in East Asia, shall be appointed by the delegates to this Conference. The first President shall be Sjt. Rash Behari Bose and the four members shall be: :

1. Sri N. Raghavan
2. Captain Mohan Singh
3. Sri K.P.K. Menon
4. Colonel G.Q. Gilani.

(xii) Any vacancy in the Council of Action caused by death, resignation or otherwise of Members not exceeding two in number at a time, may be filled up by the other Members of the Council, and in the event of more than two such vacancies the Council of Action shall call a meeting of the Representatives to fill such vacancies.

(xiii) The Council of Action shall be Responsible for the carrying out of the policy and programme of work laid down by this Conference and as may hereafter be laid down by the Committee of Representatives and shall deal with all new matters that may arise from time to time and which may not be provided for by of Representatives and shall deal with all new matters that may arise from time to time and which may not be provided for by the Committee itself.

(xiv) For the proper and efficient carrying out of the work the Council of Action shall have power to create as many departments as are necessary and to appoint and dismiss administrative officers and staff whenever necessary.

(xv) The Council of Action shall have no power to alter or amend the Policy laid down by this Conference without the sanction of the Committee of Representatives.

(xvi) The Council of Action may at any time summon a meeting of the Committee of Representatives to be held at such places as the Council may decide provided that necessary facilities for travel to Representatives and at least 14 days' notice of such meeting have been given to the Secretaries of the Territorial Committees and to the Headquarters of the Indian National Army. On a requisition by twenty members (Representatives) hailing from more than one territory such a meeting shall be called by the Council of Action and the necessary notices and facilities for travel shall be given.

(xvii) The Council of Action shall have general superintendence and control over all Branches of the Indian Independence League in all territories mentioned in article (vi) and over the Indian National Army.

(xviii) The Council of Action shall cause to be kept a register of all the territorial and local organisations and may remove there—from the names of any such organisations and withhold or withdraw recognition of any such organisation.

(xix) The Council of Action shall have collective responsibility.

(xx) The allotment of Portfolios shall be amongst the Members of the Council of Action and at the discretion of the President.

(xxi) The Headquarters of the Movement shall be at Bangkok or such other place as may hereafter be decided upon by the Committee of Representatives or the Council of Action.

(xxii) The deliberations of the Committee of Representatives and the Council of Action shall be privileged and no action of a disciplinary character can be taken against any member in consequence thereof by any Branch or Territorial Committee or by the Indian National Army.

(xxiii) Changes in the Constitution of the Indian Independence League may be made only by vote to that effect by three-fourths of the Members of the Committee of Representatives.

10. Resolved that a request be made to the Nippon Government that it may be pleased to place immediately all Indian soldiers in territories in East Asia under their control at the disposal of this Movement.

11. Resolved that the formation, command, control and organisation of the Indian National Army be in the hands of Indians themselves.

12. Resolved that it is the earnest desire of this Conference that the Indian National Army from its inception be accorded the powers and status of a free National Army of an Independent India, on a footing of equality with the armies of Japan and other friendly powers.

13. Resolved that the Indian National Army shall be made use of only:

(a) For operations against the British or other foreign powers in India,

(b) For the purpose of securing and safeguarding Indian National Independence and,

(c) For such other purpose as may assist the achievement of the object, viz : the Independence of India.

14. Resolved that all officers and men of the proposed Indian National Army shall be members of the Indian Independence League and shall owe allegiance to the League.

15. Resolved that the Indian National Army shall be under the direct control of the Council of Action and that the said Army shall be organised and commanded by the General Officer Commanding, Indian National Army, in accordance with the directions of the Council of Action.

16. Resolved that in the event of military action being taken against the British or other foreign powers in India, and for the said purpose the Council of Action may be at liberty to place the military resources available to it, under the unified command of Indian and Japanese Military Officers under the direction of the said Council of Action.

17. Resolved that before taking any military action against the British or any other foreign power in India, the Council of Action will assure itself that such action is in conformity with the express or implied wishes of the Indian National Congress.

18. Resolved that the Council of Action shall make all efforts to create an atmosphere in India which would lead to a revolution in the Indian Army there, and among the Indian people, and that before taking military action the Council of Action shall assure itself that such an atmosphere exists in India.

19. In view of the great urgency and imperative necessity of informing and convincing our countrymen in India and abroad, and friends of India all over the world, of the meaning and purpose of this movement, and in view of the fact that propaganda in and outside India is one of the most effective means of waging the war for Indian Independence, this Conference resolves to take immediate steps to carry on active and vigorous propaganda by Broadcasts, Leaflets, Lectures and by such other means as may be found possible and practicable from time to time.

20. That all foreign assistance of whatever nature shall be only to the extent and of the type asked for by the Council of Action.

21. Resolved that for the purpose of financing the Independence Movement the Council of Action be authorised to raise funds from Indians in East Asia.

22. The Conference places on record its grateful appreciation of the support and encouragement given to this Movement by the Imperial Government of Japan, and resolves that the Council of Action be authorised to approach if and when necessary the said Government with a request to render such monetary help as may be required from time to time for the successful carrying out of the object of this Movement, on the distinct understanding that such monetary help is to be treated as a loan repayable to the Imperial Government of Japan by the National Government of India.

23. Resolved that the Imperial Government of Japan be requested to be good enough to provide all facilities for Propaganda, Travel, Transport and Communication within the area under the control of the Imperial Government of Japan, in the manner and to the extent requested by the Council of Action, and also all facilities to come into contact with the National leaders, workers and organisations in India.

24. Resolved that the Imperial Government of Japan be requested to be good enough to arrange with the local authorities concerned that in matters of administration affecting the Indian Community, the Indian Independence League in the respective places, and in places where there are no branches of the League, recognised leaders of the community approved by the League Branch nearest to such places, be consulted.

25. Resolved that the Government of Thailand be requested to be good enough to consult the Indian Independence League (formerly known as the Indian National Council and the Independence League of India) in matters of administration affecting the Indian community in Thailand.

26. The Conference, while recording its grateful appreciation of the various pronouncements made by General Tojo, the Premier of Japan, expressing the preparedness of the Japanese Government to give its unstinted support to the cause of Indian Independence, reiterates the Resolution of the Tokyo Conference that in further clarification of the attitude of Japan towards India, the Imperial Government be good enough to make a formal declaration to the effect :

(a) That immediately on the severance of India from the British Empire, the Imperial Government of Japan shall respect the territorial integrity and recognise the full sovereignty of India free from any foreign influence, control or interference of a political, military or economic nature.

(b) That the Imperial Government of Japan will exercise its influence with other powers and induce them to recognise the National independence and absolute sovereignty of India.

(c) That the framing of the future Constitution of India will be left entirely to the representatives of the people of India without interference from any foreign authority.

27. Resolved that this Conference is Committed to a definite policy of close cooperation with Japan and it shall, on eliciting an official definition satisfactory to this Movement of the term 'Greater East Asia Co-Prosperity Sphere' and its implications, endeavour to persuade Independence India :

(a) To be a member of such Sphere or a member of any other international combine of which Japan is a member, on a footing of equality with Japan; and

(b) To confer on Japan the most favoured nation treatment on a reciprocal basis.

28. Whereas it has come to the knowledge of this Conference that Indians in the territories which are now freed from the domination of the Anglo-Saxons and their Allies by the Imperial Forces of Japan own considerable movable and immovable properties in these territories; and

Whereas owing to the exigencies of war a number of Indians had to leave these territories, leaving behind their properties without making arrangements for their care and management; and

Whereas the Imperial Government of Japan has promised its unstinted support to the cause of Indian Independence; and

Whereas an enormous amount of money is required to carry on and complete the object of the said movement in East Asia; and

Whereas an appreciably steady income is likely to be derived from the said properties in the said territories; and

Whereas in the opinion of the Conference, the handing over of such properties to the Indian Independence League by the authorities concerned, on the distinct understanding that the said properties are to be returned to their rightful owners when claimed, will be welcomed as a sign of goodwill and encouragement towards this Movement.

Now this Conference Resolves

That the Imperial Government of Japan may be pleased to arrange with the authorities in the territories now freed from the domination of the Anglo-Saxons and their Allies by the Imperial Forces of Japan, to hand over the properties owned by the Indian (including those owned by Indians Companies, firms and partnerships) and left by them owing to the exigencies of war, to the Council of Action in this Movement in trust for their rightful owners, to manage and control the said properties, and advance the income thereof for the use of this Movement, to be repaid as and when claimed by the said owners.

29. This Conference having learned with regret that Indians residing in certain countries under the occupation of the Imperial Forces of Japan are being treated as enemy aliens, and suffer hardship and loss in consequence; resolves that the Imperial Government of Japan may be pleased to make a declaration to the effect :

(a) That Indians residing in the territories occupied by the Imperial Forces of Japan shall not be considered enemy nationals so long as they do not indulge in any action injurious to this movement or hostile to the interest of Japan, and

(b) That the properties both movable and immovable of those Indians who are now residing in India or elsewhere (including the properties of Indian companies, firms and partnerships) be not treated by Japan as enemy properties so long as the management or control of such properties is vested in any person or persons residing in Japan or in any of the countries occupied by or under the influence or control of the Imperial Japanese Forces, and to instruct the authorities concerned in the respective territories to give effect to this policy as early as possible.

30. That this Movement adopts the present National Flag of India and requests the Imperial Government of Japan and the Royal Government of Thailand and the Governments of all other friendly powers to recognise the said flag in all territories under their jurisdiction.

31. This Conference requests Sjt. Subhash Chandra Bose to be kind enough to come to East Asia, and appeals to the Imperial Government of Japan to use its good offices to obtain the necessary permission and conveniences from the Government of Germany to enable Sjt. Subhas Chandra Bose to reach East Asia safe.

32. That no unauthorised publicity be given to any of the Resolutions adopted at this Conference, but a manifesto be issued by this Conference setting out the purpose and policy of this Movement, and incorporating such decisions and details as may be found proper and beneficial to be made public.

33. This Conference places on record its deepest appreciation of and grateful thanks for the cooperation, assistance and support extended to this movement and its objective by the Imperial Government of Japan.

34. This Conference gratefully acknowledges the sincere and friendly attitude the Governments and the peoples of Germany and Italy have adopted towards our struggle for freedom and places on record its deep appreciation and thanks for the offer of assistance and cooperation extended by them to this Movement.

35. This Conference places on record its grateful thanks to the Government and people of Thailand for the opportunity given to hold this Conference at Bangkok, for their kind hospitality, and for their sympathy and cooperation in India's struggle for freedom.

24

Rash Behari Bose to Colonel Iwakuro Requesting him to Forward the Resolution Passed at the Bangkok Conference to the Imperial Japanese Government for Approval

22 June, 1942

As President of the Indian Independence Conference held at Bangkok this month (and now in session) I have the honour to convey to the Imperial Government of Japan the following Resolution which was unanimously adopted :–

> Whereas it is the objective of the War of Greater East Asia to destroy the British Imperialism in Asia, and
>
> Whereas it gives an opportunity for India to realise its goal of complete Independence and
>
> Whereas it is the belief of this Conference that a new and regenerated Asia of free nations is certain to arise as a result of the said war,
>
> This conference expresses its sincere gratification at the War Policy of Japan and conveys to the Imperial Government its best wishes for the continued successes of the Imperial Japanese Armed Forces.

---

1. K.P.K. Menon Papers; File No. 1. Nehru Memorial Museum and Liberary, (NMML) New Delhi.
2. Col. Iwakuro Hideo, was a senior officer of Imperial Guard Regiment. He succeeded Fujiwara as head of the liaison agency (Iwakuro Kikan) to assist the Indian Independence movement. his attitude towards the expansion of INA. and the questions of antonomy led towards the deterioration of relations between General Mohan and the Japanese. Iwakuro had very little interest in the question of Indian Independence and was replaced, when Subhash Chander Bose took over the command of the Indian National Army.

This conference conveys to all the Powers Fighting against British Imperialism its sincere congratulations and prays that their efforts may meet with complete success.

2. Further various resolutions with a view to achieving "the immediate independence of India, defined as complete independence of India free from any foreign control, domination or interference of whatever nature" were adopted. The sense of the Conference as was evident from the Resolutions adopted and opinions expressed was that such independence could not at present be achieved without the goodwill, of cooperation and full support of the Imperial Government of Japan. The conference which knows the various declarations of Policy and statements by His Excellency Premier General Tojo had little doubt that the Imperial Govt. of Japan recognised that the time had come for India to have immediate independence and that the Imperial Govt. of Japan would place every facility in the hands of the sponsors of the Indian Independence Movement and of the people of India to achieve the immediate independence of India.

3. It is with this firm conviction that we hereby place before the Imperial Government of Japan some of the conclusions arrived at the Conference with the earnest request to the Imperial Government for assistance and support in giving effect to them.

4. Some of the guiding principles of this Movement were indicated as follows :–

That Unity, Faith, Sacrifice shall be the motto of the Indian Independence Movement. That India is considered as ONE, and indivisible.

That all activities of this Movement be on a National basis and not on Sectional, Communal or Religious basis.

That in view of the fact that the Indian National Congress is the only political organisation which could claim to represent the real interest of the people of India and as such be acknowledged the only body representing India, this Conference is of the opinion that the programme and plan of action of this Movement must be so guided, controlled and directed as to bring them in line with the aims and intentions of the Indian National Congress.

That the framing of the future constitution of India be only by the representatives of the people of India.

That a joint axis policy favourable towards India will be advantagious towards India.

That the sympathy, cooperation and support of Japan is invaluable in securing the object of this Movement, namely, the Independence of India.

5. The Conference resolved for carrying on the Independence Movement to start an organisation called the Indian Independence League.

6. On the assumption that the Imperial Government of Japan will be pleased to place in our hands every facility for this move, the Conference resolved that the Indian Independence League shall immediately proceed to raise an army called the Indian National Army from among the Indian soldiers (combatants and non-combatants) and such civilians as may hereafter be recruited for military service in the cause of Indian Independence. With the same object the Conference authorised me to make a request to the Imperial Government of Japan that they may be pleased "to place immediately all the Indian soldiers in territories in East Asia under their control at the disposal of this Movement". The request is being made on the same assumption that the Imperial Government would place in our hands the necessary material for achieving the object of this Movement in their declared Policy for helping India in the attainment of complete and immediate independence. It was also the desire of this Conference that "the formation, command, control and organisation of the Indian National Army may be placed in the hands of Indians themselves". I may be permitted to point out that a good deal of assistance and guidance in this connection may be required by our Army in order to make it an efficient fighting unit. We fully hope that this desire of this conference will be viewed with approval by the Imperial Govt. It was "the earnest desire of this Conference that the Indian National Army from its inception be accorded the powers and status of a free National Army of the independent India on a footing of equality with the Armies of Japan and other friendly countries". In your helping us to create a National Army of our own to fight our battles against the British in India and to regain our Independence we feel certain that the Imperial Government would be willing to confer on that Army the powers and status asked for as without such powers and status the Army may not be spiritually free, and may suffer from an inferiority complex, and may be regarded by India not as an Army of freedom and of Free India but as a reaction to our for some other purposes. It will be of immense advantage to our Movement if we can convince India that the Imperial Government has of its own accord given such a status to the Army which it helped to create for the liberation of India and which may in due course form the

nucleus of India's National Army. Another Resolution in connection with the National Army was as follow :–

Resolved that the Indian National Army shall be made used of on only :–

For operations against British or other foreign powers in India
For the purpose of securing and safeguarding Indian National Independence and
For such other purposes as may assist the achievement of the object viz. the Independence of India.

This Resolution if accepted by the Imperial Government will re-assure public opinion in India that the object that we have in view is only the full and complete independence of India by ejecting the British and other foreign powers and establishing a National Government in India.

7. The Conference decided that all officers and men of the proposed Indian National Army should be members of the Indian Independence League and should owe allegiance to the League.

8. The Conference also decided that subject to approval of the Imperial Government, the Indian National Army which may be created may be placed under the direct control of the Council of Action of this Movement and should be organised and commanded by the General Officer Commanding the Indian National Army in accordance with the directions of the Council of Action.

9. Another direction to the Council of Action was that in the event of military action being taken against the British or other foreign powers in India and for the said purpose the Council of Action may be at liberty to place the military resources available to it, under a unified command of Indian and Japanese Military Officers under the direction of the said Council of Action. We hope that when the time comes the Imperial Govt. will be willing to agree to such unified command. We shall gratefully appreciate such an act as a great favour done to this Movement for Indian Independence.

10. There were two resolutions as to the time for taking such action and we hope that they will also find approval with the Imperial Government. They were as follows :–

Resolved that before taking any military action against the British or any other foreign power in India the C/A will assure itself that such action is in conformity with the express or implied wishes of the Indian National Congress.

Resolved that the C/A shall make all efforts to create an atmosphere in India which would lead to a revolution in the Indian Army there and among the Indian people and that before taking any military action the C/A shall assure itself that such an atmosphere exists in India.

The reasons for the said Resolutions were the anxiety of the Conference in making the move to be on the side of the Indian people as represented by the Indian National Congress without whose assistance there may be various difficulties and repercussions in the achievement of the object we have in view. The adoption of the Resolution meant that every endeavour should be made by this Movement that the support and co-operation of the Imperial Government to carry on effective propaganda in India with a view to converting the Indian masses and the premier political body in India to the view held by this Conference. The resolution will also presuppose that complete reliance is placed by this Movement in the Imperial Government to enable us to do our work in such a way as to convert India to our view. The success or otherwise that we may be meeting with in our convincing the people of India that this Movement is a thoroughly bona fide Movement on our part for securing complete independence for India.

11. It was also with the view that the Conference adopted the following resolutions :–

> In view of the great urgency and imperative necessity of informing and convincing our countrymen in India and abroad and the friends in India all over the world of the meaning and purpose of this Movement and in view of the fact that propaganda in and outside India is one of the most effective means for waging the war for Indian Independence, this conference resolves to take immediate steps to carry on active and vigorous propaganda by Broadcasts, Leaflets, Lectures and by such other means as may be found possible and practicable from time to time.

12. Another resolution that was passed was as follows :–

That all foreign assistance of whatever nature shall be only to the extent and of the type asked for by the C/A.

We, who implicitly trust in the sincerity of Japan's intentions, believe, that such assistance when requested by the C/A of this movement will without doubts forth coming from the Imperial Government in as ample measure as may be required.

13. There was a resolution passed "that for the purpose of financing the Independence Movement the C/A be authorised to raise funds from Indians in East Asia", but the Conference also resolved "that the C/A be

authorised to approach if and when necessary the Imperial Government of Japan with a request to render such monetary help as may be required from time to time for the successful carrying out of the object of this movement on the distinct understanding that such monetary help is to be treated as a loan repayable to the Imperial Government of Japan by the National Government of India when it come into being". We shall be for ever grateful for this favour.

14. The Conference also requested that the Imperial Govt. of Japan will kindly see its way and be good enough to provide "all facilities for propaganda, Travel, Transport and Communications within the area under the control of the Imperial Govt. of Japan in the manner and to the extent requested by the C/A and also all facilities to come into contact with the National Leaders, workers and organisation in India". This provision we may be permitted to point out is very important for the effective commencement and culmination of our Movement for Independence.

15. In order to give a clear status to this Movement in the territories under the control of Imperial Government there was a request by the conference that the authorities in the various places may be good enough to consult in matters affecting the Indian Community in such places the Indian Independence League and in places where there are no Branches of the League recognised leaders of the Community approved by the League Leaders nearest to such places. Such action, we need hardly say will establish this Movement in the confidence of the Indian Public of the various localities.

16. This conference while recording its grateful appreciation of the various pronouncements made by General Tojo, the Premier of Japan expressing the preparedness of the Nipponese Government to give its unstinted support to the cause of Indian Independence reiterates the resolution of the Tokyo Conference that in further clarification of the attitude of Japan towards India, the Imperial Government of Japan be requested to be good enough make a formal declaration to the effect :–

(a) That on the severance of India from British Empire, the Imperial Government of Japan shall respect the territorial integrity and recognises the full and absolute sovereignty of India free from any foreign influence, control or interference of a political, military or economic nature.

(b) That the Imperial Government of Japan will exercise its influence with other powers and induce them to recognise the National Independence and absolute sovereignty of India.

(c) That the framing of the future constitution of India will be left entirely to the representatives of the people of India without interference from any foreign authority.

This was substantially the Resolution adopted at the Indian Independence Conference held at Tokyo in March this year.

17. This Conference also resolved that :–

This conference is committed to a definite policy of the closest cooperation with Japan and it shall on eliciting an official definition satisfactory to this Movement of the term "Greater East Asia Co-Prosperity Sphere" and the implications endeavour to persuade Independence India :–

(a) To be a member of such sphere or a member of any other international combine of which Japan is a member, on a footing of equality with Japan ; and

(b) To confer on Japan the most favoured national treatment on a reciprocal basis.

18. The Conference also requested that the Imperial Government of Japan may be pleased to direct by making a declaration to the effect that Indians residing in the territories occupied by the Imperial Forces of Japan shall not be considered enemy nationals so long as they do not indulge in any action injurious to this Movement or hostile to the interest of Japan".

19. The conference adopted the present National Flag for the Movement and in order to give the flag, which is the Flag of Indian Freedom, a real status appeal to the Imperial Government of Japan and to other Friendly Government to give recognition to the said Flag as the Flag of this Freedom Movement in all territories under their jurisdiction.

20. There was also an appeal to the Imperial Government of Japan "to use its good offices" to obtain the necessary permission and convenience from the Government of Germany to enable Sjt. Subhash Chandra Bose, the Indian Leader, to reach East Asia safe.

21. The conference placed on record "its deepest appreciation of and grateful thanks for the cooperation, assistance and support extended to this Movement and its objective by the Imperial Government of Japan".

22. It is our earnest hope that the Imperial Government will see nothing objectionable in these resolutions, a copy of which is attached hereto. We appeal to the Imperial Government of Japan to be kind enough to give effect to these and earnestly and entreat that the Resolutions will receive the most favourable consideration from the Imperial Government

The future of our country depends entirely on the success or otherwise of this Movement and such success in its turn is entirely dependent on the support and cooperation that the Imperial Government may be extending towards it. From the various pronouncements of His Excellency, Premier General Tojo, this Conference implicitly believe that the resolutions would find acceptance and that every facility will be given to this Movement and to Indians to win the complete Independence of India.

25

From Iwakuro to Rash Behari Bose Informing him that the Imperial Japanese Government would Extend Whole-hearted Support to the Indian Independence Movement; but no Specific Reply was Necessary as Regards Resolutions

10 July, 1942

Dear Mr. Chairman,

I have the honour to inform you that the Imperial Government is determined to extend whole-hearted and unstinted support, as evidenced in the repeated statements made by Premier Tojo, and also in his recent message of facilitation to the Bangkok Conference, in regard to the request dated on June, the 22nd, 1942, from the Indian Independence League to the Imperial Japanese Government with the object of attaining complete independence for Indian by supporting the Independence Movement in India and removing Anglo-American influence.

The Imperial Japanese Government agrees with your view to keep the resolutions of the Bangkok Conference secret, and it is also the wish of the Imperial Japanese Government that this reply will be kept under strict secrecy.

I wish to take this opportunity to pay my profound respect for your brave and strenuous efforts and earnestly wish you all the success in trying to shake off the yoke of despotism, which Britain has been imposing on your Fatherland.

1 K.P.K. Menon Papers; File No. 1. NMML.

26

British Assessment of the Indian National Army After its Expansion and Formation in the Light of Bangkok Conference[1]

17 July, 1942

The "Indian National Army" is the title given by the Japanese to a force which they intend to use to attack India's war effort. The existence of the nucleus of this "army" is established; the following account of its nature and purpose is, however, largely unsubstantiated, and must be treated with reserve.

The Japanese claim that the I.N.A. now numbers 70,000, and an establishment of 90,000 has been mentioned. This figure is considerably in excess of the total number of Indian and Gurkha prisoners of war in Japanese hands, and there is no proof that any substantial number of these prisoners have become pro-Japanese in sympathy. The Japanese claim may therefore be regarded as a target, which must include a considerable proportion of the civilian population in Japanese occupied territories.[2]

The professed objects of the I.N.A. are espionage: subversive propaganda directed, in particular, against the Indian Army: and military operations aimed at the "liberation" of India. As regards operations, it has been suggested that the Japanese intend to use elements of the I.N.A. to precede their troops in the advance, with the object of exhorting Indian troops to lay down their arms and, in general, to cause confusion

1. Weekly Intelligence Summary, General Headquarters-India F. No. 6017668/ Historical Section, Ministry of Defence, New Delhi. These reports are also available at the Public Record office London.
2. It is known that by the end of August, 1942, nearly forty thousands soldiers had given the pledge to join the Indian National Army. For details see. Mohan Singh, *op. cit.* pp. 100-150.

amongst our forces. This employment would be in accordance with Japanese methods, as exemplified in Malaya and Burma.

The I.N.A. is open to all Indians, and determined attempts appear to have been made to enlist Gurkhas. Potential recruits are subject to intensive propaganda stressing Japanese goodwill towards India, and in the case of Gurkhas, laying claim to an alleged Mongol affinity. More material inducements probably include promises of quick promotion, high pay, and money awards for specific services. In this connection a first hand, but unconfirmed, report states that Japanese attempts were made in Burma as far back as 1931, to induce pensioners, deserters and discharged soldiers to enlist in the Japanese Army. Sepoys, or the equivalent, were offered Rs. 60/- per mensem, with other ranks in proportion. Colour is given to this account by independent reports of a Gurkha "Captain" in the Japanese army, who interrogated Gurkha prisoners of war, and told one of them that he had been with the Japanese for a long time.

Independent, but unconfirmed reports suggest that the advanced Headquarters of the I.N.A., under an Indian "Chief of Staff", may be in Rangoon, where a "Spy and propaganda" school is said to be established under an ex-V.C.O. General control is probably exercised from Bangkok. It is certain that the Japanese have bribed and released prisoners of war in the hope that they would spread pro-Japanese propaganda on return to their units. A number of Indians with military titles have been employed as broadcasters and commentators at Japanese controlled wireless stations. In one case an I.N.A. "Captain" has been fairly definitely identified with an Indian V.C.O. captured in Malaya, and certain other possible identification have been made.

The I.N.A. is stated to be under the direct command of the movement's Working Committee. The following is information regarding the I.N.A., additional to that published in a recent Summary. Japan is to provide 1000 tanks and 400 planes. After the conquest of Burma, the plan envisaged was that Japan would concentrate on China and Australia, leaving India to the I.N.A.; if this failed, the Japanese would then attack India themselves.

Many of our prisoners of war (stated in one report to have been released) were taken to Rangoon, where Indians and Gurkhas were strictly segregated from the British. The Indian Wing of the prison camp was divided into companies, apparently with an eye to the future organisation of the I.N.A. Indians and Gurkhas were subjected to propaganda lectures. Volunteers were called for to carry out espionage and anti-British propaganda. Small parties were then organised, some to move with Japanese troops and shout "Stop! You are surrounded!" and the like, in Indian dialects. Others were to return to India to spread anti-British propaganda; they were then given money (about Rs. 40/- each), a *lungi* and P.T. Shoes and sent off in small parties. Two parties of Japanese spies were to go to India through Chittagong to contact Gandhi and Nehru.

To sum up, Japan is fostering, among Indians in the Far East, a movement of dangerous potentialities. It seems evident that she is attempting to give her plans the air of a spontaneous move, controlled and developed by Indian patriots, and to persuade the world that the "Free India" movement directed from Bangkok is in effect linked with the policy of Gandhi and the Congress. So far as can be judged, this new political front against India has had little effect on the public of this country. Several reports have, however, been received which refer to the departure from occupied China of bodies of Indians for fifth column work in this country.

27

Rash Behari Bose to Iwakuro Requesting him Again to Get Specific Clarification from the Imperial Japanese Government regarding their Attitude to the Resolutions Passed by the Bangkok Conference; Refers to Differences Emerging in the Council of Action on Lukewarm Response from the Japanese High Command[1]

5 September, 1942

Sir,

I have the honour to inform you that your kind communication dated 10th July, 1942, was considered by the Council of the Indian Independence Movement and, while we appreciate deeply the promise of support and sympathy contained therein we feel it our duty to point out that the said communication does not

(a) Specifically reply to the requests contained in our latter, dated 22nd June, 1942, and

(b) does not specifically clarify the attitude of the Imperial Government on the various points raised in the said letter and in the resolutions of the Bangkok Conference.

2. Your communication also does not indicate whether our said latter dated, 22nd June 1942, was referred to the Imperial Government and, if so, whether any reply was received from the Imperial Government thereto. When we forwarded our letter dated, 22nd June, 1942, and the resolutions, we were already in possession of the declarations made by His Excellency Premier General Tojo and our intention was to have further clarification

1. K.P.K. Menon Papers, Nehru Memorial Museum and Library, New Delhi. This is also reproduced by Mohan Singh in his hook *Soldier's contribution to Indian Independence*, New Delhi, 1974. p. 189.

of the position of the Imperial Government on specific matters raised in the Resolutions.

3. We shall deem it great favour if a reply to the Resolutions and my letter to you, dated, 22nd June, 1942, could be obtained from the Imperial Government.

4. We thank you in anticipation.

28

Memorandum by Mr. W.W. Coultas. His Majesty's Consul–General in Bangkok on the Development and Organisation of Indian Independence Movement in Thailand after the Outbreak of War in Far East; Refers to Indian Soldiers who are Still Loyal to the British[1]

20 September, 1942

1. The first enclosure[2] to this memorandum comprises a summary of notices and reports dealing with the Indian Independence Movement in Thailand as published in the *Bangkok Times* newspaper during the period from February 1st to July 20th 1942. The second enclosure is a list of the names of Indian mentioned in the first enclosure. Reports published prior to February 1st are not available, save for a few extracts from copies of newspapers obtained from members of the British community, since it was not until that date that permission was granted by the Siamese authorities for the *Bangkok Times* newspaper to be received by His Majesty's Legation.
2. A perusal of the enclosures will acquaint the reader with the progress of the Indian Independence Movement in Bangkok during the period immediately following Japan's entry into the war as well as furnish him with information regarding its development and organisation, culminating with a description of the Conference held in Bangkok during the latter half of Jun, 1942, for the furtherance of the aims of the Indian Independence League, which was attended, it is said, by over one hundred delegates from the Pacific area.
3. Before commenting on the information contained in the enclosures, it will be useful to describe briefly the situation in Bangkok as regard

1. Foreign Office, 371/31870, Public Record Office, London.
2. Enclosures have not been printed.

India British Subjects prior to December 1941. The Indian population in Thailand, including residents in Bangkok and the provinces, is believed to number about 50,000. The races included in this number comprise Hindus, Muslims, Sikhs and a small sprinkling of Christians. Apart from a numerous watchman class, all, except a negligible minority, are engaged in various branches of commerce. Few are wealthy and the great majority are uneducated. Some years prior to the outbreak of war in Europe, the leaders of the various Indian communities had, with the approval of His Majesty's Legation, united in forming an association of an undenominational character styled. "The Indian Association of Thailand." The objects of this society were the furtherance of common social and economical interests, to the exclusion of matters relating to politics or religion. The Association, which appears to have founded about the year 1928, continued to function as a common meeting ground of Indians in Bangkok and as their representative body, without, however, encroaching on the right of individuals or communities to approach H.M. Minister or Consul-General on matters affecting private or communal interests; (e.g., representations made by the local Sikh community against the hair-cutting regulations imposed by the Siamese educational authorities on boys attending state schools). Its direction remained until the year 1940 in the hands of a few senior members of the various Indian communities, most of them old residents of good standing who had been brought up in the extra-territorial tradition and had reason to remember with gratitude the unremitting interest taken in their welfare by His Majesty's Legation and Consular officers. Whilst these old-timers remained in control there was little danger of the Association's activities going beyond the limitations imposed by its articles. A change, however, came with the elections of the new committee for 1940, when, owing to a lack of vigilance on the part of the senior members, a majority of seats on this body was captured by younger and disaffected elements. On account of the dubious methods employed by the latter in achieving this 'coup', a bitter feud, which was still unhealed at the time of Japan's declaration of war, divided the Bangkok Indian community into two camps. In consequence of this feud, since neither side would give way to the other, the Indian Association of Thailand practically ceased to function; nevertheless it was only due to the unyielding opposition of the loyal elements that the Association was not immediately converted into an active centre of disaffection. This check to the machinations of the more radical group was, however, overcome by the intervention of Swami Satyananda Puri, a Hindu of some pretensions to culture and scholarship, the details of whose career will be found summarised in the entry under April 9th in the first enclosure. This individual appears to have seen an opportunity in the then existing situation both for fostering subversive propaganda amongst Indians in Bangkok and for obtaining financial support for his own cultural activities. With this object in view he started an institution which he styled a "Dharmasharam", with himself as head, to which he invited subscriptions from local Indians. At the outset his appeal met with but little support, and it was not until the autumn of 1940 that, with the cooperation of Debnath Das, who had arrived from Tokyo with the object of organising anti-British activities in Thailand, that he achieved any success. This was accomplished by converting the so-called 'Dharmashram', an institution for the promotion of Indian cultural research, into 'The Thai-Bharata Cultural Lodge', a society founded ostensibly for the fostering of interest in the Indian origins of Thai culture, in which object Swami SatyanandaPuri was able to interest several prominent Siamese, including His Highness Prince Varnvaidya Varavarn. The latter, as President of the Royal Institute, and himself a scholar of some distinction, gave his patronage to the new body, and actually read an address at the inaugural ceremony. How far he was privy to the real objects of the Society, for which its alleged cultural activities were merely a cloak, it is difficult to say. It will suffice to mention here that His Highness was warned by His Majesty's Legation of the suspicions attaching to the new body and that, at its suggestion, H.M. included in his inaugural address a watching hint that politics lay outside the field of cultural pursuits. Notwithstanding these warnings, however, it was remarked that the hoisting of the Indian Congress flag played an important part in the opening ceremony, convincing evidence, if it were needed, of the political motives underlying its creation.

4. The inauguration of the 'Thai-Bharata Cultural Lodge' in Bangkok took place towards the middle of November, and a full report of this event and of the attendant circumstances was sent at the time by H.M. Minister to the Government of India, who had been kept abreast of the 'Indian' situation in Bangkok as it had developed since the outbreak of war. For nearly twelve months following the inauguration of the 'Thai-Bharata Cultural Lodge', however, little progress appears

to have been made, while there was a noticeable waning of interest on the part of the local Indian community in the new institution. There were several factors to account for this. First of all, the return to Japan of Debnath Das and, with his departure, the dwindling of the fervour aroused by his eloquence; secondly, the fact that Satyananda Puri, despite his nationalist convictions, was at heart more of a scholar and ascetic than a politician; thirdly, and most important, the deterrent effect of the steps taken by H.M. Legation, in collaboration with the Indian authorities, to penalise Bangkok Indians participating in anti-British activities. These steps amounted to an embargo on travel, since, on arrival in India on business or otherwise, such person found themselves deprived of their passports and thus immobilised during the pleasure of the authorities. These penalties far outweighed any pleasure derived by the politically minded in indulging their anti-British inclinations, and were effective in preventing any wholehearted support of the Thai-Bharata Cultural Lodge during the period mentioned. The Swami, indeed, was reported to have been much discouraged and to have decided at one time to abandon politics and devote himself entirely to religion and literature. It was during the same period, however, that Baba Amar Singh, the ex-convict of the Mandalay Conspiracy Trials of 1915/16, is now known to have evaded the Indian passport authorities and to have established himself at the Sikh Gurdwara in Bangkok, and it is evident that from this retreat this political fanatic was quietly playing the Japanese game with the assistance of Giani Pritam Singh, the ex-Sikh missionary, whose subversive activities were not fully disclosed until after his death in February, 1942; (See entry in enclosure under date April 2nd). On the whole, however, it may be said that this was a period of marking time during which the anti-British movement amongst Indians in Bangkok, so far as overt action went, rather hung fire.

5. This was the situation in the late autumn in 1941 when the reappearance in Bangkok of Debnath Das in October/November of that year gave food for thought to those who had followed his activities in that city twelve months previously. No definite information was at the time available regarding the object of his visit, though in the light of later events it seems clear that he came on instructions from his Japanese masters with orders to stand by and await events. At the same time, some speculation was aroused by the visit to H.M.C.G. of an emissary from Baba Amar Singh, the

reprieved ex-convict of the Mandalay Conspiracy Trials mentioned in paragraph 4 above. This emissary (an elderly gentleman, named Lal Singh), stated that Baba Amar Singh wished to denounce to the British authorities the treasonable activities of Giani Pritam Singh, the ex-Sikh missionary, who, he said, was actively engaged as a Japanese agent in anti-British and pro-Japanese propaganda amongst Indian troops in Malaya. When asked the reason why Baba Amar Singh did not make this important communication in person, Lal Singh stated that gentleman had recently left Bangkok for Nakawn Lampang in North Thailand, information which was afterwards verified by H.M. Consul at Chiengmai. It would appear, therefore, that late in November Baba Amar Singh either knew or suspected that the zero hour in the Far East was approaching and had decided to play for safety. We learn, however, that after the fall of Singapore he visited that city, together with S. Amar Singh and Swami Satyanandapuri, to attend a meeting of the Independent League of India, (see entry in enclosure under date of March 27th). There were however, no further developments in the local situation before communication between H.M. Legation and the outside world was severed in consequence of events following the Japanese declaration of war. It should be made clear, however, that all information concerning the local Indian situation was passed to the Government of India as and when it became available. There is accordingly nothing in the above summary which has not been the subject of an official report from His Majesty's Legation Bangkok, to the authorities in India, whose information from this source was thus completely uptodate on December 8th, 1941. His Majesty's Legation was also the channel for communication to the Government of India of a number of valuable reports received from His Majesty's Consul at Songkhala, South Thailand, regarding similar activities in the Southern provinces.

6. The summaries of press announcements and reports contained in the first enclosure to this memorandum give a picture of the development of the Indian situation in Siam from day to day following Japan's aggressive action in that country, with an interval, however, previously referred to, of nearly two months during which no newspapers were received inside His Majesty's Legation. These summaries deal mainly with the activities of the Independent League

of India in Bangkok and in Malaya after the fall of Singapore, and also furnish a fairly detailed account of the Indian Independence Conference which was opened in Bangkok on June 15th. 1942, and which is stated to have been attended by over a hundred delegates from territories included within the so-called Greater East Asia Co-Prosperity Sphere. In this connection, the "Bangkok Times" issue of June 13th published a list of the names of delegates to the Conference from Malaya and Hong Kong, while later issues give some account of the subjects dealt with in its public sessions.

7. On of the first steps taken by the Siamese Government after that country's adhesion to the Axis cause was to issue a proclamation stating that none of the Asiatic subjects of Great Britain residing in Siam would be treated as enemy aliens provided they did not attempt to leave the country. In this category were included all local residents of Indian, Burmese, Malaya or Chinese (British born) race. This attitude had been expected and Asiatic British Subjects, who had sought advice previously on the subject of evacuation, had been told that in the opinion of H.M. Legation they had little to fear by remaining in Siam, since the Japanese would most certainly pose as their protectors and "liberators", while the large number involved rendered any kind of wholesale evacuation impracticable.

8. The following facts emerge from the press summaries under reference:–

   (1) The activities of the local branch of the Independent League of India commenced very shortly after Japan's declaration of war and invasion of Siam.

   (2) Indian groups took part in a mass parade organised by certain local authorities on February 6th for the purpose of demonstrating their solidarity with the Siamese Premier in Siam's declaration of war against Great Britain and the U.S.A.

   (3) The control of the *Bangkok Times* newspaper, formerly the only British-owned journal in Bangkok, was almost immediately taken over by the Japanese under the editorship of an Eurasian from Rangoon named EARDE, who had previously been employed on the reporting staff, and who, from accounts received, had not been thought to bold anti-British views. It appears that this newspaper became the main instrument of Indian anti-British propaganda in Bangkok during the months that followed. It was used also as the chief organ of publicity for the Indian

independence movement in Siam.

(4) At the outset, at least, the Indian independence movement did not receive the unanimous support of all classes of Indians in Bangkok. An article published in the issue of February 12th., concludes with a complaint that the well-to-do classes of Indians in Bangkok had shown no interest in the work of the Indian Independence League and had kept themselves aloof. On the other hand, it is to be noted that the telegram addressed to the "Tokyo Independence Mission" on March 25th purported to be signed by the Presidents of the local branches of the Hindu Dharma Sabha, the Sikh Community and the Arya Samaj.

(5) Prior to the Conference held at Bangkok during the second half of June 1942, a delegation of some 60 Indian soldiers arrived in Bangkok from Malaya on February 17th: (see under March 4th in enclosure). This mission was headed by Captain Ram Sarup and by Captain Nazara Singh. The members of the mission were lodged on the premises of the Indian Independent League of Bangkok.

(6) Great publicity is given to the tragic fate which overtook Swami Satyanandapuri and his companions, who perished in an aeroplane accident on 24th March whilst on their way to Tokyo to attend an important conference there, and the memorial service held in their honour (see under April 20th) was on a scale which was evidently intended to elevate them to the rank of national heroes.

(7) The organisation of the Indian Independence Movement in East Asia is described in the text of a Trans-Ocean message from Bangkok dated Berlin June 26th. (See entry under date of June 27th). According to this message and a similar communication from Tokyo published on the authority of the "Asahi Shimbun" correspondent in Bangkok :–

(a) The headquarters of the movement will for the time being remain in Bangkok.

(b) Regional Headquarters will be established in various centres.

(c) Branches will be established in each city under the control of Regional Headquarters, which, in their turn, will be subject to the guidance and control of Bangkok.

(d) Regional Headquarters will appoint delegates to a Committee of Representatives. This body will sit in Bangkok and will be composed of 90 members, of whom 57 will be civil and 33 military representatives. This Committee, or Council, will function as a Parliament and will be the representative organ of the two million Indian residents in the Southern Regions". It will be the task of this Committee to work out concrete measures for the attainment of Indian Independence.

(e) Finally, the policies mapped out by the Committee will be submitted to the Supreme Council of the Indian Independence League, which shall consist of 5 members; including Mr. Rash Behari Bose. (It is stated in the *Bangkok Times* issue of July 2nd that this Supreme Council, which appears also to be called the "Council of Action", is composed of the following members :–

Rash Behari Bose, Captain Mohan Singh, N. Raghavan, K.P.K. Menon and Colonel C.Q. Gilani.

(8) The Movement will operate under the name of the Independence League (AZAD HIND SANGH) in conjunction with an Indian National Army which will be created under the command of Captain Mohan Singh.

(9) The role played by Subhas Chandra Bose from Berlin in relation to the direction of the Indian Independence League is not disclosed. He would appear to have no official position on the Council of Action, but see texts of telegrams addressed to him from Bangkok as reproduced in the enclosure under dates March 27th and July 22nd.

(10) The objects of the Indian Independence League are, according to an advertisement inviting membership first appearing in the *Bangkok Times* of July 9th, "to secure complete and immediate independence of India free of any foreign control or interference of whatever nature".

(11) As distinct from the Indian Independence League, there would appear to have been another and earlier organisation established in Bangkok, styled "The Indian National Council" and working for the same objects. In the title of the article printed in the *Bangkok Times* issue of April 14th, Debnath Das is described as "General-Secretary of the Indian National Council" while

under date of March 30th Swami Satyanandapuri was described as its Chairman. Again, in the issue of April 20th, the memorial service held in honour of the last named is reported to have been conducted under the joint auspices of Thai-Bharata Cultural Lodge, The Indian National Council and the Independent League of India. There is, however, no indication of the origin or functions of this body. Anti-British broadcasts from Siam reported in the *Bangkok Times* from time to time are described as being given "under the auspices of the Indian National Council". The latter is probably to be identified with the "Indian National Committee" mentioned under date of February 5th in the enclosure as having made a donation to the Nippon Red Cross Society. The possibility that the "Indian National Council and the Indian Independence League were originally rival organisations is suggested by a Notice to Indians published on December 19th in the *Bangkok Times* newspaper, which endeavours to give the lie to so-called false rumours, that there are two parties in Bangkok canvassing for the support of local Indians. A copy of the text of this notice is attached.

(12) Nothing has appeared in the *Bangkok Times* to suggest that the Indian Independence Movement has found any enthusiastic support in Siamese circles either official or unofficial. The Siamese Government was officially represented at the memorial service for Swami Satyanandapuri and his companions, of which so much seems to have been made both in Japan and Siam. A reception was given by the M.F.A. in honour of the delegates attending the Independence Conference (June 20th), while calls were made on the same Minister by Ras Behari Bose and other members of the Council of Action on the eve of their departure from Bangkok. On the whole, however, the attitude of the Siamese Government towards the movement may be said to have been perfunctory.

9. According to reports received from non-interned individuals amongst the allied nations resident in Bangkok, the Indian Independence Conference held in Bangkok was far from being the success it was advertised to be, owing to a failure to reach agreement on a working policy. One informant, who had an opportunity of talking with a delegate, was told that several had attended under compulsion,

having been pressed to do so by the Japanese military authorities in Singapore. Although there is no means of checking this statement, it may well be true. Moreover, it is interesting to note that, according to information received from another source, there were in Bangkok Indian troops interned as prisoners of war, who had either remained loyal to the Raj or were at least still being treated as enemies, since they were being forced to give their labour in the local Railway Workshops and on the Bangkok Harbour Extension Scheme. Finally, it is believed that, although Debnath Das was duly elected President of the Indian Independence League (Bangkok branch), there has been some difficulty in forming a local committee, which is yet another pointer to the lukewarmness of local Indian residents to the movement.

29

Major Himmat Singh Report on Development of Indian Independence Movement in South-East Asia with the Help of Japan; gives Assessment about Bangkok Conference

22 October, 1942

Sir,

I have the honour to submit report of my observations as regards the Bangkok Indian Independent Conference held at Bangkok on June the 10th 1942. As I was interned from the beginning of the war until repatriation this information was entirely gathered from the newspapers and from various Allied officials whom I met on the repatriationship. Among those I am most grateful to are His Norweign Majresty's Minister at Bangkok Mr. Hassell and his wife and also to the British Consul General at Bangkok. Some of the Indian repatriates have also given me some valuable information.

The development of organisation of the Indian Independence League Movement

2. The moment kept its activities underground although in fact it began one year prior to the war, when D.N. Das of Kobe visited Thai and with Swami Satyananda Puri established the first Thai-Japan Society, both in Bangkok and Kobe. Again just before the war. D.N. Das without the knowledge of the British authorities slipped out of Japan to Thai where he has remained since.
3. It was on February the end of this year that the Indian Independence

---

1. Foreign Department, File no. 313-X/1942, N.A.I.
2. Major Himmat Singh was the younger brother of the Nawab of Nawanrage. From 1930 onward he was Military Attache, British Embassy in Tokyo and carried on propaganda against the Indian nationalist in Japan.

League came out into the open showed their line of policy. First of all, on this occasion the League sent the following address to Field Marshal Plaek Khitasangka Pibulsonggram, the Thai Premier, on his declaring war on Britain and U.S.A.

"We feel happy to see that the Thai and Japanese nations are united together to face their common enemy. It is our earnest desire to see our motherland free from the British with the assistance of these nations."

4. When Malaya fell, this League became very active in inducting the captured Indian prisoners to become disloyal and join the so-called Indian National Army to fight the British. On February the 12th, 1942, according to the *Bangkok Times,* this was stated to number about 40,000.
5. It seems that the formation of the Indian National Army was first organised by a Captain Ram Sarup and Captain Hazara Singh who visited Bangkok on March the 4th 1942, with 60 other Indian army military prisoners. There is no doubt that several of the captured military officers and men of the Indian army have taken part in these anti-British activities by joining the Indian Independent League.
6. It is well known that the movement of the Indian Independent League in Bangkok was given full guidance by Rash Behari Boss and the Foreign Office of Japan; also by Subhas Chandra Bose and his forward Bloc in India, supported by the German Ambassador in Thai. The aims and objects are no doubt, similar to the resolutions passed by the preliminary Indian Independent League Conference held at the Sanno Hotel in Tokyo on March the 28th, 1942.
7. As delegates from the Indian Independent League, Swami Satyananda Puri, Sardar (Giani) Pritam Singh, Captain Akram and N. Iyer were flown from Thailand in order to attend this conference but the aeroplane containing them crashed near Nagoya Bay and they were said to have been drowned. It is interesting to know that the Indian repatriated from Shanghai on the "Tatuta Maru" were of the opinion that this was not an accident, but think that the four delegates were purposely got rid of by the Japanese. When asked what reasons the Japanese had for doing so, they replied that the Swami from Siam was a most powerful personality and did not approve of Japanese interference in gaining the Independence of India; also that he

strongly disagreed with Rash Behari Bose being made President of this conference as he considered Bose, who had been neutralised almost a decade ago, to be Japanese subject. Whether the Japanese really got rid of these leaders in order to have any interference with their programme one cannot say definitely, but there is no doubt that we could make good propaganda out of this incident. The British Consul General at Bangkok told me that the Swami was a great personality and Sanskrit and Buddhist scholar; and also a great friend of the Thai royal family in close touch with the highest official authorities in Thai. His influence with the Indians in Thai was so great that if he really opposed Japan in her policy he could have been a great obstacle to the Japanese in carrying out their policy as regards India. For Swami's record see Appendix no. under April 9th. Japan made a great fuss over the ceremonies of the last rites of these four drowned delegates. The Prime Ministers, General Tojo, attended the ceremony and read the obituary message.

8. The public speeches delivered at this conference in Bangkok are shown in Appendix No. 'A'.[2]

9. The Bangkok conference kept its resolutions most secret and therefore they are not yet known but the Minutes of the preliminary conference held at Sanno Hotel in Tokyo in March, obtained from loyal Indian subjects, clearly gives one an idea of what they might be. (See Appendix No. B) These resolution include :–

"Agenda 1. The attitude of the Indian regarding this war........."

"Agenda 2. Complete Independence of India

(i) Ideology of independence

(ii) Nature and time of Independence

Agenda 3. To spread independence movement to east to Asia and in India. Under Agenda 3 are details of policy which include :–

(i) method of propaganda and contacts with leaders in India.

(ii) Organisation of the League with the Council of Action.

(iii) administration. Departments include :–

(a) Foreign department or Liaison department

(b) Finance department

(c) Legal department

(d) Propaganda department

2. Not given here.

(e) Relief department

(f) Civil Police and Intelligence department

(g) Civil volunteers department

(iv) Indian National Army organisation which includes :–

(a) War department

(b) Recruiting department

(c) Military Intelligence and Military department

(d) Prisoners of War department followed by the method of military action against India by the so-called national army as under:–

(1) It is resolved that, if in the discretion of the council of action it is feasible to summon a meeting of representatives and take their advice on matter of the general Policy the Council shall do so.

(2) It is resolved that, before taking any military action against India, (including Ceylon) contrary to the wishes, policy or opinion of the Indian National Congress, the Council of action shall first get the approval of the committee of representatives and act as directed.

(3) We request that military action against India will be taken only by the Indian National Army and under the command of Indians, together with such military, Naval and air-cooperation and assistance as may be requested from the Japanese authorities by the council of action.

(v) Request to the Imperial Japanese Government. Six resolutions were passed as follows :–

(1) In further clarifications of the attitude of Japan towards India, the Imperial Japanese government be requested to make formal declaration to the effect that :–

(a) That Japan is willing and ready to give all possible help to India to sever its connection from the British Empire to attain complete independence.

(b) That on such reverence of India from the British Empire Japan would recognise the full sovereignty of India of India on attaining independence.

(c) That absolute independence of India would be guaranteed by the Imperial Japanese Government.

(d) That the Imperial Japanese Government of Japan would

recognise its influence with other powers and induce them to recognise the independence and sovereignty of India.

(f) That the framing of the future constitution of India will be left entirely to the representatives of the people of India.

II. The Imperial Japanese Government be further requested to render such financial help for the successful carrying out of our object as may be required from time to time on the distinct understanding that such help is to be treated as a loan to be repaid to the Japan by the National Government of Independent India, when it comes into being.

They should give all facilities for propaganda travel, transport and communications within the area under this control of the Imperial Japanese Government, in the manner and to the extent requested by the Council of Action also all facilities to come into contact with the National Leaders, the worker, and organisation in India. Also to clarify the position of Indian troops now under the control in occupied territories. To recognise and facilitate the use of the present National flag of India in all territories under the Imperial Government of Japan. Finally to consult in all matters of administration affecting the Indian community, the Indian independence Leagues of various places where these exist and in places where there are no branches, recognised leaders of community approved by the League branch nearest to such places.

(vi) Resolution re-interim work. See Appendix No. B.

10. Under Appendix B of this minute interesting items are :–

1. Specific instructions should be given to any troops attacking India to refrain themselves and to stop others from destroying places of worship belonging to the various religious bodies in order to avoid any sort of friction liable to be caused by such acts.
2. As soon as possible the property of the Indian Government and other rich Indians considered Pro-British including the Indian princess should be placed under the joint control and custody of the occupying Indian troops to avoid embezzlement or looting

etc. so that on expiration of the war the Indian Government may be in position to cover any expense incurred.

3. In all kinds of Government affairs, external or internal and the Indian religious leaders should not be consulted and their membership could never be taken in various states councils.
4. Able and patriotic volunteers should be enlisted from every part of East Asia including Shanghai, Hongkong, Java, Sumatra, etc. so that all can enjoy equal privilege in order that they also partake in serving their motherland.
5. In the war time just as women in all countries of the world are allowed to take full share in rendering their best service for the freedom of their respective countries, similarly Indian women are also anxious to fulfil their duties, every possible way for the freedom of our country. But under the British regime the women of India have not been given the same power and freedom which the men have been so far as a result of which women in India have not been allowed to take part in Government affairs. In order to raise them to the same discretion to take an active part in serving mother land even against the wishes of their parents, husbands, and other relatives supposed to be pro-British. Military training should be considered as compulsory part of education.

11. In conclusion I consider this Bangkok conference was a new and significant step taken by the Indians residing in the Far East, when they held at Bangkok the first general conference of the newly organised Indian Independence League at which Rash Behari Bose of Tokyo, head of the Asiatic section, presided.
12. According to the Japanese press more than 6,000 Indians attended and there were also present 100 delegates representing the 2 million Indians residing in the Japanese occupied areas. Among them, there were two representatives each from Japan, Hongkong, Maci, Manila, Borneo, French Indo-China, Java, Sumatra, and Shanghai, three from Thailand, four from Burma, six from Malaya, and one representative of the newly formed 'Indian Militia', Colonel Mohan Singh-a sikh, who is probably a deserter from the Indian Army,
13. The Conference elected a working committee of 36, among them a certain Raghava of Malaya and D. S. Pande (alians Deshpande) of Tokyo. Although their policy is to be kept secret, some of their aims are :-

(1) An immediate and full acquisition of Independence for India.
(2) Dissemination of propaganda throughout in India and East Asia.
(3) Appeal to Japan and other Axis powres for practival help.
(4) Formation of the Conference, messages of congratulation and promises for support were read from the Japanese Prime Minister, General Tojo, the Japanese Foreign Minister, Mr. Tojo, the Thai Prime Minister, Subhas Chandra Bose of Berlin, and other important personages in the Far East. In General Tojo's message, a definite promise was given that Japan would back the Indian Independence movement.

15. The most significant and note worthy fact in connection with this conference was that Japan and other Axis powers caused their Ambassadors and Ministers to attend the meeting in which these latter not only gave promises of the active support of their respective countries, but also made a clear and joint declaration to the effect that, while, both wish and are prepared to help India to obtain her independence, they have no territorial or other interests of any kind, in India. This new policy of soft-pedaling, however difficult to believe, may have some effect on the Indian politicians of the Forward Bloc and the other doubtful elements, but no effect whatsoever on any of the other political parties, who have seen Japan at work in China for the past 5 years. For Japan to have any success at all in this policy, it will be necessary for her to avoid attacking India and making a second China out of that country, since such an attack in whatever guise it is delivered, will tend to unite the Indians and curse them to oppose her on the side of the British.

16. The conference at Bangkok marks the end of the first stage and the beginning of the second, viz, that of anti-British activity on the part of Indians residing in the Far East. This means that they have reverted from the stage of underground organisation to that of open and positive action.

17. It should be stressed that the only way in which the movement started at the Bangkok conference can effectively make itself felt outside India, is timing its actions with a Japanese move into India. For this reason it would appear that the conference is in some way connected with Japan's next phase of operatoins, namely an advance into India, which, however, would produce a contrary reaction in India to that hoped for.

18. I had hoped to obtain a copy, of the secret resolutions passed at the Bangkok Conference from a person in Shanghai who attended the Bangkok Conference. This person was going to be repatriated on the "Tatuta Maru" but at the last moment the Japanese authorities got suspicious and stopped him from boarding the ship. However, it may be possible that these resolutions may be obtainable from other sources. It is believed however, that the Bangkok Conference elected a supreme executive committee with its headquarters at Bangkok.

30

Outline of the Propaganda Scheme of the Indian Independence League; Makes Special Reference to the Need for Fomenting anti-British Feelings Amongst the Overseas Indians and Mobolising their Support for the Liberation of India[1]

24 October, 1942

(I) The Object of Propaganda

The object of our Propaganda is to prepare India to overthrow the British rule and to establish Swaraj or self-rule.

(II) The Aims of Propaganda

In order to achieve this end quickly the propaganda had to be carried on keeping in mind the following aims :–

1. The creation, fomenting and strengthening of anti-British feeling among Indians
   (a) By pointing out the wrongs and misdeeds committed by the British in India.
   (b) By showing how the British were using the men and materials of India to serve their own selfish ends.
   (c) By drawing specific attention of the people to the inhuman cruelties, such as Jallianwala Bagh murder and other innumerable atrocities, committed by the British in India.
2. The rousing of national spirit and patriotism of the people to a high pitch
   (a) By dealing on their national virtues as a highly civilized people.
   (b) By recalling the brave deeds of their ancestors.

1. F. No. 101, I.N.A. Papers.

(c) By telling them the stories of the lives of their great men.

(d) By emphasising the fact that to Indians patriotism forms part of their religion.

3. There must be ceaseless endeavour to stir the people to action
   (a) By making them feel passionately proud of the past glory of India.
   (b) By creating great discontentment in their mind regarding their present humiliating position.
   (c) By inspiring them with faith in, and courage to make, their own destiny.
4. Try to convince them that there is no salvation for their country so long as even a shadow of British domination remains in India.
5. To instil confidence in their strength, ability and determination to bring about the revolution.
   (a) By telling them what their forefathers did during the war of Independence 1857.
   (b) By recalling to their mind the remarkable unity and enthusiasm manifested by the people during the non cooperation and Salt Satyagraha movements in recent times.
   (c) By taking parallel instances from the histories of other countries similarly placed such as America, Ireland, Turkey, Italy, and showing how they were able to overcome difficulties and attain their objective.
6. To impress on them the imperative necessity of taking full advantage of the present world situation to regain India's freedom:
   (a) Make them understand that England's difficulty is India's opportunity.
   (b) Britain is meeting with disaster in all theatres of war and her collapse is inevitable and certain.
   (c) If we do not act now, an opportunity like this might not occur again.
7. To draw an imaginative picture of a free India and show how she would be enjoying material prosperity, cultural amenities, political status and international prestige, commanding tremendous influence among the free nations of the world.
8. Incessantly deal on national unity and the great necessity for keeping the nation united to achieve its end. Tell them that 100 per cent unity would be impossible in any country. There is enough unity in India now. Whatever disunity that exists is the creation of the British Government and it would disappear when

that Government ceases to exist in India.

9. Any attempt by any party to enter into any sort of compromise with Britain should be promptly condemned
   (a) Let the people know how the British were ready to make promises when they were in difficulties and how they broke them when those difficulties were over. What happened during the last war and after.
   (b) Firmly assert we want independence now and not a promise for granting independence in future.
10. We have to seek the sympathy and support of other nations in our struggle. Our propaganda will be so formulated as to convince other nations the justice of our cause and to show that we deserve their help.
11. Tell the people the ways and means of achieving their end
   (a) By having recourse to strikes.
   (b) By terrorising the British Officials.
   (c) By refusing to cooperate with the Government in the administration.
   (d) By not rendering them any help in the prosecution of the present war.
   (e) By stirring up revolt.
   (f) By such other means intended to paralyse the British Government.
12. Make the people believe that in achieving the Independence of India we are not only liberating a great people from their thraldom of centuries, but we are also laying the foundation for world peace. Show that without the independence of India peace would be impossible in the world.

(III) The Means of Propaganda

Since the purpose of propaganda is to present an idea in the most attractive and effective way–possible so as to produce a desired opinion in the minds of the public we have to use all possible vehicles of expression by which the people could be reached. The means may be varied to suit special times, places or circumstances. But the following may generally be adopted for our purpose ;–

(1) Radio
(2) Press
(3) Leaflets
(4) Books, pamphlets and booklets
(5) Pictures and cartoons

(6) Lectures

(7) Dramas and moving pictures.

(IV) The Methods of Propaganda

In utilising the means mentioned in Section-III we have to adopt varying methods to produce the desired result. But three things have to be borne in mind when we consider the method of propaganda generally :–

(a) How effective it can be

(b) How lasting it can be

(c) How extensive it can be.

Let us now take each of the meansf mentioned in Section III.

1. Radio: The only direct and effective propaganda that could be carried on in India from this part now is through the medium of the short—Swave stations yonan, ⅃angkok, Saigon, and Rangoon. Absolute care, caution and vigilance must be preserved in using these stations for independence propaganda. A radio network on a systematic basis has to be made which would pour out revolutionary fire in India.

(a) Care must be taken that as far as possible the programme of one station does not conflict with those of others. There is bound to be some overlapping. But this must be minimise.

(b) There must be perfect coordination of policy among the four stations. They may present the same point from different angles. But some of them should not express a view which would be contradicted by others.

(c) The listening public in India must not be judged by the number of Indians who own radio sets, since considerable groups of Indians listen-in-every private set and coffee shop set. While plenty of educated Indians welcome serious talks on current events and other topics the average India wants a racy programme in his own mother tongue. Political happenings must be explained to him in a manner which he would understand easily. The usual news service and commentaries should met by literal translations of the English.

(d) Persons who are in charge of these stations must be picked man actuated with revolutionary fire and high sense of patriotism, who would inspire enthusiasm among the members of the staff working under them.

(e) Programmes must be so arranged that entertainments and serious talks must take their proper places with a view to attract and retain the interest of the listeners.

(f) Officers in charge of these stations must carefully watch the programme of the important stations of the world and modify or change the programme of our stations, from time to time, to meet the changing circumstances.

(g) Only men absolutely essential to run a station efficiently should be taken. Keep the members down, but see that the men that you take are those who are prepared to work with conviction and purpose. Increase in number would make the administration rather cumbersome. For the smooth working of the station administration should be subordinate to programme.

In view of the restrictions imposed on the use of short wave sets in Malaya and other parts it is necessary to provide facilities to the listeners of medium sets by repeating the more important programmes connected with the Independence propaganda through the local stations, which would also set up loud speakers in important public places where they could listen in.

It is necessary to keep up the spirit and enthusiasm of the Indians of East Asia at a high pitch and this would be difficult if they are not sufficiently supplied with Indian news and are not provided with facilities to hear more important talks on Indian Independence.

The four short wave stations would be directly controlled by the Headquarters in such manner as the Member in charge may decide from time to time.

The Indian section of the medium wave stations will be run in consultation and cooperation with the Propaganda Department at each territory.

2. Press: The function of the press is

(a) To keep the people informed about the world events generally and events in India particularly.

(b) To rouse up their spirit and enthusiasm.

(c) To formulate and focus public opinion concerning Indian Independence.

For this purpose the press must be encouraged.

(i) To give plenty of Indian news of the right type.

(ii) To express their views boldly.

(iii) To give circulation to their papers widely. Now, restrictions are imposed on the circulation of papers. Some papers are not allowed to be circulated beyond their respective states. These restrictions must be removed and all papers must freely circulated through the whole country.

This part of Propaganda is mainly intended for people in Malaya, Burma, East Indies and other places in East Asia living in their respective territories. It could not for obvious reasons help the propaganda in India. In each territory in East Asia there must be some papers in English and in more important Indian languages directly controlled by the Independent League while the policy of other papers owned and conducted by private individuals must be guided by the Independent League. The Indian Press *in Syonan* would be controlled by the Headquarters in such manner as the Member in charge may decide from time to time.

3. Leaflets: Small leaflets for throwing in India by bombers may be prepared. They must be very carefully done. Through them different classes of the people must be appealed to. They must be prepared in the more important languages of India and in English.

4. Books, pamphlets and booklets: These are mainly intended for the people in East Asia. Informative booklets and pamphlets in simple language dealing with the different aspects of Indian Independence must be printed and distributed in such languages as are necessary.

5. Pictures and cartoons: Even illiterate people could be attracted by this method of propaganda. The cartoons must be simple but attractive. Pictures drawn from history and current events showing. British attrocities and misdeeds may be specially useful.

6. Lectures: Specially trained speakers must carry on propaganda. Irresponsible and ill-equipped persons should not be allow to speak in the name of Independent Leagues. Every Leagues must have a list of such speakers.

7. Dramas and Moving Pictures: Wherever possible these also could be made useful for propaganda. There is enough talent in Malaya for dramatic entertainment. It only requires to be organised.

The Strategy of Propaganda

It is propaganda that prepares the soil for the growth of revolution. So it must precede any organisation for carrying out the revolution. The strategy consists in adopting the mode, net and means of propaganda to changing circumstances. The following hints may be noted in this connection : –

1. Events in India should be carefully observed and mass reaction on our propaganda noted. Misrepresentation of facts by the British will have to be corrected. Advantage should be taken of

Allied defeats to tell the people of their weakening powers. Any tendency to despair or to be despondent should be promptly checked.

2. The allied propaganda must be closely and continuously watched. Our propaganda Executives must think out and give directions so that opportunities are seized as they arise and new situations do not take us by surprise.
3. Japanese intentions regarding India must be tactfully handled. There is no use telling India that in offering to help her to gain her independence, Nippon actuated by altruistic motives and nothing else would not carry convictions to the minds of intelligence and practical men. Our propaganda must convince India that it is as much to our advantage as that of Japan to destroy British domination. Japan does not want India to be used by Britain as a Military and naval base against Japan. And India does not want British domination to be continued. So there is something in common between India and Japan. This common basis of their comradeship must be emphasized in all our propaganda.

(V) The Organisation for Propaganda : The member in charge of Propaganda of the Council of Action is responsible for entire control of Propaganda in the whole of East Asia. For purposes of Propaganda the whole of East Asia may be divided into following 10 territories :–

1. Philippines
2. Thailand
3. Malaya
4. Burma
5. Borneo and Calebes
6. Hong Kong, Canton & Macao
7. Indo-China
8. Java
9. Sumatra
10. Andamans

In each territory the propaganda activities will be guided and controlled by an officer called the Controller of Propaganda assisted by an Advisory Committee consisting of not more than six and not less than three members. The Member in Charge shall appoint a Controller for each territory who shall nominate the members of his Advisory Committee in consultation with the Executive of the Territorial Committee. As far as possible the Controller of Propaganda must be a member of the Territorial Executive.

Each State or District within a territory shall have a State or District Controller of Propaganda through whom the Controller of Propaganda shall put into execution the policy and programme of Propaganda as laid down by the Member in charge of Propaganda. District and State Committees shall give all help and facilities to the State or District Controllers to carry out the instructions of the Controller of Propaganda and for this purpose shall constitute Propaganda Advisory Committee for their respective territories.

(VI) Propaganda in the Indian National Army

This may be divided under two heads :–

1. Propaganda among non-volunteers.
2. Propaganda among volunteers.

1. Propaganda among non-volunteers: The existence of a large number of non-volunteers may be due to one or other of the following reasons :–

(i) Either they have no faith in the movement or

(ii) They may be actuated by motives of self-interest such as fear of loss of pay or property or

(iii) Some of them might be sitting on the fence to see how things progress.

Propaganda among these must be carried on in such a manner as to counteract all these evils and to convert them into–enthusiastic supporters of the revolution.

The policy must be to win them over to the movement not by compulsion or coersion but by persuation. To take in men who are not convinced of the cause would weaken the movement. The propaganda to be carried on among them should be more or less on the lines specified in Section-II dealing with the Aims of Propaganda. But the following points may be noted in this connection.

1. Every unit must have its Propaganda Officer who should organise the propaganda work in his unit. There must be a man on whom the troops depend for the quantity and palatability of their political and educational rations.
2. No restriction is to be put on the men for expressing and discussing their problems frankly and clearing their doubts.
3. There must be quite a number of men with special knowledge on

political and kindered problems and who are willing and able to give talks and lead discussion groups in their units. To discover them and to utilise their talent is the business of the Propaganda Chief of the Army.

4. The services of civilians with special knowledge on any subjects could be requisitioned whenever necessary.
5. Some measure of compulsion would be necessary to make the troops attend the lectures. You cannot expect people, many of whom left schools years ago and left the habit of technique of learning, to attend the lectures without compulsion.
6. The Propaganda Officers will not only ascertain but stimulate educational demands in the army.

2. Propaganda among the Volunteers must be directed on the following lines :–

(a) To make them feel that they enjoy the proud privilege of being soldiers of liberty to free their motherland from the bondage of centuries.
(b) They have the strength and ability to achieve their end.
(c) They are the forerunners to the creation of a new India.
(d) To serve India at a time like this must be considered the highest end and aim of every Indian.

There must be separate propaganda for officers and for men. Propaganda among officers must be conducted with greater precision and thoroughness. The following points may be noted in this connection :–

1. The Officers are interested in questions of military strategy and policy, the other ranks are mainly–interested in general political problems.
2. It is no use telling them simply it is their job to fight. We have to tell the meaning and the background of the conflict and the purpose we have in view.
3. Special emphasis must be laid on the fact that only when our faculties are trained and our ambitions developed can we rise to our proper stature as free men.
4. Political education should be considered not as an isolated activity, but in general setting of the soldiers work, welfare and needs.

The Propaganda Officers of the Indian National Army must constantly keep in touch with the member in Charge of Propaganda and seek his advice and assistance in whatever manner required.

(VII) General Hints on Propaganda : It would be advantageous to keep in mind the following truisms in connection with propaganda generally :–

(a) 1. Military attack the body physically and crush it; Propaganda attacks the mind, ruins the morale and create within the enemy self-destructive emotion and eventually let the enemy destroy himself.

2. We must aim to wake up the mass mind of Indians and fill it with hope, faith and courage.

3. Always state the truth and then put the interpretation most favourable to support our cause.

4. The Propagandist must firmly believe in what he wants to convince others. He must hypnotise himself before he can mesmerise the public.

5. What we think strongly we generally accomplish because our sub-conscious thoughts tend to realise themselves. We have therefore to build up in our sub-conscious mind a great and overwhelming faith in our country's cause and ultimate victory.

(b) The following seven secrets of propaganda success are mentioned by a great authority on Propaganda :–

1. The first essential in\propaganda is Repetition. In the short memory of the public lies the propagandist's greatest asset and his greatest handicap. The repetition carries with in no doubt the danger that the public may be bored and lose interest in the arguments advanced. But if the propagandist persists and secures a sufficient number of new "slants" to his appeal he is bound to impress certain section of the public.

2. The second essential of sound propaganda is colour. The average individual is not interested in abstractions; but he is intensely interested in facts and personalities. The propagandist should not try to force his arguments upon the public; but he should endeavour to influence them by reports that rouse sympathy for his own cause or antagonism towards his opponents. Such propaganda can be very effective; by stringing together a few incidents, for, the man in the street is always prone to argue from the particular to the general.

3. The third major principle of propaganda is that it should contain at least a kernel of truth. The most remarkable application of this principle in post-war years was the German campaign against Czechoslovakia between May and September 1938. The sudeten Germans notoriously suffered from grievances and

injustices, economic hardships and the non-fulfilment of pledges solemnly given when the Czechoslovakian State was formed.

4. The fourth principle of propaganda is that it should be built round a slogan. The slogan is the supreme illustration of the power of brevity in propaganda. The average modern reader does not go in for long closely reasoned, arguments. He had neither the time nor the inclination to digest them. His news is served up to him in short, bright articles, and the propagandist, to succeed, must follow the fashion of the times.
5. The fifth principle of propaganda is that it should be directed towards a specific objective. The application of the principle would involve a careful study of the habits and characteristics of the people sought to be served. To fire off propaganda bullets at random is a wasteful policy.
6. The sixth principle of propaganda is concealment of motive. Propaganda is a campaign camouflaging its origin, its motive, or both, conducted for the purpose of–obtaining a specific objective by manipulating public opinion. When propaganda is disguised the subject is more open to suggestion than would otherwise be.
7. Timing is the seventh principle of propaganda success. It is a recognised maxim of publicity that once the initial groundwork has been performed, a mass attack is the best possible method of launching a campaign. The propagandist has to display opportunism to reap the reward. It dictates the time at which propaganda should be released. Allied with this principle is the recognition of the value of reticence in a propaganda campaign. Frequently a propagandist will succeed by knowing, not when to speak, but when to keep silent. When his opponent has a powerful case, it merely plays into his hand by attempting on explanation. The proper course here is to lie low and wait for the public to forget, hastening that desired end by launching a counter-offensive on a totally different subject.

31

The Aims and Objects of the Indian National Army after its expansion by General Mohan Singh[1]

30 October, 1942

1. Object : The object of the Indian Independence League (of which the Indian National Army is a part) is to unite all Indians in Japanese occupied territory in the struggle for India's "Independence". It aims at a 100% membership and to this end all civilians are compelled to 'volunteer' for membership.

In March, 1942, a Conference was held in Tokyo which was attended by several of the more important members of the I.I.L. and the following resolutions were adopted :-

(a) "We are confident of the complete elimination of the British influence from Asia and of the rebirth of the new Asia, as well as of India after the war. We should accept General Tojo's generous offer of help and work in close co-operation with Japan to emancipate our country.

(b) Complete independence implies full freedom of action and thought without the least foreign interference or influence.

(c) Only Indian forces under Indian commanding officers will attack India.

2. The Conference placed the following demands before the Japanese Government:-

(a) Japan will recognize the Indian National Government after the elimination of the British one.

(b) Japan will guarantee complete independence to India.

(c) Japan will persuade other foreign. Government to recognize the Indian National Government.

1. F. No 601/7378/H.S.

(d) The Indian representatives will frame the future constitution of India.

(e) RASH BEHARI BOSE will be the President of the Council of Action.

3. The Conference gave the following undertaking :

(a) The Indian National Government would be responsible for the repayment of the loans which the Japanese Government will make in India's struggle for freedom.

Punjab Regiment. His second-in-Command was Captain "Mohan (Mohammed) Akram", (unidentified) who is believed to have been killed in an aeroplane crash.

Other identified personnel of the I.N.A. include :-

Lt. Col. G.Q. Gilani, Ist Bahawalpur Infantry.

Major Naranjan Singh Gill, 4/19 Hyderabad Regt., who made an anti British speech at the Bangkok Conference.

Major Mirza, Field Accounts Officer, who broadcast an anti-British speech from Saigon.

Jem Ram Sarup, 4/19 Hyderabad Regt: who organizes recruiting in Rangoon. In addition a number of men' suspected of being members of the I.N.A have been identified.

12 names of men known to be in the I.N.A. are unidentgified.

13. An unreliable statement by an I.N.A. agent gives the northern land routes used for infiltration into India as :-

(a) Monywa – Kaleva – Tamu Manipur

(b) Mandalay – Myitkyia (or Mogaung) – Naga Hills – Ledo

(c) Through China into Bhutan and Nepal and thence to India (improbable).

This agent states that route (b) was used by the first parties of 5th Columnists who came to India under cover of Indian refugees from Burma.

32

British Analysis and Reaction to the Activities of Indian National Army Directed Towards Indian Army[1]

6 November, 1942

1. No one knew anything about the I.N.A. before the fall of Singapore. It came like a bombshell after the capitulation. It seemed that the Japanese had made some pre-arrangements to tamper with the loyalty of the Indian Army. A man called Giani Pritam Singh had come to some understanding with the Japanese Embassy at Bangkok. He was secretly publishing posters and training 5th columnists before hostilities broke out. His understanding with the Japanese was that the Indian civilians should not be treated as enemy subjects and that Indian soldiers too should not be treated as enemies. He said that he complained to the Japanese that Indians have no enmity with Japan and the Indian soldier does not want to fight Japan. He is being misled by the English and made to fight for Rs. 14 per month. He was sure the Indians would not fight when his men told them not to do so. He met with varying success he said. He has since been killed in an air accident.
2. His methods were to send Indians right to the frontline and then shout to the Indian troops not to fire. The other method was to send the Indian prisoners back after treating and feeding them well, thus showing that the Japanese treat Indians very well. All the soldiers captured up country owing to the difficulty of terrain while withdrawing, he attributed to have deserted due to his propaganda. It is certain some people must have been influenced by this, especially near the end of the campaign when morale was low.

---

1. Military Department, File No. L/WS/1/1576, Indian Office Liberary and Records, London, (I.O.L.R.).

3. After the withdrawal from Jitra position, Capt. Mohan Singh of the 14th Punjab Regiment, was left behind and started working with the Japanese. It was he who brought the I.N.A. into existence. He is feeding it with his ideas and is influencing it with his personality. He has got no weakness in the form of greed, lust, drink, women, etc. as far as one can find out. At the time when [the Informer] left Singapore there was a general feeling among the officers, that right or wrong, one thing was certain, that Mohan Singh was sincere and not acting a part. His assistant when he came to Singapore after the surrender was Capt. I.J. Kiani of 5/2 Punjab.
4. Capt. Mohan Singh lectured to the 60,000 Indian troops assembled in Farrer Park and 90 per cent of them went wild with the idea of Indian Independence, and the National Army. They cheered Mohan Singh at the end of his speech most enthusiastically. Major Fujiwara decided to keep the Indian soldiers who surrendered in the general capitulation as P.W. for some time.
5. The inadequate supplies of food, the lack of medicine, the extremely brutal and barbarous treatment, the beating of officers and soldiers alike, set in a reaction. By April the Japanese were universally hated and the idea of I.N.A. had lost momentum. At the end of April Mohan Singh came back from Tokyo and started his propaganda lectures. After a few days, lists were asked from officers showing whether they elected to volunteer for I.N.A. or not. Along with it were implied threats by the Japanese that the non-volunteers would be badly treated and non-cooperative leaders even shot. These threats had their effect. It was evident that, not for love, but to avoid torture, many officers volunteered. At that time of indecision [Informer] although still under treatment for his wound, as outdoor patient, escaped as he had decided not to volunteer.
6. A few months after his escape [Informer] heard that in Burma, with the exception of a few officers, all had volunteered. The Japanese made capital out of the arrest of Mr Gandhi and Pandit Nehru which caused many people to go over to thē I.N.A.
7. The idea of a National Army has a great attraction for the rank and file. If one thinks "From where do our recruits come?" It will be found that they are the same material and come from the same places where the Congress made frantic efforts to win over 'the rural population of India'. These seemingly inarticulate millions have in fact been made politically conscious to an appreciable degree by Congress propaganda. The modern recruit of the Indian Army is very different

to his predecessor of 1914-1918. Hence this lurking danger, this already prepared foundation for I.N.A.; is always there. A little real or imaginary grouse, a little subversive propaganda, and a reverse to the Allies have their hidden possibilities. This monster will not care to show its face till the last minute when prevention or cure may be impossible. This idea of I.N.A. will be exploited to extremes by the Japanese to make the Indian Army in India ineffective. They will use radio, secret agents, leaflets, promises and every other ingenious method to get at the sepoys and officers. They intend putting Indians (I.N.A.) against Indians (I.A.) and thus bank on their brotherly feeling which will make their loathe firing on each other.

8. Next, one thinks what is the remedy for all this. It is a terrific problem and all the suggestions here have been put down with a spirit of humility, that they may per chance do some good. Actually, one does not feel qualified to say anything on such a grave problem.

9. The most ideal solution of course is to have a National Government in India. That will nip all this idea of I.N.A. in the bud, and make the I.A. [Indian Army] impervious to any form of foreign propaganda. The government has made perhaps all efforts to come to some understanding with the Congress and if the Congress is not prepared to cooperate, then perhaps the remaining elements, who are cooperating sincerely may be helpful. The Japanese do not want India to come to an understanding with England. That is why they made super-human efforts to bomb India and Ceylon while Sir Stafford Cripps[2] was in India. They wanted to impress India with their might. They wanted to frighten India. If India comes to an understanding with England it will be a death blow to Japan.

10. The ideal perhaps is not attainable. A thing that struck one in Malaya was the tremendous power and influence of I.C.O.'s over the men. If the officers of some unit were prepared to volunteer then the whole unit would volunteer without hesitation and if the officers did not want to volunteer then the man and V.C.O.'s would also be disinclined. Hence if the I.C.O.'s wholehearted cooperation can be enlisted to combat this menace, then a great degree of success can be assured. Now the I.C.O.'s as a class have been labouring under

---

2. Sir Stafford Cripps (1889-1952) - British Statesman. During the War was ambassador to Moscow 1940-42, Minister of Aircraft production 1942-45. Was sent to India to negotiate with the Indian National leaders to solve the constitutional problems in 1942.

some imaginary or real grouses. The Indianisation Committee, 1939, looked into this matter and made some recommendations. Its report was never made public. Its recommendations were (i) throwing open all the I.A. to Indians, (ii) bringing back V.C.O.s into the Indianized battalions, (iii) and the basic rates of pay to be the same for all the officers (Indians not getting overseas allowance in India). The first two recommendations have been acted upon, if the third is also adopted it will make I.C.O.s happy and contented. Their feelings will reflect on the whole of the Indian Army. There is another type of grouse on which bitter comments are sometimes heard–"The complete, reluctance of the B.G.Rs to salute I.C.Os". These are little things but sometimes they assume great proportions in people's minds.

11. The other remedy is propaganda. Let the I.A. know what the Occupied Countries are like under Japan, how the Japanese treat the conquered peoples, their atrocities, greed and ambition to role the whole of Asia. Radio and press are very useful for propaganda, but nothing can better a talk from a living man, where the audience can ask questions and the personality of the speaker can impress the listeners.

33

Mahabir Singh Dhillon's Escape from Burma; his Interrogation by the British Provided Detailed information about the Indian National Army to them[1]

11 November, 1942

1. In forwarding Major M.S. Dhillon's diary of events while in Japanese hands, the following note on his attitude is added for the information of the D.M.I.
2. During interrogation Major Dhillon has shown the utmost anxiety to give us information detrimental to the Japanese. He conveys the impression that he is entirely out to help us.

   He is politically minded and is, in my opinion, pro-Congress (he describes this as "Nationalistic" which is presumably the Indian National Army's name for the same attitude).

   Reading between the lines of the account, it seems probable that he has been of use to the Japanese during the past eight months.

   He is much impressed with the Japanese fighting spirit and their determination to spare no trouble and expense to get things done quickly. He does not think much of their equipment however.
3. Three points which struck me as suspicious are :
   (a) He was anxious to send his signet ring by an agent to Hav. Udai Singh, who was promoted by the Japanese and given charge of one of the fifth column camps in Rangoon. He claimed that Udai Singh would send us valuable information. The latter is now at Kalewa.
   (b) He appeared to think that we were not enthusiastic about this idea and suggested that a radio message enquiring about Udai

1. Military Department, File No. L/WS/1/1576, IO.L.R.

Singh's welfare would inform Udai Singh that the Dhillon was safe.

(c) Dhillon is not married. He had trouble with his family over refusal to marry in his own caste. He wanted to marry a girl outside it. This might loosen his ties with India and single him out as a man whom the Japanese might expect to return to them.

4. In my opinion, Major Dhillon is uncertain in his own mind as to his future attitude.

5. It will depend a good deal on our attitude towards him. He is clever and potentially very useful to us. He might cause dissension in the I.N.A. through propaganda. It remains for decision whether we are to trust him or not. Half measures would be useless, he is much too clever to be taken in by eyewash.

Major Mahabir Singh Dhillon, R.I.A.S.C.

Unit-22 Bde. Tpt. Ccy.

Captured at Singapore on the 16th February, 1942

Took part in Malaya Campaign as Comdr. 11th Div. Amn. Coy. From Jitra to Johore Bharu. Johore Bharu-Singapore as L. of C. Tpt. Coy.

Original plan to escape immediately after the General Surrender together with Major A.N. Weinman (A.I.R.O.) miscarried due to the four sons of the civilian through whose agency the steamer was to be obtained not having been released from the Volunteers.

17th February, 1942: On this date all Indian and British troops were separated. The Indians collected at Farrer Park. Lt. Col. Hunt handed them over to the Japanese on behalf of the British Government. Major Fujiwara, the Japanese Intelligence Officer took them over on behalf of the Japanese Government. Col. Hunt then left the parade and Major Fujiwara made a speech. He read out Premier Tojo's declaration about the Japanese desire to seek an Independent India, and handed over the Indian prisoners to Capt. Mohan Singh C.O., I.N.A. Fujiwara's speech was translated into English by 2nd Lt. Kunizuka. Lt. Col. Gill was told to interpret it into Hindustani. Gill made it perfectly clear both before, during and at the end of the speech, that he had been told to translate and what he said was not his own personal view. Capt. Mohan Singh then made a stirring, emotional and anti-British speech, at the end of which there was great excitement and wild cheering. The Officers' lines were quiet, but the troops appeared to be deeply move. Mohan Singh announced the creation of the I.N.A. and told the men that they were not prisoners. This emotional display worried Gill and me considerably. In the evening Mohan Singh asked me to go and live with him and help him administer this huge force. I tactfully declined to do so. With the others I went to Neesoon Camp on the 18th February. Life there became difficult owing to volunteers coming in and delivering lecture. Discipline was getting bad, and for the first time I began to wonder if my refusal to live with Mohan Singh was a wise step. Living with him I might have prevented quite a lot of trouble to other Prisoners of war. Gill also thought the same. Therefore, I was sent to Mohan Singh's H.Q. as the Prisoners' Representative on the 25th February, 1942. It was not difficult for me to persuade Mohan Singh to send out a letter saying that the I.N.A. and Prisoners of War were two quite different organisations, and that volunteers should not live with the Prisoners of War also that there should be no political lectures. Gill wanted this point settled. I have no doubt that for the time being, this broke the backbone of the I.N.A. With the help of Gill and Mehtab we were also able to organise the food and medical services. Rations had to be collected from all over Singapore, and there was a great shortage of medicines, which had to be collected from various dumps with the Japanese assistance. Gill also did everything possible to get the water supply functioning. We also arranged for a wider distribution of our men in order to avoid overcrowding and disease.

25th February, 1942. Sent to H.Q., I.N.A. (Capt. Mohan Singh) as Prisoners of War Liaison Officer.

28th February, 1942. Taken by the Japanese to Saigon together with Lt. Col. N.S. Gill.[2]

Route followed : by air – Singapore to Bangkok. 3 days to Bangkok.

In Bangkok taken to Col. Tamura, Japanese Military Attache. Introduced to Baba Amar Singh, Master Bhagwan Singh, Swami Satyananda Puri and Das. Also met Lt. Ito (Pilot) who was Liaison Officer for Indians in Bangkok and worked with the Japanese Military Attache. By air-Bangkok-Saigon.

We were told that the German Military Attache will also be flying in the same place as us, and that we were not to speak to him. For this reason we were provided with "Mufti".

Saigon. Stayed three days. Met only one Japanese Lt. Col. and one Major. They came to the house where we were accommodated. We found Capt. Ehsan Qadar, 5/2 Punjab, Sub. Shangara Singh 5/14 Punjab, Hav. Shiv Singh 5/2 Punjab, there for wireless propaganda.

5th March, 1942. Returned to Singapore and found Captain Mohd. Akram 1/14 P.R. living with Captain Mohan Singh. The former appeared

2. See Statement of Gill at S.No. 43.

to wield great influence on the letter, and they shared a room. My place as Prisoners' Rep. had been taken by Major K.S. Mehtab, R.I.A.D. I found a definite feeling of hostility towards me at H.Q. I.N.A. Apparently influences had been at work in my absence. Mohan Singh also warned me that the Japanese disliked me. He refused to return me to the Camp. For this reason I shifted to another house with Mehtab, giving the excuse that Mohan Singh's house was overcrowded.

15th March, 1942, Mohan Singh went to Tokyo to attend the Tokyo Indian Independence Conference. He took with him Lt. Col. N.S. Gill and Capt. Mohd. Akram and the civilians whose names are noted in the margin. A few days later we heard that the plane carrying Capt. Mohd. Akram, Ayer and Swami Satyananda Puri of Bangkok had crashed into the sea just before reaching Japan.

I had access to a radio set in Mohan Singh's house and used to collect all news, especially from Delhi and London. Thus, on two occasions I read over to the Officers in the Camps to keep them informed of world events and to prevent mental inertia. This was construed as propaganda against the Japanese and the I.N.A. and I was forbidden to use the radio set. Hostility towards me in the Japanese and I.N.A. quarters increased. In fact, I was told afterwards that I might have been shot if it had not been due to a definite request of Mohan Singh that no harm must befall me in his absence.

25th April, 1942. Tokyo party returned. I.N.A. and Japanese poison Mohan Singh against me, so much so that Mohan Singh actually avoided me.

26th April, 1942. The Japanese warn Gill that he will have to go to Bangkok. The excuse given was that he was to unite the two Indian parties there, namely the Indian National Council and the Indian Independence League. He was told that he could take me and another Officer. He selected Capt. S.M. Hessian 4/19, Hyderabad. The real reason was that before forming the I.N.A. they wanted Gill and me out of Singapore as they thought our presence would harm their movement.

27th April, 1942. Fujiwara and Capt. Mohan Singh delivered a propaganda lecture to all Officers including V.C.O.'s Gill, on my advice, refused to speak. After this lecture Gill spoke confidentially to about 20 Officers Gist of his talk was : "I have tried to serve the Indian Soldiers to the best of my ability, in an administrative capacity. I am convinced that the Japanese want to exploit the Indian Soldiers for their own purposes.

I am no longer able to serve you. I am being separated from the troops and sent to Bangkok against my wishes.

I may be exploited personally. Remember that I do not represent you now.

He also spoke to the Officers including V.C.O.'s of 4/19 Hy.

28th April, 1942. Gill, self and Hussian, with Japanese Officer, left Singapore by car, stopped en route at Kuala Lumpur and Penang. Caught the Bangkok train from Hadoyai. Reached Bangkok on the 5th May, 1942.

5th May to 1st September. At Bangkok. Our second plan to escape was made here. Got into touch with a local Indian for guides into Burma. The difficulty was to get out of Bangkok without the knowledge of the Japanese. It was eventually decided to say that Gill was not keeping well, therefore, a fortnight's change of air at Hua Hin a seaside resort not far from Bangkok was contemplated. From there the escape was to be carried out. By now the date for Bangkok Indian Independence Conference was fixed, and it was decided that perhaps the best time to escape would be after the Conference, when some useful information as regarding the Conference would be available. About the middle of June Mohan Singh and party arrived at Bangkok to attend the Independence Conference. Mohan Singh first told Gill that I could not attend the Conference, as I was not a Volunteer, but later changed his mind and told me to attend, mainly because Gill and I were so well known in Bangkok that the absence of either of us from the Conference would create suspicion. After the Conference Mohan Singh wanted to take Gill and me to Singapore. Fortunately there was only one seat in the plane and that he took himself. Gill and I stayed behind though Mohan Singh had left instructions for us to move by rail.

Our second plan to escape was formulated and amended whilst Mohan Singh was still at Bangkok. Colonel Iwakuro, the Japanese Officer after whom the Dept. that deals with Indian questions in East Asia is named, sent for Colonel Gill towards the end of July, 1942. He offered to place him in charge of the Indian Intelligence Service in and outside East Asia. This Gill refused to do. The next day he asked Gill if he would accept to run an Indian Contact organisation with his H.Q. in Rangoon. Gill promised to consider this proposal. He and I discussed this question and we agreed that here was an excellent opportunity to make good our escape with all the political information which we collected before, during and after the Bangkok Conference. Iwakuro asked that his conversation with Gill be kept secret from Mohan Singh on the I.N.A. and Bose of the Independence League. It was fully realised that this Contact Scheme, from the Japanese point of view, was no more and no less than espionage pure and simple. This appeared the only way to escape, but the idea was so repugnant (although this would have enabled us to completely deceive the Japanese) that Gill and I could not bring ourselves to accept Iwakuro's proposal.

A few days after his return to Singapore, Mohan Singh had a telegram sent to Gill to report to Singapore at once. I was able to persuade Gill to leave me behind at Bangkok, because I did not want to get involved with the I.N.A. Even my silent presence there would have been harmful. I also strongly advised Gill not to deliver any lecture etc. at Singapore, and if compelled to do so to try and get out of it somehow. The idea was that the Prisoners of War must not get the false impression that Gill was in the I.N.A. Gill was at Singapore for 10 days, and whilst he was still there the arrests of Gandhi, Nehru and Azad took place. This roused the Indian people of East Asia against the British. It also helped the I.N.A. to draw into their fold quite a lot of waverers.

Gill and I then decided it was absolutely necessary for one of us, if not both, to escape to India with full information, and to contact the Government of India without delay. With that in view it was decided to accept Iwauro's Indian Contact offer. Mohan Singh sent 20 men to Gill for this scheme. Gill selected the Officers, namely, myself, Tehl Singh 1/8 Punjab, J.B.S. Grewal 5/2 Punjab and Bakhtawar Singh (I.E.). These Officers were specially selected by Gill because they had difficulties with the I.N.A. All these came to Bangkok.

We left Bangkok on the 1st September, 1942 by air in three or four parties, and one party went by rail to Singapore and thence by sea to Rangoon. After reaching Rangoon on about the 10th Gill decided to take Tehl Singh and Grewal into his confidence about the escape plan. We decided that three forward posts be established, one at Mityaha, one at Kalewa and one at Akyab. Grewal was to go to Mitkyaha, myself to Kalewa and Hav. Shiv Singh 5/2nd to Akyab. Most of our men we could trust but Hav. Shiv Singh we suspected as a spy of Mohan Singh certainly, if not of the Japanese. We therefore arranged that Shiv Singh should go to Akyab and the pro-Japanese element must be sent through him. Both Grewal and I were to go to our respective posts at Mitkyaha and Kalewa, and to reconnoitre the routes to the nearest British post. It was agreed that we were to send Gill a code telegram, as follows :

"Routes 1st. class. Very good"

(a) This meant "you can come here even with Japanese escort, if they will not let you come alone. I can manage to get you over the border".

"Routes 2nd class. Good"

(b) This meant "I can get you over the border, but you must not come with a Japanese escort"
"Routes 3rd class. Bad"

(c) This meant "Things are very difficult and I cannot get you across under any conditions".

The message was to be handed over to the nearest Japanese W.T. for onward despatch to Gill through Iwakuro Kikan, Rangoon.

Gill was to send a party of four each to Grewal and me, followed by a second party. He himself was to come last with the balance of his organisation. This would have meant that in about 3 weeks to a month, all our men would have come to India. The men were not to be taken into confidence at Rangoon, but our Forward Post Comdrs. were permitted to tell them the plan if they considered there was no risk of the Japanese getting to know our scheme.

Grewal and I left Rangoon on the 19th September, 1942, by rail. We reached Mandalay on night 20/21st. We crossed the river by a country boat and reached Sagain on the 22nd. We spent the night at the station and left for Monyma early next morning, reaching Monywa in the afternoon. At Monywa I went to the Sikh temple and there saw Capt. Pritam Singh 3/16th, who I had left for Bangkok. I told Pritam Singh that he need not worry and that I will get him over the frontier as soon as possible. Unfortunately no steamer for Kalewa was available till the 3rd October, and we had to wait at Monywa from 23rd September to the 3rd October. On the 3rd October we were provided transport in a Japanese convoy which was conveying Col. Koba's Regt. H.Q. and a B. to Kalewa. The journey took 9 days and we reached Kalewa on the 11th. The delay was due to the unwillingness of Indians employed to run these steamers and to want of proper fuel. The steamers are being run on firewood instead of coal. This necessitates frequent stops for refuelling and firewood is not always dry.

Colonel Koba knew that I was connected with Iwakuro Kikan. He was most helpful. On reaching Kalewa I decided to go as far forward up the river Chindwin as possible in order to be as far away as possible from Japanese troops, so that Gill's escape could be arranged.

When I told Koba that I would establish my H.Q. at Mowlaik or Kindat he wanted to send a Japanese escort with me. I was able to dissuade him from this course by saying that the presence of a Japanese escort would arouse suspicion of British Agents, who might report our location to their Government.

I left Kalewa on the 12th and reached Kindat on the 15th October. On the 18th October, I sent Capt. Pritam Singh with the first party whose previous instructions, which they had received from the Japanese in Rangoon, I cancelled, and whom I told to accompany Pritam Singh. On the 20th October Bakhtawar Singh reached Kindat from Rangoon. I then had to decide quickly. There was no doubt that the Japanese would not left Gill escape, nor would they let me escape. Luckily for me no Japanese troops were where I was, and I had two courses open to me :

(a) To stay at Kindat and get in touch with Gill again.

(b) To leave Kindat and escape with as many men as possible. I decided against course (a) and for course, (b) due to the following reasons :

  (1) It would have taken me at least 6 weeks to get in touch with Gill and to get a reply from him.

  (2) The Japanese were sending troops up the Chindwin and a party of 20 had already arrived at Massein. If I did not clear out of Kindat almost at once they might arrive any day at Kinda and make my escape most difficult.

  (3) Knowing the Japanese mind I was certain that there was no hope of Gill being permitted to leave Rangoon once the Japanese had refused to let him do so.

  (4) I had valuable information which I could have sent by say 2 Lt. Bakhtawar Singh to India, but only Gill and I personally knew all the Japanese, Indian and some German personalities in East Asia, and it was necessary for Gill and me to come over to this country to convey the information to the Government of India. Gill obviously could not come and so I had to do so.

The Japanese were apparently getting suspicious of Gill and me and therefore there was a great risk of them breaking up the organisation and thus preventing any one of us escaping.

I left Kindat by boat on the 21st and reached Autong on the 22nd. I left Auktong on the 23rd and following an elephant trail reached 2 M.S. on Sittang-Tamu road. I halted the night there and on the 24th reached M.S. 22 halted there for the night and next day, i.e., 25th reached Tamu and got into touch with the nearest Bde. H.Q.

34

Rash Behari Bose to Col. Iwakuro Requesting him to get Formal Acceptance of Bangkok Resolutions by the Imperial Japanese Government; Hints Towards the Emergence of Differences in Council of Action[1]

28 November, 1942

Sir,

In further reverting to the enclosed (copy of the letter sent to you and subsequently withdrawn) we have again the honour to place before you the imperative necessity of receiving a formal assurance from the Imperial Government as to which portion of the Resolutions passed at the Bangkok Conference has been adopted without qualifications or change by the Imperial Government, which portion has not been approved, and which portion has received approval subject to alterations. We have had in the past few months certain reasons for anxieties and if we have to be true to the great trust that has been placed in us not only you but by the Indian Public in East Asia, we cannot remain any more without requesting you to be kind enough to forward the enclosed letter to the Imperial Government and vouchsafe to us a reply from them as requested.

In this our request, we fully hope that you, who have personally watched and understood our Movement, will accord to us your sympathy and support.

If a reply is forthcoming at this earliest possible opportunity, it will considerably facilitate the further work and progress of this Movement. Though this letter is being sent to you formally, we shall, if so required,

1. I.I.L. Papers; File no. 45/3, For the attitude of the Impenial Japanese Government policy towards the Bangkok Resutionols see the official publication *S.C. Bose and Japan, Tokyo,* 1956, pp. 78-82.

be pleased to wait on you at any time, and at a mutual conference have further discussions with your good self. We hope, however, that you will be good enough to act upon this letter immediately as it is our considered opinion that a reply from the Imperial Government is urgently required for the work, which is now awaiting our attention.

Thanking you in anticipation,

Enclosure

Indian Independence League,

Syonan,

29th November, 1942

Rash Behari Bose to Colonel H. Iwakuro,

Chief of the Iwakuro Kikan,

For favour of Transmission to the Imperial Government of Japan.

The Council of Action had a series of sittings recently when it took stock of the whole situation concerning the Indian Independence Movement in East Asia and the development of the revolutionary struggle in India. The enormous increase in the number of members in the Independence League, the wide network of League Organisations throughout East Asia, the tremendous enthusiasm seen everywhere for the cause which we stand for and the spirit of sacrifice manifested by all classes of Indians in East Asia have given us immense satisfaction in the progress of the Movement made possible by the help and cooperation of the Imperial Nipponese Government. The rapid march of revolutionary events in India resulting in the growing number of strikes, rebellions, sabotage and other mass actions have further raised our hopes and leave us in no doubt regarding the intentions and determination of our countrymen to overthrow British rule and to regain our independence at any cost. We have now reached a stage at which we feel that before we take any further forward move, it is necessary to clear matters, to understand our position perfectly and to cement Indo-Japanese friendship without which it is impossible for us to do any effective work for the attainment of our objective.

We are unfortunately so placed that we have not so far been able to contact with leaders in India and ascertain their views regarding our policy and our own plans. This makes our responsibility all the more sacred and onerous. The time would not be distant when we shall have to deal with a Provisional National Government in India and when that comes, we must be in a position to convince them that we have taken every possible step to maintain the safety, dignity, and integrity of our country when once our goal of independence has been reached.

We have, therefore, after very careful consideration, come to the conclusion that it will be advantageous and in the interest of our Movement to request the Imperial Government of Japan to favour us with a reply at the earliest possible opportunity, clarifying the position on the following points:

1. A copy of the Bangkok Resolutions has been forwarded to the Imperial Government so long ago as the 22nd July, 2602. Though we have been working on the basis that such resolutions would be accepted by the Imperial Government, we are not yet in a position to know exactly where we stand with regard to these resolutions. We do not want to conceal the fact that anonymous enquiries are still being made by many leading members of our community regarding these resolutions and we find it difficult and even embarrassing to give them a satisfactory reply. It is, therefore, of urgent importance to us to request the Imperial Government to be good enough to inform us, formally and at the earliest possible opportunity, regarding the acceptance of the Bangkok Resolutions and if there is any resolution to which the Imperial Government cannot give their support, we shall be glad if they would kindly define their attitude towards the same.
2. Recognition of the Council of Action as the Supreme Executive of the Indian Independence Movement in East Asia and the acceptance of their status as such is absolutely necessary in order that the Council of Action may function efficiently.
3. The Imperial Government must no doubt be aware of the propaganda that is being carried on by the British Government in India regarding the intentions of Japan, Although we had some declarations from His Excellency Premier General Tojo and other leading statesmen of Japan to the effect that Japan has no political or military ambitions in India, we would respectfully suggest that a full, formal and solemn declaration binding on the present and future Government of Japan regarding the intentions of Japan to recognise and support the absolute independence and full sovereignty of India immediately on the removal of British rule in India, is found essential to instill complete confidence and to place the Movement on an effective and proper footing.
4. As a corollary to the acceptance of the Bangkok Resolutions, it is necessary that the formation and existence of the Indian

National Army on the principles laid down in the said resolution will be formally and publicly recognised and all facilities offered for its expansion with a view to make the army a strong and efficient one to carry out the great purpose for which it is intended.

We are conscious of and profoundly grateful to the Imperial Government of Japan for the great help they are rendering to Indians in connection with the Movement and with further support, which we have no doubt will be forthcoming, we shall be able to attain our goal of independence in the immediate future.

35

Minutes of the Meeting between General Mohan Singh and Colonal Iwakuro for Resolving the Confidence Crisis between Indian National Army and Japanese Authorities on the one hand and between Indian National Army and Indian Independence League on the other[1]

2 December, 1942

Colonal Iwakuro was not in his usual happy and cheerful mood. He looked depressed. He said "I am very sorry that mutual dissatisfaction and suspicion has started and we have started thinking in these terms. I am sorry that your side has taken this attitude. I never said this a Japanese puppet movement on the contrary I have the firm conviction that this is entirely an Indian show and we are trying our utmost to help and support this glorious attempt. But I cannot understand why you have taken this drastic step. After very thoughtful deliveration we have come to this conclusion that it is of no use to continue this movement in the present prevailing atmosphere. It is much better to stop it. I entirely leave it to you to do anything you think fit and those of you who don't think it advisable to continue any further they can go back to their previous tages, i.e., the prisoners of war. Do as you please we want's impede in any way. It is very tragic that my genuine efforts have gone in vain. I am feeling very lonely and depressed. I feel I have been betrayed by my own beloved son. Visualising the whole thing I clearly see the fundamental differences of two different character.

I am very sorry that this sort of stage has arisen. This movement was a child of my dreams. All my energies were devoted day and night to bring about the successful realization of those dreams. I never started

1. Indian Independence League Papers. F. No. 45/3.

it to be ended in such a abrupt manner. It will be a tragedy from my view point if this mightly fabric fails before fulfilling the cause for which it was raised for. The Council of Action after careful deliberation and thoughtful consideration drafted the letter requesting a reply to the Bangkok resolutions. We also consider all possible reaction from your side and were prepared for all eventualities. The letter was discussed in detail yesterday in concurrence with you and it is extremely regrettable that we went back dissatisfied by the unaccommodating welcome given by you. The Japanese side should also be blamed for this.

Gen. On our return from Tokyo Major Fujiwara told us that Tokyo resolutions were accepted in principle but subsequently you told us the contrary and latter on as regards Bangkok resolutions you gave us some vague promises which never materialized. Naturally we had to become suspicious. Now we thought that time has come when we should exactly know where we stand.

Col. after Bangkok resolutions I tried my best to get the formal reply for you but unfortunately there were so many constitutional difficulties that it was impossible to get the requested reply, but at the same time our Govt. decided to give the practical shape to the various resolutions.

At such a critical moment, when Mahatma Gandhi is engaged in life and death struggle for the emancipation of India from the British yoke it is regrettable that this suspicious atmosphere has started. You are ignoring the practical application and just worrying for a mere scrap of paper.

Gen. We Indians are very accommodating. We always trust people and this has been our national character and in fact our present plight is the direct outcome of our placing too much trust in the British at one time or another. We have been repeatedly betrayed and cheated and that's why we have developed a suspicious nature. As individual's we are prepared to trust you and several other Japanese friends but our national trust is a very sacred trust and much above mere individual trusts and I am afraid we are not satisfied what we have heared or seen so far in this respect from the Japanese side.

Col. I am still trying my best to assist you in every possible way and I am sending these M.Ps to Japan with a personal message. I am also forwarding some special instructions in this matter. I have been preparing these papers for the last two months. It may be our last interview but I would like to show you my views forwarded to my government for kind consideration.

Salient Points of the Letter Forwarded

1. Japanese should fully help in satisfying the burning desire of patriotic Indians for complete independence.
2. Japan should try to bring about friendly relation between Indian and herself, i.e., the spirit of goodwill and good neighbourhood.
3. Japan should not force the Indians to join any sphere politically, economically, militarily an culturally.
4. Japan must respect the territorial integrity and full sovereignty of India.
5. All treatment should be on equal basis and under mutual understanding.
6. Japan should not aspire for new interest in India beyond already existing before the war.
7. All Indian property to be handed over to the Indian government soon after the occupation.
8. On the request of the Indian people Japan should give all technical advise and assistance.
9. Japan should not interfere in any of Indian internal affairs and all occupied territories should be immediately handed over to the Congress or Indian Independence League.
10. In case of external invasion on India's request, Japan should give all possible help. Defence of India should entirely be left in the hands of the I.N.A.

While the British are still there, the Japanese will fight the British and utilise the aerodromes, landing grounds and other strategical points.

I have been working day and night writing so many training pamphlets for the I.N.A. and it is a great tragedy to stop this now at this stage. I feel that you have let me down and betrayed.

Gen. It is none of my business to advise the Japanese Govt. but I must say Japan will make a great blunder if she invade India before absolutely clarifying her status and position. India has been fighting the British for the last 150 years with all possible means and methods at her disposal and she will continue to fight Japan till she has attained her one and one objective, i.e., complete independence. India has seen many invaders and history proves that all of them met their final end on the same side. Today India is politically awakened and she can never be subjugated. A free, strong and friendly India not only be a great asset to Japan but will also contribute for the peace, property and deliverance of

Japan but will also contribute for the peace, property and deliverance of mankind.

Col. I love my country as you love yours and quite agree with you. It is equally bad for my country to invade India with any selfish intentions. In Manchuria we have been quite true to our declarations, because we declare all five races should equally benefit by the new order. Prince Konoi's promises are still carried to the last word. (China)

Gen. Before we started this movement we knew your policy in Manchuria and China. We have been seen your ways in Malaya and heard about Burma and this is the reason that we are very careful about our commitments. Our only hope was that Japan will be wise enough to adopt a different policy in different territories. We cannot tolerate these types of government in our country, so before taking any further step we want definite assurances.

Col. I quite agree with you, India's question is a separate question and I am trying my best to request the Premier to issue a clear and formal declaration. Please understand the Japanese viewpoint; we are absolutely ready to cooperate wholeheartedly.

Gen. I will talk the whole matter with my colleague in the light of what you told me just now. Till then I am not in a position to say anything on this major issue.

Col. This Burma incident has caused great misunderstanding which was all enacted in heart tamper. Mr. Yutani is a strong supporter of Indian cause and he fully understands Indian problems and Indian character.

Gen. I beg to differ. Col. Kitabe is a soldier and head of Iwakuru Kikan in Burma and he should not have been influenced by Mr. Yutani. In fact Mr. Yutani himself said and more over I don't agree that Mr. Yutani has the foggiest idea about Indian character and Indian problems. He might have come across some labour and cooly classes of Indians or he might have associated with some rich ignorant Indians. It is only today that I have received a letter from Mr. Prashad written by Mr. Yutani ordering him to dismiss two gentlemen working in his office and employ some one else. I don't think you will appreciate if this thing is done to you by some one and yet you say that he is very pro-Indian and helping the Indian cause. I would like to point out that Mr. Deshpande who has been brought up, educated and married in Japan and who was a staunch supporter and admirer of Japanese people is at all satisfy with the whole show after working for the last few months. He is trying his utmost to get away from this movement as soon as circumstances will permit him to leave this force.

36

Minutes of the meeting between General Mohan Singh and Major Fujiwara Regarding the Arrest of N.S. Gill; Refers to Mohan Singh's Requests to Japanese Authorities to Meet Gill to Find out about the Desertion of M.S. Dhillon and other Persons of Indian National Army on Burma Front[1]

8 December, 1942

Major Fujiwara started with apologies that such an incident has happened at this time and he hoped that the G.O.C. has not taken seriously. He asked G.O.C. whether he could suspect Col. Gill G.O.C.'s replied–"Nothing doing–Not at all". He went on to explain the charges against Col. Gill. Col. Gill has been watched right from the beginning and that they were sure that he had a complete network of British spies in and out of the I.N.A. That he during March selected 6 trusted officers to convey to the British Govt. India what was happening in the Far East. Out of the 6, 2, had succeeded in crossing the border and the remainder about Col. Gill's activities. In Tokyo Major Fujiwara was warned not to trust Col. Gill by some of the Indians there to whom Col. Gill had told telephone some one that this movement was nothing and that he was definitely pro-British. However Col. Gill played so well with me (Major Fujiwara) that he had no suspicion whatsoever that Col. Gill was a British espionage agent. Col. Gill requested Major Fujiwara to make him the C-in-C and G.O.C. (Mohan Singh) was nothing. Major Fujiwara said he had already given his word and he will never divert but he said that I promised him that you will be a useful partner.

During this time Mr. Senda interrupted now and then on other matters like :–

1. Indian Independence League Papers. F. No. 45/3 .

1. Do not doubt the Japanese sincerity.
2. There were technical difficulties re-clarification.
3. The announcement was not made because of strategic reasons.
4. The Japanese C-in-C has already sent circular to the Japanese to treat Indians as comrades in arms, etc. You have a sincere and open heart and now must not crush this movement.

To these G.O.C. replied suitably in this manner :–

1. From the very beginning I came and started these activities with complete sincerity.
2. After the Bangkok Conference the formation of the I.N.A. was done in full trust.
3. Now I am honour bound to safeguard the interest of the men under me so that they may not be exploited and for this and several other reasons have taken this step.
4. Individuals do not matter and I am prepared to take all the blame.

To these Mr. Senda nodded and agreed that whatever you (G.O.C.) have done you have done in full sincerity and he wished that as soon as the matter is clarified the movement will flourish.

After this the G.O.C. began :–

What has happened is not unexpected by our side.

We were ready for this show. Re: Col. Gill I cannot believe and will not that he is working for the British. From my close association and the work he has done for me I have not the slightest doubt.

This incident can be looked at by a disinterested person in the following lights :–

(a) That I have called Col. Gill from Burma and have handed him over to the Japanese for my own personal.
(b) That you believe that the present deadlock has been created by Col. Gill and to get rid of him you taken him away.
(c) To separate him from me during this juncture.

Under all these circumstances my position become awkward. As I have told you that not one Gill or one Mohan or one Bose but Hundreds may have to be sacrificed to achieve our goal. I do not matter. It will be the greatest blot on me not to take the responsibility. I have done all these and I stand by all my actions. May I ask a few questions Re: Gill again :–

Q. Can I meet the 6 parachutist that landed in Pegu?

A. Impossible. They are under the charge of M.P.

Q. Can I meet the Officers despatched by Col. Gill?

A. I think it is not possible.

Q. Can you name these officers?

A. Yes, I shall give you detailed news after I get from the M.P.

Q. Can I see Col. Gill now and then?

A. As the M.P. have full powers it is not possible but after the investigation I think it will be possible.

Q. Can you tell me the approximate dates of the arrest of the Officers and when they crossed the border?

A. During Aug. but I am not certain.

The G.O.C. then said that "this step taken in my view by the Japanese was entirely wrong and it does not good to the Japanese. It was a wrong move yet it was expected by me. The proper thing would have been that you should have sounded me about this earlier and that would not have been so bad. All the san.. I am of the opinion that you have taken him away, for no reasons except stated before. I only regret that you are entirely wrongly informed and your move is wrong. It was I who brought about his deadlock, sincerely tool, and I should have been arrested.

I have to fight hard against my conscious and imagination to believe Major Fujiwara's story about Gill, because in 1939 after the outbreak of the European War certain officers (Sikhs) planned to capture Punjab. I was in it. We decided to put up the claim of Maharaja of Patiala and one senior officer amongst us took the scheme to Col. Gill at Army Headquarters at Simla. Col. Gill kept that secret to this date. He advised us to wait as it was not the proper time. There can be no other better proofs of his sincerity towards India. Then Mr. Senda remarked that as Col. Gill's way of living was completely Anglicised his personal opinion is that he might like the British because he had achieved highest possible post for an Indian in the Army. He was of the opinion that quite unknowing Gill was pro-British.

To this G.O.C. said, I don't agree with you because most of us army officers lived like and amongst the British yet we could never change hearts. Whatever it is. Gill is or never was pro-British. Some of us might have liked their ways but not their rule.

Major Fujiwara then requested the G.O.C. to call on Col. Iwakuro and inform him about our meeting.

G.O.C. replied that he cannot do this till he can make up his mind.

away, for no reasons except stated before. I only regret that you are entirely wrongly informed and your move is wrong. It was I who brought about his deadlock, sincerely tool, and I should have been arrested.

I have to fight hard against my conscious and imagination to believe Major Fujiwara's story about Gill, because in 1939 after the outbreak of the European War certain officers (Sikhs) planned to capture Punjab. I was in it. We decided to put up the claim of Maharaja of Patiala and one senior officer amongst us took the scheme to Col. Gill at Army Headquarters at Simla. Col. Gill kept that secret to this date. He advised us to wait as it was not the proper time. There can be no other better proofs of his sincerity towards India. Then Mr. Senda remarked that as Col. Gill's way of living was completely Anglicised his personal opinion is that he might like the British because he had achieved highest possible post for an Indian in the Army. He was of the opinion that quite unknowing Gill was pro-British.

To this G.O.C. said, I don't agree with you because most of us army officers lived like and amongst the British yet we could never change hearts. Whatever it is. Gill is or never was pro-British. Some of us might have liked their ways but not their rule.

Major Fujiwara then requested the G.O.C. to call on Col. Iwakuro and inform him about our meeting.

G.O.C. replied that he cannot do this till he can make up his mind.

37

Statement by Rash Behari Bose, President Council of Action Regarding the Crisis between Indian National Army and Indian Independence League; Requests Indians in East Asia to Continue Struggle for Indian Independence[1]

10 December, 1942

My colleagues of the Council of Action have resigned. The Constitution to that extent has broken down and, on behalf of the Indians, in East Asia, I, as President, have decided to carry on, pending the election of other members which can be done according to our Constitution only by the members of the Committee of Representatives from the various territories of the East Asia. In exercising all the powers and duties of the Council of Action, which consequent on the resignation of my colleagues, have vested in me, I believe I am interpreting the Constitution of our Movement in the most politically sound way and thus respecting the mandate of the Indians of East Asia given to me at the Conference held at Bangkok in June this year. I have, from the 9th of December onwards, taken control of the Movement and I once again pledge to serve the cause of Indian Independence without fear and without favour, loyally and conscientiously and to the utmost of my ability. I shall endeavour my very best to interpret the conscience of our people, and give effect to their wishes and dictates. I shall not, as far as humanly possible, allow anything, however powerful it may be, to come between us and our objective, namely the absolute Independence of India, free from any foreign control domination, interference or even influence of any nature. In taking over control, I know and fully believe, that what I have done—to save the Movement for Indian Independence from collapse—will meet with the approval of my countrymen wherever they may be.

---

1. I.I.L Papers F. No. 45/3.

As with many of my countrymen, the cause of Indian Independence has always been nearest to my heart. For that I had been striving my utmost to pave the way for the liberation of our Motherland. It was not only liberation from the British yoke that I wanted, but liberation from any yoke whatsoever. There was a time when even the people of Nippon, among whom I lived, viewed the question of Indian Independence with indifference. But I strove on, and today I believe that we have succeeded in securing their sympathy and support an—international asset of no mean importance for any nation to have at the present juncture and for the future. We have secured the sympathy of other nations as well. It would have broken my heart if at this moment I had let this Movement die because some of my colleagues took it into their heads that unless on every point they had their way they could not go on. On the other hand, I believe, that if there are difficulties in the Movement, they can and shall be rectified. If there are doubts and fears, they can and will be cleared. If there be even obstruction in our path, it is my firm conviction that those should be removed and the way made clear for achieving our object, the much-longed-for and long awaited Independence of Hindustan. The co-operation or otherwise of any Nation, however, valuable it may, be, is not a rock on which the ship of Indian Independence should founder. We shall fight our battles with such help if possible, but without it if necessary.

The Indian Independence Movement was, as is well known, being carried on even prior to the War. But the declaration of War and of the Japanese attitude towards Indian Independence outlined in the statement of His Excellency Premier General Tojo made it possible to work this Movement in the various committees in the East Asia openly and without hindrance. The Movement was started even prior to the Bangkok Conference. We have been carrying it on now for nearly a year. At Bangkok we were given by the delegates assembled there a definite mandate to carry it on, and as a result of that mandate more organisations, both civil and military, were established. We were making progress. Very recently my colleagues felt that some further clarification of our position was necessary for us to work the Movement. With that view I was in complete accord. Where some of us differed was in the contention that without such clarification–and that forthwith–the Movement could not and ought not to proceed. Thus arose a deadlock. In my negotiations for clarification which started immediately on our deciding in the third week of last month to secure such clarification, I found that some time was necessary to obtain results. I therefore advised the Council that we should give a little time, that having carried on the Movement all these months, it would not cause much harm, danger or hardship by carrying it on for a few weeks more in the same manner as we had been doing, and thet if at the end of our negotiations, we could not get satisfactory arrangements made, we were entitled to consider and change out policy if necessary. It required a little patience and a good deal of perserence. I felt happy when after discussions amongst ourselves, on the 4th of December, It was agreed that matters should be left for further negotiations and for report by the end of next month. On the 5th of December, however, for no apparent reason, I was informed that some of my colleagues again changed their minds and the decision arried at on the previous day was not to be acted upon. It was them that I realised there was more in the Move than what appeared on the surface. Immediately on such realisation I began my fight against the Move, against the creation of a deadlock, against the break up of our Movement and disruption of our work. I pleaded with my colleagues not to resign and precipitate crisis and a deadlock which would result in hardship, misunderstanding and unhappiness, and may ultimately damage our cause. I assured them that I was as jealous of our rights as they were. My stay in a foreign country has not made me any the less a patriot than other sons of India, but has only intensified my attachment and affection to my Motherland.

My colleagues resigned on the 8th of December, I have given deep consideration to their letters of resignation. I am of the view that they should not have resigned without consulting the representatives from the various countries in East Asia. I am of opinion also that it was not necessary for them to have resigned at all, as some of them appeared to have done, for the solution of the matters raised by them. But they are their own best judges and so I have accepted their resignations with regret. Since I am confident that the Movement can be carried on for India's and India's benefit only, and all outstanding questions solved to our satisfaction, I have taken upon myself to continue the Movement with the support and co-operation of the Indians in East Asia. While on the one hand I shall be carrying on with our work, I shall, on the other hand, also spare no pains to negotiate and secure for the Movement every facility and support for which my colleagues and I have all the while been asking. At the earliest opportunity I shall be reporting to my countrymen, the progress that I shall be making. In the meantime the work will go on, and name on the civil side or the military side of the Movement need entertain the slightest fear. There shall be as little upsets as possible. The Movement shall be carried on as heretobefore. I shall endeavour to put into it as we go along even deeper enthusiasm and more vigorous activity. I must assure every branch of the League and also the Indian National Army that my taking over on myself the rights, duties and responsibilities of the Council of Action need not in any manner mean changes in the Constitution, Organisation or development, of the civil and military Institutions that we have endeavoured to create, nurse and nurture during the last few months. I guarantee to them that I shall not be a party to any act that will jeopardise their interests or the interests of our Motherland. These interests have always formed my sole objective in the work that I have undertaken to myself

I know I have the trust and confidence of my brothers and sisters in the arduous work ahead. If my opponents call me a puppet, let them do so. But let me assure them, that they are sinning against a man whose only end and aim in life is to see his country free, absolutely free and Independent, who is as proud of his birthright as any Indian alive, and who has staked his all and who will stake the last drop of his blood in upholding the honour and integrity of Hindustan. I seek nothing from life except the success of our mission. If once it is accomplished I shall retire into seclusion in some nook or corner of our beautiful Homeland. The full and complete Independence of Hindustan is our objective and let no differences, personal or otherwise, cloud or obstruct the issue. I appeal to my countrymen, to continue to render to me and to this Movement their generous support and co-operation in abundant measure, without which nothing can be accomplished, but with which, I have complete confidence, we shall carry on our fight to its successful termination–the attainment of India's Independence.

38

General Mohan Singh to Rash Behari Bose challenging his Statement; Expresses his Unwillingness to Cooperate with the Japanese under the Present Circumstances[1]

13 December, 1942

I am in receipt of your letter of the 12th instant, I maintain that with the resignation of the four members of the Council of Action you have no authority to assume any of the powers you claim in your letter.

In the preliminary conference held at Tokyo and again at the Conference at Bangkok we were most anxious that no one individual should have dictatorial powers. We frustrated all attempts in this direction. The outcome of these conferences was the creation of a Council of Action and the limiting of the powers of the President to only giving effect to its decisions, you are now striving to invoke the constitution to do the very mischief that we took so many precautions to avoid.

We are all faced with a grave situation. All the members of the Council of Action save you have resigned. Rule 12 of the constitution provides how the vacancies of the Council of Action should be filled up, and until such vacancies are filled up in the manner stated therein you cannot arbitrarily assume all the powers and functions of the Council of Action. You may be the sole surviving member but you cannot act for the whole Council specially in view of Rule 19 of the constitution which lays down "the Council of Action shall have collective responsibility. If you do, you do it at your own risk.

It is apparent from your correspondence that you are not only totally ignorant of anything pertaining to an army but have some foolish and misguided notions about it. Let me put down a few facts concerning the Indian National Army which may help to clear your mind.

(a) The members of the Indian National Army are pledged to me and

1. I.I.L. Papers; F. No. 45/3,

me alone by name and I am pledged to safeguard the honour and dignity of the I.N.A. We form one indivisible whole. It was raised and trained for an honourable cause; that of securing the unfettered independence of India and not to satisfy the passing whims and fancies of any particulars individual.

(b) This army will only be part of any movement if it is convinced that that movement is conducted in the interests of India. It has been found necessary under the circumstances in which the army was raised and trained to depart from normal practice and keep the officers informed of the trend of political events. They are fully aware of the position you have played and the manner in which you have played it. There is nothing but disgust and contempt for you. In fight any person or persons for the attainment of its goal.

The events of the last few weeks, however, have convinced us that, under the existing circumstances, we cannot usefully serve our motherland through the Independence League in East Asia and we have accordingly thought it fit to sever our connection with it.

I have had the opportunity to come across the false and malicious reports including your statement issued on the 10th instant "To the Indian patriots of East Asia" concerning our resignations. They constitute a deliberate attempt to misinform and mislead the public as to the true facts. The varsions given are all of your own manufacture and one-sided. I am most anxious that the public should be acquionted with the true facts in order to ensure that their patriotism should not be exploited by unscrupulous people wishing to serve their own selfish ends.

I therefore challenge you to face the public at a meeting at which I shall take the opportunity to present the facts to them and let them decide the correct standpoint for themselves. If you do not call such a meeting forthwith I will be compelled to issue a statement placing all the facts before the public.

The above letter has not been written to contest or disprove the position you hold for yourself in your imagination. You to me have only been the sole surviving member of a defunct Council of Action since the resignation of the others. It is merely written as a courtesy and to avoid future unnecessary instructions by you to the Army. Needless to say that if you still persist in writing anything it will not be answered.

---

2. The text of the pledge was "I will be an unconditional volunteer for the Indian National Army under General Mohan Singh, which will fight for the liberation of India".

39

Secret Orders of Mohan Singh for Dissolution of Indian National Army in the Event of his Arrest by Japanese Military Authorities[1]

21 December, 1942

The Indian National Army will be dissolved shortly. It is with deep regret and great reluctance that this decision has been arrived at. Circumstances have arisen under which it is impossible for the Indian National Army to forge ahead to achieve its goal, i.e., the complete Independence of India without any foreign control, influence or interference.

I thank all ranks of the Indian National Army for their loyal and enthusiastic support in this great undertaking. Though we have not been able to achieve our final object, the movement has not been in vain. It has inculcated in us a true national spirit. It has brought a degree of unity among us unknown in the past, and it has shown to us and to the world at large what we are capable of, if only we are left to ourselves.

All the members of the Indian National Army are welded into a patriotic group. We were and are prepared for supreme sacrifices. It is up to everyone to ensure that those sacrifices are directed in one and only one direction–the achievement of our goal of independence. Let us never forget that we are not concerned with ourselves alone. We have at stake that great and beautiful land of ours with its 400 millions—our brothers and sisters. To her freedom we are wedded. I, therefore, appeal to you all to continue demonstrating that solidarity that you have so admirably manifested before. I know you will now and always continue to do so. Remember our strength is in our unity and our life is for our country.

1. I.I.L. Papers; File no. 45/3, This special order was to come into effect as soon as General Mohan Singh was separated from the I.N.A.

A confirmatory order will be sent out as soon as arrangements, with the Nipponese are complete. In the event of my being separated from you before such an order is issued, the dissolution will take place automatically and immediately. Also at the same time, the resignation of all members of the Indian National Army and their release from all obligations and undertakings to me and the Indian National Army will be taken for granted.

India First and India Last.

Long Live India.

40

Statement by Rash Behari Bose Supporting Japanese Policy and Condemning Mohan Singh for his Non-cooperation; gives Details about the Crisis between the Indian Independence League and the Indian National Army; Defends Japanese Policy[1]

27 December, 1942

It has been my desire for sometime to clear the existing misunderstanding between the Indian National Army and the Indian Independence League, but unfortunately, owing to the extremely heavy pressure of work I have not been able to express my views in public though I did manage to talk to the military officers and some civilian officials of the League. Later I wish to speak before a mass meeting on the whole issue but for the present, wish to circulate this statement for your immediate information.

It is a known fact that our Motherland has been exploited and looted by the British for the last two centuries and during the period thousands of our patriots and leaders have sacrificed their lives for the emancipation of Hindustan. Even today thousands of our brethren in India are being murdered daily. This is the reason that not only in India, but all over the world every Indian is clamouring for the freedom of India. Remember the words of our leader Mahatma Ji "Do or Die."

It is about thirty years ago that I threw a bomb at the Viceroy and as I was an active member of the Lahore—Delhi and Benares conspiracies, I had to leave my country and to seek foreign help. With the aid of Germany I was able to send home two ship loads of arms and ammunition but unfortunately they were confiscated before reaching India. What was

1. F. No. 311/I.N.A. Papers. The statement was published by the I.I.L. Headquarters, Singapore under the litle "Our struggle" by Rash Behari Bose and was widely distributed amongst the members.

the motive behind this all? Freedom of my country, which is very dear to me. I feel confident that everyone of you have the same love for the freedom of our fair land if not more. As for me I have forsaken everything–life, wealth, relatives and all other things which were dear to me for the sake of our country. The British offered thousands of rupees as a reward for my head. They succeeded in persuading the Japanese Government, through their ambassador to hand me over to them, and I was ordered by the Japanese Government to leave Japan within five days, but fortunately some of my Japanese friends concealed me in their house and there I lived in obsecurity for seven years. Had the British been successful in taking me back to India I would have been killed long ago. That is why I have great belief in the Almighty God who has helped me and guided me all through these pertious years and I hope He will not forsake me in this sacred work, which you have placed on my shoulders by electing me as the President of the Council of Action at the Bangkok Conference. I shall see that our mission does not fail, and the trust put in me faithfully carried out.

Comrades: Let me tell you that we in the Far East shall soon join hands with our brethren at home and shall create such a revolution in India that we will achieve our most cherished purpose—complete freedom of India. He reads to die as free men rather than to live as slaves. The time has passed for India to stay under a foreign power. India must be free during this struggle. India would have been free long ago if we had been in possession of arms and ammunition. History tells us that many nations have fought their battles with foreign help. In our struggle for Independence, the more the Congress fought with non-violence methods the more brutal became the methods of the British. For this reason I worked in Japan with a view to asking for help when the occasion arises. I am glad to tell you that my work and labour of last thirty years has borne fruit.

On the outbreak of the Greater East Asia War I interviewed the minister of Home Affairs and other important officials of various departments, as well as members of the General staff in our struggle for freedom and I was promised such support and cooperation in our struggle for freedom and I was promised such support I can assure that in Japan you will find a true and sympathising friend. She has very clear intention about the independence of India. The help she is offering to the Indians is not because she wants to dominate India but because the enemies of India are also her enemies, and, therefore, cooperation and unity between the two peoples is essential. I can tell you that Japan will not rest until the last soldier of Anglo-Saxon race is removed from India, she is determined to destroy British-American influence in Asia. So why should we not grasp this God send opportunity and fight for the complete freedom of India?

Before I go any further I want to say very clearly that the Indian Independence Movement is ours and ours alone which has been specifically formed to fight for the independence of India. Remember this Movement is neither of the Japanese people nor of their Government. They have nothing whatsoever to do with it except that they have offered all their help for the defeat of the common foe, for which we are indeed grateful. But suppose a time were to come when we begin to receive not sufficient help or say nothing at all, are we to give up our Movement? The answer is No. The Movement must continue until our country is completely free from any kind of foreign domination or influence. It is our Movement, our struggle and we alone shall have to decide its fate. It is therefore imperative for every true son of India who loves freedom to join this Movement with heart and soul and move forward with complete determination until our independence is achieved. You will have to face several drawbacks, discouragements difficulties and obstructions in the attempt but you should not be disheartened as you have shouldered a most sacred cause and have become the custodians of four hundred millions of India. You should therefore see that this Movement is not used by anyone for any other purpose, except the gaining of Indian Independence. It is equally the duty of every one of us to be ready to crush any opposition or die in the attempt. Remember that at the declaration of the Greater East Asia War this Movement was at full swing in Japan, Shanghai, Canton and Bangkok. The Indian Independence League was established by me in Japan in 1924. As I was perfectly aware of the position of Indians during and after the war I had a clear understanding with the Japanese Government on this matter and it was through this process that Major Fujiwara asked for the cooperation of Indian patriots and our late beloved Sardar Pritam Singh took a major part in the pageant of the Malai campaign. Captain Mohan Singh joined hands with Sardar Pritam Singh on 12th December, 1941, with a party of a few persons. Sardar Pritam Singh being a civilian and Major Fujiwara being a Japanese Officer, did not know very much about the Indian soldiers and officers so the administration and command of Indian military personnel was given over to Capt. Mohan Singh. It was desired to teach to them nationalism, patriotism and love for freedom and to prepare them for struggle for the freedom of India, I realised that the organisation of the Independence Movement in East Asia was not merely my affair but the concern of my countrymen residing there. It was for this reason that arranged for the Conference of some of the leaders in East Asia including military officers, which was held at Tokyo in March last year. The fundamental principles of this Movement were laid down at that Conference. Subsequently at the Bangkok Conference I received the mandate of our countrymen in East Asia to carry on this Movement in the best way possible. Nobody can ever doubt that considerable progress has been made in the great work we have undertaken and in which Capt. Mohan Singh played a major part. There are great possibilities of our succeeding at attaining our objective. The Bangkok Conference was held in June last year and certain resolutions were passed for the guidance and working of the Movement. In accordance with these resolutions a Council of Action was elected as the Supreme Executive Body of the Movement.

Prior to election, Mr. Mohan Singh in his speech made statements which now appear to be misrepresentation of facts because he solemnly gave us to understand that the majority of the Indian Army personnel were prepared to join this Movement without any threat or force and that they had acclaimed him as their military leader. I was horrified at a later date to learn of the atrocities meted out to officers and men of the Indian Army for which the blame naturally falls on Capt. Mohan Singh. Many of our poor brethren were shot while many were tortured, humiliated or sent to concentration camp and thus by sheer threat and violence he demoralised the majority of officers and men and compelled them to become volunteers, which is against our principle. I for one will be the last man to see my countrymen shot in cold blood. This is what we are fighting for against the British and I personally cannot afford to see Indians tortured in this manner.

In accordance with the resolutions of the Bangkok Conference Indian National Army is a part of the Indian Independence League and every officer and man of the I.N.A. is a member of the Indian Independence League and owes allegiance to the League. It must be understood that an army is an army of a country and not of an individual so it was wrong of I.N.A. personal to give allegiance to an individual without raising an objection. I was under the impression that the whole I.N.A. was well aware of resolution because an Officer was purposely sent down as a representative of Mr. Mohan Singh to explain in details the resolutions to Army which I understand he did from camp to camp. Not only that I am further given to understand that on return of Mr. Mohan Singh a few conferences were held at his bungalow and the position was clarified to the officers who later join the I.N.A.

I however was being informed of the situation in Syonan and I felt it desirable to hold a meeting of the Council of Action in Bangkok but unfortunately the members could not come for some reason or the other, and under the circumstances I was forced to come to Syonan for discussion.

There was however, at any moment, any divergence of opinion on the broad principles along which this Movement should continue, nor, were there any difference of opinion as to the necessity of obtaining sufficient assurances from the Imperial Government of Japan regarding their acceptance of the basic principles enunciated at the Bangkok Conference. The reply to the Bangkok resolutions which was delivered to us dated the 10th July was not so satisfactory. I was in agreement with my colleagues that a further clarification of the Imperial Government's attitude towards the resolutions adopted at the Bangkok Conference was desirable. On 5th of September 1942, a letter was addressed to Colonel Iwakuro requesting that the Imperial Government should give us a more specific reply to the Bangkok Resolutions. On receipt of this letter, Col. Iwakuro intimated to me that such a request to the Imperial Government might be misconstrued and lead to a good deal of misunderstanding and suggested that the letter should be withdrawn. An emergency meeting of the Council of Action was held on 7th September at which all members were present except Mr. Raghavan. The meeting decided to withdraw the letter which was done accordingly.

This matter again came up for a good deal of discussion in the meetings of the Council of Action during the latter part of November. The necessity for requesting a further clarification of the Imperial Government's attitude on these important issues was found essential. We, therefore, formulated our proposals and submitted them in Col. Iwakuro for transmission to the Imperial Government of Japan, and at a joint conference we explained to Colonel Iwakuro the necessity of giving us more formal assurances than we had had up till then. Although the discussion with Col. Iwakuro did not give us full satisfaction, I pleaded with my colleagues in the Council of Action that they should give me time to enable me to take up these important issues with the Imperial Government of Tokyo. On the 20th of November, the Council of Action had already decided that my colleague, Sri N. Raghavan, and I should visit Tokyo if need be and take up these important matters directly with the Tokyo Government.

In the latter part of November, it came to light that Mr. Mohan Singh as G.O.C. of the I.N.A. had arranged with the Iwakuro Kikan for the transport of some I.N.A. troops to Burma for purposes of training. An advance party was sent by the G.O.C. to Rangoon without the consent of the Council of Action. Naturally the Council of Action wished to know about the move to greater detail and was not prepared to sanction movement of troops without its knowledge. During the discussions in the Council of Action, Mr. Mohan Singh, for the first time since the Bangkok Conference placed before the Council the state of affairs existing in the Army. It was then that the Council of Action, was in a position to realise that if the Indian National Army was to become a strong and efficient fighting force for the purpose of achievement of our freedom, a radical change in the existing organisation was absolutely necessary. It is perhaps essential to state here the reasons why I, as President, Council of Action, left all questions relating to the Indian National Army in the hands of Mr. Mohan Singh. I was of the opinion before these facts became known to us that it would be better to entrust the organisation of the I.N.A. in the hands of our G.O.C. and to give him that confidence which he said, was essential for him to carry on the great task. I therefore refrained from interfering with the work of the G.O.C. in the belief that the latter would, in turn, keep the Council completely informed of the position of the Indian National Army from time to time. There have been ample opportunities for the G.O.C. to appraise the Council during its sittings in September and October of all the difficulties which he was facing in relation to the organisation and expansion of the I.N.A. but unfortunately in these matters either no information or very meagre information was supplied to the Council of Action.

I regret to have to say that in matters connected with the I.N.A. the G.O.C. arrived at important decisions without reference to the Council of Action. In fact the Council was kept almost in darkness with regard to various important activities of the I.N.A.—a state of affairs which we tried to rectify. I thought it was vitally important that the Council of Action should immediately take control of the policy regarding the Army and all questions of major importance should be decided by the Council and not by the G.O.C. I had to write to Col. Iwakuro to that effect so that no further mistakes would be committed.

Because of all this muddle which could have been avoided Mr. Raghavan, who was all the time advocating better coordination between the Army and the Council, resigned. I asked him to withdraw his resignation as matters were now getting better. On the 4th December, at my request, the members of the Council agreed to give me time till the end of January, 1943, to enable me to obtain full and satisfactory assurances from the Japanese Government. I was glad that I was given further time to attempt at a solution of those difficult questions before my colleagues resigned.

The next morning, that is on 5th December, I was surprised, therefore, to hear from Mr. Mohan Singh, Col. Gilliani and Shri K.P. Menon that notwithstanding the previous day's decision, they were not prepared to carry on the Movement unless an assurance was immediately given that a reply to Bangkok resolutions in detail would be obtained on or before 1st January, 1943. As far as I know, there was no one in Malai capable of giving such an assurance. Moreover it was virtually an ultimatum to the Japanese Government which would have offended them. I then realised that an attempt was being made to obstruct the solving of the questions in issue in order to wreck the Movement. This I was not prepared to agree to. I was not then, and even now I am not satisfied that the Japanese Government is insincere. At all events we have not, as yet, explored all avenues open to us to find our ourselves whether the Japanese Government is prepared to help this Movement in such a manner as we desire. If we find that they are not sincere then we shall drop their help but not till then. Notwithstanding the inexplicable attitude taken up by my colleagues, I tried to negotiate with the Japanese authorities to arrive at a formula which would help us in tiding over the present crisis.

On the 6th December, a most unfortunate event happened, namely the sudden arrest of Col. Gill by the Japanese Military Policy for certain investigations. Col. Gill was taking an active part in the present crisis however on enquiry I found out that his arrest had no connection with our crisis, although it gave an impression that it was.

On the afternoon of the same day a meeting of the Council of Action was held Mr. Raghavan being absent. However, the other members said that unless their request for sending the ultimatum, on the 5th December, were acceded to immediately, it would be impossible for them to continue in this Movement. The meeting of the Council of Action was adjourned till the 10th December for further discussions on all these questions. Later in the evening, however, I received a letter of resignation signed by all three of them. I must confess that it did not cause me much surprise because I had a feeling for some time that they were not interested in attempting to secure a settlement. So I accepted all the resignations. This being the position I had no other alternative but to take over the powers and duties of the Council of Action according to our Constitution pending the election of new members which can be done only at a meeting of representatives of various territories in East Asia and of the Indian National Army.

Mr. Mohan Singh, from the very beginning, wanted to carry on his work despotically. He wanted to have a free hand in his undertakings, and as such, he could not bear the idea of being interfered with by others in his work but constitutionally he had to work under the Council of Action. In order to sweep away this restriction, he intensified his exercise of dictatorial influence over the I.N.A. and infused wrong idea into the minds of his officers and men that the army belong to him, and that he was its master.

Moreover in the last meeting of the Council of Action Mr. Mohan Singh tried to blot out the Council of Action pressing upon the Council to get an immediate clarification of a few questions from the Japanese authorities which as I have stated above was impossible because there was none in Malai who could answer on the spot. On receiving no reply, he, as well as the other two members of the Council of Action tendered their resignations the same evening without waiting to meet on the 10th December as was previously arranged. Col. Gillaini, in his capacity as an officer of the I.N.A. under Mr. Mohan Singh, had no alternative but to comply with the wishes of his superior and thus relinquished his post.

Since Mr. Mohan Singh was instrumental in the election of Mr. Mennon as a member of the Council of Action and his election was mainly due to the military votes, he was obliged to resign together with Mr. Mohan Singh.

Two of the highest military officers having resigned I wished to call the rest of the senior officers in order to acquaint them with the whole situation and inform them of my plans. So, I asked the G.O.C. to sent these officers to meet at the Sea View Hotel on 12th December. The G.O.C. however, thought it necessary to enquire in what capacity I had called that meeting and what the purpose of that meeting was. As President of the Council of Action and, as such, the Head of this Movement, I am entitled to meet any officer of the I.N.A. and the G.O.C. is not at liberty to ask for an explanation from me. However, I pointed out to him that the powers and duties of the Council of Action were vested in me as the President and the sole surviving member of the Council of Action. The G.O.C. not only ignored my directions but stated in his letter to me dated 12th December, 1942 that :-

(a) "the members of the Indian National Army are pledged to me (i.e., Capt. Mohan Singh) and me alone by name" and

(b) "under the existing circumstances, we (meaning, I presume, the Army) cannot usefully serve our Motherland through the Indian Independence League in East Asia and have accordingly though it fit to sever our connection with it."

The tone and contents of this letter came to me as a great shock. I could hardly imagine that any officer appointed G.O.C. of any army would disown the very Movement of which the army forms an integral part and claim that that army is his own private personal army. I could not for a moment believe that any officer or any man who had volunteered for service in the I.N.A. did ever imagine that he was pledge loyalty to an individual and not to the Movement which brought into existence that army.

When Mr. Mohan Singh had resigned from the membership of the Council of Action and said that he had nothing to do with this Movement he should naturally have washed his hands off the command of the I.N.A. but he did not. He waited for further three weeks, thinking that as the Council of Action does not exist, any decision reached between the Indian side and the Japanese would be between him and the Japanese Government. But his idea did not materialise because the Japanese authorities stuck to the Bangkok resolution by recognising the Council of Action as the Supreme Body of which I was the only surviving member. As a matter of fact Mr. Mohan Singh approached Col. Iwakuro with a letter stating clearly that the Indian National Army belonged to him and that he wished to dissolve it. On the other hand he informed his officers that if anything happened to him they should dissolve the army immediately.

In the face of the above facts, I had to take the most painful but the only course open to me namely the removal of General Mohan Singh from his post as G.O.C. of Indian National Army.

Before closing the facts of the case I want to give you extracts from the speeches of the Premier General H. Tojo at the various occasions concerning India and from which I hope you will be able to know the intention of the Japanese Government towards India.

1. In his address before the Diet on the fall of Singapore on 16th February 1942 the Premier General Tojo said :–

   It is a golden opportunity for India having, as it does, several thousand years of history and splendid cultural tradition, to rid herself of the ruthless despotism of British and participate in the construction of the Greater East Asia Co-prosperity sphere. Japan expects that India will restore its proper status as India for the

Indians and it will not stint herself in extending assistance to the patriotic efforts of the Indians. Should India fill too awaken to her mission forgetting her history and tradition, and continue as before to be begailed by the British cajolery and manipulation and opportunity for the renaissance of the Indian people would be for ever lost.

2. In his Message to the Imperial Diet on 12th March, 1942 the Premier said :–

   It is my firm belief that now is the time to establish India for the Indians, which has for many years been the aspiration of the 400 millions Indian people.

Great Britain has for long deceived and continued her arbitrary rule over India. What the reality of the British promise made to India in the last Great War must be still fresh. I believe, in the memory of the Indian people. Now Great Britain is trying again to deceive India with all sorts of cajolery. If the leaders of India, misled by such British cajoleries, betray the long cherished aspiration of the Indian people and thus fling away this heaven-sent opportunity, I believe there will no chance for saving India for ever and there will be no greater misfortune befalling the 400 million Indian people.

While India rise as India for the Indians to have the honour to co-operate for the establishment of the Greater East Asia Co-prosperity Sphere, or will she permanently stoop under the shackless of the Anglo-American Powers to leave her name as a slave to posterity? She is now face to face with the time, when she should liquidate her past, see the new situation correctly and make her final decision.

3. In his advice to India on 7th April, 1942 General Tojo said :–

The Imperial Forces which previously occupied Rangoon, and important base in Burma, and then took possession of the more strategic point in the Eastern Indian Ocean, the Andaman Islands, which have hitherto been a place of exile for patriots of Indian Independence, have now at last dealt severe blows to the British forces, and military establishments in India.

The grim determination of our Empire to crush the United States and Britain is thus being steadily translated into action. If India should remain as before under the military control of Britain, it would, I am afraid, be unavoidable that, in the course of our subjugation of the British forces there, India will suffer great calamities.

As it is, of course, fartherest from the thought of Japan to consider the Indian people as an enemy, Japan deeply sympathise with them who are likely to suffer the ravage of war.

What Japan's intentions are toward the Indian people was made clear in my address delivered before the Imperial Diet on March 12th (see I. above). In short, I am firmly convinced that now is the golden opportunity for the Indian people to exert their utmost efforts in order to secure India's status as it ought to be.

The British influence in India is now about to be exterminated. I wish once again to repeat at this juncture Japan's expectation that not only the leaders in India but the four hundred million people there, while avoiding unnecessary calamities which will result from their being misled by sweet flatteries of Britain, the nation destined to downfall, will take full advantage of this heaven-sent opportunity and break away from the British bonds which have so long shackled them and thus go vigorously forward to realise truly their long cherished aspiration, of "India for the Indians."

4. In his address before the Lower House of the Diet on the Progress of the War and on Economic Problems of the Greater East Asia on 28th May, 1942 the Premier General Tojo said :–

> There still remains in India a framework of British possession with various military establishments, and the military forces are being steadily increased. As long as there remain Anglo-American Military forces in India, Japan determined inflexibly to crush them thoroughly. To our regret, it is, indeed, unavoidable that in the progress of such campaign some misfortunes may befall innocent Indians. What I expect at this juncture, however, is that the Indian people will rise with an intrepid spirit, expel the Ango-American forces as well as their influence completely from India and thereby realise the independence of their Fatherland.

I must emphasise that before we can take a final and decisive step to completely stop this Movement, we have got to be satisfied beyond doubt that the Japanese Government are not sincere in their desire to assist us and that they want to use us mere fifth-columnists or puppets. It is also necessary before the final step is taken to consider the repercussions of such a step on the two and half million Indians in East Asia and 400 millions in India, a matter which seems to have escaped the attention of my three colleagues. I would have been untrue to the trust reposed in me by you all if I had allowed any wrecking of the Movement immediately and before we could even find out the attitude of Tokyo.

I have given you a true pen picture of the whole situation and I leave it to your good judgement to decide. You must always remember that this Movement and the Army do not belong to any one can and they can never be so. The foundation of this Movement was laid, years ago. Despite all opposition to the struggle it is gaining a momentum. Many die in the struggle and a greater number take their place. Many have played their part in this drama of Indian freedom and disappeared from the stage of sacrifice but the Movement continues to expand and is gradually carrying us to the ultimate goal. I may die tomorrow but one of you should be ready to take my place and when he dies there should be another to take over the responsibilities. It is the most sacred duty of every Indian to sacrifice his all for the complete independence of India and the Hindustan of tomorrow will be proud of you. If you survive in the struggle, you shall be called heroes and if you died in the attempt you shall be martyrs.

I therefore appeal to you in the name of our Motherland to set aside all petty differences, make one unit and brotherhood and move forward as one team and the freedom of our country is assured. Remember you are born only once and will die only once; whether it is on a sickbed or whether it is on the battlefield. Come forwards as men, live as men and die as men, so that the India of tomorrow can be proud of you.

The Indian National Army does not belong to me or to Mr. Mohan Singh or to any one of you, but it is the vision of four hundred millions of Indians. Remember, when it did not exist; it did not exist; but once it is formed, see that nobody can break it. It shall only break when no trace of an enslaved India is left. If you have the feeling of nationalism and want to live as a free citizen of the world then answer the call of your Motherland and join this Movement. This is your work just as much as mine so there shall be no force and threat of any kind. This is merely a service for your country. By serving your country you are serving yourself. A small party of true and patriotic men is worth more than any army of hundred thousands which may betray India at the time of her need.

Comrades, it is a God sent opportunity. Everything is in our favour. One of the world's greatest powers is prepared to help us, and even the inner voice of the heart tells me that India must be free during this struggle.

41

Statement by Iwakuro Kikan Clarifying Japanese Policy Regarding the Crisis, Arrest and Dismissal of General Mohan Singh; Reafirms Japanese Government's Policy to help Indians to Gain Independence[1]

29 December, 1942

On receiving a report from the Indian Independence League to the effect that General Mohan Singh has been dismissed today from his present position of G.O.C. of the Indian National Army becoming a mere Mr. Mohan Singh from today, the Japanese side has to recognise the action taken by the League to my great regret.

Your glorious Indian National Army has been established according to the resolutions of the Bangkok Conference as an Army belonging to the Indian Independence of India. I cannot but admire the level best with which you have been striving day and night to attain the sublime ideal for the sake of your mother country.

Mr. Mohan Singh, however, has of late had an opinion which is fundamentally different from that of the League regarding the Indian Independence Movement in East Asia, holding a serious doubt about the sincerity of Japan. He himself has declared that he has severed all his connections with the Indian Independence Movement in East Asia and arbitrarily made a proposal to me about the dissolution of the Indian National Army, under the wrong impression that it is his own private army. Thus he has reached a conclusion which is not acceptable both to the Indian Independence League and the Japanese side.

1. I.I.L. Papers; File no. 45/3; on 29 December, Mohan Singh was removed from the INA command and was taken into custody by the Japanese Military Police. He was kept at an Island in Sumatra and gave a statement after the War explaining his position. See. Appendix II.

Mr. Mohan Singh's reasons are as follows :–

1. That the Japanese reply to the resolutions of the Bangkok Conference is not itemised with the management of the properties of absentees Indians in Burma.
2. That the Japanese side has an intention of using the Indian National Army.
3. That the Japanese reply to the resolutions of the Bangkok Conference is not itemized article by article, hence unsatisfactory.
4. Japanese side has not given recognition to the Indian National Army by publicly announcing its existence.
5. That there have been several happenings of assult and insult inflicted by Japanese on the officers and men of the Indian National Army.

Out of these instances, he seems to have reached the wrong conclusion that Japan's real intention must consist in the utilisation of the National Indian Army as its 5th column with the aim of controlling India in place of Britain and therefore he further concluded that seeking the help and cooperation from the Japanese side will not be good for the I.N.A. which is loyal to India. Thus he came to the conclusion of dissolving the Indian National Army.

I feel extremely sorry about the present issue for the sake of Japan as well as India, and I would like to appeal to your good judgement by reviewing the issue from the Japanese standpoint, clarifying its real facts. First of all, I must make a strong protest, for the sake of Japan's honour, against the wrong assumption that Japan is going to control India in place of Britain. I, as a representative, of Japan, declare hereby the Japan's real intention as follow :–

1. Japan has no territorial, political, military or economic ambitions at all toward India. Any assumption, therefore that Japan is going to control India by replacing Britain is nothing but a malicious enemy propaganda of Britain and America.
2. India should be a complete independent country as India of Indians. Therefore the two nations, Indians and Japanese, will stand on an equal status as friendly nations, on her attaining independence.
3. As the Indian Independence League is an organisation of Indians themselves whose movement should be developed by keeping inseparable relations with the major current of the National Movement within India, Japan has got the slightest intention of utilising it for Japan's 5th column. However, the Indian

Independence League, being a political organisation should be carried out in such a way that they will not infringe on the sovereignty of the respective country, before its advancing into India. But, after it has advanced, it will receive no restriction or interference whatever from any country other than India.

4. The Indian National Army is an Army belonging to the Indian Independence League, and it is by no means a private army belonging to an individual and Japan has no idea that the Indian National Army will be used for any purpose other than those provided in the resolutions of the Bangkok Conference.
5. Japan's aid of establishing peace in Asia and India's aim to secure her complete independence, both is not, therefore, motivated by any selfish ambition. The Japanese wish for India's complete independence is a natural expression of the Japanese national sentiment, with which they have regarded India with respect and love for the past 2,000 years. Therefore, there is no intention on our side of demanding, at present or in future, from you any consideration whatever in exchange for our support.

Although the principles as above mentioned have several times been expressed by the Premier General Tojo in his statements and the Japan's real intention has been clearly explained, I am prepared to recommend to the Japanese Government to issue another Official statement which may be more satisfactory to you at an early opportunity.

I am, further, prepared to request the Government to formulate a concrete policy as to how to support the Indian Independence League and clearly indicate the contents of such policy.

The several instances, which have been utilized by Mr. Mohan Singh for his twisting Japan's real intentions, are no doubt regrettable matters and yet most of them were caused by the differerce in ethical ideas, customs and language between the Japanese and Indians, which will be naturally corrected and improved by the mutual understanding and sincere effort, and by no means constitute problem which is so fundamental as to destroy the friendship and confidences existing between the two nations. The creation of an unfortunate breach between Japan and India may virtually mean to you the loss of a great opportunity of attaining India's Independence and I firmly believe that such a happening will be by no means favourable to both Japan and India, which otherwise shall be friendly nation in the future. If Japan deals with the Indian question with such an attitude as mentioned above, there can be no fundamental question between the two great nations which cannot be solved, unless, of course, you are contended with being a faithful watch-dog of Britain, or are mislead by Anglo-American propaganda.

It will serve some useful purpose, I believe, to explain at this opportunity about some questions which otherwise, I am afraid, may lead Japan and India to estrangement :

1. On the Itemized reply by the Japanese Government to the Resolutions of the Bangkok Conference

Although I consider that your request for an itemized reply is reasonable. I regret to say that the Japanese Constitution does not permit the Government to issue a written reply in such a form as desired by the Indian Independence League for the reason that the same is a mere political organisation and cannot be regarded as a state. The Japanese Government, however, fully recognising the existence of the League and its movement, have issued a written reply promising general support, and instructed the Iwakuro Kikan to meet with the wishes of the Indian Independence League to the greatest possible extent. I am sure that you will readily admit that we have already done a great deal in this connection. It is my wish therefore, that you will not regard our replies as similar to the empty promises of Britain.

2. On the Public Announcement of the I.N.A.

We have been refraining from making a public announcement about the existence of the I.N.A. simply because we thought that a greater strategical effect could be gained, if it is done simultaneously with the start of the Indian campaign. However, should the Indian Independence League prefers the present political effect to the strategical one, I shall not be reluctant to make a public announcement of its existence after the settlement of the present issue.

3. On the Handling of the Indian Prisoners

We cannot agree to the proposal to put the Indian prisoners under the supervision of G.O.C. of the I.N.A. because of the rules and regulations of the Japanese Government. The manners and purposes of using the prisoners shall be solely decided by the Japanese according to the discretion of its own.

However, we have no objection to grant authority either to the I.I.L. or to the G.O.C. of the I.N.A. of inculcating anti-British independence spirit into the prisoners, as well as of selecting the members out of them for the I.N.A.

4. On the Arrest of Col. Gill

Regarding the arrest of Col. Gill there was current a rumour, I have heard, that it was a political engineering to separate him from Mr. Mohan Singh. The fact is that, while he was executing a special mission in Burma, he was connected with a case of his subordinates Major Dhillon and several others, who had jilted away to the British side and also with a case of sending a secret correspondence from Col. Gill to a senior adjutant of the British General Headquarters in New Delhi. In this connection, not only Col. Gill but several others who are connected with these cases have been also taken into custody for examination in Bangkok and Rangoon.

5. On the disarming of the I.N.A.

The Japanese army has never attempted the dissolution of the I.N.A. or its disarmament.

6. On the Future of Mr. Mohan Singh

Mr. Mohan Singh, driven by a impulsive sentiment, blinded by a narrow minded subjective idea, has made indiscretly an error this time of hampering the Indian Independence Movement and his sincere devotion to this mother country, we Japanese will regard him with honour and respect his own will as regards his future movement, as long as he refrains from any conduct that may injure the Japanese Indian relations or Indian Independence Movement.

7. On the Insult of the Officers and Men of the I.N.A.

Regarding the assault and insult inflicted by the Japanese upon the officers and men of the I.N.A. We have already made an arrangement wilh all those concerned in order to guard against such happenings with full precaution, and therefore in future the situation will be better. Should such things happen again, we shall deal with each case on its merits in good faith.

With the above I have explained the attitude of the Japanese side toward the various questions which seem to have been the cause of the present unfortunate situation.

With this statement, I believe that you have now understanding of Japan's real intentions and will remain in the I.N.A. as hitherto and work for the progress of Indian Independence movement.

Friends : I sincerely ask you for your calm and careful examination of the present issue lest you should be dependent, or you will disappoint your fellow countrymen who are courageously fighting at this movement the anti-British war in your country, India.

Premier General Hideki Tojo, replying to an inter-pellation posed by Ryo Koyama in the Budget Committee Meeting of the House Representatives this morning, reiterated the statement that the Nippon Government has no territorial ambition in India but rather, on the contrary desires to see India regain its independence as soon as possible. He said that, whatever propaganda the enemy nations may send out to countreact and discredit the oft repeated statement, it will amount to nothing before the overwhelming realities, indicating as shining examples the ever growing empire of Manchukco and the up and coming of the National Government of China at Nanking. He continued that the Nippon Government is a staunch upholder of righteousness and shall at all times abide by its promises. He asserted that Nippon had stood by its assurances given to Thailand to respect the sovereignity and territorial integrity, as a consequence of which Thailand is now fully collaborating with Nippon in the prosecution of the Greater East Asia war.

Nippon's attitude towards Burma has already been clarified, continued Premier Tojo, adding that the Philippines too has been assured independence provided it comes to realise its place in Greater East Asia to collaborate fully with the Nippon policy. Asserting that realities speak more eloquently than any malicious enemy propaganda aimed to discredit Nippon, Premier Tojo declared that India at the present juncture needs only to turn a deaf ear to enemy propaganda and concentrate its efforts in its immediate task.

He concluded saying that Nippon has no territorial ambition whatever in India.

42

British Assessment of Indian Independence Movement in East Asia; Examines its Repercussion on Indian Army and Japanese Policy Towards their Position in India[1]

30 December, 1942

The Pre-War Situation

1. In 1937 there was a Conference at Tokyo attended, among others, by Rash Behari Bose, Hari Singh alias Osman Khan, Giani Pritam Singh, and Swami Satyanand Puri. (The two lastnamed were subsequently killed in an air crash flying to Tokyo in March, 1942 together with Capt. Mohd. Akram and K.A.N. Iyer). This conference planned anti-British propaganda in Siam, Malaya, Burma and India. It gave special attention to Indian troops in the Far East and, it is thought, made a general plan for an organisation on the lines of the Indian National Army to operate in the event of war. The foundations of this fifth column work were built around Congress and Revolutionary organisations by the Japanese Intelligence.

2. Colonies of disaffected Indians existed at centres in the Far East for many years before the war. In Japan, Siam, Shanghai and Canton their activities were encouraged by Japan and, when the war with Japan commenced in December, 1941, there wee Indian fifth columnists ready to take the field, advance with Japanese troops and start subversive activities among both our Indian troops and Indians residing in Far East territories. In this connection, a report received just before Japan's entry into the war mentioned a Fifth Column School at Tsingtao in China, the recruits for which were drawn from Far Eastern countries, special attention being paid to British Indians.

3. The Indian Congress Party, Bangkok, was founded by Ram Seth

---

1. Military Department, File No. L/WS/1/1576, I.O.L.

Pande in 1937. In 1937 Giani Pritam Singh enrolled volunteers for "fifth column" activities and by 1939, 40 batches of volunteers were ready for despatch to Malaya for propaganda work.

Activities after Japan's Entry into the War

4. On the outbreak of war, or just before, Giani Pritam Singh, accompanied by Sudarshan Adha of Gorakhpur, Anrudh Shukal, Kartar Singh, Jhanda Singh, Qadur of Kedab Chand Khan and probably others opened an office at Haadye in Siam (a few miles from the Malaya frontier), where Kartar Singh and Jhanda Singh had previously resided. From here the party moved forward as the Japanese advance under the direction of Major Fujiwara of the Japanese Army. The activities of these parties were assisted by leaflets dropped from the air.

5. Where Indian disaffected organisations already existed these were, taken over, officials being changed and new branches opened as appeared desirable. In non-British territories, i.e., Siam and Shanghai, the removal of British influence allowed the anti-British element to come into the open. Where there was no suitable organisation in existence, such as in Hong Kong, one was quickly started. These local associations were represented to be a combination of social welfare societies and influential mediators between the Indians and Japanese. Gradually, but without delay, the position was reached whereby the local association became apparently all powerful so far as Indian affairs were concerned; it became the "go between" for complaints and petitions to the Japanese, and controllers of rations and privileges generally, and was thus able to discriminate against no association members. Consequently many probably joined the associations from motives of self-interest.

6. Another method of recruitment followed gangster lines. This is particularly apparent in the case of Hong Kong, where the original Indian Independence League workers, Sohail Khan (formerly a night watchman of Hong Kong and a Japanese spy), Zahoor Ahmad (a pre-war military deserter) and M.R. Malik (absconded from Hong Kong about a year before the war for "financial reasons") establish something of a reign of terror amongst Indians under presidency of D.M. Khan (formerly a clerk in government service at the Queen Mary Hospital). Rich and influential Indians were despoiled and forced to throw in their nominally with the Indian Independence League for fear of physical reprisals, or of denunciation to the Japanese authorities.

7. There were, however, many Indians in the Far East, already possessed of anti-British feelings, who welcomed Japanese assistance

against Britain and needed no incentive to join these associations. Following the conquest of Malaya a belief gained ground amongst Indians that the British would be expelled from India and this gave considerable impetes to the Indian Independence movement which spread rapidly.

Fifth Column Activity in the Field

8. As already stated the Japanese had Indian Fifth Columnists ready to take the field in conjunction with their troops, with the task of starting subversive activities amongst local Indian residents, and to influence Indian troops captured or otherwise encountered. These parties supported the Fifth Columnists already in the country and met with considerable success in their task of shaking the confidence, and thereafter undermining the loyalty of Indian troops and civilians.

The Suborning of Prisoners of War

9. Whether or not there was, before hostilities, any definite understanding between disaffected Indian officers of the Army in Malaya and Hong Kong and the Japanese (as has been suggested) there is no doubt that the latter soon had a following of traitors, real or assumed, from amongst captured Indian personnel of all ranks. Having first won over a few officers, the general technique has been for them to work on others by propaganda, Japan's role as a friend of India is stressed–her alleged aim, so far as India is concerned, being that of assisting her to attain complete independence. Probably, however, a much strong argument in winning troops over has been the promise of better conditions of living; in nearly all cases condition for Indian P.W. have been bad in the first instance but have then been steadily improved as men have been won over in accordance with the policy that all Indians who shower signs of responsiveness should be accorded greatly preferential treatment as compared with other P.W. In the case of Indian officers, one of the inducements held out has been promotion by a stop in rank, and promises of his office when the "Independence" of India had been won. There is evidence, however, that, in individual cases, no apparent inducement has been necessary to cause Indian P.W. to transfer their allegiance.

10. From the earliest reports the name of Captain Mohan Singh has been prominent. There is unconfirmed information that this officer, and others, were in touch with the Japanese before hostilities; and one report says that he telephoned to the Japanese in Alor Star asking them to come and take his party over as prisoners. Mohan Singh is a Sikh, a King's Commissioned Officer of the 1/14th Punjab Regiment, who passed out

from the Indian Military Academy in 1934, having previously had several years service in the ranks. One report suggests that he was disgruntled at not having received acting promotion in his turn; at all events there is no doubt that little persuasion was needed to win him over to the side of the Japanese; he took with him a Capt. Mohd. Akram of the same battalion who was later killed in an air crash on his way to the Tokyo Conference. Both these officers quickly rose to prominence, and on 24th June, 1942, the Berlin Radio announced "Captain Mohan Singh of East Asia fame" to be a member of the Council of Action of the Indian Independence League, and Chief of the General Staff of the Azad Hind National Army. Later reports all refer to Mohan Singh as the G.O.C. of the Indian National Army, and I.N.A. leaflets recently addressed to Indian troops on the Arakan front have been signed by him. One of his qualifications for leadership is a marked gift of eloquence.

The Tokyo and Bangkok Conferences

11. In spite of the good start made in winning over Indian nationals to the support of Japanese aspirations, things were not moving altogether smoothly. In places like Shanghai and Bangkok there were independent Indian National Associations, the leaders of which did not relish the idea of being submerged by the new Japanese controlled organisation. In the Japanese sponsored organisations also there were intrigues, peculation and fighting for position and, in consequence, no real unity of effort.

12. To remedy this state of affairs the Japanese, probably in consultation with Rash Behari Bose and other Indian renegade, decided to attempt to weld the various Indian associations into a single Indian Independence League; the Tokyo Conference of March, 1942, was accordingly summoned for this purpose, but owing to conflicts of personal ambition was not an unqualified success. It was therefore considered necessary to hold a further conference this time at Bangkok.

13. The Bangkok Conference was held from the 15th to 25th June, 1942. The conference was well stage–managed, Gandhi's portrait and Congress flags being widely displayed in imitation of the approved Nazi practice at such "party" meetings. Rash Behari Bose led off with a long speech intended to convince the delegates that Japan was India's truest and best friend; this theme continued to be stressed or possibly overstressed, by messages from Togo and Tojo, and addresses by the Japanese Ambassador. The German, and Italian Ministers harped on the same string, but somewhat naturally hinted at the claims of their respective countries to be regarded as India's sincere and disinterested

supporters. Other speakers included D.N. Das, A.M. Sahay, N. Raghavan, Capt. Mohan Singh and Lt. Col. N.S. Gill; Lt. Col. G.D. Gilani moved the vote of thanks. Mohan Singh's speech was long and emotional and is said to have deeply affected the audience.

14. The Conference resolved to sponsor a movement for achieving the complete independence of India through the Indian Independence League. It was also resolved, in furtherance of the Indian Independence League's objective, that the Indian National Army should be raised immediately from among Indian soldiers, combatant and non-combatant, and such civilians as might be recruited for that purpose. Another resolution involved the Council of Action in an undertaking to create an atmosphere in India which would lead to a revolution in the Indian Army and among the people; the creation of such an atmosphere was to be a prelude to the invasion of India. A further resolution accepted the burden of propaganda inside and outside India, by broadcasts, leaflets, lectures and any other means; these other means may in the light of later events be defined as espionage and sabotage. The Conference also laid down certain principles, amongst which were :

(a) That India should be considered as one indivisible whole.
(b) That all Indian Independence League activities should be on a national basis, not sectional, communal or religious.
(c) That the Indian Independence League's policy and programme must be in line with the aims and intentions of the Indian National Congress.
(d) That India's future constitution must be framed by representatives of the people of India.
(e) That a joint Axis policy favourable to India was accepted as advantageous, and that Japan's support was invaluable.

15. There was also a number of resolutions apparently designed to safeguard the independence of control of the League and Indian National Army and to ensure the good faith of the Japanese. These resolutions, it is interesting to note, were for the most part, not for general publication; the deduction is that (with good reason) a measure of distrust regarding Japanese intentions existed amongst the delegates, but that the Japanese, backed by Rash Behari Bose and his clique, insisted that a solid front should be presented to the outside world.

16. Constitution of the Indian Independence League.

The constitution of the League was laid down as follows :

(a) Council of Action
(b) Committee of Representatives

(c) Territorial Committees

(d) Local Branches.

17. The Council of Action elected consisted of :

President	:	Rash Behari Bose
Civil	:	N. Raghavan
		K.P.K. Menon.
Military	:	Capt. Mohan Singh
		Lt. Col. G.D. Gilani.

Its function, as laid down, is to carry out the policy and programme of the League, and to deal with any new matters which may arise; also general superintendence and control over all Indian Independence League branches and over the Indian National Army. It also had powers to create departments as necessary and powers to appoint and dismiss administrative officers.

18. The Committee of Representatives was to be elected by Territorial Committees and to include representatives selected by the Indian National Army. This committee was also to be responsible for general policy, and its decisions were to be binding on every member. Representation on this committee was to be as follows :

	I.I.L. Members
Japan and Manchoukuo	4
Philippines	2
Siam	6
Malaya	14
Burma	21
Bornoo and Colobos	1
Hong Kong, Canton and Macao	2
Other parts of China including Shanghai	2
Indo-China	1
Java	2
Sumatra	1
Andamans	1
	57 or 50
I.N.A. Members	30
Total	87 or 80

19. There is some doubt regarding the figure from Burma out the probability is that the first figure quoted is correct, for this would roughly agree with one of the Bangkok resolutions which appears to aim at keeping the Indian National Army representation at 1/3rd of the total of the Committee of Representatives.

20. Territorial Committee were to be formed by representatives elected by Local Branch Committees, for organisation and control within the territory concerned. Local Branches would be formed by meetings of local Indians above 18 years of age, subject to approval by the local territorial committee, with the provise that branches of the Indian Independence League already in existence would continued to be recognised. The Headquarters of the movement were initially at least to be located at Bangkok.

21. Particulars of known Indian Independence League branches with office bearers are not complete or authoritative, and much of the information awaits confirmation.

Strength of the Movement

22. Many reports on the strength of the Indian National Army have been received placing it as between 60,000 and 90,000 but for the Indian Independence League no estimate exists. Whether the figures quoted for the Indian National Army are correct is very doubtful; they probably represent a target strength. It is also difficult to assess at what stage a P.W. becomes a recognised member of the Indian National Army. In Rangoon Jail, for instance it appears that personnel "unlisted" into the Indian National Army, and told off the companies, etc. are still, in some cases, subjected to bad treatment to induce them to "volunteer" for the fifth column parties. It follows that many men who are nominally members of the I.N.A. are probably not prepared to carry out executive tasks in support of the enemy. This presumption is strengthened by the fact that a number of the members of intercepted I.N.A. infiltration parties do not appear to have had the intention to carry out tasks to which they were assigned.

Japanese Intelligence Organisations

23. The departments in charge of intelligence affairs are known in Japanese as Kikans and the name of the Japanese director is added as a prefix. The combination, e.g., Iwakuro Kikan, is generally used as a password for agents. Thus, early in Malaya there was the Fujiwara Kikan, Major Fujiwara being then in control of this activity. In Burma, Minami

first controlled the Kikan. Later, in June 1942, Col. Iwakuro took over general control. Iwakuro, a middle aged man who does not speak English, was Japan's representatives at the Tokyo Conference in March, 1942, and was doubtless behind the scenes at the Bangkok Conference in June. The second in-command of the Iwakuro Kikan is Lt. Col. Saito, and the staff at the H.Q. in Bangkok is believed to be over a hundred strong. Extensive records are maintained and besides intelligence the Kikan looks after Prisoners of War and Indians generally; it is the Japanese link with the Indian Independence League, of which the Indian National Army is an integral part, and is responsible for co-ordinating the subversive activities of Indians in the East.

24. There are Iwakuro Kikan branches at Singapore, Penang and Rangoon. A branch at Akyab is possibly a sub-branch under Rangoon. Each Branch is in the charge of a Japanese Lt. Col. assisted by Japanese officers and civilians, and Indians of the Indian Independence League and Indian National Army. Lt. Col. Kitabe is in charge at Rangoon and Lt. Col. Matsua at Akyab.

25. Amongst their activities the Kikans control the sending out of espionage, fifth column and "contact" parties. Contact parties were quickly formed during the Malayan Campaign from amongst P.W. with the tasks of contacting and subverting our troops, and to round up stragglers and isolated parties into the Indian National Army fold. Apparently the scheme was of sufficient success to justify sending a large party of some 50P or 60 prisoners of War under a renegado officer, Jemadar (Captain in the Indian National Army) Ram Sarup, of the 4/19th Hyderabad Regiment, from Malaya to Burma as early as February, 1942, for similar work. There are grounds for believing that these parties had some influence on the behaviour of portions of certain Indian units during the fighting in Lower and Central Burma. Subsequently also, the various Kikans, arranged the despatch of parties, military, civil and mixed, into India. A further survey will describe this activity in detail.

26. Under the auspices of the branches at Rangoon and Penang, instructional institutions have been set up. There are probably others. In Rangoon, there is the military institution accommodated at Mohan Camp (Boundary Road) and the Akram and Gilani Camps, on Kokino Road, and a civilian institution at Cushing High School, where training in espionage and fifth column work is imparted.

43

Statement of N.S. Gill given at the Time of his Arrest Explaining his Position with Regard to Desertion of M.S. Dhillon; Expresses his Faith in Sincerity of Japan; Apologises for Misunderstanding between him and Japanese[1]

31 December, 1942

1. I have had the pleasure and privilege to come into contact with Nippon since the fall of Synon[2] on 15th February this year and I have been working in close touch and cooperation with Iwakuro Kikan ever since then. In March and April, I visited Japan and attended the Tokyo Conference of Indian Independence. Later in June, I also attended the Indian Independence League Conference at Bangkok. During these conferences and on many other occasions, during the period, February to December, I made many anti-British speeches, both in public and private and in all places, Thailand, Burma and Malaya. From the very beginning, I associated myself with the Indian Independence Movement which aims at the destruction of the British. I was the one who with General Mohan Singh held the first conference of Senior Indian Officers shortly after return from Tokyo. This Conference passed strong anti-British resolutions and was attended by the prisoners of war as well as Volunteer Officers. Everyone agreed. I am of the opinion that news of my anti-British work must have reached India, as although I have high connections in India, not a single message of welfare has come for me while most of the Officers, and many sepoys have got messages. The British authorities obviously do not allow a message for me. My anti-British feelings and

---

1. I.N.A. Papers; File No. 295. This statement may be read with the record of his activities, which he sabmitted to the History of Freedom Movement when he was sarving as India's Ambssadre in Ethopia at Appendix I
2. Japanese Changed the name of Singapore to Synon.

activities should be clear from the foregoing. Indeed, I can indeed, have nothing at all to do with the British now or in the future.

2. Further more, I definitely belief India's only salvation is in the destruction the British and now is the time for it. I also believe that with Nippon's leadership, Asia must again regain its former glory and play its rightful and dominating part in the world of the future. Again, now is the time for all Asiatics to combine with Nippon and gain that goal, otherwise we may be left behind and America may gain the upper hand in the world, same as Europe had in the last 100 years. If that happens (God forbid) then Asia's lot will be (as) unfortunate as it has been while Europe was in ascendancy.

3. I therefore beg to point out that holding the views given in paragraphs 1 and 2, how can I possibly, even remotely, have anything to do with Espionage for the British. That would mean being the enemy of my own country, and enemy of Asia. Can I be such a low creature, God Forbid. I shudder to think of it even. Please do not even, for a moment, think so. No! no! I love my own country too well and hate the enemy off my country, British, again too well.

4. I was told on the morning of 8th December, that I was suspected of Espionage on behalf of British. After my ten months work with the Indian Independence League, this charge came as a great shock to me and I confess I was deeply hurt. No other charge would have heart me or degraded me so much. I was too astonished, too worried to think of it even. I could not believe it, and can hardly believe it now that such a charge has been brought against me. However, misunderstandings do often arise but they are also cleared soon.

5. Ever since I have come here (8th December morning) I have been constantly considering and reviewing all my actions, since 15th February to trace as to what event could have possibly let to even a remotest suspicion against me. During this period I can only think of my stay in Burma, which may possibly have to do anything with this. Then again, after carefully reviewing everyday's work in Burma, I can only think of one event which could have thrown even a suspicion, and that event is the actions of my 2nd officer, Mr. Dhillon. Here I would like to say that I had gone to Burma after arrangement with Col. Iwakuro to run an India contact organisation with a view to getting information from India and spreading our propaganda there. I had taken on this work after hesitation. On arrival at Rangoon, I found others doing similar kind of work. So again, I asked Captain Sakai (Colonel Iwakuro,s representative with me) that I do not want to do this work.

I only quote the last two sentences to show that had I ever thought of espionage, I would not have acted like this. Later even, I told Captain Sakai (even before Dhillon's departure) and once Colonel Iwakuro that the work was not to my liking. Again, please think, would I have acted like this, if I had any thought of espionage, for without this work I would return to Syonan and espionage would be out of question. Again all my men were selected on the qualification of being anti-British and pro-Japanese. Some of these men were well-known past revolutionalists. Could I have made such a selection if espionage had ever entered my mind?

6. Reverting to Dhillon's[3] actions, on arrival at Rangoon, I decided to open up posts at Mytkyina, Kalewa and Maymyo. I decided to send my three senior officers to these posts. Later Maymyo was abolished, and that officer stayed at Rangoon. Dhillon's post was Kalewa. My orders were for officers to establish the posts, carry out the reconnaissance supervise the first party entering India through their post, and Akyab had been captured. Immediately I thought if it was Dhillon's work, they came to the conclusion that it was not because the captured party entered Indian about the same time of not earlier, than Dhillon could have done. They entered by an entirely different route to the one decided when Dhillon left Rangoon. So I concluded that the capture was just luck. The reason for the capture was being investigated when I left. Later on, on Captain Sakai's advise we decided to send my two officers and some men to do propaganda work in the Army. It is my firm belief that to do spy work most effectively, officers must manage to rejoin the Army in India and then work hidden. So instructions were issued by me to these officers and they were given some letters to be used if they helped them to join the Army. They were to go by Kalewa so as to make sure of truth about Dhillon and if Dhillon had really gone, these lettered again may come useful. Their effort must be to get back into the Army. Captain Sakai was informed about this and he agreed if necessary hand yourself over and join the Army in India. Please note that I never gave any letter or instruction to Dhillon because he was never meant to go to India. Whereas these officers were definitely to go to India and if necessary use false pretences, including my name so as to gain their object. I made these officers sign an oath in our secret temple in Rangoon that they would be true to our country's interest. That oath is somewhere in my papers here and can be found in the luggage. I need not say that our

3. See Document No. 33.

country's interest automatically mean anti-British. No true Indian can say otherwise and this is what Mahatma Gandhi the most respected man in India says. In fact our interest in India can only be anti-British and nothing else. So you see, my intentions and Anti-British feelings in this oath as late as middle of November. These officers were definitely going to India to do anti-British work by hook or by crook and all means and instructions were issued to that end. One more factor about Dhillon's case. If the news is correct then it appears that he has taken everybody in the post with him. How if I was implicated in this, could I issue such an instruction which will straightaway bring doubt and suspicion. Obviously, Dhillon got all his men together, I don't know why, except for some selfish interest of his own and went. If it is true, he has deserted nothing else. My fault in this, has been misjudging him, and he will pay for it when we meet him in India. I had told the other two officers going to India to watch Dhillon carefully. These two officers were still in Rangoon, when I came here. So my blame in this has been misjudging Dhillon and I am sorry for this, but I am not alone in this. General Mohan Singh also trusted him and they knew each other much longer. He wanted to keep Dhillon as his military secretary, and only because I had no senior officer, I kept him, otherwise I would have sent him back.

7. The only other thing which may raise doubts in our minds possibly is my past career. I was educated at English schools and spent my time with Englishmen. Let me tell you that among this type of Indian (who has got to know the Englishmen well) that strongest anti-Britishers are found. Mr. Nehru was an English School scholar, and he intensely hates the British. Mr. S.C. Bose (now in Berlin) went to England and passed Indian Civil Service and now is the terror of the British. Many other examples, even with Indians with English wives, are like this. I have, from a long time, disliked the English because they brought slavery to India. Twice in my service of eighteen years, I was nearly turned out of the Army, and once because I fought for India's dignity, and once when I fought over Mahatma Gandhi's policy and views and this was in 1931, during the second civil disobedience movement and during his famous Salt March to Dandi.

8. To sum up therefore, I sincerely hope that the foregoing paragraphs have proved beyond the shadow of doubt that leave alone an act, I have not been even guilty of thought of espionage for the British. I never was, and never would be such untrue Indian. On the contrary I fervently hope that I will prove in these critical days, a true Indian, by taking my share of the work in the Independence movement.

My conscience and heart are so clear of any thought of espionage that I am prepared to take an oath to that effect.

Part Two

PRESENT FEELING AND FUTURE

1. My own feelings and convictions and actions are based on following two salient points :–

(i) British must be defeated in this war.

(ii) Japan must come out victorious.

I want (i) because that means Independence for India. I want (ii) because that is necessary if India is to get Independence and because it will mean Asia under Nippon's leadership playing the leading role in the world after the war. That is only right and just as Asia has practically half the population of the world. Any other course will be disastrous to India and Asia. It is on these two principles that my actions are based and will be based. Further my trip to Japan has strengthened my respect for that country.

You may well ask that if these had been my principles, why some of our actions have not entirely been consistent with that. That is what I will explain in the next paragraph which will show the principles have remained the same, but some incidents, now and then have affected our actions.

2. Now that I have time, calmly, cooly and with detachment to review everything I fully see that our chief mistake has remained suspiciousness. I remember Col. Iwakuro, at Bangkok Conference, saying that we Indians were suspicious. I have to admit that his words have proved true and this may have marred our vision. Perhaps it is true due to period of slavery under British. This is unfortunate but I do say that it has not affected our sincerity.

When I review the generous treatment given to Indians in East Asia by Nippon, it is amazing that sometimes we have failed to appreciate it. Indians have been treated extremely well. Their prestige has gone up. In Thailand it has gone up 100 per cent. Then again, see how-well Indian prisoners of war have been treated. National spirit and army have been created. Indians in East Asia have became one with no Hindoo-Muslim disunity. It is therefore surprising that we have failed to appreciate fully the attitude and generosity of Nippon. I am afraid, I, among others, have also to take this blame that I failed to understand this position fully well.

I would ever say that it was an act of ungratefulness not to appreciate the position and still be suspicious. It was most unfortunate. Also, if even I had not come from Rangoon, events will have happened the same, but I did associate with them and an surprised now how we failed to realise the rear position. Mr. Bose, our President, was wisest of all and we should have followed him implicitly and should do so now.

I will take the liberty of saying that you please on your side must also realise why this happened. We were mostly young, inexperienced in politics, or big dealings. We had got certain large powers and this may have marred our outlooks. It was due to all these combined that we showed suspiciousness when it was not justified.

I don't know what has happened since I was arrested, But I sincerely hope and pray, that everything is all right and the Independence movement and Army are as strong as ever. Our movement, and our service to India. Any damage to it will be a serious loss to us, and at this time which may never come again. As soon as I got this realisation, I wanted to come out and do my very best, but my presence here, prevented me. To sum up, therefore, I may say, that it was our foolishness and inexperience that made us think of asking for conditions. Now when I quietly think that when such powers as Britain and America failed to make conditions with Nippon, what made us think of such ridiculous ideas. All I can say is that it was not insincerity or lack of confidence.

3. I hope I have made up my position and outlook quite clear. Where my wording is not fully understood, I will be only too glad to explain. I have only to add that I have made this statement in absolute sincerity and honesty.

4. I am anxiously waiting to come out and work for the independence of India in the closest cooperation with Nippon and that I may be of good use because (a) I have quite high connections, relatives and friends in India, particularly northern India, (b) I know the Indian Army and senior Indian officers better than anybody else (c) I am well known in the extremist and other Sikh parties, perhaps better than any other Sikh in East Asia. I say this, not in any self praise, but to show that in my humble way, I could be of use to our movement and I want to do so honestly and faithfully.

I request, therefore, that a copy of this statement be sent to Colonel Iwakuro and a copy to Mr. Bose, for their consideration if there is any part which Police authorities would not like to forward, that part may be erased, and the rest sent, although I hope as complete a part as possible of my statement will be kindly forwarded to give them the complete picture, for which I should be very grateful indeed.

5. Last but not least, I must once more, express my gratitude to you and your soldiers for the kind and polite treatment given to me here. On my going from here I would like to give you a short statement to be published in my name, or anonymous, (as you consider fit). I want to say in that, about the good food, etc. given to prisoners, even now in wartime. If you would permit me, I would get that statement ready.

Signed N.S. Gill

Appendix-I

N.S. Gill's assessment of Indian National Army and Indian Independence Movement in East Asia under the Patronage of the the Japanese[1]*

Introduction

1. I write this for the consideration of the "Compilers of the History of India's Freedom Movement" for there is just a possibility that the earlier phases of the Indian National Army formed in the Far East during 1942 may not be known to the extent required for an accurate history; at least I have not seen such an account. I dare to do so because I was intimately and directly concerned with these events. My task and duty will be fulfilled if this article throws even a little new light and so helps the compilers, however little that may, in the formation of their final judgment.

2. I find it easier and quicker to write in the first person. The concerned events are over 12 years old, and I am 12 years older too. Hence I feel reasonably confident of recording the happenings impersonally to the best of my knowledge and with a view to accuracy. For the same reason I give no comments, and only state the facts.

3. This article is divided into the following three parts :–

(i) Brief outline of the events leading to the formation of the I.N.A.

(ii) I.N.A. during 1942 (Parts 'A' and 'B').

(iii) Imprisonment under the Japanese and the British.

My main purpose is to bring the contents of Part II (B) to the notice of the compilers. I also wish to add, that if due to this article or even

---

1. History of Freedom Movement Papers B 5/3.
2. The above Account was written by N.S. Gill after more than 20 years of the events. It is included here in order to show as to how Gill changed his opinion of the Japanese after the War. Gill could not forget his loyalty to the British and created a near crisis in the relations between Indian National Army and the Japanese by sending M.S. Dhillon to India. (Doc. No. 33)

otherwise the compilers wish any additional information from me or have any queries, I shall try to answer the same frankly, realizing it is for history and not for any books or novels.

Part I

BRIEF OUTLINE OF EVENTS PRECEDING THE FORMATION OF I.N.A.

4. By the middle of 1939 war had become imminent. So as a precautionary measure and before the actual declaration of the Second World War, the British despatched one brigade of Indian troops, known as Force EMU to Singapore in early August. My battalion (4/19 Hyderabad Regiment, now the Kumaon Regiment) was a part of this force. It was an Indianized battalion and among other officers of this unit were the present Commander-in-Chief General Shrinagesh and Lt. General K.S. Thimayya, all three of us being Captain then. This was the first Indian army fighting force to reach Singapore. War was declared shortly afterwards. In December 1939 as I had graduated from the Staff College, Quetta, I was posted to Army Headquarters and returned to India.

5. My stay in India was however short. In October 1940 I was promoted and posted as a Staff Officer on the newly formed 11 Indian Division (11 Ind. Div.). Our destination was Malaya. It appears the plan for the defence of Malaya was enlarged. It was decided to defend Singapore by defending the whole of Malayan mainland. Hence, as there were no troops in Malaya proper, this newly formed Division was posted on the mainland with Headquarters at Kuala Lumpur. The Division was in position by the end of 1940. In early 1941 another Indian Division, the 9th, was also sent to that country. The 9th Indian Division replaced the 11th which moved north with Headquarters at Sungei Patani near Alor Star. A little later an Australian division also arrived in Malaya. There were thus 3 divisions (in addition to Singapore Fortress troops) in Malaya when the war opened; viz. the Australian, 9th and 11th divisions, being posted in southern, central and northern Malaya respectively. 9th and 11 divisions were formed into an Indian corps with Headquarters at Kuala Lumpur. I happened to be the seniormost combatant Indian officer of the Indian Army in Malaya then.

6. It was generally expected that the Japanese would concentrate and attack from Indo-China, and that the first landings would be in south Thailand near Singora and north-east Malaya near Khota Baharu. The latter was in our actual occupation. To learn something about the former,

a number of officers were sent in disguise and under false names and passports to reconnoitre south Thailand in particular from Haadyai to Singora and from Haadyai eastwards to the Malayan border. I was one of these officers, who crossed the Thai border as a barrister. I was also given the task to visit Bangkok, as news had been received that a number of Indians were secretly in league with the Japanese. This was in November 1941. By the time I returned on 2nd December, we all were under battle conditions expecting fighting any moment. But the big surprise was, that we were not allowed to cross the Thai border and capture Singora, where the landing was expected. Yet the plans were made and based on the capture of this port so as to hit the Japanese at their weakest time, i.e., when landing. Weather it was due to the fear of violating Thai neutrality, or fear of thrusting our forces too forward or something else, I am not in a position to say. But the plan was not followed. And the Japanese landed exactly at the expected places and were totally but pleasantly surprised at no opposition. This was in the early hours of 8th December 1941, when Japanese simultaneously attacked Pearl Harbour. Only then were we ordered to cross the Thai border. But it was too late. Japanese had obtained a base and an aerodrome and had won the first vital round without battle. The Malayan plan of defence was to cause the maximum delay to the enemy, so that sufficient troops would be rushed to reinforce the Singapore fortress for its proper defence and later reattack.

7. To what extent this unopposed landing was responsible for the rapid retreat of British forces, I am not in a position to say, but a good chance of delay had been lost without a battle. There were other causes for retreat also. We had no air force, perhaps its vital role was not realized. The Japanese did, air bombing at their leisure. They also had armoured units, when a number of our military leaders had considered the terrain of Malaya impracticable for such vehicles. Furthermore after the successful attack on Pearl Harbour, and sinking of the 'Prince of Wales' and of the 'Repulse' a few days later, the Japanese had complete command of the sea. No wonder the retreat was quick and the whole of Malaya and the so called mighty fortress of Singapore fell to the Japanese within 2½ months of the attack, to be exact on 15th February 1942.

8. There is no doubt that the quick and ignoble defeat of the British forces hastened the process of a national movement. There is also no doubt that the Indian troops were in the main mercenary and there was no real cause for them to fight. Yet the Indian soldiers fought well under difficult and adverse circumstances. My division, i.e., the 11th fought from the first to the last day of this campaign, without any rest, reserves or

reinforcements. Of course such a fight without any patriotic motives cannot create heroes! But the troops fought well with heavy casualties, as a matter of discipline and training. They were however only too relieved the battle had ended.

Part Two

INDIAN NATIONAL—IN ARMY 1942, 'A'–FORMATION

9. After the fall of Singapore, the Japanese insisted that all Indian officers and soldiers be segregated from others. Hence we all gathered at the Farer Park, on 15th and 16th February 1942. It was then that I and Majority of others learnt that a group of officers and men had been helping the Japanese during the battle under the charge of captain Mohan Singh and the seeds of the I.N.A. had already been sown. They had been cut off after the first long attack in the North of Malaya about the middle of December. They had found some civilian Indians under S. Pritam Singh with the Japanese troops, through which contact had been established between them and the Japanese. For the first few days after the fall of Singapore we devoted ourselves looking after the men's health, a dysentery and cholera were taking their tolls. Various camps were established and doctors did a very good piece of work. At the same time talks about forming a movement went on. The Japanese informed us that in Japan an Indian Independence League had already been formed under the leadership of that well-known revolutionary Ras Behari Bose. Consequently a deputation of officers and civilians proceeded to Tokyo in April 1942, to have talks with Shri Ras Behari Bose and Indian from the other parts of the Far East with a view to forward to help the cause of Indian Independence. The three military officers selected for this meeting were Captain Mohan Singh, Captain Mohd. Akram and myself. Among the civilians were Mr. R.N. Raghavan, India's Ambassador-designate to Argentina and Mr. K.P. Kesava Menon, ex-High Commissioner to Ceylon.[3] Unfortunately one of our planes crashed in Japan killing all occupants. Among them were Captain Mohd. Akram, Shri Ayer and Shri Satyanand Puri a Bengal revolutionary. Among the Indians residing in Japan was Shri A.M. Sahay, though to our surprise we only met him after some difficulty. Raja Mohendra Pratap was also there. Our

---

3. They were appointed after independence.

surprise was greater still, as we were not allowed to meet him, and only did so secretly on our own. He immediately warned us that Japanese wanted to use us as puppets. This caused a disturbance in our minds, which later was to mount up. However, this meeting of Indians from Malaya, Japan, Thailand, Hong Kng, Indonesia and Manchuria decided to hold a bigger meeting of Indians in the Far East Asia at Bangkok in June-July, 1942, and meanwhile to proceed with the preliminary arrangements for the formation of a strong Independence League and I.N.A. We returned to Singapore towards the end of April or early May.

10. The Japanese had sensed my hesitation. They were correct too, for I could not bring myself to look at them as pure liberators without any other motives; I could not adjust myself to the Axis views, of which Japanese were a part. So immediately on return to Singapore, the Japanese sent me to Bangkok ostensibly to organise the Indian Independence League there, but in reality to get me away from Singapore and other officers and men. In June-July the big conference took place at Bangkok. It was a very well represented meeting of Indians from every country in the Far East. A Council of Action was formed to direct the activities of all Indians in territories under the Japanese occupation. It was formally decided to form a national army. While in Bangkok I noticed another incident. Whenever diplomats from the German Embassy would come to see me, the Japanese would question me, and ask me not to meet them again. This was a strange behaviour for allies.

11. Towards the end of July I was called back to Singapore to help in the organisation of the I.N.A. There were over 40 thousand Indian prisoner of war soldiers. Of these the vast majority volunteered to join the I.N.A. But of the volunteers only about half could be got ready. The Japanese could not equip all, or perhaps they hesitated to do so. It was amazing how quickly and successfully we instituted Hindi words of command for the English. Questions of caste and creed, which the British for their own reasons had nurtured vanished overnight. All ate together from the same cook house. Nobody thought of provincialism or communalism. All considered themselves Indians. Within a few months a disciplined body of Indian soldiers with a new spirit of nationalism was ready, to act. The basis of the I.N.A. was a division divided into three brigades named Gandhi, Nehru and Azad Brigades. It was of course not equipped with modern arms. But a guerilla force of about 20,000 was ready to act, admirably suited to act in the jungles of Assam and Bengal. It was realized that this force alone could not defeat the British forces in a direct battle, but its impact on the whole of India and on the Indian Army in

particular was our primary motive and the main weapon. And the spirit behind the I.N.A. soldiers was the real asset and the main force. Everyone was ready to march into India, no matter what the obstacles.

12. It must be recorded however the Japanese response to our spirits and views was not as hoped for. So during these days I often felt perturbed. On the one hand I went forward fully helping the organisation of the movement as its advisor, on the other hand I was more and more troubled by the motives and behaviour of the Japanese. The Japanese sensing this again sent me to Rangoon to organise the forward headquarters and espionage into India. I went to Rangoon via Bangkok in August. Here in Burma also the majority of Indians were awaiting to be organised and led forward. The start was made. Four bases were established and a number of parties were sent to filter into India. In Burma also the treatment and outlook of the Japanese left much to be desired. We constantly felt that we were merely being fitted into Japanese plans and no more. Indians were ill-treated. No real power or freedom of action was given to us. My fears and doubts only increased in November 1942. I was suddenly flown back to Singapore.

'B'

DISSOLUTION

(It is for this part that I have mainly written this article).) After I had written this article I have seen the book *The Two Great Indians in Japan* by J.G. Ohsawa. On pages 58 and 59 of this book are the following pertinent sentences :–

"In Indian National Army, a big disorder begun. Captain Mohan Singh and Lieutenant-Colonel Gill were its leaders. They were not satisfied with the G.H.Q. of Tokyo, because all resolutions of the Bangkok meeting had not been implemented. I.I.L. too were not satisfied, they were revolting."

These sentences however hardly explain the reality and it is this important phaze I want to clear.

13. On my return to Singapore I found the situation tense. My fears and worries about the Japanese had affected other also. And there were good reasons for these suspicions, major ones being –

(i) Japanese were ill-treating many Indians and complaints brought no results.

(ii) A large number of our anti-air craft gunners had been taken away and posted in various parts of Singapore as part of the Japanese defences. We were not even allowed to see them. They were made to wear Japanese uniforms and shout 'Banzai' (Three cheers) for the Japanese Emperor.

(iii) Our request that the formation of the I.N.A. be proclaimed to the world was side-tracked.

(iv) Our request that India's complete independence be declared by the Japanese was ignored.

(v) Our wish that Netaji Subash Chandra Bose be brought to lead the movement also drew no favourable answer.

(vi) We were merely being fitted into the plans of the Japanese General Staff, no more, no less.

14. Thus it became clear to me and many others that we had no real powers and the intention was to use us in accordance with the Japanese policy and strategy more or less as puppets. Naturally resentment arose among us and I was perhaps the spearhead of this resentment. Instead of satisfying our reasonable requests and winning us over, we were threatened and tempted both, particularly Mohan Singh and myself. We managed to stand firm. I, whom the Japanese considered the centre of opposition to them, became their first victim. In the early morning of 8th December 1942 (exactly one year after their attack and entry into the war–a day considered auspicious by them), the Japanese Gestappo arrested me and put me in an underground dark cell in solitary confinement. And I remained a prisoner (the word 'prisoner' cannot explain the conditions of arrest under the Japanese secret police for which please see Part III) till the end of the war, when I believe I escaped because news had filtered out about my whereabouts. After my arrest Mohan Singh and others stood firm and now demanded another condition–namely my release–before they could negotiate. So a fortnight afterwards Mohan Singh was arrested and the first I.N.A. stood dissolved. From here on the story can be better told by others who were direct participants in the later events. I personally remained a prisoner till 22nd August 1945, when I was released and sent to a camp from where the British arrested me in September. I then remained their prisoner till April 1946, when I was released from the Red Fort–thanks indeed to the great support of our nation led by our Prime Minister.

15. At the beginning of this sub-part 'B', I have made a note that my main reason for writing this note is this part. I repeat it. It should be known that while Indian soldiers and officers were ready to fight for their country, they refused to be puppets. It should be known that they knew something of the world events going on, The stand of the axis and allies

and that they tried to work for the real interests of the country according to their right and understandings in difficult circumstances and were not merely 'Yes Men". And for this stand the Japanese never forgave them and made many of them their worst victims, such as myself and those who were sent to new guinea. I think it is fair that this phase of the Indian National Army should be known also, as many foreigners are too prone to dub the I.N.A. as a puppet of the Japanese. If this part of the I.N.A. was fully known, then the posterity can pass the correct judgment on them, i.e., they were ready to die for their country but not as puppets of anyone. True, various individuals joined the I.N.A. with varying motives in those difficult conditions. But in general the above remarks hold true and hence I consider it my duty to bring the same to the notice of the compilers, so that justice is done to those who worked and suffered in those days and so to India's sons and to our country.

16. I have only to add that the above stand which surprised the Japanese, and for which they inflicted heavy punishments nevertheless brought desired results. Netaji came over, most of the things we asked for were generally accepted and second phase of I.N.A. started under the dynamic leadership of Shri Subash Chandra Bose, a phase which is now history. It appears the two phases were complimentary. Without the first, the second would not have been feasible. Without the second, the first would have been of no value. Hence both phases should be known, viewed in the right perspective to make the whole story, for both should reflect credit to India and her sons, though the first did not have the good fortune of having a famed person to lead it, nor is it so known as it should be. Yet individuals are a part of a phase or a movement. Therefore it is essential on that the movement be known from all its aspects and to give one such aspect, which I consider an important one, is my present task. I seek forgiveness of the compilers if it was already known in which case I am only happy to confirm it. As I said at the start I will only be too happy to give any additional information required or answer any queries.

Appendix-II

Statement by General Mohan Singh after his Release from the Prison at the End of the War; throws Light on the Events Leading to his Surrender in Malaya and Formation of the Indian National Army; Explains his Differences with the Japanese and Rash Behari Bose, his Arrest and Internment during the War; gives Assessment of Japanese Policy Towards Indian National Army[1]

I was arrested on 29th December, 1942 at Singapore by the Japanese for reasons clearly stated by them in a comprehensive statement (copies of which were freely distributed to Indian soldiers and civilians in Singapore) issued by Major General Iwakuro on the day of my arrest.

I was released on 26th August, 1945 in Sumatra after 32 months of confinement and at the conclusion of the war.

I have been awaiting the arrival of a responsible Allied Officer in this country to hand over myself to him. This I am going to do tomorrow and before doing so I have decided to issue a statement for the general information of my countrymen.

1. W.O.F. No. 208/810, Public Record Office, (P.R.O.) London.
2. General Mohan Singh (1909-1989) was born in a Sialkot village in 1909. After matriculation, he joined the Army as a Sepoy. He was trained at Kitchner college and was made Captain in 1940 and Major in 1941 before he left for Malaya. Before the outbreak of the Pacific war, he was attached to the 1/4 Punjab Regiment. He surrendered to the Japanese on 15 December. After discussion with Fujiwara and Pritam Singh he agreed to organise the Indian National Army. Was dismissed by Rash Behari Bose on 29 December 1942 and was kept unde detention for two months at a sea side Bungalow in Singapore. He was afterwards removed to a near by island (Puloou Ubin) and kept there till the end of December 1943. Later he was taken to Sumatra and detained there till the surrender of the Japanese. After the War, joined politics and was member of Lok Sabha.

STATEMENT[3]

1. Before Surrender

War with Japan broke out on 8th December, 1941. My battalion, the 1/4th Punjab Regiment, was the foremost battalion on Thai-Malaya border in the well known position of Jitra. Till the evening of 11th December, 1941, I fought on the British side as dutifully as any soldier should do. At about 1700 hrs., the same day, a Japanese tank unit broke through our dispositions. The battalion was completely disorganised and dispersed in small parties to various directions in the jungle. My small party consisted of Lt. Col. Fitzpatrick (Commanding Officer) myself and two N.C.Os Till midday, 14th December we remained lost in thick jungle and heavily flooded marshes; all the time trying and struggling to find our way out. On 13th evening Captain Mohd. Akram, also of our battalion, with a small party of Pathans met us accidentally. On 14th we reached Kuala Narang, a small town, 22 miles away from Alor Star. Here we were reliably informed by a Malay Civil. Official and local Indians that the Japanese were already in ALOR STAR and that they were pushing forward.

Lt. Col. Fitzpatrick Captains Akram and I held a brief conference and we decided to surrender.

1. Mental Picture

I must state here that when the war on the Eastern theatre broke out and even before that I was mentally greatly disturbed by the British War Aims.

I could not convince my conscience that it was correct for Indians to shed their blood for an end which was not applicable to them. Britain, faced with an imminent invasion danger of England itself, had declared to the world that she was fighting for freedom, democracy and other high sounding principles. She beseeched Allied Powers to come to her help. Even at the time of the most critical period of her National history and when she was utilising India to fight for her own freedom, she refused to consider the question of India's freedom. Instead she ordered the arrest of Indian leaders because they were considered guilty for asking freedom

3. The above statement was issued on 26 August 1945 in Sumatra and clarifies many points not mentioned by either Fujiwara or Gill in their account of the events leading to the collaboration between the Indian National Army and the Japanese General Headquarters.

for India. Why should, then, we Indians fight for a thing, the mere mention of which, was considered sufficient crime for the greatest of us, to be put behind the prison bars?

The obvious deductions which I could draw from the British attitude at that time were :–

(a) That British will never give India freedom unless she was compelled by force of weighty circumstances, which circumstances we Indians must create. In other words she will not grant freedom but we will have to take it from her.
(b) That Britain will never release her hold on India as long as Indian soldiers, paid, fed, clothed and armed by poverty stricken India, remain loyal to the British, irrespective of India's own fate.

Then why were we Indians fighting? The only answer which I could find was that we were fighting merely as dignified, befooled mercenary heroes at the expense of poor India for the sole benefit of Britain and thus helped Britain to keep India in Subjugation with Indian men, money and materials.

This was my mental picture just before surrendering and I am absolutely sure was the mental picture of most Indian officers, N.C.Os and other ranks of the Indian Army.

Here I also want to take it absolutely clear that before my surrender I had no connection whatsoever with any Japanese or any of their agent. In fact I had never seen a Japanese before.

2. After Surrender

At the time of surrender Major Fujiwara, representative of the general staff of General Yamashita, told me that I was not a prisoner. He also said that all Asiatics and particularly the Indians were their friends and that Japan was prepared to extend all help towards the attainment of Indian Independence. This was not what I expected and naturally I was very much impressed but not convinced. Lt. Col. Fitzpatrick was separated from us.

After this, and till the end of December, 1941 I carried on many long discussions with Major Fujiwara. Captain Mohd. Akram and Mr. Pritam Singh who was brought by the Japanese from Thailand to be made leader of the Indian Independence League movement, also attended these discussions. In these talks Major Fujiwara tried his best to convince me that the Japanese were absolutely sincere regarding the question of India and said that if I could raise a patriotic Indian army they would give all aid.

From these talks it was not difficult for me to see that the Japanese had their eyes on India as well. It looked to me that if they meet cheap victories they would at least try.

They had brought with them from Thailand a band of Indian civilians headed by Mr. Pritam Singh who was opening Indian Independence Leagues. Without meaning any ill will to any of these Indians, I must state that I was shocked with their intellect and the utter lack of understanding of what they were talking about. They might have been sincere and I think Pritam Singh was but sincerity alone is not sufficient. They were quite unconsciously playing directly in the Japanese hands.

In the light of two week's continuous discussions I was convinced that the Japanese were seriously determined to create some sort of movement. I had no doubt that in order to achieve their end they would apply all imaginable and even unimaginable methods. There was no such thing as neutral in their dictionary. They looked at every one either as a friend or a foe. A group of Indians attracted towards them was prepared to take the leadership to mislead Indians. Under those circumstances to stand aloof meant inconceivable damage to the Indian cause. My clearest and definite aim at that time I had in my mind that if the Japanese prove sincere, I would after consulting leading Indian civilians of political reputation, do my best for the furtherance of India's cause.

In that short time I had heard and seen enough of the Japanese atrocities on Prisoners of War and civilians. I wanted, even at the risk of my life, to spare Indian soldiers, that inevitable fate which was then befalling Chinese, British, and Australian soldiers. I also wanted to save Indian civilians from terrible hardships and atrocities.

To sum up, my aims for joining the Japanese were :

(a) Further the cause of India's freedom.

(b) Save Indian prisoners of war from certain and lingering death.

(c) Try to save Indian civilians and their property from the Japanese.

It is a matter of great satisfaction and consolation to me that in all these aims I succeeded to a great extent.

It must also be remembered here that the British forces were running as fast as they could, leaving all of us to our own fate, our own resources and in the hands of victory drunk Japanese who respected no laws and no moral codes of honour except their own.

On joining the Japanese I immediately started to teach patriotism to Indian soldiers. Throughout in my patriotic education I stressed this point that at this moment India's enemy No. 1 was Britain and India's enemy

No. 2 would be that nation who had designs on India whether it be Japan or any other.

So I organised Indian prisoners of war in a strong patriotic body fully determined to die only for India.

In doing this I had these objects at the back of my mind. Firstly a patriotic soldier will not be easily exploited. Secondly the British in India would also think twice before transporting ship loads of Indian soldiers to serve as gun fodder to various theatres of war without recognising them as men fit for Independence. Thirdly the world would also be awakened to the faet that Indian soldiers also love their country and wanted freedom as much as any other people.

As regards the practical cooperation with the Japanese I did only that such or even less than that which no prisoner of war could avoid at that time.

3. Alternative Plans

Whether I believe the Japanese to be sincere or not at that time it was very difficult for me to decide. Even if changes of sincerity were only 1 to 10 I wanted to test it. It was worth it. In any way it was going to bring out the truth. If they were trying to use us as it suited them we were also trying to use them as it suited us. I was prepared for both eventualities.

The Plan which Did Not Materialise : I was never in favour and I made it very clear to the Japanese that I would never consent to take Japanese into India.

Forces to liberate India should consist purely of Indians. I wanted to raise and train a patriotic force of 200,000 to 500,000 strongly united, well disciplied and completely independent. This entire force was then to be taken on Indo-Burma border and when there I wanted to give an open challenge to the British to come to an agreement with the Indian National Congress, that being the real voice of India, or fight. At the same time, I wanted to make an appeal to America, Russia and China to back our just demand and also wanted to make it clear to them that we were not Japanese puppets. If even then Britain remained adamant I wanted to fight and die to the very last man at Indo-Burma frontier.

I had strong conviction that that action would alarm the world. America, Russia and China, acting that we were not Japanese puppets and knowing our demand to be a just one, would not keep quiet and would certainly press Britain to accede to our demand. I also knew that the death of about 400,000 Indians would count more than 100 millions alive.

Alas ! Japanese were to prove beyond all doubts, insincere for they did all in their power to hamper the creation of such a force because it did not suit them and it only suited INDIA. They wanted a puppet army only for propaganda.

The one That Materialised : My plan in case the Japanese proved insincere from the very beginning was that at the appropriate time, I would challenge them and put their sincerity to a very severe test before taking any action that may jeopardise India's cause. At that proper moment I wanted to demonstrate, openly, publicly and boldly and expose once for all the Japanese designs. That moment would come when I was fully convinced about the solidarity and patriotism of Indian soldiers. Only then it would be proper, I thought, to give Japanese designs a shattering death blow and so expose them that it would be impossible for them to exploit Indians.

As it happened only this plan came into operation and for six months after my arrest the Indian Independence Movement in the Japanese Occupied countries was for all practical purposes dead. Only the arrival of Mr. S.C. Bose, whose name dazzled and blinded many sincere Indians that it came to life again. Even then thousands of Indian officers and other ranks and civilians, who were whole-heartedly in the moment before, did not join and have consequently suffered considerably.

The Japanese were under the impression that I was just a captain and it could not be possible for me to raise, organise and train such a force as I intended. Therefore they were very liberal on all verbal support. Thanks to the hearty cooperation of the officers and men and also Indian civilians that all my plans began to materialise far quicker than my own expectations. It was only when the Japanese realised that my plans actually started to take shape that they were alarmed. The Materialisation of my plans meant the complete destruction of their own.

4. Leadership in the Army

I do not feel happy to speak on this delicate question but now; on my release from the Japanese, I have been told by some Indian friends that the late Mr. Rash Behari Bose, the well-known Japanese puppet, had tried to mislead the Indian public by misrepresenting the real causes of my arrest. I am also glad to hear that the public, especially in Singapore, was too well informed to believe him. Still I want to clear this point here.

Mr. R.B. Bose in his campaign of lies, to hide his own weakness, levelled certain charges against me which included that I had designs for a dictatorship. How on earth he believed that he could convince the public by such lies is beyond me; when his own official statement and the official

Japanese statement issued by Major General Iwakuru, stated clearly and which conclusively proved that the principles involved were mainly Japanese insincerity and mistrust, their designs to use the I.I.L. Movement as a puppet movement and the I.N.A. as their 5th columnist, their misbehaviour towards Indian officers and men, the question of Indian civilian property etc., etc.

It was never my desire to create myself a general or a political leader. I remained a captain all through till after Bangkok conference held in June, 1942. If I had any such aim, there was nothing in my way to stop me from creating myself anything. I knew, I was an average army officer and I had no misunderstanding or complex about my military or political abilities. I was always sincerely prepared to give place a better man.

Until the fall of Singapore about 8,000 Indian soldiers had united under me ready to sacrifice everything for the Indian cause. As it happened, no officer senior to me surrendered. All the men declared their complete faith in me and accepted me as their leader.

A few weeks after the fall of Singapore, I collected about 30 senior officers (all majors and colonels), briefly explained to them what I had done so far, requested them to investigate fully and critically examine all my works and if in their honest judgement I was found guilty of injuring the Indian cause; or if proved that I was a Japanese paid man, I should be duly punished. I also appealed to them to carry on the work of Indian freedom and that they were free to select their own leader for this work, under whom I would gladly serve to the best of my ability in whatever capacity he decided to utilise my services. They unanimously selected me again as their leader and I had to accept their decision. This decision was again confirmed by the representatives of Indians in East Asia at the Bangkok Conference held in June, 1942, where I was unanimously elected member of the Council of Action and again appointed General Officer Commanding, The Indian National Army, by the Council of Action.

I may add here that it was repeatedly proposed in the Bangkok conference that I should take over complete control of the moment and I rejected even to hear such a proposal.

5. Council of Action and Col. N.S. Gill

The members of the Council of Action, as every one known were as follows :–

Mr. Rash Behari Bose (President), Messrs. K.P.K. Menon and N. Raghavan, Lt. Col. G.Q. Gilani and myself.

It must be mentioned that Col. N.S. Gill, although not elected member, C of A (for reasons I do not want to state here) played as important a role to serve India, as any other member of the C. of A.

Col. N.S. Gill : He was my chief military adviser. He was in my humble opinion the ablest military brain (Indian) in the East. I am not aware of the charges invested against him by the Japanese but I can declare that he is a true and great patriotic son of India. I maintain that after knowing the true intentions of the Japanese and having seen their treatment of the other Asiatics, particularly the Chinese, no true Indian with the least sense of justice, courage of conviction and strength of character could work with the Japanese.

At this time I do not know whether he is still alive or has already been tortured to death by the Japanese. It is my humble request to the Indian nation, that if he is not alive, those responsible for his death, whether Japanese or Indians, should be brought to justice. I may mention here that a very senior Japanese Officer, who was by no means his friend, said to me once that men like Gill are presented to nations once in centuries. I did all in my power to get him released but I too followed him soon.

Mr. Rash Behari Bose : It may be interesting to know that why we elected such an incapable man, a well-known Japanese puppet, whom no one trusted, as our President. That was the most unpardonable and historic blunder. We were under the impression that influence for India's benefit. At the same time we made it doubly sure that he had no power whatsoever as President of the C. of A. He was also our puppet. But when we all resigned he made use of some sort of a legal clause and declaring himself as 'the sole surviving member of the C. of A' assumed a dictatorial role with the help of Japanese bayonets.

Messrs. Menon and Raghavan : Both these gentlemen were very able and sincere Indian patriots. The organisation of the Indian Independence League, Far East was their creation. Their chief fault from the Japanese point of view was that I must add that during the most critical and trying time of crisis, Mr. Menon played a very bold and noble part at the risk of not only his life but also of his large family, I have the greatest admiration for his brave stand.

For shattering R.B. Bose's and his henchmen's plans of preconceived dictatorship, the drafting of the Tokyo conference's resolutions and the drafting of the constitution at Bangkok Conference were the fruits of the labour of M/s. Raghavan and Menon.

Lt. Col. G.Q. Gilani : He too joined the movement with great enthusiasm but after seeing the Japanese, his confidence too was shaken.

During the time of crisis he stood with me as a true soldier and colleague.

I may be pardoned for developing on leadership and the C. of A but it was essential to say a few words.

6. Indian Soldiers

It will, I am sure, gladden the hearts of Indian people in India to known that out of about 55,000 Indian prisoners of war about 45,000 had volunteered for India's cause (although the Japanese did not allow me to raise an army of more than 20,000). These volunteers included men from all classes recruited into the Indian Army including a large number of Gurkhas as well. Out of the remaining 10,000 nearly half were such who were prepared for India's cause but who did not trust the Japanese. Officers belonging to this group rendered me very valuable service. The rest I am ashamed to say were either too selfish or too coward. Some of them do not deserve to be called Indians.

I am proud to state here for the information of my countrymen that the army that I raised was truly a patriotic Indian Army. It was the only Japanese sponsored Army in the East which had no Japanese advisers, instructors, symbols, words of command, uniform, badges or their flag and which demanded equal respect. This was no easy task. I had to fight for every single item.

7. Crisis

Having worked for about a year with the aims and motive mentioned above and having perceived the Japanese evil designs and being firmly convinced that they just wanted to exploit us, I put forward this my opinion in the C. of A. This was done in the second half of November 1942.

All my colleagues of the C. of A. agreed with me except the 'brave' President. We agreed to demand an explanation from the Japanese and very strongly requested the President to put forward our view to the Japanese asking them to.[4]

Next day the President replied that he had accepted our resignations. On the same day I delivered two open lectures to all the officers (about 1,000) placing before them clearly all the facts, proving the insincerity of the Japanese and Mr. R.B. Bose. I told them that this was the trial for which we had been preparing for so long. I warned them that the trial would be very severe probably entailing the loss of lives of many of us but it must be undergone calmly and bravely as befit true soldiers. Only then would the world know that we were patriots and not puppets of the

4. For details see Appendix IV.

Japanese. I also told them that since we could no longer serve the cause of India I was taking steps to dissolve the army which was unanimously approved.

As already stated, Mr. R.B. Bose assumed the role of a dictator, declaring that he derived that right because he was the sole surviving member of the C. of A. So he declared himself as Commander of the Army as well. Needless to say that the Japanese bayonets were supporting his actions. But when he tried to interfere in the Army by ordering me to send certain officers to him, I gave such a rude and threatening reply, stating in it what I thought of him and what other officers and men of the I.N.A. considered him to be also telling him to keep his hands off the Army. Today, when I recollect the wording of that letter I myself feel ashamed for having sent him such a reply. But with that letter his interference in the Army ceased once for all. Far from wanting to meet officers of the I.N.A. he was afraid of coming out of his rooms which were heavily guarded by the Japanese,

Dissolution of the Indian National Army : On the 15th I sent a letter to the Japanese stating that I had absolutely no confidence in the Indian Independence League Movement conducted by the Japanese in the East and that the Army should be immediately dissolved and the members of the I.N.A. should again revert to the status of prisoners of war. In reply to this Major General Iwakuru told me that having once declared these soldiers to be free, they could not be reverted to the status of Prisoners of War. He asked me that if I had no confidence in the moment in the East whether I had confidence in the freedom movement in India and if so, he was prepared to allow me to take the army inside India, to work there for India's cause. I must confess that I was completely surprised but I immediately accepted his proposition. Later on after consulting my senior officers, who all heartily approved of it, when I re-enquired, nothing came out of it.

On 21st December, 1942, I issued open warning orders thanking all officers and other ranks for the sacrifices which they were prepared to make for India's cause and warning them that as the army could no longer serve India's cause, I was going to dissolve it.

An other secret letter was sent to all battalions which was to be opened in case I disappeared secretly, removed, arrested or shot. This letter contained the final, dissolving orders freeing all ranks from all obligations and from their personal pledge given to me and I took all the responsibility.

The long awaited day came at last. I was arrested on the morning of 29th December, 1942 and the secret letter was opened in all battalions and was strictly obeyed.

It is not correct for me to say what happened after my arrest clearing the situation. The President was so afraid of the Japanese that he wanted to run away. Of course we did not allow him to do that. Eventually we compelled him to put our demand which he did tremblingly.

The Japanese flatly refused to consider these demands and instead threatened us for daring to demand from the mighty Imperial Government.

But we expected this and were not frightened.

On 4th December, 1942, having consulted all my senior officers, I again, put up in the C of A. a 'Minimum demand' which included besides others, a demand to give me a free hand to raise an army not less than 200,000 strong. This was again supported by the C. of A. except of course the President who shed considerabl amount of tears, remarking that that would mean his death. In that demand I made it very clear that if the Japanese did not accede to my demands in toto by 1st of January, 1943, the Indian National Army would have nothing to do with the Indian Independence League Movement or the Japanese after that date and would be automatically considered dissolved. This was considered an ultimatum on any part by the Japanese who said that even the U.S.A. had not dared to insult the Japanese with such an ultimatum.

I was threatened, cajoled and begged not to make such a stand and finally pressed to resign. I stood firm and refused to do anything of the sort. The whole I.N.A. united as one man, stood behind me. In vain did the Japanese try to split the officers. The splendid united stand made by the Officers deserves the greatest admiration. Only two men failed in their duty, both of whom had in fact nothing to do directly with the army. One of them was a medical man and the other a regular infantry officer. I knew they were Japanese informers. I allowed them purposely to attend all secret meetings of officers which I was conducting daily in those days so that the Japanese may be duly and truly kept informed about the attitude of the I.N.A. At that time we were already armed and were not afraid. The Japanese knew this too and were very cautious.

Arrest of Col. N.S. Gill : Very early in the morning of 8th of December, 1942, when it was still dark, 17 members of the Japanese Military Police headed by a colonel, the chief of the M.P., whose name I have forgotten, raided my house and demanded Col. Gill who was sleeping in my bungalow. He gave me a written promise that if I permitted the arrest of Col. Gill, they promised that in future no member of the I.N.A. would be touched. I strongly protested and did not agree and asked him to arrest me also. This he refused. They took Gill away. I became furious on such high handedness. Till midday, various high ranking Japanese officials tried to pacify me. I, however, refused of listen to any of their excuses and demanded Gill back which was not done.

Resignation from The Council of Action : Calling an immediate meeting of senior officers I placed the facts before them. They unanimously agreed with me that the time for a decisive step had come. In the afternoon, a meeting of the C. of A. was held, which Mr. Raghavan did not attend and who we came to know had already resigned on some other issue. We three, Mr. Menon, Lt. Col.G.Q. Gilani and I, submitted a joint resignation from the C. of A. Besides various other reasons for our resignation we strongly protested against the Japanese high handedness in arresting the Gill.

It was Year 1942 : Finally in connection with my work I want to state that all this happened in the year 1942 when the Japanese were intoxicated, maddened and blinded with victories, when every member of the Japanese armed forces considered himself no less than a personal representative of their Emperor, when the slightest disobedience or difference of opinion with the lowest Japanese meant certain death, when famous Allied generals were not only forced to sign unconditional surrenders but had to bear quietly several personal insults, injuries and indignities, when Allied soldiers, British, Americans, Australians and Dutch were dubbed as white slaves of the descendants of the Sun Goddess. It was in that very period that I took the gravest decision of exposing Japanese insincerity publicly. Those; who have the slightest experience of the Japanese and their ways in the war, particularly in the year 1942, can well visualise the sort of punishment that I was expecting for my action at that time.

I myself am surprised to find myself alive today. I know that I owe my life to the splendid stand of 20,000 armed Indians in Singapore on that day and the backing and sympathy of all Indians in the East.

I am not sure of my fate and before handing over myself to the British I think it my duty to thank all the members of the C. of A. all the officers, N.C.Os and men of the I.N.A. who stood so loyally and firmly united with me and Indian civilians for their sympathetic support extended to me all through in the movement.

I must also thank Major General Iwakuru (I do not know whether he is dead or alive) for publishing a comprehensive statement stating clearly, openly and boldly the reasons of my arrest. By doing that he did a service to India.

8. Before handing over myself to British

As I may not have another opportunity of meeting them I want to express my heartfelt gratitude to the following, who, at the personal risk of their lives helped me in several ways during the days of my confinement:

Corporal Abdul Rahman of Singapore Police

Mr. Teja Singh of Anti-Malarial Dept., Singapore.

Mr. Cheah, a Chinese gentleman of Singapore.

All the Chinese inhabitants of Ubin Island (off Singapore) especially Messrs. All Bhoe and Tan pang Ling. S. Pritam Singh of Sumatra.

Dr. Roesm and his wife of Manindjau. S.W.K. Sumatra. Miss Soefjani Mawani of Matoer S.W.K. Sumatra.

And also Lt. Col. Ogawa who sincerely sympathised with me and who saved my life at a very critical time in my confinement.

Appendix-III

MEMOIRS OF FUJIWARA IWAICHI
pertaining to his role in the formation
of the Indian National Army (Extract)

War History Document No.70
August 1959, Tokyo

This was written after the release of Fujiwara from Singapore. It should be read with the Interrogation Report included in this Volume. This account was written in Japanese from which portions relevant to the study of the Indian National Army were translated.

Section 1: Patriots' Leap into the Dark

On a chilly December day of 1940, a secret confidential telegram was delivered on the table of Lt. Col. Kadomatsu[1] of the 8th Section of the Army Department of the Imperial Headquarters located at Miyakezaka of Tokyo. It was from the chief staff officer of a certain division of the Japanese 21st Army stationed at Canton. It was addressed to the deputy chief of staff, and to convey the following request of three Indians who had contacted the Japanese army Headquarters at Canton after leaving Hongkong secretly. That they were confined in the jail of Hongkong on charge of anti-British activities, but had escaped. They wanted to go to India, Berlin and Malaya secretly to establish contact with their comrades and carry on their fight against the British. For that they wanted Japanese protection to go to Bangkok if possible, otherwise to Indo-China, from where they proposed to go their destination overland on foot. Although the names of these three persons were not mentioned in the Telegram, yet in the footnote it was appended that they were Sikhs, and confirmed their claim of being anti-British patriots.[2]

Lt. Col. Kadomatsu and Maj.-O (Ozeki) spent some time in studying the implications of this telegram, and came to the conclusion that a reply should be sent to this telegram. Thereupon they sent the following reply after obtaining the approval of the higher authorities. 'The Japanese army in Canton should investigate the anticedents of these persons in more detail carefully, and should try to comply with their requests as far as possible'. Even before this telegram reached Canton, the following telegram was received from Canton. 'The three Indians in question have been placed on board a steamer bound for Kobe, and the general staff office is requested to take the necessary steps in this regard.

Thereupon Lt. Col. Kadomatsu entrusted the task of ensuring safe and secret, transportation of these three persons to Bangkok to Maj. Fujiwara, I myself, (At that time I was a captain). A certain Capt. K. was allotted the task of assisting them. After confirming that the Imperial Headquarters did not have any special project about these three persons. I started making arrangements for their journey by boat to Bangkok, and

---

1. Lt. Kadomatsu Shoichi, was in-change, Intelligence operations towards India at General Headquarters in Tokyo.
2. The names of the three Indians were Kartar Singh Quami, Harnam Singh Dhillon and Hari Singh.

at the same time sent a telegram to Mr. Tamura, our military attache at Bangkok, to make arrangements for their safe and secret landing in Bangkok.

Just at that time a boat was spotted which was about to sail for Bangkok for bringing back a cargo of rice. Unfortunately I have forgotten its name.

Capt.-K (Koi Wai) immediately left for Kobo, and succeeded in enlisting the cooperation of the captain of the ship with the assistance of local police. On a dark night, the three Indians were put on board the ship in great secrecy.

In fact they were transferred from the incoming boat straight to the outgoing vessel, without even giving them time to land on the soil of Japan. They were accommodated in a hold of the ship, and remained there till they reached Bangkok.

Capt.-K reported that the three Indians did not utter even a word of complaint over the extremely uncomfortable conditions. On the contrary they were moved to tears over the goodwill and warm gesture of the Japanese army. Again, they assured that in case of their detection on the way by British or Thai police, they would immediately commit suicide so that Japan did not get implicated and showed the knives they had kept ready for the purpose. They showed their firm desire to bear the heat in the hold during the voyage through warm South China Sea, and would try to do their best to stand upto the expectation of Japan.

As we did not have any political or military scheme whatsoever about these persons, their names even were not recorded on the files, which I regret now very much. We were extremely happy over the fact that we could offer our humble assistance to these three patriots fighting for their country's Independence just out of friendship, transcending above narrow nationalistic designs.

The ship slowly moved south across the South China Sea where the temperature was above 100°C with the three Indians on board. The condition inside the hold was unbearable like that in a boiler room. The presence of these three Indians was known only to the captain and purser of the ship. The purser carried day's food only once during the night stealing the eyes of the crew, and encouraged them as much as possible. Although it was unbearable, yet they did not express the desire to come to the deck at night to get fresh air even once. As they did not have valid travel papers, they were transferred to a small boat from the ship under the strict supervision of the Military Attache Col. Tamura. The three Indians left the ship passing off as coolies, and reached the residence of the military attache near Lumbini Park. Presently we received a telegram from the military attache informing the safe landing.

The colonel acted as an ideal host, providing the three tired and exhausted Indians with cool bath, cool drinks, Indian food and good place to sleep.

The next night Col. Tamura asked these men about their future plans. When the colonel expressed his concern over their prospective difficulty in an unknown city, one of the three Indians with great self composure said that the old veteran Amar Singh was there in Bangkok. He was the leader of the Indian Independence League with Headquarters in Bangkok. A young Indian Pritam Singh was there to assist him. The IIL was a secret society of the Sikhs set up with the sole objective of liberating India from the British rule, and had members in Hongkong, Shanghai, Tokyo, San Francisco and Berlin. The three Indians next vanished in the darkness of Lumbini Park after expressing gratitude and soliciting Japan's help for the forthcoming Independence struggle. After a few days a tall Sikh priet called on Col. Tamura at his residence secretly and solicited his interview to the Sikh guard. He was Pritam Singh, and this was the first step in the contact between the IIL and the Japanese army.

Following this, both Pritam Singh and Amar Singh met Col. Tamura a number of times.

Although Thailand at that time was showing pro-Japanese leanings, yet it was within the sphere of influence of Britains and had turned into a hot bed of intelligence warfare by Japan, Britain, USA, China and Germany. Hence extreme caution was called for. The talks did not go beyond a certain point because the Anglo-Japanese relations had not deteriorated during the early summer of 1941 yet to the extent where war become a probability. However, through these talks Col. Tamura was convinced that the IIL was a secret society with a membership network spread over Tokyo, Shanghai, Hongkong, Southern Thailand, Malaya, India, Berlin and other places, and committed to anti-British struggle, if possible with arms. He also saw the prospect of obtaining military and political intelligence regarding Indian and Malaya through the IIL. Again, Pritam Singh and Amar Singh also could confirm the good wishes of Japan through the talks held with Col. Tamura. It was in this way that the bridge of friendship was build between Japan and the IIL.

In the midst of such quick changing situation Lt. Col. Kadomatsu, who was the staff officer of the Imperial Headquarters in charge of propaganda arrived at Bangkok in plain dress towards the end of July 1941. In case war broke out between Japan and Britain, then Burma, Malaya and the Eest Indies would become the main scenes of war. The attitude of the people of these countries as well as of India would be decisive. Although these countries were under imperialistic occupation for a long time and apparently had lost national consciousness, yet there were very strong nationalistic movements in India and Burma. In case Japan took the initiative to study the national aspirations of these peoples and assist their struggle with proper understanding then they would become the most valuable ally of Japan in the event of war between Japan and Britain. As this is quite obvious to those who have studied the rudiments of war strategy, Lt. Col. Kadomatsu also probably had this conviction when he came to Bangkok. However, this is not possible overnight. When he left Tokyo he had one very important objective in view, viz., to assist the movement of the Thakin Party of Burma which was established towards the end of 1934. This was also not particulars in view of any war between Japan and Britain, but to hamper the assistance to Chiang Kai Shek through the Burma-China Road by Britain. However, as war between Japan and Britain was apprently round the corner, he advised Col. Tamura to step up all his schemes related with enlisting the support and cooperation of Singapore. He was very familiar with the situation in Singapore involving the Chinese by virtue of his long stay there and had a large number of acquaintances among the Chinese. The trail of Sumatra and Java was totally missing. After promising to send the officers required for the job and money to Tamura, Kadomatsu returned to Tokyo. I was at that time working as the youngest officer in charge of news and propaganda of Section 8, and I was under the belief that Kadomatsu had gone to Indo-China on an urgent work. I came to know that he actually went to Bangkok for the first time when he reported to Col. T, the head of the Division, on the developments there on his return.

Although the whole idea was in a nebulous stage, yet I felt that a firm ideological conviction normally required for sponsoring such a project was totally lacking. However, it was mentioned during the trips that I myself and Capt.-K had some providential connection with the IIL source. As this did not involve our main duty, and as no comment was invited, we kept quiet. In the mean time the Japanese forces marched into South Indo-China, in July, and the Anglo-Americans retaliated strongly by freezing Japanese assets abroad, abrogating trade treaties, prohibiting sale of petroleum, and bringing about rupture in Dutch-Japanese oil negotiations. Thus the destiny was slowly leading us towards war.

I continued with my cautious life renting a room in Thailand Hotel. Apart from that I was cautious over the movements of the boarders and the waiters. After a few days I realised that there were a few military officers whom I had seen before somewhere. They were the officers who had come to train the Thai soldiers to handle Japanese planes and tanks supplied by Japan. Besides there was Lt. Col. Y who was a member of the committee set up for determining the national boundary between Thailand and Indo-China. The waiters, however, apparently overlooked my presence. In order to avoid my becoming a topic of discussion among the Japanese boarders, and thereby attracting the attention of Thai police and the agents of the big powers, I requested the military attache to find out a house for me in a very non-conspicuous locality. After a few days, 2nd Lt. Yonemura came to this hotel as an employee. It was indeed painful for me to see one of my assistants and comrades just pretending to be a waiter in this hotel just for the sake of our fatherland. He had to maintain rather cold and formal relation between a guest and a boy not acquainted to each other. Only our eyes expressed our feeling.

He played his part very skilfully. That made me feel all the more pity for him. At night he came to my room stealthily for contact.

I think it was 10th of October, the day when I met Pritam Singh, the representative of IIL, with which my destiny was going to be tied up. It was decided that we would meet at the residence of the military attache at noon. He came in a Samlom, at the appointed time. I was waiting rather impatiently and longingly for him alongwith the military attache. As he was led in by a boy, I had the shock of my life. I had expected a rough and tough looking revolutionary, but contrary to my expectation he was a lean and thin tall and somewhat nervous and soft looking Sikh youth. Another shock was his greeting with folded hands, which we do at the time of prayer to God, whereas I had expected to shake hands. After formal introduction by Col. Tamura, he said that he had heard a lot about me, and was waiting to meet me longingly, and shook hands with me. In reply I said that I would feel it a great honour to be able to associate myself in realising their lofty ideal. I came to Bangkok with the firm conviction that their fight for Independence would be crowned with success ultimately, and I would cooperate with them whole heartedly. Col. Tamura acted as the interpreter, and on hearing my wishes he was very happy.

Then we made ourselves comfortable, and I asked about the three Indians of Canton. He thanked me profusely on hearing that I had arranged their passage to Bangkok. He continued that the three Indians were very much grateful to the Japanese general staff office, and that they had already reached their respective destinations safely. And he added that our cooperation and joint work became more or less a settled fact at that time.

In that sense we were old comrades. Then he related about their political struggle. He had plunged head long in the country's political movement in 1939, and had to leave India as his life was in danger. He came to Bangkok via Singapore, and was working as an assistant to Amar Singh.

He expressed his anger at the British deception of India at the time of First World War, and confided his conviction that Independence of India could not be achieved without the uprising of the Indian people. Thereupon he asserted that the Second World War should be taken advantage of for starting armed struggle for Indian Independence. He also expressed great respect for Subhash Chandra Bose who was in Berlin at that time and pledged consolidation with the movement headed by him in Europe. He supported the stand of the leaders of Indian National Congress in not welcoming assistance from the big nations in the Independence struggle as this would mean inviting an evil to get rid of another evil. The sole objective is to attain Independence of India without any strings attached from any country. He said "In case we seek assistance of foreign countries for our Independence struggle, we would lose the support of our countrymen. Even then, we believe that we should not let this golden opportunity slip, and hence should not hesitate in seeking foreign assistance. This situation has created a great and painful dilemma for us." Even when we were discussing this hot topic, he remained very cool, and not even once did he betray his excitement. It became very clear to me that I had a very cool and rational man of firm conviction to deal with.

Even in this first meeting I got a hint of our future course of action. After this political talk was over, I asked him about his turban, long beard and the iron ring on his wrist. In that connection I came to know a rough outline of Sikh religion. This first confidential meeting lasted for two hours, Col. Tamura acting as the interpreter.

In this very first meeting a bond of friendship was established between us, where we could express our view without reserve. I felt that there was a path of glory lying ahead of us.

At the time of parting he expressed his desire to meet after three days. He proposed the house of a cloth merchant as the next venue of our meeting so as not to rouse suspicion with his frequent visit to the military attache house. Col. Tamura immediately approved of it. It is needless to say that I was also of the same opinion. I was slightly worried over this meeting. This was because I was very bad in English. I had neglected it during my middle school days, and ever since the cadet schools days, I had to concentrate on Chinese. I was also worried over the health of Pritam Singh, as he had fits of cough during his talks.

Two days after the first meeting, Col. Tamura introduced me to an young man called Otaguro. He was about thirty, dark and was a teacher of English in the Japanese primary school in Singapore. He had come over to Bangkok following deterioration in Anglo-Japanese relations. He was quite affable and appeared to be sincere. After talking with him I got the impression that he had neither understanding of nor interest in nationalist movement, and did not care much over the political developments in the region. However, he was prepared to do anything and everything in case it was for our fatherland.

In this way I got another comrade who was to become my ear and speech. Another happy thing occurred on this day. A house was finally spotted for me in a very ordinary locality near the Bangkok railway station. It had become vacant as a Japanese professor of Taipei Medical College, who returned to Japan after completing his assignment of research on certain tropical diseases. I inherited both the maid servant as well as the furnitures. It was a very inconspicuous house, with five bed rooms on the first floor and a big hall and dining room on the ground floor. As the stay at the hotel was telling on my nerves. I practically grabbed the opportunity and shifted on the very day the professor vacated it.

On that very day I instructed Otaguro to find out the house of the Indian in whose house the meeting had been fixed. He located in the venue on the first floor of a pickle godown behind a dilapidated house inside a narrow lane about four kilometres from the Lumbini Park. He also made a report on the distribution of the houses in the locality. As well as the residents and the details upon the topics that were likely to be discussed the following day with Pritam Singh till late; and I was extremely related over the prospect of gaining a first hand knowledge of the activities of the IIL in Southern Thailand and Malaya besides the activities of the Indians in Bangkok. I also decided to discussed over his own idea of Indian revolution. I was also supposed to exercise extreme restraint in not allowing Pritam Singh to know anything about Japan's preparations for war against England and America.

When I left Tokyo in early October, there were rumours over war with the Anglo-Americans, but even though middle of October had passed, there were no such signs. However, the coded message of the state of war could come in any day. In that case what a pity it would be that I had not yet succeeded in evolving any viable policy to implement the task for which I had come. Most of my assistants had not yet arrived, nor there was any information from Tashiro (Shigeto) and Kamimoto (Toshio) in Southern Thailand, who had been summoned to Bangkok. I passed the night sleeplessly. As it dawned, I jumped out of the bed, took a good shower, and had a gulp of whisky straight. It was only after this I had a sound sleep.

I left my house at about 7 P.M. telling my maid servant that I was going to dine with our ambassador, and after walking some distance with great care to ascertain whether someone was following me. I picked up a Samlom and went to the China town, just in the other end of the town. From there I came back to the Lumbini Park after changing the Samlom a number of times, where I found Otaguro waiting for me. Next we both started for the destination on foot, with great caution.

We reached the house 10 minutes before the appointed time. There was a man in flowing white robe standing under the eves of the house. As we tried to pass him, he stopped both of us. He led us to the first floor of the pickle godown, where at a corner I found a small table, a small chair and a simple dirty bed, besides the suffocating smell of the pickles. There Pritam Singh was waiting for me. As usual he first greeted us with folded hands, and then shook hands. He apologised for the dirty venues but added that it was necessary for precaution. As a man was standing below on watch, we could proceed with our talks with ease. Although it was very oppressive there, yet I requested him to be at ease, and said that I was very happy over his caution.

The night was very oppressive and sultry without even slightest breeze, and there were hordes of mosquitos feasting on us. The talks went on for about five hours over tapid water to quench our parched throat. He first of all expressed his views of the Indians in Bangkok.

In Bangkok there was Indo-Thai Friendship Association besides the IIL. This organisation had its allegiance to Indian Nation Congress, and two of its active leaders were Swami[3] (a professor of Bangkok University) and Das. This organisation had connections with the German Embassy, as well as the backing of the local Indian businessmen, and as such was much more powerful than the IIL. This organisation was at daggers drawn with the IIL the latter being supported mostly by the Sikh.

This Mr. Das had in the past lived in Japan, leading the anti-British movement in Japan together with Sahay. I had the occasion of meeting Anand Mohan Sahay and Das (Deb Nath) in Tokyo in spring this year. I immediately realised that the rivalry between the two organisations was a very delicate matter; and apprehending the likelihood of exposure of the

3. This refers to Swami Satyanand Puri and his associate Dab Nath Das who were very prominent in Thailand.

IIL activity because of the rivalry. I enquired from Pritam Singh whether some sort of cooperation could be ensured between the two organisations. He ruled out any such possibility. I had a great impulse to develop separate contact with my old acquaintance Das. but realising that this would give Pritam Singh a very adverse impression, I decided to postpone the question of cooperation between the two organisations till the outbreak of hostilities. I was also afraid that such a move might expose the Japanese contacts with the IIL. However, I tried to press the necessity for cooperation between the two organisations for the success of the Independence movement, and if this was not possible, then at least to reduce the friction to the minimum for the sake of the greater objective.

Next I came to know about the presence of the supporters of the IIL at Hatai, Yala in Southern Thailand and at Kotah Bahru on the north-east coast of Malaya. Pritam Singh made monthly trips to these places under the pretext of preaching, but mainly to maintain contact with these people as well as to distribute IIL propaganda pamphlets. He reported a heavy concentration of British Indian forces along the Thai-Malaya border, and the comrades of Pritam Singh in the region are trying their best to propagate the cause of the IIL, but has so far failed to attain any tangible result because of frequent rotation of the forces. Because of antipathy towards the Britishers at the bottom of their hearts, the British Indian forces accepted and read the pamphlets with great delight. He expressed his confidence that in the event of war in case Japanese forces invaded Malaya and he went alongwith the Japanese forces and made appeal directly to the Indian soldiers, then there would be very good response.

As he related, I had hoped in the beginning for the penetration into Malaya and to a certain extent into the British Indian forces by his organisation, but was slightly disappointed on hearing the full report. However, he dropped hint about his earnest desire for Japanese declaration of war against Britain, but I refrained from making any comment on this socre. I urged him to continue with his propaganda among the Indian soldiers in Malaya as the situation was rather tense. I also could hear his future plan about his movement. He was apparently convinced of the inevitability of war between Japan and Britain, and in such an eventuality he wanted the Japanese assistance in raising an Indian Independence Army from among the Indian officers and men of the British Indian army, as well as from among the Indian living in Thailand, Malaya and Burma, and take up arms against the Britishers. At that stage he wanted to develop the IIL in global scale.

My response to this plan of Pritam Singh was spontaneous, and I promised all helps possible. He solicited Japan's cooperation in Asia establishing contact with Bose in Berlin, and the privilege to use Saigon Radio and Tokyo Radio for anti-British propaganda for Indian Independence.

At that time Pritam Singh had all his attention focussed on the broadcasts by Bose. He wanted me to help him in exchanging messages with Pratap in Tokyo and his comrades in Shanghai. Although the fateful day was approaching fast and I was tempted much to encourage him by confiding the fact, yet I exercised restraint. It was indeed regrettable that the talks could not touch upon the vital points at such a crucial stage. The Indian who was standing on watch below was trying his best to keep of the mosquitos, and everytime he slapped against his body we lowered our voices and tried to judge the situation. During the talks Pritam Singh had fits of cough, and as the night advanced he betrayed signs of fatigue. Finally I enquired about his health.

With slight worry he said that he had been suffering from some throat trouble, but it was nothing serious. He ruled out his death before accomplishment of the noble task assigned to him by God. I was very much impressed by his resolution. We suddenly realised that it was already past 2.00 A.M. Finally he said that he would be away the whole of last week of October for making contacts and propaganda in Southern Thailand. We parted after agreeing to meet again during early November. We both left the quiet and sleepy lane cautiously and emerged on the main road.

On the way back also, we changed Samlom a number of times covering almost half the city and finally returned home. Although I was extremely tired, my mind was very fresh. After ordering the maid servant to bring whisky and cold water, I recollected the words of Pritam Singh, and wrote them down in my memo while wetting my throat with whisky. It was already dawn when I got into the bed ultimately. Next day I reported the contents of the discussion to Col. Tamura, who in turn forwarded it to the Imperial Headquarters. It was quite apparent that the situation was worsening consequent to the oil embargo imposed by Britain, USA and Holland. In the mean time Kamimoto and Tashiro came to Bangkok from Southern Thailand and reported on the situation there.

As expected, Tashiro failed to make any appreciable headway with his project with the Chinese. After they returned to Southern Thailand, Uemochi, Nakamiya, Yamaguchi, Segawa, Takimura, Ishikawa and others came to Bangkok from Tokyo together with Masufuchi. According to my plan, I retained the charge of IIL, with Yamaguchi, Nakamiya, Ishikawa and Otakuro as my assistants. Nakamiya acted as an employer of Nikku Yoko

Co. and Ishikawa and Takimura as the employees of the military attache. All others were sent to South Thailand as employees of Mitsubishi Co. and Dainen Koshi Co., to assist Tashiro and Kamimoto. As all these people were new to the place, it was necessary for them to get accustomed. Again, it was also necessary to make reasonable progress with our projects so that any sudden outbreak of war did not take us by surprise. I lodged them for a few days at my house, and tried my best to convince them of the ideological aspect of our projects. Yamaguchi and Ishikawa started living permanently with me and they were very pleasant company indeed. At night Nakamiya and Segawa came to my residence for contact.

We discussed till late on the ideals inspiring us as well as the policy to be adopted for accomplishing our mission. These were our happiest moments in Bangkok. In case the Far East became the field of war, in that case the ideal of Japan should conquer all the obstacles and confrontations for building up coprosperity sphere, in which there would be no place for any feeling of being ruled by the conquered nations, or any pride of conqueror.

The nations of East Asia should be liberated from foreign rule and exploitation, and a new order of peace and welfare should be ushered in where all the nations would get proper opportunity to achieve political goal and maintain their cultural tradition. The Japanese nation has the obligation to stand in the vanguard and accomplish this mission. The religious belief, customs and manners and attitude towards life of all these nations should be respected. Moreover, we should avoid having a subjective attitude towards these things. We should try to gain appreciation and approval of our ideal from other nations through the sincerity of our action.

The British and Dutch rule was about hundred years old, and has thoroughly pacified the local people through skillful policy and rewarding the collaborators. As against this we are not only inexperienced, but also we were inadequately prepared. Hence the only way before us to break the stranglehold was to appeal to the national aspiration of these peoples with great sincerity, Indeed sincerity is the key that opens all doors.

Our movement should assume the shape of assisting the spontaneous movement of our comrades among these nations who would respond to this idea of Japan. There should be no place for coersion or interference, and they should not get any impression that they were being exploited or used as puppet. We should set at the work sincerely without any ulterior motive. Our dedication should match the patriotism and spirit of sacrifice of the freedom fighters of the various nations of South Asia and India.

Another important aspect of our work was that we were supposed to act the mediator in between these nations and the Japanese forces, and check the repitition of violence committed by a section of the Japanese officers and men in China against innocent population and prisoners of war.

A firm commitment was to be obtained from the operational forces to this effect. We had to be reconciled with the difficult demands imposed on us as the intermediary standing in between these peoples and the Japanese operational forces. And we would have to fulfill this difficult task with boldness and firmness.

For the present the most important question was the understanding and unity of the team. The harmony existing among the team members should automatically influence the leaders as well as the common people of this region. In my talks with my comrades at night I emphasised the above points citing numerous examples. All agreed to whatever I said.

Pritam Singh returned from Southern Thailand in the beginning of November. We had another meeting at the above place. This night he introduce me to Amạr Singh, who wore a white flowing beard and appeared to me not less than seventy years old. The old man quietly walked upto me and stood in front of me just like a statue. With both his hands across his breast he looked at me intently through his beard which reached upto his waist. And he offered prayer to God reciting something.

I felt as if a messenger of God was standing in front of me. In his stern looks and solemn face I could read inviolable sincere feeling, and indomitable spirit. My face surely had expressed my respect and relianee for this old patriot about whom I had heard so much.

After finishing his prayer, he pulled a chair and sat besides me. I was rather overwhelmed in his august presence. Next he started speaking in a low but forceful voice emating from deep down his chest which could be singled out even from among million. He talked without stirring his body, and his eyes moved either on my face or on that of Pritam Singh. Sometimes he looked at the ceiling as if thinking of his distant home. During his talk he often prayed for God's help with closed eyes. As he talked, he often got excited, and I could read his feeling in the tightening grip of his right hand. In no time the ascetic turned into a fiery revolutionary and I was easily overwhelmed by his solemn attitude.

He branded the British conquest and rule of India as a case of immorality and deception. Since his early youth he had dedicated his body and soul to fight for the freedom of his country and his compatriots. He had spent, consequently, ten long years in the prisons of Andaman and Rangoon, where he was mostly kept in fetters. He related his tortures and consequent hardening of his conviction as if chanting prayers. And even at this fag end of his life he has lost none of his ardour to stand at the vanguard of his country's freedom struggle. He also expressed his confidence that God's blessings were with the IIL and the Indian people. I must confess that the talks of the old man were not wholely ratio ıal or logical, yet I was very much impressed. I was not very optimistic about the capacity of the old man to lead freedom movement of grand magnitude. Somehow he lacked political consciousness and capacity to plan required of such a leader. He appeared to me as an emotional man rather than a logical man, instinctive man rather than a man with deep insight. And I felt that the old man and Pritam Singh were a very harmonious pair.

After the old man had finished, I enquired about the situation in Southern Thailand from Pritam Singh. He related that he could contact his comrades in Kuantan and Kotah Bahru, who were very active, but had again failed to establish cells in Kedah area.

He also regretted the failure to carry out proper propaganda and win over supporters among the British Indian forces because of frequent rotation of the forces assigned to border protection duty. Next I wanted to know about the distribution of his comrades in Southern Thailand, especially around the Thai-Malaya border, as well as in Kotah Bahru, and the mode of their operation. But I did not press the point as he was reluctant to speak on the subject. This was because I knew that for success mutual confidence was of paramount importance, and all cooperation should be on voluntary basis.

The talk next shifted to the attitude of the Indian people and leaders towards Japan. I solicited their frank opinion about the thinking of the Indian people in general towards Japan. This was because I thought that this would provide me with better understanding of the situation and would help me in evolving the plans for fulfilling my mission. In the beginning Pritam Singh was a bit hesitant, and started with Japan's failure on the propaganda front vis-a-vis Britain, America and Chungking. However, as talks proceeded, he expressed his views rather frankly. Japan's policy towards its colonies of Formosa and Korea, and the military action and policy of Japan in Hanchuria and China have created the image of an warlike aggressor in the Indian mind.

Again, citing the cases of violence and cruelty of the Japanese officers and men against the Chinese masses, obtained from British, American and Chungking sources, he expressed his profound shock. He warned me that the Japanese propaganda was incompatible with the actual deeds of the Japanese forces. He emphasised that as the Indian people were more sensitive towards colonial policy and military and immoral actions than the Chinese people. I however, tried to blame the malicious propaganda of the enemies of Japan for creating such an impression of Japan. Moreover, I frankly admitted the necessity of correction of Japan's policy after criticising Japan's colonial policy towards Formosa and Korea, as well as its policy and military action with respect to Manchuria and China. I also expressed my disapproval of the violence and immoral actions of a section of Japanese army officers and men in China. I took great pains to explain the imperial will of establishing a new order of peace and prosperity in the Far East based on liberty and equality of all the oppressed nations of the region. I also emphasised that steps were being taken to correct the Japanese policy and that actions were being taken against the guilty officers and men after the fall of Nanking. As evidences, I cited the declaration of our Prime Minister Koneo and the pamphlet titled 'Dos and Donts for the Expeditionary forces' by Gen. Hata, the commander in chief of the China Expeditionary Forces. I also tried to enlighten him on the traditional virtues of the Japanese people in an attempt to solicit his understanding and related my belief that Japan, being the motive force in establishing new order in East Asia, was on the process of reflecting upon its own policies I actions in order to effect necessary corrections. We agreed that exploitation, coersion and domination should be totally banished from the idea of Indo-Japanese cooperation, which should transcend above piety nationalistic rivalry and confrontation, and that respect for the traditional cultural values and political ideals of various nationalities should form the very basic of coexistence and coprosperity in the Far East.

Moreover, we took a vow to stand in the vanguard in the struggle for realising the above ideals. Amar Singh listened to our talks with great interest and satisfaction, and when we ended our talks with the above vow, he rejoiced slapping against his thigh. And standing up he prayed to God for protecting us and said that God would be with us in our noble mission. The perspitation drops oozing out from the face of both Amar Singh and Pritam Singh were shining like oil. We were recalled back to the realistic world with crowing of the first cock. With a start we looked at our watch. It was past 4.00 A.M. After fixing our next meeting five days hence, we left the place after agreeing not to use the place for such meeting any more.

As we were trying our best to develop mutual understanding and grasping the significance of the basic ideals necessary for our future work, the situation in the Pacific went on deteriorating from bad to worse. Towards the middle of October, Tokyo News reported the fall of the third

Koneo cabinet. With the formation of Tojo cabinet on the 18th October, I intuitively felt that the Japanese-American talks were on the verge of collapse and the Imperial Headquarters was going to opt for war in a very near future. The Japanese people in Bangkok somehow became restless around this time, probably reflecting the above developments.

I found myself in a position where it was impossible for me to know beforehand anything about the strategy and line of action to be adopted by the Imperial Headquarters and the Southern Forces in the event of hostilities. However, from the emphasis on reconnaissance of Southern Thailand and east coast of Malaya by the Japanese army, discussions among the Japanese service personnel, and my own knowledge on strategy. I was quite certain that occupation of Thailand and landing in Malaya were now just a matter of time. In view of iron wall like defence of Singapore on the side exposed to the sea, the range of the Japanese army and navy aeroplanes based in Southern Indo-China, and the objective of occupation of Singapore, it was quite inevitable that landing of Japanese forces in Southern Thailand and Kotah Bahru was already a foregone conclusion.

I also came to know that Lt. Gen. Yamashita had been assigned the job of capturing Singapore. He had shifted his Headquarters to Saigon, and was concentrating his 25th Army at Hainan Island for the purpose.

As I realised that the war was round the corner, I found myself faced with a dilemma the necessity to keep the war preparations of the Japanese army a closely guarded secret was rather incompatible with the necessity for drawing up a concrete plan for our project. As we were practically unprepared at that time, it was absolutely necessary to explain the resolution of the Japanese army to Pritam Singh in order to persuade him to draw up a concrete plan and start the necessary preparations. On the other hand any leakage of the operation plan of the Japanese army would have a very serious repercussion.

Pritam Singh probably got an air of this development from his sixth sense, and asked me several times about the real intension of the Japanese army. However, I was unable to give any satisfactory answer to him. During the first half of November, I had a number of meetings with Pritam Singh, changing the venue with every meeting. These meetings cemented our friendship and mutual reliance. These meetings helped me in obtaining a first hand knowledge of the Indian Independence movement and the conception of movement sponsored by the IIL. I also succeeded in catching a number of hints over the question of assisting and cooperating with the IIL.

I was somewhat worried as I realised that the Imperial Headquarters would be in for a great dissolution in case it had placed too much hope on the capability of the IIL in winning over the local Indians and Indian soldiers in Malaya at the time of Anglo-Japanese hostilities. This was because the IIL had not succeeded in penetrating these targets appreciably as was claimed by Lt. Col. Kadomatsu of the Imperial Headquarters. Moreover, the feeling among the Indians was far from being pro-Japanese. What was more important was that very little time was left. I racked my brain in conceiving the plan of fulfilling my mission on the basis of my faith and ideal, the suggestions provided by Pritam Singh and the stern reality of our unpreparedness. The rough outline I had chalked out was that with the outbreak of hostilities the members of the IIL would be urged to penetrate the enemy line and win over the Indian soldiers after making appeals to them directly. Again, efforts should be made to bring the Indian masses in Malaya and Thailand within the folds of the political movement of the IIL as quickly as possible. After the opening of the hostilities, the IIL movement would proceed with the dual objective of winning over the Indian soldiers of the British Indian army in particular and the Indian nationals in general.

The programme for the Indian soldiers was as follows. The members of the IIL and the F-Organisation (F-Kikan) would dedicatedly protect the Indian war prisoners and explain to them the ideal of the IIL and the real intension of the Japanese army, in order to raise a volunteer army for Indian Independence as quickly as possible. The programme for the Indian people in general was also almost identical. The members of the IIL and the F-Organisation would protect and allay the fears of the Indian people living in terror in the midst of hostilities, explain the political aims of the IIL and Japan, and attempt to persuade them to join the IIL movement and set up the IIL units all over the occupied territories and then go in for reaching the Indian masses under the enemy sphere of influence.

These two programmes were complementary to each other as the two wings of a bird. Spreading the IIL movement among the Indians living in Burma and other East Asian countries and seeking support from the Indians in India were of vital importance.

The members of the IIL and the F-Organisation should dedicate themselves to the movement of the Indian people and their interest and freedom, guarantee their safety, and try to gain confidence through their bravery and modesty. Again, the Japanese forces should not commit even the slightest violence on the Indian residents and soldiers, rather should support their patriotic movement, ensure their life, property and freedom, and show proper understanding and enthusiasms. Again, the IIL being a voluntary and spontaneous movement of the Indian people should transcend above the narrow provincial and religious bias, and adopt a policy with an appeal to all the Indians. Again, it was also necessary to impress the Japanese people, especially the Japanese military and government leaders with proper understanding of India and the Indians, especially their freedom movement. (Indeed, the Japanese people had a very meagre knowledge of India and the Indians).

When I thought over this problem, I felt that it was more necessary to create proper understanding and atmosphere of cooperation among the Japanese military officers and men rather than seeking Indian response. Besides looking after the Indian affairs, I had to give proper guidance to Tashiro and Kamimoto over their Chinese and Harimau projects respectively. Towards the end of November, a new question of establishing contact with and enlisting cooperation of Malay Youth League cropped up.

Towards the middle of November, the Japanese Consulate General of Singapore supplied me with information on the anti-British Malay socialist group Malay Youth League. This secret organisation of the Malays worked under the cover of the newspaper 'Warta Malayas' and had its base in Singapore. It had established cells all over Malaya, receiving enthusiastic support from the Malay intellectuals and proletarians. The object of the movement was to gain freedom from the British, and neutralise the propertied Malays acting as the tools in the hands of the British.

I also came to know that this group had established contacts with the Japanese Consulate General in Singapore. As the activities of Harimau[4] was motivated only by anti-Chinese grudge devoid of any principle whatsoever, it was not possible to place much reliance on him to appeal to the Malays for their nationalistic cause. Moreover, his influence was restricted only to Kuantan State. Thus it is needless to say how welcome this news was to me and the military attache. I immediately started chalking out plans to enlist the cooperation of the Malay Youth League.

I got a detailed first hand information on the subject towards the end of November when the Japanese Consul General Tsurumi posted in Singapore came over to Bangkok. I tried to evolve plans to bring about cooperation between the active workers of Malay Youth League and the members of the F-organisation already working in South Thailand. However, the time at disposal was too short.

On 28th November, I went to the Japanese embassy as usual in the

4. This was a pseudonym for Tani Yutaka, a prominent leader of Malaya.

morning, and after talking with the ambassador for a while I proceeded to meet the military attache. As I entered his room, his assistant twinked at me and whispered to me to go down to the lounge. His action sent horror creeping through my mind at the prospect of getting out plans exposed. I was overwhelmed with only one worry; whether my twelve comrades deployed in Southern Thailand had been captured by Thai police or British and Chinese agents because of their over enthusiasm. However, he conveyed to me a message in a very low voice for which I was least prepared. He said that the talks between Japan and America had reached a deadlock, and that war would start sometimes early December. The work of the F-Organisation regarding Malaya would then pass into the jurisdiction of Gen. Teraushi, the Commander-in-Chief of the Southern Forces. The general would place the organisation under the command of Gen. Yamashita, commander of the 25th Army. I also had expected such a development, but when I came to know about it finally, I felt unprecedented excitement. Immediately two thoughts came to my mind. One was to contact Pritam Singh and discuss about concretes plans of our work. The second was how to rush to South Thailand without delay together with Pritam Singh, the members of the IIL and the organisation so as not to be too late at the start of hostilities. I requested to keep a Douglas aeroplane ready for me there and was glad to receive his immediate approval.

I immediately took steps to meet Pritam Singh that very night. I sent Yamaguchi to the manager of Mitsubishi Co. with a request to use his house for the meeting, and sent Otaguro to inform Pritam Singh. The tension of the military attache and his assistant was reflected in the behaviour of all the members of his office, and when I stepped on the road the peaceful atmosphere struck me as a grim contrast.

Although we were drawing up plans on Malaya, yet we were not very sure about the attitude of the Thai government, on whose soil we were hatching our plans. I was under the impression that the Japanese ambassador and the military attache would try to persuade the Thai government to permit peaceful stationing of Japanese forces in Thailand. However,, the Thai reaction was anybody's guess in view of complicated national and international situation. In case the Thais decided to disagree then all the Japanese in the country would be taken into custody. In that case all the members of the organisation including myself would be taken into custody in Bangkok and Southern Thailand, and the whole work would come to a standstill. Even the thought of such a prospect sent chill through my spine. The safest course appeared to be to withdraw to Saigon immediately and then to land in South Thailand alongwith the operational forces. But the snag here was that it was impossible to take all the members of IIL including Pritam Singh to Saigon together with us. There was almost no prospect of Thai government's permitting Pritam Singh to leave the country legally, and any attempt on his part to leave the country illegally was surely to be watched. Even if it was possible, it was already too late. (It would be an extremely dangerous step to try to smuggle out Pritam Singh in a Japanese plane). As there was no official communication about the start of hostilities, discussions with Col. Tamura drew blank. There was no way left but to resign to our fate.

That night I met Pritam Singh at the residence of the manager of Mitsubishi Co. As luck would have it, the manager was absent. Carefully avoiding any hint at the intention of the Japanese army, I explained to him about the impending rupture in the Japanese-American talks, and that Japan was expecting Anglo-American attack any moment. In that case, I added, the Japanese army would go into action, Malaya becoming the prime target. I cautioned him that the time for us to act might come much earlier than expected. I expressed my views over the necessity to start discussions on concrete plans for action. As expected I could read tension on the face of Pritam Singh.

That very night we held four rounds of talks on our future plans. I listened to Pritam Singh passionately explaing his conviction frankly with great attention. Fortunately as there was identity of view over the concept of ideal and there was proper understanding, his line of thinking agreed with that of mine this time also. Excepting for very minor technical aspects, there was no serious divergence of views. The plan we finally drew up had to be a very abstract one since we had no idea of the army's operational plan or the course the operation might actually take.

We agreed to have the following points as our ideal and basis of cooperation, and vowed to each other to do our best for realising them.

1. The principle objective of our cooperation will be to realise friendly relation between Japan and India, both the countries constituting partners as independent, free and equal nations. The two countries will cooperate with each other with the ultimate aim of bringing peace, freedom and prosperity in East Asia.
2. The IIL will take up armed struggle for achieving quick and complete Independence of India, and will welcome overall support from Japan. However, in this connection Japan will guarantee that it will not have any territorial, military, political, economic and religious design against India in return for its help.
3. The IIL will transcend above narrow provincial, religious and party

bias, and will welcome all the patriotic Indians willing to fight the Britishers within its fold. Again, it will try its best to create an atmosphere of cooperation and harmony between the local people and the Indians in the zones of military operation.

4. Immediately on the outbreak of Anglo-Japanese hostilities, the IIL will implement the following programme.
   (a) The IIL will advance to Southern Thailand and Malaya alongwith the Japanese army and establish itself among the Indian people living there, trying its best to rouse anti-British feeling among the local Indians and the Indian soldiers and to create an atmosphere of cooperation with the Japanese forces.
   (b) The IIL will raise a volunteer army from among the Indian soldiers of the British Indian Army and the Indian civilian population of Malaya, and will make preparations for the future fight for freedom.
   (c) Depending upon the situation, the IIL will try to enlarge the above movement of item (b) to encompass the other territories of East Asia.

5. The Japanese armed forces will take the following steps for ensuring success of the various aspects of the IIL movement mentioned above.
   (a) The Japanese army will confer freedom of activity to the IIL in its occupied and operational territories as much as operational considerations can permit. It will also ensure safety and assistance to the members of the IIL.
   (b) The liaison work between the Japanese armed forces and the IIL as well as direct assistance to the IIL will be entrusted to the Fujiwara Organisation (Fujiwara Kikan). This organisation will try its best to facilitate the promotion of the IIL movement. (The Fujiwara Kikan will be organised formally as soon as hostility breaks out).
   (c) The Japanese forces will not treat the Indian prisoners of war and the civilian Indian population in the operational zone as hostiles, rather they will be treated as the compatriots in general are treated. The life, property, freedom and honour of the Indians will be protected and respected. Again, the places of worship will be protected and these will not be used by the Japanese forces for any military purpose. The Japanese officers and men will be apprised of this and will be forbidden to violate these.
   (d) The Japanese army will permit the IIL to use Radio Tokyo and the other radio stations of the occupied territories as well as

Bangkok Radio for carrying out effective propaganda activity. Again, the Japanese army will provide aeroplane facilities to the IIL for distributing propaganda literatures.

(e) The Japanese army will lend its good offices to arrange liaison between Subhash Chandra Bose in Berlin and the IIL.

(f) The Japanese army will provide necessary money and material to Pritam Singh considered essential for carrying on the IIL activities on demand, and will not hinder collection of voluntary contributions from the Indians in the operational zone.

Besides preparing the above Tamura-Pritam Singh Memorandum we discussed about the following items.

(a) Just after the start of war, the members of the IIL and of Fujiwara Organisation will proceed to Southern Thailand in a Japanese plane provided by the Japanese army for the purpose.

(b) The IIL will prepare propaganda materials on the basis of the above memorandum.

(c) A symbol will be fixed for discriminating the IIL members from the enemy and ensuring freedom of movement and activity in the battle zone. All the Japanese officers and men will be enlightened on the symbol.[5]

Note : Later on the letter F was fixed as the symbol after discussions with Pritam Singh as it could be readily recognised by the Japanese soldiers. The letter F was selected out of consideration that it was the initial letter of 'Friendship' and 'Freedom', not to tell of 'Fujiwara'.

(d) The IIL will make preparations to organise a number of propaganda squads immediately on arriving at Southern Thailand, and send them behind the enemy lines for carrying out propaganda among the Indian soldiers of the British Indian Army and the civilian Indian population.

The above memorandum was prepared in English and Japanese, and was formally signed by Col. Tamura and Pritam Singh on the Ist of December. As it was signed, we forget all our painful sleepless nights spent on discussion and were pervaded with a great sense of joy and success. And we vowed to each other to stand at the vanguard of the two nations and accomplish our mission with all earnestness, by cooperating with each other.

Incidentally this was also the day when the meeting in the Imperial Diet decided to go in for war.

---

5. See the Interrogation Report of Fujiwara. Document. No. 10

The main strength of a Japanese navy task force was proceeding towards Pearl Harbour for launching a surprise attack, and a massive force of Japanese army and navy had collected at Hainan Island for attacking Malaya. Of course, we were in complete darkness of these development. This was indeed a fateful day when Japan got into the whirlpool of the great Pacific war.

Copies of this memorandum were forwarded to the Headquarters of the Southern Forces and that of the 25th Army at Saigon. The approval came immediately. Another copy was also sent to the Military Section of the Imperial Headquarters in Tokyo.

Now started the busiest period of my life. I had to discuss with Pritam Singh over the steps to be taken for implementing the programme chalked out in the memorandum. Again, I had to maintain contact with the Malay Youth League, and exchange messages with and send instructions to the members of F-Organisation in south Thailand. Pritam Singh also sent his secret messenger to South Thailand, and tried his best to evolve an operation plan.

In Bangkok, the members of the F-Organisation had to remain in battle readiness for any eventuality.

It was rather impossible for a Japanese to conceive of a soldier without bald head and a sword on his waist, probably because of the long tradition of feudalistic administration ever since the militarists grabbed the government. Again, the atmosphere in the army also gave absolutely no scope for deviation from the traditional values. Anybody seen without bald head and a sword by his side was likely to be branded as coward immediately. Even the reporters, authors, artists and monks accompanying the armed forces as non-combatant without exception put on military uniform and took sword gladly. It was the custom of the time for the military civil administrative officials and businessmen sent for reconstruction and rehabilitation after military operations to aspire to have some sort of military rank, however, nominal it might be.

As all my associates and myself had entered Thailand as diplomats or employees of commercial firms or hotel employees, it was not possible for us to have our formal military uniforms with us. The job assigned to us was neither to subjugate the enemy and the local people by brute force, nor to overwhelm them by weilding authority. The only arms we had at our disposal in confronting the enemy and the local people were our virtue, integrity and sincerity. We were not supposed to carry even a bit of iron, and hence the stern military uniform was not for us. We had to put on dress that would bring us close to the people among whom we were expected to work. Considering from the conventional contempt of the Japanese army towards the people engaged in pacification work it was certain that we with long hair and plain dress would not be welcome guests running about in the battle field. A large number of obstacles were bound to be placed on our way. Even then I had no intention to procure military uniform as such a step would betray our antecedents immediately.

After considering the various *pros and cons* of the problems, we decided to get simple khaki riding-dress made by some local Chinese tailor. I also decided to get a number of pistols sent from Saigon for self protection of the IIL members and the F-Organisation members who would have to move about in the front. I personally decided not to carry either sword or pistol. However, I decided to put on my rank marking and staff officer's badge, and to carry a silver baton.

I sent orders to all the members of F-Organisation to retain their long hair.

With these rapid developments we became very nervous about the move of the Thai government. At night information was sent round to the Japanese residents to collect at the Japanese primary school in small groups. All the military personnel gathered in the military attache's room, at night. An ominous silence, as if precussor to the events to follow, befall the street in front of the military attache's room and some doubtful figures, apparently Thai secret police, started moving about suspiciously on the street. An uncanny tension gripped everybody in the place. However, we did not take up sieze-like position in order not to provocate the Thais. Although the night of seventh with a likely threat to our life was advancing fast, yet the fortunate development was that the movement of the Japanese forces was still shrouded with great secrecy. Reports started pouring in that the foreigners in the Oriental Hotel were still peacefully gossiping around the dining tables and crowding the dance floor. Finally the time has come to inform Pritam Singh about the development.

However, the Thai attitude towards Japan was not yet clear. In case the Thais adopted an anti-Japanese posture, then just like the local Japanese Pritam Singh was also surely to be put behind the bars alongwith associates. In order to prevent Pritam Singh from visiting me, I sent Odakuro and Yamaguchi secretly to the house of Pritam Singh to inform him about the war. He was to be informed that the war would start on the following day dawn, and as the Thai attitude was not very clear he was to remain very careful. However, he should make preparations to go to Southern Thailand on the day following the start of war, i.e., on the seventh alongwith me. My two informants related to me on return that even cool and calculating

Pritam Singh was besides himself with excitement. With a very happy expression he had offered prayers to God muttering that at last the long waited time had come, and God would be on his side.

I felt a great burden releaved from my breast, which was torturing me eversince I came to know about the war. I could easily guess the feeling of Pritam Singh who had waited all these years just for this day, and could feel the echo of this feeling in my mind. And I took the vow afresh that as the representative of the Japanese nation I would live upto the expectation of Pritam Singh and would try to render all possible help for fulfilling his lofty ideal.

The night started dawning slowly. The distant cocks started crowing. Still there was no news on the whereabouts of the Thai Prime Minister Phibun Songkram. The negotiations were at a standstill. The movements of the foreigners did not betray any sign of abnormality. The number of uniformed Thai police started increasing around the Military attache's office. Probably the Japanese forces had already landed at Singora and Patani in Southern Thailand and Kotah Bahru in Malaya.

In the Gulf of Thailand also a Japanese convoy must have entered by now. The Konoe Division was probably moving towards Bangkok in lightening speed overland from Indo-China. There might have some skirmishes also with the Thai forces. In the morning, a Japanese plane was supposed to come flying over our building for contact. Day before yesterday at the time of arriving at an understanding the signal informing that Thailand was neither as enemy nor a friend had not been agreed upon. There was no other way out other than writing down the signal 'Not known' on a piece of cloth and displaying it at the race course. Presently a Japanese army plane came flying from the east and started circling over the military attache's office. Immediately a few persons ran to the race course carrying the signal cloth. As soon as they started unfurling the singal, scores of Thai police who were watching the situation came running and forcibly snatched the cloth and took all the Japanese alongwith them towards the stand. The whole thing happened in a few seconds. Immediately the assistant to the military attache ran to the place in a car. The plane circled over the building vainly for a number of times and then vanished towards east. Almost simultaneously with this disturbing news started pouring in. 'The Japanese forces landing at Bangkok port ran into resistance from Thai police and Thai people'. 'Clashes have occurred between Thai forces and the advancing Japanese forces along the Thai-Indo-China border.' 'The Thai army in Bangkok are getting ready for action.' etc. The Japanese employees of the embassy and military attache's office knowing Thai language hurried to the troubled spots and tried their best to stop the incidents. Although the Thai attitude was not very happy, yet there was no varulous anti-Japanese feeling. We all in the military attache's room clung to the radio for news from Radio Tokyo, and did not leave the radio even for a moment.

Declaration of the state of war with Britain and America in West Pacific, Imperial announcement of declaration of war, speech by Premier Tojo, success of the surprise attack on Pearl Harbour, surprise landing on South Thailand. Such good news came pouring out of the microphone of the radio one after another. All of us were overwhelmed with emotion, and there was none whose eyes were not wet. Finally, we heard out national anthem followed by martial music, which only went to highten our excitement even further. At about 11 P.M. a messenger came hurriedly from the residence of the ambassador bringing the message of reappearance of the Thai Prime Minister and successful conclusion of negotiations. He also reported that the Konoe Division was almost on the outskirts of Bangkok. At a stroke we were relieved of the oppressive apprehension that had gripped up since the night before. I again sent my messenger to Pritam Singh to set his worries at ease relating the latest developments. The time finally had come where we could meet each other openly and start out work.

Within a few minutes we arrived at a decision. It was decided to send a propaganda squad of the IIL alongwith the main strength of the advancing Fifth Division. Two of Pritam Singh's associates who had accompanied us from Bangkok were selected for the purpose, and I ordered my three assistants, Lt. Nakamiya, the old man Shiba and Susuki to accompany the above two persons for liaison work. The group boldly started for Alor Star front in the midst of heavy rains.

After seeing off the group, I accompanied Pritam Singh to a rally of his associated living around the Thai-Malaya border. Next we inaugurated a conference of Indians in Hat Yai, established the Southern Thailand branch of IIL, and undertook the task of organising IIL propaganda squads for sending them to the Kotah Behru front. Capt. Tsuchimochi remained busy converting the two story residence of Tashiro on the outskirts of Hat Yai into the Headquarters of the IIL, and the office of Tainan Koshi Co, into the office of the F-Organisation. Next I went to inspect the IIL Headquarters alongwith Capt. Tsuchimochi. A large number of Indians had already gathered there, and they were very happy to see both Pritam Singh and myself.

I was very happy over Capt. Tsuchimochi's arrangement. Pritam Singh was also very happy. Pritam Singh immediately went to the first floor and unfurled an Indian national flag from the verandah, I could see his hand shaking with emotion as he unfurled the national flag. For a while he prayed to the national flag, bathed in the western sun just like an erect statue. We standing down below were also overwhelmed with emotion. Next, a strip of cloth with the words IIL written on it in Indian language and Japanese was hung from the railing of the verandah. This was for he first time that the IIL came out of hiding, and in effect declare war for liberating motherland. Thus a new dimension was added to the war that was progressing in the South.

Next Pritam Singh announced the convening of a conference of local Indians on the following day. Thus we passed the first night in the front. Throughout the night, a continuous stream of Japanese forces moved south towards the Alor Star front.

As we were proceeding along the road to Sadao, our vehicle entered a side road on instruction from Pritam Singh. After advancing along the zigzag road of the rubber plantation, we stopped in front of a ramshakle hut. A Sikh appeared from inside in a hurry, surprised by the sound of the motor engine. He was just like a recluse seeking salvation away from human habitation. He was about 50 years old.

Pritam Singh who had got down in a hurry ran to him and embraced him as soon as he saw him at the door. As soon as Pritam Singh saw me, he introduced his friend to me. I have forgotten his name. We were ushered inside the house. He praised the bravery of the Japanese forces which had put the British Indian forces to flight in the vicinity of Sadao on the day before. He hurriedly prepared tea and made preparations to leave with us. All his possessions were a bedstead made of bamboo and rope, some sooty pots and pans and a set of dirty dress which he was mending. Even if he left the house unlocked, there was nothing inside worth for a thief to steal. I was very much impressed by this man who had voluntarily chosen such an austere life gladly in such a God forbidden place for the sake of motherland. In this way, Pritam Singh picked up two more of his associates living in the region before returning to Hat Yai. On the street crossing of Hat Jai I could see propaganda posters of IIL pasted prominently. These were brought from Bangkok by Pritam Singh, and a large number of Indians were reading them avidly.

In the afternoon, about two hundred Indians, men and women, young and old gathered in front of the Headquarters of the IIL. Almost all the Indians living in the town had gathered here. Pritam Singh made the maiden speech of his life addressing these people from the balcony. One Indian interpreted his speech in Tamil. Every sentence of Pritam Singh was greeted with wild applause by the people. The tone was low, but very forceful. It was a passionate speech expressing firm desire to fight for the freedom of Motherland.

The Indian, who were in a state of terror ever since 8th December when their dream was rudely broken by the guns of the Japanese forces, had their fears set at rest as a result of this meeting. They also recovered their national consciousness.

On the following day, i.e., 12th, Pritam Singh gathered his comrades from Yala, organised them into two propaganda squads, and sent one of them to accompany the A-Detachment, which was advancing along the Yala-Beton Road. 2nd Lt. Yonemura and Kamimoto accompanied this equal as liaison officers from the F-Organisation side. Again, the Harimau band also penetrated behind the British lines in this sector under the guidance of 2nd Lt. Yonemura. The second propaganda squad proceeded to the Kotah Bahru front by train, with 2nd Lt. Segawa and Nagano of F-Organisation accompanying as the liaison officers.

That night I held a very friendly discussion with Capt. Mohan Singh and Pritam Singh. During the first part of the talks I related my happy experience over the surrender of the Indian soliders led by Capt. Mohan Singh. We both appreciated the smooth way the whole thing had been arranged. Both Capt. Mohan Singh and Pritam Singh again sympathised with my sincere regret over the two unfortunate incidents of the afternoon. During the later part of the talks I explained the Japanese army's views over assistance to the Indian Independence movement, and the details of cooperation with the IIL as seen from the angle of the Japanese forces. Herein I also expressed my own views on the success of the Indian freedom struggle. I pointed out the dishonour and sad plight of the conquered nations. I also related my firm conviction that the Independence of India should be won by the Indians primarily through their own struggle. I emphasised that the Second European War followed by the great East Asian War has provided a unique opportunity to the Indian people to rise in revolt and win back their glorious freedom. In that connection I related the Japan's committed objective of supporting Indian Independence struggle with all understandings as one of the goals of the present war. Besides I also related four of my personal views frankly. *Firstly*, both Japan and India should take the enemy as the common enemy for realising the Indian objective. *Secondly*, Japan is historically bound to India through religion and culture. *Thirdly*, location in East Asia has bound the destiny of the two nations. *Lastly*, people in general are extremely angry over the servile position of the Indian people.

Capt. Mohan Singh also cited a large number of instances of British misrule of India and discrimination of the Britishers against the Indians, and explained his pains over the unhappiness and dishonour of a survile nation. He also agreed with my view that the Indian Independence can be achieved only through the revolution of the Indian people. He finally concluded by saying that he would be in the vanguard in case such a revolution breaks out for the Independence of India. He appreciated my conviction over the sincere desire of the Japanese army to give all out support to the freedom movement of India. However, he sought my assent to discuss something, which was not be very complementary. For the sake of future happiness of the two nations of India and Japan, after tendering proper apology. It was regarding the colonial rule of Japan over Korea and Formosa, and the Japanese policy towards Manchuria and China. All these, he added, coupled with the actions of the Japanese armed forces have created a very adverse impression of the Japanese people on the Indian people in general. The content was more or less the same as that already discussed by Pritam Singh before. I listened to his views very attentively and expressed the same views which I had expressed to Pritam Singh earlier.

After relating the above views, the captain emphasised that whatever method may be adopted for achieving the Indian Independence, it is imperative that, this should receive the approval and whole hearted support of the Indian National Congress, the mainstay of the Indian nationalist movement. This view of Capt. Mohan Singh was contrary to the view held by Pritam Singh and myself, and I realised that this view had moderated his enthusiasm for Indian revolution with Japanese support. I tried to convince him by arguing that the form of political struggle adopted by the Indian National Congress should be very flexible and should change with the changing international situation. I also related my assessment of the situation that in case international situation ripens in favour of armed struggle as advocated by the great Indian revolutionary Subhas Chandra Bose, or the movements launched by Subhas Chandra Bose and the IIL succeed in producing encouraging results and become a real force for the Indian Independence, then the Indian masses would come forward to support this struggle and the Indian National Congress also would find it difficult to stand aloof. Our talks were held in a very friendly atmosphere where we expressed our views frankly, nevertheless passionately. I was very happy to learn about the latent patriotism of Capt. Mohan Singh, and his grudge against the ruling English people.

This talk, however, dashed all my hopes of enlisting Capt. Mohan

Singh's support to our movement in a foresee-able future, but I felt convinced that he could be won over in the long-run. It was already 3.00 A.M. when the talks ended. We had talked almost the whole day since morning without break, but the talks were so interesting and earnest that I was totally oblivious of fatigue. We went to bed after agreeing to continuing our talks the following night.

The prospect of the eleventh Division of the British Indian Army making any firm stand in the region north of Perak river following the collapse of the Jitra Line appeared to be very dim in the face of heavy pressure of the pursuing Japanese forces. The English forces beat a hasty retreat to the south of the Perak river leaving the vast military installation at Sungei Patani. There was no sign of organised resistance at Taiping either. In case the Japanese forces succeeded in capturing the vital bridge over the Perak river before the British forces could destroy it, then the front would shift to Central Malaya at a stroke. A fierce battle was also likely to develop over the capture of the Penang Island.

The work of the F-Organisation was showing all the symptoms of enlarging manifold. The time had come to mobilise all our strength to work all along the front for the welfare of the local people and the Indian soldiers of the British Indian Army. Again, urgent work was piling up like protecting, accommodating, feeding and medically assisting the ever increasing number of Indian soldiers in Sungei Patani and Alor Star areas. Again, discussion with Capt. Mohan Singh was also very vital. The IIL organisation also had to be established in the various regions north of Perak river. A liaison officer had also to be sent to Kotah Bahru area to substitute 2nd Lt. Segawa. Protection of the Sultan of Kedah, and negotiations with the Sultan and the Malay Youth League were also a very tricky affair. We were desperately short of hands. I also had only one person capable of interpreting talks in English in my team. I had no spare hand to look after our safety, accommodation and food. I had to select persons for these duties from among the persons who came to us on recommendations from the IIL or just out of goodwill for our work. As for meals, we had to pull alongwith Chinese and Malayan dishes exclusively.

I was very much worried over the slowly accumulating fatigue because of my hard work. On 16th, ultimately I succeeded in procuring the services of two persons for our work. One was 2nd Lt. Kunizuka, an interpreter of the Fifth Division. He had graduated from Yamaguchi Higher Commercial School and was an employee of a certain trading firm of Kobe before he was drafted for service. He was indeed a genious so far as English language was concerned. The other person was one Ito, an employee of the Japanese consulate at Singora. He was fairly conversant with day to day spoken English, and volunteered to join the F-Organisation on hearing about its activities. He was also very young in age. I entrusted all the jobs connected with looking after all the Indian prisoners of war in Alor Star and Sungei Patani area, as well as the liaison work between Capt. Mohan Singh and the F-Organisation, to these two enthusiastic members. At that time the number of the Indian prisoners had, in all probability, reached the figure of 700. And I requested these two members to be constantly by the side of the Indian prisoners and share their food and lodging just like any other Indian.

Of course they were not given even a bit of iron. Although they were very talented and earnest, yet they lacked experience. Indeed I had entrusted them with very heavy responsibility, and I expected that they would fulfil their mission magnificently. I solicited Capt. Mohan Singh's good offices for discipline and positive cooperation of the Indian prisoners, and I got his ready approval.

With their sincerity, kindness, earnestness and amiability they immediately won over the Indian prisoners, who started treating these two young members as their darling. They slept amidst the Indian soldiers, shared their food with great relish, and worked like a clock without any sign of fatigue or grudge. From the very first day they started learning Indian language from the soliders. On the 16th, the Indian soliders taken prisoner by the 5th Division in the battle of Jitra were handed over to the F-Organisation, and they came and joined the group of Capt. Mohan Singh. The new arrivals were very happy to find their old comrades in this camp. Which was free from any restriction expected on such occasion.

On the 17th noon, I arranged a luncheon party with the members of the F-Organisation, IIL and the officers and NCOs of the Group of Mohan Singh. I wanted to have it in Indian style to cater to the taste of the Indians, and requested Capt. Mohan Singh for cooks. The backyard of the police station became alive with the busy cooks since early morning. At the stroke of twelve, we stopped all work and went to the venue. The table were full of strange looking dishes, and there was an orchestra of strange musical instruments.

I was very much surprised by the deep impression this luncheon created in the minds of the Indians, although I had just casually arranged it thinking that such a step would help fraternisation. Capt. Mohan Singh stood up and gave a table speech on the following line. 'For a staff officer of the victorious army to invite his Indian prisoners of war, and that also who have just surrendered hardly two days back, even down upon the level of NCOs to Indian style luncheon and partake Indian food with them is something rather inconceivable for the British army. In the British army, the British officers never take meals together with their Indian fellow officers, although they may fight shoulder to shoulder in the same unit. In the officers club any suggestion, however, earnest it may be, put forward by the Indian officers for Indian style meal is rejected outright. This earnest invitation of Maj. Fujiwara transcending over the petty bias of enemy and friend, victor and vanquished, or race is a singular proof of his friendship which he has been showing to us since day before yesterday, and which even a thousand words would have failed to convey. We all are so deeply impressed by this gesture that we fail to find adequate words to express it. It is needless to say that todays food and arrangement are thoroughly inadequate because of the abnormal conditions prevailing presently although we have tried our best to satisfy the request of Maj. Fujiwara. Capt. Mohan Singh spoke each and every word of his speech with deep emotion, and that he spoke the views of all the Indians present there was corroborated by thunderous applause that followed the speech.

Although most of the F-Organisation members including myself had left Bangkok in October, yet this was the first occasion for most of us to have an Indian meal together with the Indians. As we were at a loss since we could find neither chopsticks nor forks, our Indian friends taught us the way to partake with hands, as was the custom in India. Kunizuka and Ito, who had picked that up the day before immediately, started eating with hands feigning great ease and were warmly applauded. Yamaguchi started such a terrible hiccup after swallowing the first morsel of curry that everybody burst out laughing. It was indeed a grand success for forging Indo-Japanese understanding.

Sweet rice cooked in ghee, unbearably hot curry, fowl meat with skin and bone on, all these were too much for me to eat with ease. I wetted upto my wrist with curry. All the officers sharing my table including Capt. Mohan Singh smiled at my clumsiness. I felt as if whole of my oral cavity was on flame. At last, Capt. Mohan Singh also could stand it no more, and brought a fork for me alone. I appreciated his gesture, but I declined it because I was very happy to try to eat just like all other Indians although somewhat clumsily.

Around this time Capt. Mohan Singh was very busy during the day time discussing various things with Pritam Singh and his fellow officers, and looking after the accommodation, provision, health etc. of the Indian prisoners. We brought in tents, provisions cooking utensils, clothing and medical stores from the Godown of the British army in Jitra and Sungei. As the Japanese forces were preoccupied with pursuing the enemy, they did not have any time either to spot out the British military stores; and even when these were located there was nobody to look after these properly. Taking advantage of this volatile situation, I permitted Capt. Mohan Singh to bring the goods required for the Indian prisoners from the British military stores under Japanese occupation. I took this step out of my own discretion as I thought that any formal request to the Japanese high command or the commissariat department would invite unnecessary restrictions and imposition of ceiling, etc.

Kunizuka and Ito developed very good understanding with Capt. Mohan Singh, and assisted him very well in avoiding unnecessary troubles with the Japanese soldiers. The Indian officers also proved to be very loyal assistants to Mohan Singh. The Indian NCOs and soldiers also carried out all the orders loyally and sincerely, and there was not even a single case of contravention of discipline. It was indeed commendable that they strictly observed all the military discipline and did not behave like prisoners at all. The luncheon party of the 17th helped in creating a feeling of brotherhood between the members of the F-Organisation and the Indian officers and men. When the Indian soldiers saluted me with sincere look, I felt the illusion as if I was being greeted by my own men of my unit. Again, when I exchanged salute with the Indian officers, I felt as if I was exchanging salute with the fellow officers of my regiment. The propaganda squad led by Gopal Singh with Capt. Tsuchimochi as the liaison officer reached the camp of Sungei alongwith a large number of Indian prisoners after carrying out successful propaganda among the Indian army stragglers in Taiping area. Lt. Nakamiya, who had been assigned the duty of protecting the Sultan, reached the Sultan's palace at Alor Star successfully, and his work there received high praises from both the Malays and the Japanese forces. Later on, he left the old man Shiba with the Sultan and rushed to the Perak river front alongwith the propaganda squad of the IIL. There was also a very sad news. It was the death of 2nd Lt. Segawa Kiyoshi in engagement with the enemy. Hence I had to hurriedly send the only officer left with me Lt. Yamaguchi to Kotah Bahru by plane to look after the work there.

Although Pritam Singh was very busy with discussions with Capt. Mohan Singh and organising the IIL propaganda squads, yet he found time to establish IIL branches in the areas around Alor Star. Our life in the IIL Headquarters and the F-Organisation Headquarters was indeed a very busy one.

Although I was extremely busy, yet I made time at night to have a very through and frank discussion with Capt. Mohan Singh for four consecutive nights following 16th December. From these meetings I realised that the captain was a man of excellent character, and I could also get a clear insight about his convictions. Mohan Singh also on his part appeared to understand me, and as such did not hesitate to bare his mind. I discovered his ardent patriotism, and his sincere desire to dedicate himself for the liberation of his motherland. I discovered all the qualities of a leader of revolution in him. He was very friendly to his colleagues and subordinates, he reasoned rather than following blindly, had a very sincere and plain attitude, firm resolution, capacity to carry out resolution, and impressing all with modesty and frankness. We agreed on a number of points like follows. That the Second World War has brought a grand opportunity at its wake for the Independence of the various nations of the South East. Asia including India, and that the Indian people should garb this chance to win back their freedom. That the newly liberated nations should rise above petty rivalries and strive for mutual prosperity and co-existence treating each other as equal partners. That there is not a single field where the national interests of the Indian and the Japanese people can clash with each other, and that the two nations are destined to remain good friends cooperating with each other with no scope for military confrontation between the two nations. That the lofty goals described about can be achieve only by mobilizing the patriotic young people of the various nations of South East Asia. During the talks he expressed great respect for Subhash Chandra Bose, and expressed the view that all the Indians in South East Asia will unanimously place themselves under the leadership of Subhash Chandra Bose in case he come over to East Asia to lead the freedom struggle.

I was very much impressed over the great esteem in which the Indians in general held Subhash Chandra Bose. He was almost a divine figure with them. I, in my turn, communicated this view to the Imperial Headquarters whenever I got any opportunity. I was of the view that the Germans may not approve of any proposal to send Bose to East Asia in view of their campaign towards Middle East. However, the thing that pained me most was that not a single revolutionary leader of the subjugated nations of South Asia, who could rightfully claim to represent his people, had come over to the Japanese side, although it had been advocating great East Asia Co-prosperity Sphere in its life and death struggle. This could be attributed to the callous attitude Japan had shown till then towards the nationalist movement of the peoples of the region.

I confided to Capt. Mohan Singh that it might be difficult to invite Bose to East Asia at the moment because of the international developments therefore the IIL should try to organise freedom movement in East Asia for the moment, and next associate this movement with the great enterprise of Bose in Europe, thus giving it a global status scale. I also assured Capt. Mohan Singh that I would try my best to persuade the Imperial Headquarters to convey to Bose his feeling. I also tried to encourage him to take bold step as taken by Bose.

After five nights of discussions, it appeared to me that I had almost won him over. He was apparently thinking to accept the sincerity of Japan as a real one. This was because he promised to try for gaining the support of his countrymen, especially Congress party, and try to gain unanimous approval of his fellow officers and men. I knew it very well that any hasty emotional step to organise a revolutionary army to win over freedom through armed struggle was bound to end in a failure in the long run. Voluntary participation of all the officers and men dedicated to the cause in the Indian National Army was the only way to achieve success. So I requested Capt. Mohan Singh once again to consider the whole question coolly and carefully without making any haste. Pritam Singh also approved of what I had said.

At that stage I felt that a meeting of Pritam Singh and Capt. Mohan Singh with the commanding officer of the Japanese forces Lt. Gen. Yamashita would be very useful as this would provide a very good opportunity to both my friends to ascertain directly the Japanese army's intention over the question of supporting the Independence movement of the Indian people. So I proposed such a meeting. As both of them welcomed this meeting, I called upon Lt. Gen. Yamashita around 20th afternoon alongwith Pritam Singh, Capt. Mohan Singh and four Indian officers of the INA.

Lt. Gen. Yamashita greeted us warmly. He ushered us to the operation room, and standing before the operations chart, he explained the overall war situation in the Pacific. Next he explained frankly the Japanese army's earnest desire to give all out support to the Indian Independence movement, and requested my friends to put forward all the demands without hesitation as that the Japanese army could give all the necessary support and assistance to the IIL movement. The Chief of Staff, Maj. Gen. Suzuki was also present in the meeting. Both Pritam Singh and Capt. Mohan Singh thanked the two generals sincerely. This meeting lasted for about 40 minutes. It appeared to me that all the Indians were very much impressed by this giant of a man (Lt. Gen. Yamashita) who expressed all his sympathies over the question of Indian Independence.

Two days before this meeting I came to know about the sudden withdrawal of the British force from Penang and liberation of all the Japanese confined in the Jail of Penang by local Indians and Malay. One of the Japanese confined in the jail had come to inform me with the assistance of the local people. This news came as a great surprise for me as the Japanese army assessed that the British forces would try to retain Penang at all cost. All started slowly realising the gravity of situation created by the start of hostilities. One phase of discussions with Capt. Mohan Singh was thus over, and as the prospect of settling down of the Indian prisoners of war into a peaceful life was very rosy. I started considering plans for my next move.

It was the last day of the year 1941. Suddenly Capt. Mohan Singh came from Alor Star to visit me without any prior intimation. He was accompanied by Capt. Akram and 2nd Lt. Kunizuka. I received the party at the porch. Just at a glance I could read great tension on the face of Capt. Mohan Singh who seldom betrayed his feeling. When I shook hands with him I found his hand burning hot. His lips were dry and he was gasping for breath. His face also appeared very emaciated.

I was taken aback and practically shouted involuntarily "Captain, what is the matter? You are running such a high fever, and yet why you have taken such a rash step in coming to visit me? " He replied that he had caught malaria, and although it was a bit rash, yet he had rushed to see me in order to intimate me the important decision he and his comrades had taken and had a thorough discussion over the subject. Although his eyes were bloodshot, yet they bespoke of firm resolution. I could not help getting overwhelmed by this resolute captain. Although I knew that his talks would be of very important nature, yet in view of his serious condition I forced him to take some malaria medicine and take rest in bed.

I requested Masubuchi (Sabei) and Capt. Akram to look after him. He might have caught this disease when he was engaged in Jitra operation. Methodical Capt. Mohan Singh with strong sense of responsibility did not have a moment's rest eversince his surrender, carrying out discussions with me and Pritam Singh day and night, looking after accommodation, food and sanitation of the officers and men, thinking over the questions of joining the patriotic a movement and discussing the topic with his fellow officers and men and the cause of this attack could probably be traced to his over work and fatigue. I felt like bowing down my head when I realised that he had come all the way to discuss with me despite his serious illness.

After some time, Mohan Singh recovered slightly and then had a discussion with Pritam Singh. Next he came to my room and thanked us. With the coming down of fever, he appeared to be slightly better, but he was very tired. I offered him to be comfortable in the sofa so that we could continue with our talks with ease. Next Capt. Mohan Singh stated that following a number of meetings over the question of armed struggle for the liberation of India, the officers and men had unanimously decided to take up arms for the freedom of motherland provided the Japanese authorities agreed of the following conditions beforehand. The conditions put forward by him were as follows. (1) That Capt. Mohan Singh will organise the Indian National Army, (2) That the Japanese army will give all possible assistance and support to this army, (3) That the INA and the IIL will have independent existence, both cooperating with each other as brother organisations, (4) That the Japanese army will entrust the supervision of the Indian prisoners of war to Capt. Mohan Singh, (5) That the Japanese army will treat the Indian prisoners as friends, and will release those aspiring to join the INA, (6) That the Japanese army will treat the INA as an ally, both sides bound by alliance, etc. I personally had no objection to all these conditions put forward by him. However, as this was a matter of great importance, I refrained from making any reply immediately pending the approval of the army high command.

After expressing my above views over the proposals of Capt. Mohan Singh, I tried to emphasise the instance of cooperation between the INA and the IIL. I said that the two were like two wheels of a vehicle with two wheels, and a revolutionary army should be organised on the overall support of the people for achieving success. Capt. Mohan Singh replied that it was that very reason why they selected the name of Indian National Army for this liberation army instead of Volunteer Army for Indian Independence. Next he added that instead of keeping the INA prerogative for the ex-British Indian service personnel, its doors would be thrown open to all the Indians, and in view of the army's role in liberating motherland, emphasis would be laid on ideological indoctrination. I was very happy to see that he listened to my views attentively and appreciatively. After further discussions we agreed on keeping the two organisations separate from each other bound by the bondage of friendly cooperation, and organise the INA mainly from among the volunteers of the Indian prisoners with active support of the IIL. The indoctrination aspect would be entrusted to the IIL. In order to raise the strength of the INA rapidly Capt. Mohan Singh decided to send some of his excellent comrades into the British lines and make propaganda among the Indian soldiers.

One of the conditions put forward by Capt. Mohan Singh, viz. the question of official declaration on treating the INA as an ally, posed some technical difficulty. So it was decided to accede to the condition in effect, and postponing the official and formal declaration on the issue till the INA took proper shape. Capt. Mohan Singh thereupon decided to organise the INA headquarters, and proceed to Ipoh in near future.

As we arrived at a very good understanding. I called upon the Headquarters of Gen. Yamashita, and explained the conditions put forward by Capt. Mohan Singh and the details of discussions to his chief of staff Suzuki and staff officer Surgita. The chief of staff Suzuki also expressed view similar to those of mine on the question of according the INA the status of ally formally. He agreed with the other conditions of Capt. Mohan Singh, and received the official approval of Gen. Yamashita. I also utilised this opportunity to make a detailed report on the contacts with the vice-chairman of the K.M.M. Mr. Onan Siraji[6] and the youth from Sumatra, Mr. Said Abu Bakar. Chief of Staff Suzuki was very happy after these two contacts.

I immediately returned to my Headquarters and reported the approval of Gen. Yamashita to Pritam Singh and Capt. Mohan Singh. Both of them were extremely pleased. By chance, Col. Tamura had also come to visit us from Bangkok on this very day. He was very happy that we had indeed succeeded in taking our first step towards success. We all drank toasts after toasts to our success. I requested Capt. Mohan Singh to be my guest for the night and proceed to Alor Star on the following day; but he explained the urgency of communicating the decision of the meeting to all the officers and men back in the camp as quickly as possible, and take up the task of organising the INA without any delay. While taking leave, Capt. Mohan Singh warmly shook hand with me and said "Although I am, by nature, rather slow in arriving at a decision, yet once I decide I try my best to accomplish it. I have left my newly wed wife in India. As soon as my activities become known to the British authorities they will subject her and all other members of my family to inhumane torture. I have decided to dedicate myself and my dear family to the cause of my country. As has been said by Gen. Yamashita the other day, I have acquired a new friend in you, of course at the cost of my wife. I hope you will realise that all the officers and men have decided to fight for our motherland knowing fully well that their families in India will be subjected to barbarious treatment by the British authorities in India. The fighting spirit of these men who have decided to sacrifice everything for the noble causes of motherland's freedom is thousand times stronger than that they had when they were

---

6. One of the most active leaders of K.M.M. (Kesatuan Malayu Muda) a political organisation is Malaya.

just the members of the British Indian Army. "I on my part listen every word he uttered with chocking emotion. I vowed in my innermost heart to contribute my might to the noble cause that inspired the soldiers to organise the INA. Despite his high fever Capt. Mohan Singh set out for Alor Star that very night alongwith Capt. Akram and 2nd Lt. Kunisuka.

Thus the crusader for achieving the noble goal of liberation of motherland was born at last for which Pritam Singh had struggled for all these years. Thus it was in Taiping the capital of Perak state that the curtain was raised on the last day of the year 1941 of a new and glorious chapter of the Indian Independence movement that ultimately culminated in the end of century old British rule of India.

As we both, Pritam Singh and myself, stood at the porch silently watching the party vanish in the darkness of night with deep appreciation Pritam Singh grasped my hand and said only one word 'thank you'. I don't think that any other expression could have expressed the depth of feeling he was having. Pritam Singh immediately took a steps to inform the leaders of the IIL in Northern Malaya of the decision of Capt. Mohan Singh.

The year 1942 dawned. After Defeat in the Kedah plains the 11th Division of the British Indian Army reinforced with the 12th Brigade and the 28th Brigade, which was deployed in Ipoh area, took up position in the Kanbaru-Slim area after destroying all the bridges during retreat. Again, the Kwamura Brigade of the 5th Division came across stiff resistance from the British forces in the vicinity of Kohon, north of Kanbaru. Thus, there were all symptoms of a grim battle developing in the region.

In the morning we all in my headquarter together with our honoured guest Col. Tamura gathered in the lawn in front of our building raised our national flag in the acacia tree, and prayed for our success facing east towards our fatherland . The red ball of our national flag appeared to be all the more beautiful bathing the morning sun. As if it was also blessing us for success.

The Indian Independence Army had become a reality and the contacts with the Young Malaya Association as well as the Sumatran youths were also established. Harimau also probably had succeeded in penetrating behind the British lines. The Kanbaru-Slim front was also warming up. This battle held the key to the capital of Malaya, Kuala Lumpur. The day was not far when the Japanese army would become undisputed master of the Malacca Straits. A golden opportunity was coming for the F-Organisation to expand its activities all over Malaya and Sumatra. We drank toasts for our success with champaign, and then started packing our things to proceed to Ipoh.

The members of the INA propaganda squads were handpicked by Capt. Mohan Singh himself after very careful screening of the volunteers. During the last few days Capt. Mohan Singh had devoted almost all his time with these people training them in the art of penetrating the enemy line and gaining friends, after explaining the ideals of the Indian Independence movement. This training programme continued even when they came over to Ipoh. The handpicked volunteers were divided into a number of groups. They were dressed as army stragglers and ordinary local inhabitants for penetrating the enemy lines with ease. Preparations were also made so that they could dress up as the regulars of British Indian Army. Besides carrying armband with the letter 'F' written on it and certificate from the F-Organisation for facilitating their passage through the front line Japanese forces, they carried INA propaganda leaflets calling upon the Indian soldiers to join the Indian National Army. Tauchimochi, Nakamiya and Yonemura, who had successfully smuggled a number of IIL propaganda squads carrying propaganda leaflets as calling upon the Indian soldiers to join the INA, returned to my Headquarters to smuggle these INA propaganda squads behind the enemy lines. They came alongwith about one hundred Indian soldiers who had surrendered in Kanbaru area. As soon as the trucks carrying them stopped in front of my headquarters, scores of officers and men from the nearby INA camp came running and embraced them as they got down. Capt. Mohan Singh also came hurriedly and gave them a word of advice and encouragement. These people, who were very apprehensive over the treatment they were going to receive in the enemy hands, had all their fears set at rest on seeing correctness of what they had read in the propaganda leaflets. Nothing could have made me happier than this.

The battle line was slowly moving south towards Sunkai. That night the 1st propaganda squad of the INA started for the front accompanied by Nakamiya as the liaison officer. Prior to their departure Capt. Mohan Singh tried to inspire them as much as possible. I also spoke a few words in encouragement. All of them vowed that they would accomplish their mission with all their might even at the cost of their life. Everybody in the camp was present there surrounding the squad. All were chocked with emotion. At last the time of departure came. As they boarded the truck and the engine was started, all present raised cheers.

The next day the 2nd, the 3rd INA Propaganda Squads departed for the front accompanied by the F-Organisation liaison officers Nakamiya. Tsuchimochi, Yamaguchi and others went on running to and fro in between my office and the front. The liaison officers first went to the front line

Headquarters together with the INA propaganda squad, ascertained the war situation and the exact location of the front line, and studied the location and topography suitable for penetrating the enemy line easily. Next they went to the commanding officer of the front, requested for safe passage of the propaganda squad, and discussed with him further on the situation and topography. After pin pointing the places where the enemy vigilance was, tax apparently lax, they proceeded to the foremost line. There were very few convenient places for slipping through in this region excepting the battle line, as the whole territory was one of vast jungle excepting for a narrow strip of rubber plantations on the two sides of the sole motorable road. Again, the rubber plantations could offer very little shelter to them in the face of saturated shelling by the trench morters of the British Indian forces. The brave members of the F-Organisation and the INA propaganda squads crawled to the foremost Japanese position braving the enemy shelling and sniping. There they shook hands with the soldiers and got a first hand knowledge about the enemy skirmish line and topography. The members of the INA propaganda squads were excellent in judging the enemy situation. There the members of the propaganda squads bade farewell to the liaison members and penetrated the enemy line. They tried to spot Indian units having no British Commanding Officer or British soldier amongst them. After ascertaining safe penetration, the liaison officers withdrew to the rear and returned to the Headquarters collecting the Indian prisoners from the various units. There were three hurdles not the way of successful accomplishment of mission by the F-Organisation liaison officers.

Firstly, there was the likelihood of misunderstanding between the members of the IIL and INA propaganda squads and the Japanese officers and men. Again, they might be shot at mistaken as enemy. To avoid these the liaison officers accompanied the squads upto the skirmish line. Extreme care was taken so as not to bring any physical harm to the propaganda squad members.

The second difficulty involved in persuading the Japanese staff officers and front line Japanese commanding officers, who lacked proper understanding over the significance of our work. A large number of these people suspected that the INA soldiers who were the members of the British armed forces till the other day might be in league with the British Army. Whenever enemy shells landed near the command posts or artillary positions by chance, they suspected that their positions had been betrayed by the propaganda squad members who had crossed the front line a little while ago. The F-Organisation members had to do their best to explain that the suspicion was unfounded. Even though they were convinced of the sincerity of the Indians, yet they thought that the Indians might have betrayed the Japanese positions which they had seen just a little while ago during interrogation following capture. We firmly rejected any such eventuality and sought their cooperation agreeing to shoulder all responsibilities. It was not a very easy task for a 2nd Lieutenant and 1st Lieutenant to convince a regimental commander or a brigade commander. I must confess that when we sent the first propaganda squad to the front, we were very much worried over the way they would act once get reached the enemy lines. I was at that time mentally prepared for a few black sheep, but even then in view of greater interest resolved to proceed with the work.

However, within ten days, it became very clear that all our apprehensions over the activity of the propaganda squad members behind the enemy lines were totally unfounded. When the battle line shifted to Kuala Lumpur following the battle of Slim, both myself and Capt. Mohan Singh could confirm that none of the ten propaganda squad members belonging to the IIL and the INA defected to the enemy. When I came to know this. I was all the more impressed by the firm determination of the members of the IIL and the INA, and this served as a great inspiration to me for devoting myself wholeheartedly to my mission with the belief of unlimited success.

I was also convinced that with such firm conviction the INA was bound to write a glorious chapter in the history of Indian Independence struggle. The third point which worried me was the distance the liaison officers had to cover in fulfilling their duty. These four or five persons were running to and fro in between the Headquarters and the front about two hundred kilometres away just like a piston, as well as all over the front. Although such activity was fraught with great danger, the members of the propaganda squads were exposed to yet greater danger. Supposing that they succeeded in penetrating the enemy line and persuade the Indian soldiers to come over to our side, yet it was extremely dangerous to cross the Japanese line with a large body of soldiers. In this jungle territory it was extremely difficult to cross the shirmish line at night without being mistaken by the battle weary and trigger happy Japanese soldiers. If these surrendering soldiers came under Japanese fire even one due to misunderstanding, it would render the future work of the propaganda squads extremely difficult. Capt. Mohan Singh and myself had a very careful discussion over these problems and the possibility of capture of the propaganda squad members by the British forces. On the basis of this, Capt. Mohan Singh issued the following sinstructions to the members of the INA propaganda squads. 'Search for the units without British officers' 'Next spot individual soldiers or small groups', 'if possible, search for the men of your own unit', 'If you find a reliable Indian soldier, speak to him about the IIL and the INA, 'Tell them the treatment the Indian prisoners are receiving in the hands of the Japanese', 'In case they agree to surrender, persuade them to convience their close comrades', 'Brief them as follows on the procedure of surrender', leave the front, and hide in the dense jungle nearby', 'In case of strict vigilance by the commanding officer, wait till the skirmish line plunges into confusion with the Japanese breakthrough', 'Instead of firing directly against the Japanese forcers, fire at the sky', 'when the time is ripe, take advantage of the confusion and hide in the Jungle,' Even if the British commanding officer orders retreat, do not accompany him'. 'Hide your weapons in the jungle'. 'After the 1st line Japanese forces pass, raise white flag and come out,' 'show the INA propaganda leaflets to the Japanese soldiers'. These instructions were also printed in the form of propaganda leaflets in case it became impossible to explain these orally.

In view of the rapidly developing situation I thought of shifting my base to Kuala Lumpur by the 8th January morning. But I was forced to spend one more day at Ipoh as I had a very important guest. Moreover I had to dispose of some work connected with the newly developed contacts in the Straits of Malacca area. This important guest was my old colleague in Section 8 of the Imperial Headquarters, who was at the moment in charge of my work. This Maj. - Ozeki had come to get a first hand knowledge of our work and the latest developments achieved by us. As I was convinced of the human quality of the IIL and the INA, and their dedication, I tried to drive home the importance of Japanese assisting this movement in all possible ways. Although I did not have a clear picture of the future course of this movement, as well as all the plans I had in my mind were still in very nebulous state, yet I tried to explain all the ideas I had in my mind after making a report on our work till date. I promised to make an official report at a later date after seeing the developments further which would help me in evolving concrete plan. The main points on which I tried to convince him are as follows :

1. The great ideal of establishing a new order of Coprosperity in East Asia will succeed only after it gets the support of the thirty-five crore people of India.

The war between Japan and the allied countries is likely to be a protracted one. An early settlement of the war can be achieved only through an early capitulation of Britain. The attitude of the Indians will be a decisive factor in bringing about British capitulation. It will be too foolish to rest on the laurrels of Philippines, Malaya and Pearl Harbour. Policy should be evolved to incorporate India in the camp of the nations of East Asia as quickly as possible. It will be too late to just wait for the war situation develop necessitating this. Japan's military might will be stretched to extreme limit with the annexation of Burma. It will be just impossible for Japan to reach for India militarily, and even if such an action is taken, it will immediately meet with the resistance of the Indian people, if the primary object of such a move is just dislodging the British forces. This resistance will be inspired by two factors, their sensitivity to foreign domination and their impression about Japan. Japan should adopt a policy of wining over the Indians without taking recourse to arms and try to persuade them to cooperate with Japan in setting up a new order in the Far East. For this Japan should give all possible support to the Indian Independence movement standing on the footing of equality, without any ulterior motive. Not to have any design of any type on India is of primary importance here. Again, any interference in their political movement or any attempt to control such movement should be strict taboo. Only through this it will be possible to inspire the Indians to become an enthusiastic member for setting up a new order in the Far East.

2. On the basis of the above understanding the Japanese government should make public its basic attitude towards the Indian Independence movement, as well as Japan's policy towards India.

3. The Imperial Headquarters and the Japanese government should sit together for evolving a policy towards India, that will cover all the aspects.

4. The activities of the F-Organisation should be extended to Burma so that a call can be given directly to India.

5. Again, Japan's policy towards India should be evolved in global perspective. For this contact should be established with Subhash Chandra Bose in Germany, so that the policy will have its effect both from the east and from the west. However, emphasis should be laid so that impact will be greater from the east in view of the prevailing conditions. From this viewpoint, the best course will be to invite Subhash Chandra Bose to come over to the east for leading the movement.

6. The basic tenet of Japan's policy towards India will be to give all possible support to the spontaneous movement of the Indian people living in East Asia. In this policy there should be adequate provision to support both the political movements and military actions at present under

consideration of the leaders of the IIL and the INA. In the political field, Japan should encourage all the Indians living in East Asia to join the movement of the IIL . On the military front, a very strong INA should be organised with the help of the volunteers of the Indian prisoners of war and ordinary Indians living in the region. Both these wings should be helped to go to India and build up massive and powerful nationalist movement.

7. The members of the IIL and the INA, not to tell of the Indian people, are watching with great interest the way Japan is going to implement the New Great East Asian order in Burma, Philippines, and other occupied territories of South Asia. It can be easily understood that the approval of the thirty-five crore Indians depends wholely on this. Japan should put the ideal of the new order in practice in Burma, Philippines and other occupied territories of South Asia.

8. The Fujiwara Organisation should be properly reorganised so that it can make useful contribution for realising this ideal when the time becomes ripe. I shall try my best to prepare ground so that the imperial government can implement this policy without any difficulty.

Maj. -O listened to my views very attentively. He also promised that he would try his best so that the ideas proposed by me could be realised.

After the Slim battle, the Indian soldiers who surrendered started pouring in into the camp of Kuala Lumpur, and their number crossed the figure of one thousand in no time. There was also a company which came from the vicinity of Port Swatenham carrying a leaflet calling for surrender dropped by a Japanese plane. The camp was located in the heart of Kuala Lumpur city. Previously housing British troops. The barracks were of thatched roofed, and were in a fairly good condition. There were some permanent structures also. Especially the structure housing the command office was a beautiful two storeyed concrete building. There were also a number of structures for the officers.

The capacity of the camp could be increased to accommodate about three thousand soldiers just by adding a few structures. Although the Japanese army had initially decided to take over the camp, but after negotiations they agreed to step down in favour of INA. It was estimated that already the number of the Indian soldiers surrendered all over Malaya had reached the mark of two thousand five hundred.

Capt. Mohan Singh expressed his desire to concentrate these Indian soldiers in Kuala Lumpur in order to consolidate and strengthen the INA, as well as to facilitate overall supervision, training and policing. To ensure military discipline and to provide with adequate supplies and medical facilities. I readily agreed with this view of Capt. Mohan Singh as this would mean strengthening both the INA activities and the INA command. Thereupon Capt. Mohan Singh started taking steps to bring the Indian prisoners to Kuala Lumpur from Alor Star, Sungei Patani, Ipoh, Pinna and other places. Capt. Mohan Singh took a special care about the rest and recuperation of the inmates, as well about the treatment of the sick and wounded. These instantaneously won over the soldiers, and they found in him a person on whom they could rely upon. This loving attitude of Capt. Mohan Singh towards his followers instantly found response from the IIL, which started door to door campaign for donation in cash and kind for the Indian soldiers. The local Indian population responded to this call generously. An old Sikh resident called Budh Singh made a huge contribution in the form of provisions and clothings. He even sent fruits and flowers to the convalescing soldiers.

After becoming convinced of the sincerity of his comrades as a result of their splendid achievement during the Slim battle, Capt. Mohan Singh draw up three new plans and sought my cooperation. One of it was to arm a section of the INA soldiers and start training. The second plan was to build up a very powerful propaganda wing for persuading the Indian soldiers in the British army to defect in a large scale and join the INA. He drew up this plan as he was very much apprehensive that the British might give up the idea of making a decisive stand at Singapore and might prefer to retreat. The third plan was to utilise the facilities of Saigon Radio for carrying out effective propaganda to the Indian people. I supported these Ideas of Capt. Mohan Singh enthusiastically, and promised all help. After getting the approval of Maj. Gen.-Suzuki, the chief-of-staff, light weapons sufficient for two companies were handed over to the INA. Some talented officers of the rank of captain were selected and sent to Saigon. As the Japanese army hurriedly moved south, Kuala Lumpur remained practically free from Japanese forces excepting for the military administration personnel after a few days. The INA soldiers remained in the camp with Indian sentry standing at the gate with rifle in hand. The camp was fenced nominally with barbed wire. There were only two Japanese officers, 2nd. Lt. Kunizuka and I to for liaison work in the camp. Even then, not a single soldier tried to escape, nor did they have any trouble with the towns folk. Staff officers of the Imperial Headquarters and high command as well as newspaper reporters who came to the front to gain a first hand knowledge of the developments were taken aback on seeing the management of the camp, and many of them expressed grave doubts. On hearing their remarks often I thought that such a possibility was indeed there, but even then the overall situation was so natural and we were so accustomed to it that we felt such an eventuality inconceivable. The 3rd Air Group Command moved into Kuala Lumpur immediately after its occupation. I sent 2nd Lt. Yonemira to the command and reported the misbehaviour of some of the officers and men of the unit at Lipis, and requested for appropriate action. The next day the deputy chief of staff Maj. Gen.-E (ENDO) visited the F-Organisation office alongwith a second lieutenant, who was responsible for the Lipis affair. Maj. Gen. -E had punished the officer immediately, and had sent him together with his deputy to apologise to Capt. Mohan Singh and me, promising to return the articles taken away from the Indian soldiers.

I was deeply moved by the action of Maj. Gen.-Endo Suburo, and while reporting this to Capt. Mohan Singh I also tendered my apology for the misbehaviour of the Japanese soldiers. Capt. Mohan Singh also was deeply moved by the action of Maj. Gen. - E, and profusely thanked him. He said, "Such misbehaviours by some officers are but natural in any army. And it is very rare for a general of the victorious army to apologise to the lower ranking officers and men captured during fighting. This splendid action of the Japanese has only heightened our esteem for it. This will indeed have a tremendous input on our psychology for voluntarily observing the military discipline strictly. Next, he enquired from me on the punishment meted out to the 2nd lieutenant. He asked me to request the general not to punish the young officer severely.

This compassionate attitude of Capt. Mohan Singh impressed the deputy chief of staff deeply. During my talks with the deputy chief of staff casually he mentioned about the difficulty he was facing with the Kuala Lumpur airport. In view of the war situation, this airfield was of vital importance, but had been rendered unservicable firstly by Japanese bombing, and secondly by the British forces during withdrawal. It was urgently needed for, mounting air strikes against the enemy. Reading the signs of vexation on his face, Capt. Mohan Singh enquired about the cause. On being told the reason, he immediately offered to undertake the repair work with the help of the INA.

Maj. Gen. -Endo was very happy over this offer. As the preliminary step Lt. Nakamiya visited the command Headquarters and solicited understanding and respect after explaining the manners and customs of the Indian soldiers as well as enlightening them about the INA. Proper cooperation was solicited from the employees and officers of the air field. It was decided to attach one of the E-Organisation members with the Indians going for repairs. From the following day about one thousand

INA members went to the air field for carrying out repair works. They worked so earnestly from 9.00 A.M. to 4.00 P.M. that they immediately won the hearts of the Japanese present there and who became very good friends, eventually.

The work proceeded very smoothly and there was not a single dispute. Gen. -E rewarded the Indian soldiers with money, food and other articles of day to day use. The INA soldiers put the air field back into service within a week. Maj. Gen. -E won the heart of the Indians to such an extent that they held a ceremonial parade in his honour on the day the work was completed.

From the very first day Pritam Singh reached Kuala Lumpur, he went round visiting the leaders of the Indian community, discussing with them over the question of unifying the Indians politically. On 15th December a delegation of seven or eight leaders of the local Indians headed by Dr. Lakshmi visited me, and thanked me for the protection given to the service. They were also very grateful over the support accorded by the organisation to the Indian Independence movement. The delegation also frankly expressed its views on Indian Independence movement and on the interest and protection of the Indian community in Malaya. I, on my part, explained the oral motive of the Japanese government and the plans of the Japanese army on military administration. Our discussions went on for about two hours in a very cordial atmosphere. The delegates expressed their intention to join the IIL, and promised all help to the Japanese army. That night I was invited by the Indians to an Indian style dinner, which helped in cementing our relation. I was impressed by the views of Dr. Lakshmi, as well as his concern over the welfare of the local Indians. I was also deeply moved by Budh Singh who earnestly advocated the cause of the IIL and the INA, and who had already shown very good attitude towards the INA officers and soldiers. A meeting of the Indians in Kuala Lumpur was held on 16th January where the branch of the IIL was established in the city. This was followed by a series of similar meetings in the cities of Central Malaya just like Surenban, Klan, Malacca, etc., where resolution on establishing IIL branches was adopted. The IIL movement spread through the Central Malaya just like forest fire. With success in Central Malaya, the IIL movement was poised for grand success in Malaya. The Indians made all possible contributions for the INA officers and men.

All of us, Pritam Singh, Capt. Mohan Singh and myself, became confident of the success of our movement after seeing the response from the Indians whereever we went. We also discussed plans for spreading our movement to Burma and all over East Asia, with Malaya as the base, with the ultimate objective of spreading it into India proper.

Although I was extremely busy with the work of the F-Organisation yet I availed of every opportunity to come in contact with Pritam Singh, Capt. Mohan Singh and the leaders of the Indian community in various localities, as their frank views helped me greatly in crystallising my ideas on the policy Japan should adopt towards India. As I was convinced that before long time would come when my views would be solicited by Tarauchi the Commander-in-Chief of the Southern Forces and by the Imperial Headquarters.

Again, in order to ensure smooth passage of my recommendations when officially sought for by the authorities, I tried to win over as many members of the top leadership beforehand as possible by explaining my views and requesting them to see the actual conditions whenever the staff officers of the supreme command came to Malaya to gain a first hand knowledge of the situation. With the above end in view, I also sent personal letters explaining my p ints to my fellow officers in the Imperial Headquarters and the Supreme Command Headquarters at Saigon.

About 600 Indian soldiers were taken prisoner after the Moar Battle. With these the inmates of the Kuala Lumpur camp crossed the figure of 2500. The Japanese forces were pursuing the British forces hotly after defeating them at Batbaha and Gomas. The immediate objective was Johar Bahru. The resistance of the British forces in Malayan Peninsula was practically over. The British forces were gradually withdrawing to Singapore. The fall of Johar Bahru was now a matter of days. The command Headquarters of Gen. Yamashita was advanced to Klan from Kuala Lumpur. The final scene of the war in Malayan peninsula was about to be enacted. The Japanese forces were converging on the citadel of the British empire in the Far East, Singapore.

Around this time the thing that worried us was the possible withdrawal of the British forces from Singapore. In case they decided to withdraw to Sumatra and Java the question was whether they would force the Indian soldiers, who were early waiting for a chance to join the INA, to accompany them.

Lt. Nakamiya and 2nd Lt. Yonemura proceeded to Johar Bahru front alongwith a member of F-Organisation members. The object was to assist the propaganda squads of the INA. Capt. Tsuchimochi was staying back at Moar to look after the Indian soldiers. 2nd Lt. Kunisuka and Ito remained at the INA Headquarters exclusively devoted to liaison work. The two armed companies of the INA which Capt. Mohan Singh had organised and was training were slowly acquiring fighting strength befitting revolutionary army. The will and conviction of Capt. Mohan Singh were slowly becoming firmer, and he was slowly acquiring all the qualities expected of a general of a revolutionary army.

Around this time the Japanese forces were concentrating on the Thai-Burma border to make a drive for the Salween river in Burma. The 15th Army struck on the 19th January at the vacuum behind the British forces which were pressing the Japanese units in Tavoy very hard and quickly reached the Salween river. The 55th Division advanced from occupying Kokala on the 22nd, and reaching almost Moulansin sometime later. The 33rd Division advanced to the vicinity of Kyawkala, and was getting ready to make a thrust towards Salween. The British forces in that sector consisted of 11th Burmese Brigade and a part of the 17th British Indian Army.

In the Philippines, the force commanded by Lt. Gen. Homma captured Manila on 2nd January, and from 27th started a general offensive against the American forces led by Gen. MacArthur in Batam peninsula. Borneo was secured by joint army and navy operation. Again, Oslebes and New Britain were occupied on the 23rd and 24th of January respectively. The Japanese forces were making lightening progress through the Pacific and the Southern areas.

In view of these developments I was sure that time had come for me to present my views on the policy Japan should adopt with respect to India to the Imperial Headquarters and the Supreme Command. Again, out of consideration of my duty towards Pritam Singh and Capt. Mohan Singh, I felt that it was my duty to persuade the Central authorities to accept officially the plan we had evolved. Although this was nothing but a secret desire of a petty major of the Japanese army, yet it was a very useful mission indeed. It had to be accomplished at any cost. After returning to Kuala Lumpur, from the very first night I had been preparing the draft of the India policy secretly so as to present it to the authorities when required. That very night I got a telephone call from the command Headquarters at Klar quite late. This was from Lt. Co.-O, staff officer of the Southern Command located at Saigon. He was a senior staff officer of the Southern Command in charge of intelligence and propaganda. We had exchanged a number of communications on my plans on India.

I was summoned to the Command Headquarters at Klan to report on the progress of my work, and at that time to put my views on the policy Japan should adopt towards India in writing. I replied that I would report at the Command Headquarters after two days, I was also overwhelmed with joy that I could not sleep that night. My sixth sense told me that staff officer Lt. Col. -O, in whom I had placed so much confidence, had been won over, and that he has came to the Command Headquarters with the purpose of observation of the situation and personal assessment. That very night with all my soul I poured out all my plans on paper. I read the final draft over and over again. I was swept off my feet by my own manuscript. I was so engrossed with it that I didn't know even when it dawned. I came back to myself on hearing loud notes of truck engine at the porch followed by loud talking of people . Lt. Nakamiya had returned from the front to report the developments. The sun was shining brightly. I left my manuscript on the desk and went downstairs hurriedly. Capt. Yamaguchi, Capt. Nakamiya and 2nd. Lt. Kunizuka were very happy over the manuscript, where I had put down our views in words and my firm desire to persuade the centre to adopt it. They took great pains in fairing the manuscript with great care and giving it proper shape of official document. The whole process was completed around noon.

I boarded the Studebaker with three copies of the manuscript, one for my Commanding Officer Gen. Yamashita, one for the commander-in-chief of the Southern Forces Gen. Terauchi, and the third one for the Imperial Headquarters. I was accompanied by Kitamura. In the eyes of the officers gathered at the gate to see me off I could read their feeling. 'We pray for the successes of your mission. You try to stick to your points for the sake of IIL, INA and India, for which we are working so hard. I was sure that I would have my way with all my sincerity, conviction and zeal'.

The car proceeded along the Singapore Road to Klan at break neck speed of 60 miles. On the way unfortunately there was a puncture, and hence we reached Klan towards dawn. Because of the tension, I forgot the fatigue of two days' work without a moment of rest. The command Headquarters was located in a rubber plantation in hurriedly constructed barracks, when I entered the room of staff officer Lt. Col. Cokamura, I was surprised to find there my old course mate, who was also the staff officer of the 37th Osaka infantry regiment formerly. He was also equally surprised, and jumped up and embraced me, congratulating me for the success of my mission. There was also one Lt. Col. Kondo in the room. He also congratulated me for my work. Besides there were two Lt. Cols., both staff officers of the Imperial Headquarters.

From them I came to know that Lt. Gen. Nagatomi, Chief of Personnel Division of the War Ministry and Lt. General Tanaka, Chief of Operations Division of the Imperial Headquarters had arrived at the command Headquarters only the day before alongwith a few senior officials as the personal representatives of War Minister Gen. Tojo and of the supreme chief of staff respectively, for on the spot study of the war situation.

Again, as luck would have it, these senior officials were mostly my acquaintances, under whom I had served. My confidence increased hundred folds, and I felt that I was sure to win my point. First of all I report to the staff officer of the Southern Command Lt. Col.-Okamura on the general situation, and then explained the draft I had carried, which was to be presented to Gen. Terauchi. It took about one hour. As I started making the report, the two staff officers of the Imperial Headquarters begged leave of us out of courtesy. But I requested them to stay on as no secrets were involved. My motive for requesting them to stay on was that they should report my talks to the two lieutenant generals. Both the staff officers gladly remained behind eagerly listening to the talks. From their behaviour I felt that they approved of my views. Lt. Col. Okumura approved of my views enthusiastically and requested the two lieutenant colonels from the Imperial Headquarters to lend their support to the plan.

As I was under the jurisdiction of the command of Gen. Yamashita, it was necessary to forward all official reports and my views for the higher authorities through the 25th Army Command. However, the views I was going to present did not relate to Malaya and Sumatra which were under the jurisdiction of the 25th Army. It rather related to India, which was bound to occupy a very prominent position in the Japanese place for establishing a new order in East Asia. So I felt that I should try to put forward my view directly to the leaders of the Imperial Headquarters and the War Ministry, and seek their approval. I was afraid that by the time my plan reached the proper authorities, my views would most probably get distorted while passing through the 25th Army Command and the Southern Command, not to tell of the time factor. I felt the visit of the important officials of the Imperial Headquarters and the War Ministry as heaven sent opportunity for presenting my report and views directly to them. After finishing my report, I went to staff officer S. of Gen. Yamashita to make report and solicit his support. He also expressed his approval of my plan, but he pointed out simultaneously that for the government of Japan to approve such a bold and grand policy officially, it would take a lot of careful deliberation. As I came out after making the report, I found Lt. Gen. Tanaka and Lt. Gen. Tominaga enjoying a stroll in the rubber plantation in the morning sun. As I saluted, Gen. Tanaka asked me what the hell was I doing in such a place. I felt as if all my blood rushing to my head, but realising that I had reached the most crucial point I replied boldly that I was carrying out the Indian policy, besides carrying out propaganda to the Malaya and the Sumatrans.

With a very amiable voice he enquired of the nature of the work and the way I was faring. With great firmness I replied that I was trying my best and that I was confident of success. I had come there to present a report and my views for enlarging the scope of my work and draw up a revised policy to include whole of India and immediately implement it for forwarding to the Imperial Headquarters and the War Ministry. I found Gen. Tominaga listening to my reply with great interest. Instinctively I felt that they had heard about my report and my views from their two staff officers already, and hence took some interest in the subject.

Next Gen. Tanaka asked me about the success I had achieved. As I got the opportunity I was waiting so eagerly, I immediately related the organisation of the INA at Kuala Lumpur with a few thousand Indian prisoners of war, and that the strength of this revolutionary army was bound to increase vastly once the Singapore operation went on smoothly. I also related the success of the IIL movement in whole of Malaya, and its spread to Burma and the various regions of East Asia. But its dedication, the IIL had laid the foundation for carrying this revolutionary struggle into India.

Lt. Gen. Tanaka looked at Lt. Gen. Tominaga, and after a meaningful wink at him said to me whether he could have a look at the INA whose drum I was beating so much Lt. Gen. Tominaga also immediately expressed his willingness to see the INA. The most I had expected of these two generals was that they might at best reluctantly agree to hear my views after a lot of persuation. I just could not believe my own ears when these two top ranking leaders of the Japanese army expressed their desire to accompany to Kuala Lumpur, see the INA, and have a chat with Capt. Mohan Singh and Pritam Singh, besides listening to my views. I was besides myself with joy. Lt. Gen. Tanaka immediately called his staff officer-K and ordered him to make preparations for the trip to Kuala Lumpur, and keep a plane ready for the purpose. After taking leave of the two generals I ran to the staff officer of the southern forces Lt. Col.-O and reported this development. He told me that this was due to persuation of the two staff officers of the Imperial Genaral Headquarters who had accompanied the two generals. He encouraged me so that I could boldly explain my project to them. The staff officers of the commanding officer Yamashita were literally taken aback to see me cornering the two generals and the team of the Imperial Headquarters, seven persons in all.

On that very day I reached Kuala Lumpur airport around noon together with the two generals and the Imperial Headquarter steam. The team proceeded to the local command office conducted by the local commandant from the airport, and I hurried to the F-Organisation Headquarters together with Lt. Yamaguchi who had come to receive me. Lt. Yamaguchi was also very happy to see the two generals. As soon as this news spread in the F-Organisation, all the young officers there falicitated me over the success. But they were also a bit worried over the arrangement to be made for the team as time for preparation was not there. I immediately called Pritam Singh and Capt. Mohan Singh and explained the whole positions. Both of them were also very happy. After discussions we decided to put our views frankly to the two generals and planned the whole show accordingly. I was also very happy to present our situation to the two generals without concealing anything or taking recourses to any deceit.

After careful consideration I prepared the schedule as follows. It was to start with a visit to the INA camp followed by a review of troop a meeting of the two generals with Pritam Singh and Capt. Mohan Singh at the INA Headquarters, a meeting Capt. Mohan Singh with the team of the Imperial Headquarters, and finally my report to the two generals. Pritam Singh and Capt. Mohan Singh started preparations immediately. The first two items of inspection of the camp and military review started around 4.00 P.M. Although it was a very hurriedly arranged review, they marched in regular formation under smart officers, creating a very good impressions on the two generals. Next, the meeting was held in the INA Headquarters between Capt. Mohan Singh and the two Generals. In a very serious tone Capt. Mohan Singh explained the actual situation of the INA and the firm resolution of the officers and men. He also expressed his gratitude to the Japanese army for assisting the INA movement through the F-Organisation. As agreed upon earlier, no concrete topic was taken up during the discussion both the generals were deeply impressed by the ideal of the Pritam Singh and Capt. Mohan Singh, and encouraged them enthusiastically.

After the party left, I ran to the local command alongwith Capt. Mohan Singh and his deputy Akram to meet the team that had accompanied the two generals. 2nd Lt. Kunizuka accompanied us to interpret. There was no special topic for discussion. The object was to let the officials of the Imperial Headquarters to have an idea of the character and conviction of Capt. Mohan Singh, besides developing acquaintance. It was quite obvious that the real motive of the two generals in taking so much trouble to come all the way to Kuala Lumpur and meet Capt. Mohan Singh was to ascertain Capt. Mohan Singh's personality and whether he was worth backing by Japan, I was so sure of the outcome that I did not have even slightest apprehensions. This was because I had no doubt about his patriotism and watching his eversince Alor Star. Another point in my favour was that the team consisted of my old acquaintances, who also had excellent records to their credit. The talks were very frank and continued for about an hour. As expected Capt. Mohan Singh succeeded in creating a very good impression in their minds. The talks went on also the following line. Lt. Col.-: Okamura " I must confess that most of us lack a clear understanding of the national character of the Indian people. I think by now you have studied the national character of the Japanese people. Do you think that the understanding of the national character of the two nations is very important in forging the cooperation between the two nations."

Capt. Mohan Singh : "Just like you I also lack a clear understanding of the national character of the Japanese people. However, in the past I had read a book on Bushido of Japan. There I have read of three divine objects, viz., sword, jewel and mirror. The sword signifies bravery, the jewel benevolence and mirror righteousness. It was written there that these three objects denote the spirit of Japan. Indeed I have seen the bravery of the Japanese soldiers eversince the engagements along the Thai-Malaya border with my own eyes. Again, the actions of Maj. Fujiwara and other members of the F- Organisation have confirmed the benevolence, righteousness and gentleness of the Japanese people.

We the Indian people attribute religious significance to benevolence and righteousness. I personally believe that being the nations of the orient, both the peoples have many things in common in their national characters."

Lt. Col. Okamura, "I hope you will not mind if I put a somewhat delicate question to you. We quite often hear that the Independence movement of India is very much handicapped due to religious confrontation and castism not to tell of rivalry and antagonism between various racial groups. Could you please enlighten us on this point."

Capt. Mohan Singh, "I do not agree with the above viewpoints popularised in Japan. I think that our love for motherland should transcend the narrow sense of loyalty to religion or race. Although the caste system has survived till today, yet it is a legacy of the past, and this inhuman and anti- social contradiction is slowly vanishing from the national scene. I do not think that the elimination of this evil is that difficult as some of the foreigners think. Rather this system is very much encouraged by the British rulers. We are building up the INA by sinking all narrow caste prejudices and religious and racial differences, setting the liberation of motherland as our supreme goal. Our patriotic officers and men have risen to the occasion, and there had been not a single case of trouble due to these factors. This fact will serve as an ample proof of the correctness of our conviction."

Lt. Col. - O : " I hear that the Burmese have a strong sense of antipathy towards the large number of Indians living amongst them. The Japanese army is now thinking to advance to Burma and liberate the Burmese people. As this question is of grave importance, could you please express your viewpoint over this problem?"

Capt. Mohan Singh : "We must frankly admit that there are good reasons for the resentment of the Burmese people against the Indians. The Indians there have some sort of superiority complex towards the Burmese people. The Indians are more enterprising than the Burmese, and thus have succeeded in monopolising land and business. Again, afraid of the Independence movement of the Burmese people, the British government has stopped recruiting them for military and police service. The British government is employing the Indian soldiers and Indian policemen to supress the nationalist movement of the Burmese people. These are some of the main causes of Burmese resentment against the Indians. The conflict over interest and feeling is rather very deep rooted. But even then I do not think that it is an impossible problem with no solution. If the leaders of the two countries try to sort out the trouble across the table after overthrow of British bondage keeping the greater interest of the prosperity of the nations of East Asia in view, then I think that the problem can be solved without much difficulty.

The above are some of the topics that were discussed during the meeting. The team of the Imperial Headquarters got a thoroughly clear picture of the convictions, intellectual capability, seal and personality of Capt. Mohan Singh. After Capt. Mohan Singh had left together with his deputy Akram, Lt. Col.-O (Okamura) went to the room of the two generals and made a report on the meeting. After sometime I was called by the two generals.

After offering me a chair, Lt. Gen. Tanaka practically poured cold water on my enthusiasm by saying "Fujiwara, you have dragged us all the way to this place, but from the report of the staff officer Lt. Col. - O it transpires that Capt. Mohan Singh, whom you are grooming so much, is not a person worth that much of trouble. What do you have to say on this points?"

I was simply taken aback by this question of the general. But the next instant I recovered my self composure as I felt that this was just an attempt to test my own conviction. There were of course a number of reasons for my thinking like that. Both the generals had given a very favourable impression that very morning at Klan, and during the guard of honour and talks with the Indian officers also they had shown considerable interest. Thus becoming convinced that the general was saying something which he really did not mean, I said " Sir, that is not correct. From what Capt. Mohan Singh had said during the above talks, my confidence in and respect for Capt. Mohan Singh have hightened all the more. In case any member of your team has such a misunderstanding, then I would like to hear the cause for it directly from him."

In a cold and blunt tone the general asked, whether I was challenging the report of the staff officer?

I replied : " Yes. However, reliable the staff officer may be, yet I want to assert that this particular report is wrong. I have seen Capt. Mohan Singh over the last fifty days standing on the verge of life and death. I am sure that my study of Capt. Mohan Singh is not wrong."

With this assertion of mine the general softened his tone and still somewhat ironically said, "Capt. Mohan Singh is basically a soldier of the British Indian Army. He is neither a politician , nor a revolutionary. And moreover, compared to the famous leaders of India, nobody even has over heard of his name. In the language to the king in chess he is just a pawn.

I encouraged myself by saying that the critical moment had come and but I should not give way, and said: "Sir, as you have said, Capt. Mohan Singh in a soldier. He has not been tempered by the flame of revolution. Again, he is also very young in age. But we know many instances of soldiers heading revolutions. All the famous revolutionaries were little known young men in the beginning. Selfless love for the country, passionate ardour for revolution, capacity to carry out decision, and foresightedness are the qualities which make grand revolutionary out of unknown young men. I have seen these qualities in Capt. Mohan Singh. Although you have likened Capt. Mohan Singh with pawn, yet I do not contribute to your view. Even if it is assumed that he is just a pawn at the moment, yet he has enough capability to become a queen and checkmate the king."

As I ended, the general said 'Un' in a tone of assent. I could also read signs of approval in the eyes of Lt. Gen. Tominaga, who was silently listening to the talks. Being encouraged I continued: "Independence of India and Indo-Japanese cooperation are essential for the successful conclusion of the East Asian War and realisation of Japan's cherished objective of establishing a new order in East Asia in the form of Great East Asia a co-prosperity sphere. However, out of self complacency Japan has taken no notice of India and has not taken any step to cultivate friendship with the Indian leaders. Because of this we have failed to win over a great leader like Subhash Chandra Bose on our side. However, at the moment we have succeeded in winning over Capt. Mohan Singh and a few thousands of his comrades in INA as well as the tens of thousands of Malayan Indians. In case Japan displays appropriate statesmanship as I am advocating and implement it in whole of East Asia, then it will be possible to mobilise more than a lakh of Indian soldiers whom we are going to capture in the Malayan campaign, besides the millions of Indians living in the region in our anti-British war. This is the only way for enlisting the support of free India in establishing the new order in the East. Furthermore, both Pritam Singh and Capt. Mohan Singh are committed to the Independence of India, and they do not have any adventurist ambition. They would gladly hand over the leadership of the IIL and INA to any great leader of India who would like to assume leadership and would work as his assistants without any grudge. They are sincerely hoping that Japan would extend invitation to Subhash Chandra Bose to assume leadership of the Indian Independence movement in East Asia."

After I had finished suddenly general Tanaka changed his cold attitude, and told me to explain in brief the contents of my report. He initiated the talk asking any views on the importance of Japan's policy with regard to India.

After I had talked a little, suddenly he stopped me telling that he had enough of my explanation, and told me to speak about concrete plan if any. Although I was slightly taken aback as I had least expected such an interruption, yet I recovered my composure and put forward my view as I had done in Ipoh to the staff officer- O of the Imperial Headquarters.

After I had finished, the general only curtly said that he would keep my explanation in view. Seeing my slight disappointment over the general's cold reception of my urgings, Lt. Gen. Tominaga said " Never mind young man, try to do your best." Saying this he offered me a glass of whisky following which Gen. Tanaka also offered me a glass of whisky. I could not make out whether my mission was a success or a failure. However, I felt that the net balance was in my favour. This was because, when I had expressed that the F-Organisation should be replaced by a very powerful organisation in case it was decided to implement a very vigorous India Policy. Gen. Tanaka asked my opinion about a suitable person to head this organisation. I told that the person should be politically mature, sincere and a very good diplomat. In view of the gravity of the question, he was probably trying to test me, and was telling something which he did not really mean. The reason for my thinking like this was that it was not possible for the two generals to make any firm commitment over such an important issue without the concurrence of the War Minister and the Supreme Command.

As soon as I came out of the room of the generals after thanking them for taking all the trouble of coming to Kuala Lumpur, the officials of the Imperial Headquarters accosted me asking about the interview. I replied that I had a thorough bashing.

Lt . Col. -O reassured me telling that I had indeed scored a success in case I had a good bashing from Gen. Tanaka. He also congratulated me for having found a magnificent man like Capt. Mohan Singh. Although I had enough self-confidence to accept the above verdict of the colonel, yet I had a bit of apprehension at a corner of my mind.

On my way back I called upon Capt. Mohan Singh at his official residence. He sought my opinion about the day's proceeding. I assured him that all was well. Knowing my liking for alconol, he told his deputy to bring a bottle of whisky. Over whisky we talked in a very relaxed mood, and I enjoyed the bliss of pure friendship free from any duplicity.

It was past midnight when I returned to my Headquarters. All were waiting there eagerly without going to bed. With great confidence I told them that all was well. Immediately the whole office was engulfed in a festive mood, and again over whisky I related the developments that took place since morning. On the following morning I saw the two generals and their party off at Kuala Lumpur airport. They were to proceed at right to Saigon. Here for the first time the two generals expressed deep appreciation of my work and encouraged me to go ahead with my work.

One of the staff officers of the generals took me aside and said that he had been ordered by Gen. Tanaka to express his personal appreciation of my work and the success I had achieved. As my work was of extreme importance the general wanted me to pour my heart and soul into the work. My views were also very educative and the generals were very much happy over these. I was very happy to know that the two generals had approved of my proposals, and there was every likelihood of their being adopted by the topmost authorities. I was besides myself with joy, and thanked him profusely. As soon as the aeroplane left, I suddenly felt a heavy burden removed from my chest, and simultaneously with this I was overwhelmed with terrible fatigue.

On 30th January evening the advanced units of the 5th Division of the Japanese army finally captured Johar Bahru. The only bridge connecting the island of Singapore with the Malayan peninsula was destroyed by the retreating British forces. Around this time the 6th batch of Sumitra Youth Group vanished into night darkness of the Malacca Straits for crossing over to Sumatra. With the departure of this group all information on the developments in Sumatra ceased. Again, Mr. Onam of

Young Malaya Association was busy training his comrades for starting work immediately with the fall of Singapore.

On 4th February I came to know that a general offensive on Singapore was scheduled for 9th February. On this very day I received two orders from the 25th Army Command. One was a copy of the order of Gen. Terauchi, the Commander-in-Chief of the Southern Forces, to Gen. Yamashita, the commander of the 25th Army. The other was the order of Gen. Yamashita to me. The order from Gen. Terauchi ran on the following lines : 'The 25th Army will dispatch a section of the Fujiwara Organisation to Burma, which will carry on and support the IIL and INA movement under the overall command of the 15th Army Commander Lt. Gen. Iida.' The order from Gen. Yamashita ran as follows: 'The Head of the Fujiwara Organisation will immediately bifurcate the Fujiwara Organisation and send a section to Burma to give active support to the IIL and the INA movements in the area.' It was evident that one of the earnest desires of Pritam Singh and Capt. Mohan Singh and which I had strongly advocated in my proposal had been accepted by the commander-in-chief of the Southern Forces. Burma occupied a top priority position in our scheme as it was adjacent to India, besides having about two million Indians. Thus, extending our work to Burma constituted a great turning point in our work. Yet with the decisive battle for Singapore just round the corner and advance of the Japanese forces on to Sumatra in near future it constituted a heavy burden for the F-Organisation to send some of its members to Burma as we were extremely short of hands. It was expected that the Burma campaign was going to be a tough one in view of the zise of the country, lack of communication and prevalence of diseases. However, these were problems about which nothing could be done beforehand. The Japanese forces were faced with the dual task of fighting the enemy on one hand and solving these problems on the other. Although we were extremely short of hands, yet I decided to send my best associates to Burma in view of the importance of the assignment. Thereupon, I selected Capt. Tsuchimochi, the seniormost officer in the organisation to head the team, and placed three of my most trusted associates, Ishikawa, Kitamura and Takimura, under him. Although it was extremely unfair to impose such a heavy burden like that on only four persons, yet that the best I could do at the moment. The only thing we could hope for was the positive assistance from the 15th Army.

I also immediately held a meeting with Pritam Singh and Capt. Mohan Singh and discussed about the war situation in Burma after disclosing the contents of the orders I had received. Both of them were extremely happy. After detailed discussions it was decided to send a team of three groups.

One from the IIL with Pritam Singh as the head, the second from the INA consisting of sixty propaganda cadres with a certain captain of the INA as the head, and the third consisting of four F-Organisation members including Capt. Tsuchimochi. The F-Organisation members were to coordinate the work with the Japanese forces on active duty. It was decided to start preparations immediately so that the team could leave Kuala Lumpur on 9th February by train. The Japanese forces in Burma at that time were making preparations to cross the Salween river after capturing Moulmein on the 31st January. The British forces in this area had retreated to the west bank of Salween and a section was retreating overland towards Rangoon. Intelligence reports indicated that reinforcements had reached Rangoon from India, and that a Chinese detachment was on way to Rangoon from Yunnan.

The Headquarters of the Southern Forces in Saigon was at this time busy preparing plans for the capture of Rangoon and the important enemy bases in Central Burma.

Besides preparing plans for the capture of Burma, the Japanese forces were also busy providing large scale assistance of the Thakin Party of Burma which was leading the anti-British nationalist movement of the Burmese people. Content between the Japanese army and the Thakin Party had been established as early as 1940.

About thirty young Burmese nationalists headed by Aung San representing the extreme faction of the Thakin Party had escaped from Burma by land and by sea, and at that time were receiving training in arms secretly at Hainan Island under enthusiastic supervision of the Imperial Headquarters. A cell called Minami Organisation (Minami Kikan) with Col. Suzuki as the head had been established for coordinating this work. It was a very powerful organisation composed of about ten members including the head, drawn from both the army and the navy. With the declaration of war in December 1941, these Burmese young men under the leadership of Aung San and the Minami Organisation came to Thailand and immediately undertook the task of raising a volunteer force from among the local Burmese under the name Burma Independence Army (BIA). The BIA accompanied the Japanese army when it advanced into Burma from Thailand. The BIA received very enthusiastic welcome from the Burmese people everywhere they went and the Burmese young men came forward in large number to swell its ranks.[1]

The BIA played almost no operational role as it was hurriedly raised from among people who had no military training whatsoever, but it facilitated the head, and the third consisting of four F-Organisation members including Capt. Tsuchimochi. The F-Organisation members were to coordinate the work with the Japanese forces on active duty. It was decided to start preparations immediately so that the team could leave Kuala Lumpur on 9th February by train. The Japanese forces in Burma at that time were making preparations to cross the Salween river after capturing Moulmein on the 31st January. The British forces in this area had retreated to the west bank of Salween and a section was retreating overland towards Rangoon. Intelligence reports indicated that reinforcements had reached Rangoon from India, and that a Chinese detachment was on way to Rangoon from Yunnan.

The Headquarters of the Southern Forces in Saigon was at this time busy preparing plans for the capture of Rangoon and the important enemy bases in Central Burma.

Besides preparing plans for the capture of Burma, the Japanese forces were also busy providing large scale assistance of the Thakin Party of Burma which was leading the anti-British nationalist movement of the Burmese people. Content between the Japanese army and the Thakin Party had been established as early as 1940.

About thirty young Burmese nationalists headed by Aung San representing the extreme faction of the Thakin Party had escaped from Burma by land and by sea, and at that time were receiving training in arms secretly at Hainan Island under enthusiastic supervision of the Imperial Headquarters. A cell called Minami Organisation (Minami Kikan) with Col. Suzuki as the head had been established for coordinating this work. It was a very powerful organisation composed of about ten members including the head, drawn from both the army and the navy. With the declaration of war in December 1941, these Burmese young men under the leadership of Aung San and the Minami Organisation came to Thailand and immediately undertook the task of raising a volunteer force from among the local Burmese under the name Burma Independence Army (BIA). The BIA accompanied the Japanese army when it advanced into Burma from Thailand. The BIA received very enthusiastic welcome from the Burmese people everywhere they went and the Burmese young men came forward in large number to swell its ranks.[1]

The BIA played almost no operational role as it was hurriedly raised from among people who had no military training whatsoever, but it facilitated

1. For details see, Izumiya Tatsuro, *The Minami Organ*, Rangoon 1981.

Johar Bahru Strait and launched general offensive against the citadel of Singapore. The INA propaganda squads and the members of the F-Organisation immediately proceeded to Singapore to carry out propaganda to the Indian soldiers.

I had to proceed to Johar Bahru in great haste for guiding our work in this decisive battle. Because of this I could not see off the Burma team at the Kuala Lumpur station. On 8th February I gave a farewell party to the INA squad members at my residence, and that very night I gave another farewell party to the four F-Organisation members. I felt very sad to part with these boys with whom I had shared my joys and sorrows for the last four months or so. They were proceeding to the battle field in the north, and I was proceeding to the battle field in the south. Indeed this could be our last parting. Indeed Pritam Singh and Capt. Mohan Singh were also holding such parties with such heavy heart with their associates. On the 9th February morning I bade farewell to Capt. Tsuchimochi and left for the front together with Nagano.

I shifted my office to Singapore after getting the approval of the Chief of Staff on 16th February.

At night I reached the hillock west of Raffle's University from the Bukipanjan crossing in just five minutes driving along the Bukitema Road. Just a few days on the 13th night back we had taken more than eight hours to cross this stretch of land. The houses and the trees on both sides of the road were the vivid witnesses of the fierce engagements that were fought here. I could see everywhere the graves of those heros who fell here, covered with unknown red flowers of the tropics and their water bottles hanging from their memorial slabs.

Under special instructions from Gen. Yamashita, ordinary soldiers were prohibited from entering the city proper. Only the military police and some auxiliary forces assisting the military police were permitted entry into the city for maintaining law and order. There were checkposts everywhere, and even the individual soldiers in plain dress were not permitted to enter the city not to tell of the units. There was not a single soul on the road. One million inhabitants of the city had confined themselves indoors out of sheer fear. A large number of houses were destroyed during the weeklong artillery bombardment, and rotting human bodies were befouling the air everywhere.

Lt. Nakamiya had selected a house in the residential district of British police officials near Raffle's University on the western suburbs of Singapore as the office of the F-Organisation. He had complied with my instruction of selecting a simple house in the suburbs slightly away from the city hubs but with good traffic facilities. Because this area constituted the first line of defence, the whole area including the houses was littered with war equipment and ammunitions, and all the open spaces were dug up with trenches leaving no space even to walk.

On this very day the INA command, IIL office and Sumatra Youth Group were shifted to Singapore. In the evening a joint committee of the British and Japanese forces was set up in the British High Command Office at Fort Canning for the handing over of Singapore. It was ordered that the F-Organisation also should be incorporated in this body. It was also decided that the formal handing over of the Indian soldiers will be held on the following day, viz., 17th afternoon at Farah Park.

According to the report of the British committee members, there were about fifty thousand Indian soldiers. There were also almost equal number of British soldiers. The Japanese army estimates had put the total strength of British forces in Singapore at about thirty thousand, of which about ten to fifteen thousand were Indian soldiers. The Japanese committee, members were taken aback when they heard these figures from their British counterparts. Numerically the Britishers were several times stronger than the attacking Japanese forces. In case the British forces had held out for a few more days and tried for a counter offensive, then the Japanese forces inferior both numerically and in equipment would have surely met with a serious debacle. The greatest problem that faced me right at the moment was the question of looking after fifty thousand Indian soldiers with about four army officers and about ten civilians as my assistants, with no preparations whatsoever. They had to be accommodated, fed, and controlled and their personal hygiene had to be ensured. In addition the original purpose for which the F-Organisation had been set up had to be fulfilled. My head was full of the above problems as I returned to my office in car. The previous night the F-Organisation was allotted the additional task of procuring the list of persons involved in political and ideological crimes from the detective department of Singapore. I had sent 2nd. Lt. Yonemura and Tashiro to the British Detective Department to procure this list in the morning. Lt. Nakamiya was running about in search of barracks for accommodating the Indian prisoners of war. Lt. Yamaguchi was busy cleaning the F-Organisation office littered with arms and ammunitions left behind by the British forces.

After hearing the reports from my staff, I gave them instructions on the work for the following day. I told Lt. Nakamiya and 2nd Lt. Yonemara to search for barracks all over Singapore to accommodate the Indian prisoners numbering fifty thousand, as well as to procure the necessary provisions and sanitary facilities. Some INA officers were detailed to assist them in their work. Lt. Yamaguchi was allotted the task of making preparations for the handing over ceremony of the prisoners at Farah Park. All the members scattered in all directions for discharging their duties. After the members of the F-Organisation had left, I had a discussion with Capt. Mohan Singh and Pritam Singh over the prisoners of war handing over ceremony scheduled to take place on the following day. It was decided that after formal taking over of the charge of the Indian prisoners of war from the British representative. I would first address the Indian prisoners as the representative of the Japanese army, followed by Capt. Mohan Singh and Pritam Singh as the commander of the INA and the representative of the IIL respectively. It was also decided that I would meet the Indian officers after the ceremony following which the prisoners would be dispersed in the different camps in a planned manner. All three of us were thoroughly aware of the importancc ɔf these first addresses to the prisoners. It was decided to procure very good microphones for the purpose. We also agreed to request the Japanese army propaganda division to send photographers to record this historic occasion. I was to prepare my speech by the following morning, and get the approval of the army chief-of-staff Maj. Gen.-S only after the consent of Capt. Mohan Singh and Pritam Singh. That night I was very busy preparing the speech. It ran on the following lines.

(A) One of the war objectives of Japan is to liberate the nations of East Asia.

(B) Japan earnestly hopes for the Independence of India, and is prepared to give all out assistance for the achievement of this goal. Japan does not have any design whatsoever on India.

(C) The fall of Singapore has brought a golden opportunity for bringing about Indian Independence.

(D) The Japanese army holds the freedom movement of the INA and the IIL in high esteem, and with this in mind is giving all possible support to these movements. Both these organisations are showing extremely good work in protecting the Indians in the war zone and the Indian army stragglers.

(E) The Japanese army treat the Indian prisoners as brothers.

(F) Those prisoners desiring to join the INA for liberating India will cease to be prisoners. They will be given total freedom and all help will be given to them.

(G) The Japanese army will deal with the Indian prisoners through Capt. Mohan Singh.

(H) The Japanese army will try its best to provide the Indian prisoners with all the necessities. However, because of the situation arising out of rapid advance of the Japanese forces, adequate supplies have not come up yet. If there is any temporary shortage because of the circumstances stated above, you are requested to show proper understanding.

It was almost midnight when I completed my speech. When Capt. Kunizuku just started to translate it, Capt. Mohan Singh suddenly came into my room in a very agitated mood.

With visible expression of anxiety on his face he said that one of the INA propaganda squad members had been arrested by some British officers and had been kept in confinement. There was a likelihood that he might be tried for treason. It was indeed very difficult to watch the execution of a comrade. So he had come to discuss with me on the question of getting him released at any cost. I was very happy over this fresh proof of Capt. Mohan Singh's love and friendship for his comrades. I immediately took a resolution to save his comrade who was my comrade as well. The name of the British officer concerned and his address were also known. Although the instruments of surrender had already been signed, yet the issue concerned the enemy who had fought desperately even the day before and who were still carrying arms. I felt slightly worried. But any delay might bring about irreparable harm to the arrested person. It was not possible to hesitate either. I decided to go to the unit concerned and talk to the particular officer directly. Capt. Mohan Singh tried to dissuade me as he realised the danger involved. As there was the likelihood of the whole issue getting very complicated in case I entrusted the job to the young officers or I sought the assistance of the Japanese units or military police, I decided to stick to my decision. As Mohan Singh also wanted to accompany me, we both went to the unit concerned guided by an INA propaganda squad member who had witnessed the arrest. We also took an escort of a few INA soldiers. I strictly forbade my companions to commit any violence unless the British troops initiated such a situation. Entering the room of the battalion commander I resolutely protested against the impropriety of keeping in confinement of an INA soldier, who had been assisting the Japanese forces, disregarding the signing of surrender on the 15th. The battalion commander accepted my protest and immediately handed over the INA propaganda squad member in his custody to me.

I was extremely happy that the matter ended so amicably. I could not contain my joy when I saw Capt. Mohan Singh embracing his released comrade with tears in eyes.

On our way back Capt. Mohan Singh thanked me profusely. Although it was past midnight, yet both Mohan Singh and myself had to study the rapid advance of the Japanese forces, adequate supplies have not come up yet. If there is any temporary shortage because of the circumstances stated above, you are requested to show proper understanding.

It was almost midnight when I completed my speech. When Capt. Kunizuku just started to translate it, Capt. Mohan Singh suddenly came into my room in a very agitated mood.

With visible expression of anxiety on his face he said that one of the INA propaganda squad members had been arrested by some British officers and had been kept in confinement. There was a likelihood that he might be tried for treason. It was indeed very difficult to watch the execution of a comrade. So he had come to discuss with me on the question of getting him released at any cost. I was very happy over this fresh proof of Capt. Mohan Singh's love and friendship for his comrades. I immediately took a resolution to save his comrade who was my comrade as well. The name of the British officer concerned and his address were also known. Although the instruments of surrender had already been signed, yet the issue concerned the enemy who had fought desperately even the day before and who were still carrying arms. I felt slightly worried. But any delay might bring about irreparable harm to the arrested person. It was not possible to hesitate either. I decided to go to the unit concerned and talk to the particular officer directly. Capt. Mohan Singh tried to dissuade me as he realised the danger involved. As there was the likelihood of the whole issue getting very complicated in case I entrusted the job to the young officers or I sought the assistance of the Japanese units or military police, I decided to stick to my decision. As Mohan Singh also wanted to accompany me, we both went to the unit concerned guided by an INA propaganda squad member who had witnessed the arrest. We also took an escort of a few INA soldiers. I strictly forbade my companions to commit any violence unless the British troops initiated such a situation. Entering the room of the battalion commander I resolutely protested against the impropriety of keeping in confinement of an INA soldier, who had been assisting the Japanese forces, disregarding the signing of surrender on the 15th. The battalion commander accepted my protest and immediately handed over the INA propaganda squad member in his custody to me.

I was extremely happy that the matter ended so amicably. I could not contain my joy when I saw Capt. Mohan Singh embracing his released comrade with tears in eyes.

On our way back Capt. Mohan Singh thanked me profusely. Although it was past midnight, yet both Mohan Singh and myself had to study the distribution of the fifty thousand Indian soldiers in different camps on the to their camps. I requested Lt. Col. Hunt to hand over the Indian soldiers who had already arrived, and to hand over those yet to arrive directly to the Japanese army. So we immediately started the ceremony. Through the mike, all the Indian soldiers were ordered to sit down facing the dias. The officers were told to sit in the front row. Lt. Col. Hunt took up position in front of the mike. All the Indian soldiers packing the park looked at Lt. Col. Hunt with great attention. In a very business like manner he said the Indian soldiers that they were being transferred to the Japanese army, and as such they should obey the command of the Japanese army in future. After speaking these few words, he handed over the list of names to me. The list contained about forty five thousand names. By this all the Indian soldiers came under the jurisdiction of the Japanese army. After telling the colonel that I had taken over the charge of the Indian soldiers. I requested him to leave the place. According to the schedule already drawn up, I stood in front of the mike. I felt ninety thousand eyes focussed on me. Suddenly there was pin drop silence. To my right stood 2nd Lt. Kunizuka for translating my speech into English, and to his right stood Lt. Col. Gill for translating my speech into Hindi. I was about to make a historical declaration of the philosophy of my work as the representative of the Japanese army to the forty five thousand Indian soldiers sitting in front of me. I felt all my blood roaring through my body and rushing to my head. With my manuscript in my hand I first made obeisance to the Indian soldiers respectfully in order to show the sincerity of friendship to all the Indian soldiers who had assembled there. The Indian officers and men seated there responded rather reflexively, some by folding their hands and some by touching their forehead with their right hand. At that very instant I felt that a bond of friendship was established between me and the Indian soldiers. Then I introduced myself to the Indian soldiers by saying "My friends, the soldiers of India, I am Maj. Fujiwara, the Head of F-Organisation, who has come here to take over the charges of you all from the British authorities on behalf of the Japanese, and for establishing the bond of friendship between the peoples of India and Japan. "As soon as this was translated into English by 2nd. Lt. Kunizuka, I saw nods of approval in the front row where the officers were seated. As soon as this was retranslated into Hindi by Lt. Col. Gill, I saw the same nod of approval among the thousands of soldiers in the rear. I felt that I had succeeded in touching the hearts of all those seated in front of me. After explaining the philosophical background of Japan's intension to establish a new order of Prosperity in East Asia based on liberty, equality and fraternity of the liberated nations of the region, I proceeded to assure them of Japan's earnest desire to give all possible support to the Indian Independence movement. The last part of my speech was drowned in deafening applause of my listeners. The next part of my speech also received similar welcome when I expressed my firm conviction that the fall of the British citadel in the Far East Singapore signalled the collapse of the empires of England and Holland in East Asia and liberation of the nations of the region from imperialistic fetters. The listeners went so wild with enthusiasm that it was not possible for me to continue my speech for a while till the applause subsided.

Next I introduced the glorious achievements of the IIL led by Pritam Singh and the INA led by Capt. Mohan Singh, and declared the Japanese army's all out support to these two movements. This was also received with similar applause. I explained to them that the Japanese army will not treat the Indian soldiers as prisoners of war, rather they will be treated as friends and brothers. The Japanese army had always regretted the sad destiny of confronting you all in the battlefield with arms for no fault of yours or ours. However, today we have been freed from that destiny, and have succeeded in establishing the bonds of friendship and brotherhood, with the blessing of God. The Independence of a nation should be won over by the nation through struggle that should arise from within the nation. I also declared that those soldiers willing to join the INA after taking the vow of loyalty to India and to fight for the freedom of motherland, will cease to be prisoners forthwith, and they will be given all possible help. Not only that their right to fight will also be recognised. As soon as I finished this line I saw thousands of caps flying into air besides deafening cheers. My speech lasted about forty minutes. This speech of mine can be considered as one of the landmarks in the birth of the Indian National Army. Together with the speeches of Pritam Singh and Capt. Mohan Singh, this speech also can be taken as a historical declaration deserving due recognition in the history of India.

Pritam Singh and Capt. Mohan Singh took the mike after me. Both of them spoke in Hindi. Both of them described the activities of the IIL and the INA, and expressed their firm conviction of gaining India's Independence through armed struggle, with both of them standing in the vanguard of the fight. After describing the state of the Indians as living corpses because of servitude, they appealed to all those present to join the struggle for the liberation of motherland and put an end to the shame of foreign domination. Each and every word they uttered went home deep into the hearts of the Indian soldiers. As their speech ended the crowd burst out into thunderous applause, the caps went flying into air, and all tried to come near the dias. For some time chaos reigned supreme. All of them were imbued with inspiration for dedicating their lives for the cause of their motherland. Thus ended the meeting of the Farah Park amidst great success. Next I proposed to Capt. Mohan Singh and Lt. Col. Gill to have a meeting exclusively with the officers in the hall. Lt. Col. Gill immediately ordered the officers to assemble in the hall. We all sat around a round table, and I proposed to the officers to have a frank discussion over their questions and doubts on the Japanese army in particular and Japan in general.

The officers put questions on the motive of Japan in supporting the Independence of India, the extent of support Japan was prepared to give to the Indian Independence struggle, cooperation between the INA and the Japanese army, organising the INA and arming it etc. I replied to these questions on the basis of the memorandum of Pritam Singh and Col. Tamura and the discussion I had with Capt. Mohan Singh at Taiping. I frankly admitted that the question of organising and equipping of the INA and its cooperation with the Japanese army should be settled by bipartite talks between the Japanese authorities and the Indian leaders. I succeeded in winning over the understanding and friendship of the Indian officers through these talks. After the end of the talks, Lt. Col. Gill issued instructions on the accommodation of the soldiers. The Indian soldiers assembled in the park started moving towards their camps just like flood water breaching the dyke. All the members of the F-Organisation and of the INA were mobilised to guide them to their camps. It was night by the time the last soldiers reached their camps.

Immediately after the meeting I returned to my office alongwith Pritam Singh. This was because there was a scheduled meeting with two representatives of the local Indian community Goho and Menon. Pritam Singh had briefed them beforehand over the nature and function of the F-Organisation, as well as about me. They were well versed with the activities of the IIL and the INA, and also knew about the grand spectacle of the Farah Park, Pritam Singh had also briefed me about these two persons beforehand. As we settled down for discussion after an exchange of greetings, we felt as if we were old friends. I was very much impressed by Goho who initiated the discussion on the subject of freedom, honour and interest of his compatriots. He appeared to me as a person with strong character and will, with capacity to enforce decision besides having great political consciousness. In this sitting we discussed about the support of the IIL by these two gentlemen, appointment of Goho as the President of the Singapore chapter of the IIL, and the meeting of the Singapore Indians tried to come near the dias. For some time chaos reigned supreme. All of them were imbued with inspiration for dedicating their lives for the cause of their motherland. Thus ended the meeting of the Farah Park amidst great success. Next I proposed to Capt. Mohan Singh and Lt. Col. Gill to have a meeting exclusively with the officers in the hall. Lt. Col. Gill immediately ordered the officers to assemble in the hall. We all sat around a round table, and I proposed to the officers to have a frank discussion over their questions and doubts on the Japanese army in particular and Japan in general.

The officers put questions on the motive of Japan in supporting the Independence of India, the extent of support Japan was prepared to give to the Indian Independence struggle, cooperation between the INA and the Japanese army, organising the INA and arming it etc. I replied to these questions on the basis of the memorandum of Pritam Singh and Col. Tamura and the discussion I had with Capt. Mohan Singh at Taiping. I frankly admitted that the question of organising and equipping of the INA and its cooperation with the Japanese army should be settled by bipartite talks between the Japanese authorities and the Indian leaders. I succeeded in winning over the understanding and friendship of the Indian officers through these talks. After the end of the talks, Lt. Col. Gill issued instructions on the accommodation of the soldiers. The Indian soldiers assembled in the park started moving towards their camps just like flood water breaching the dyke. All the members of the F-Organisation and of the INA were mobilised to guide them to their camps. It was night by the time the last soldiers reached their camps.

Immediately after the meeting I returned to my office alongwith Pritam Singh. This was because there was a scheduled meeting with two representatives of the local Indian community Goho and Menon. Pritam Singh had briefed them beforehand over the nature and function of the F-Organisation, as well as about me. They were well versed with the activities of the IIL and the INA, and also knew about the grand spectacle of the Farah Park, Pritam Singh had also briefed me about these two persons beforehand. As we settled down for discussion after an exchange of greetings, we felt as if we were old friends. I was very much impressed by Goho who initiated the discussion on the subject of freedom, honour and interest of his compatriots. He appeared to me as a person with strong character and will, with capacity to enforce decision besides having great political consciousness. In this sitting we discussed about the support of the IIL by these two gentlemen, appointment of Goho as the President of the Singapore chapter of the IIL, and the meeting of the Singapore Indians

YMA supporters from the jail. He said that he wanted to work for the cooperation of the Malayan people with the Japanese army under the support and guidance of the Japanese army. After felicitating him for safe release from jail I promised all cooperation for fostering friendship between the Malayan and Japanese peoples. I proposed to him that for the moment we should concentrate on bringing out the banned paper *Warta Malaya* and helping out the poverty striken supporters of the YMA financially. After the departure of Ibrahim, I called upon the deputy chief of staff Maj. Gen. -M, (Manaki) and solicited his approval for converting the YMA from a political organisation into a cultural body for the cultural uplift of the Malayan people. At that time the army authorities were thinking of adopting a short sighted policy of derecognising all the political, cultural and economic bodies of the local people. This was motivated either by its complacency over the success in Malaya, or by the apprehension of the attitude of the local Chinese who had till then carried out a boycott Japan movement and who might take advantage of these organisations for carrying out anti-Japanese movement. At any rate such thinking was totally incompatible with the professed lofty ideal of establishing a new order of coprosperity sphere in the Far East by liberating the nations of East Asia. Such breach of trust has resulted in trampling of peoples reliance in Manchuria and China. All my associates and myself were trying to mobilising the peoples of India, Malaya and Sumatra for the noble cause with all our zeal sincerely believing the imperial rescripts and messages issued on this lofty ideal. It was impossible for me to tolerate this duplicity. I expressed my conviction to Maj. Gen. -M. and requested him to lend his support to the YMA as an organisation for fostering cultural understanding of the Malays. After somewhat heated argument for more than thirty minutes he finally consented to allow the YMA to function as an organisation purely for cultural uplift of the Malays. He immediately agreed on the republication of the party paper *Warta Malaya* and giving priority to the YMA members in appointments. Next I called upon the head of the propaganda division of the army and succeeded in getting his approval for free supply of the materials and rent free use of press for its publication. By this I succeeded in discharging a part of my obligation to the YMA. Encouraged by this success I resolved in my mind that in future also I should hold my ground like this in face of all difficulties in order to discharge my part of the duty towards my comrades. The time had come at last to part company with the YMA. It had already been decided that the military administration will incorporate the YMA, which will in turn devote exclusively to peaceful cultural activities. I introduced my friends Ibrahim and Onam to Maj. Gen.-M and solicited his support and understanding. To my friends I promised all possible help for all the time to come even though our official relation was going to be snapped. On the 19th, a general meeting of the Singapore Indians was held at Farah Park, the meeting which has made a lasting impression on all those who have witnessed it. Tens of thousands of Indians filled the park, and the dias was decorated with flowers and cloth. Goho, the chairman of the Singapore branch, gave an inflammatory speech to the crowd, which was cheered repeatedly. After Goho, Pritam Singh, Capt. Mohan Singh and myself addressed the crowd one after another. Thus was established the Singapore Branch of the IIL, and with this, the IIL, ultimately succeeded in embracing all the Indians living in Thailand and Malaya. On this very day it was decided to bring all the INA units scattered all over Malaya to Singapore on the basis of the proposal of Capt. Mohan Singh. This task was assigned to 2nd. Lt. Yonemura. By this Singapore became the main base of the IIL and the INA, and these two organisations reached what we may say as the offtake stage.

Around this time, Premier Tojo delivered his historic speech in the Imperial Diet where he promised liberation to the peoples of East Asia, Independence of Philippines, and all our support to the Indian Independence struggle. Thus at long last one of my dreams which I had been trying hard to push through was realised. The only drawback of this declaration was that it was too abstract.

At a time when Pritam Singh was busy convening a meeting of the heads of the IIL branches spread all over Malaya and Singapore in Singapore and Capt. Mohan Singh was busy in enlarging and consolidating the INA which had now assembled in Singapore, I received a telegram from the Imperial Headquarters of Tokyo via the Supreme Command of the Southern Forces. According to it, Rash Behari Bose, a veteran Indian revolutionary and an old resident of Tokyo had convened a meeting of the leaders of the Indian Community of various regions of East Asia in Tokyo with the good offices of the Imperial Headquarters for discussing the political problems related to the liberation of India. Another objective was to establish cordial relation with the Japanese authorities. In all about ten leaders were invited; to be selected from among the IIL leaders of Malaya and Thailand and the INA. The delegation was expected to reach Tokyo by 19th March. In this telegram I was instructed to accompany the delegation to Tokyo, besides one Col. Iwakuro. Intuitively I felt that the exclusively to peaceful cultural activities. I introduced my friends Ibrahim and Onam to Maj. Gen.-M and solicited his support and understanding. To my friends I promised all possible help for all the time to come even though our official relation was going to be snapped. On the 19th, a general meeting of the Singapore Indians was held at Farah Park, the meeting which has made a lasting impression on all those who have witnessed it. Tens of thousands of Indians filled the park, and the dias was decorated with flowers and cloth. Goho, the chairman of the Singapore branch, gave an inflammatory speech to the crowd, which was cheered repeatedly. After Goho, Pritam Singh, Capt. Mohan Singh and myself addressed the crowd one after another. Thus was established the Singapore Branch of the IIL, and with this, the IIL, ultimately succeeded in embracing all the Indians living in Thailand and Malaya. On this very day it was decided to bring all the INA units scattered all over Malaya to Singapore on the basis of the proposal of Capt. Mohan Singh. This task was assigned to 2nd. Lt. Yonemura. By this Singapore became the main base of the IIL and the INA, and these two organisations reached what we may say as the offtake stage.

Around this time, Premier Tojo delivered his historic speech in the Imperial Diet where he promised liberation to the peoples of East Asia, Independence of Philippines, and all our support to the Indian Independence struggle. Thus at long last one of my dreams which I had been trying hard to push through was realised. The only drawback of this declaration was that it was too abstract.

At a time when Pritam Singh was busy convening a meeting of the heads of the IIL branches spread all over Malaya and Singapore in Singapore and Capt. Mohan Singh was busy in enlarging and consolidating the INA which had now assembled in Singapore, I received a telegram from the Imperial Headquarters of Tokyo via the Supreme Command of the Southern Forces. According to it, Rash Behari Bose, a veteran Indian revolutionary and an old resident of Tokyo had convened a meeting of the leaders of the Indian Community of various regions of East Asia in Tokyo with the good offices of the Imperial Headquarters for discussing the political problems related to the liberation of India. Another objective was to establish cordial relation with the Japanese authorities. In all about ten leaders were invited; to be selected from among the IIL leaders of Malaya and Thailand and the INA. The delegation was expected to reach Tokyo by 19th March. In this telegram I was instructed to accompany the delegation to Tokyo, besides one Col. Iwakuro. Intuitively I felt that the

the impression I got from the telegram of the Imperial Headquarters was correct. Col. Iwakuro had held many key posts in the War Ministry, and had taken part in the Japan-America peace talks just before the outbreak of war. He was also posted in USA in that connection. He was one of the most capable and politically talented officers of the Japanese army. Many leaders of the government and of public life were his close friends. He was the fittest person for pushing through and supporting the India policy by mobilising both government officialdom and the leaders of the public life, and well as for dealing with the Indians at political level. I called upon Col. Iwakuro at his residence in the military barracks near the Menam river. I did this because I wanted to inform the colonel of the work I had done till then as well as to apprise him of the belief under which I had worked so far. During the course of talks I repeated my convictions which I had expressed to Lt. Col.-O (Ozeki) of the Imperial Headquarters at Ipoh as well as my plan on Indian policy which I had presented to this very officer at Klan. I particularly emphasised the need for abandoning the petty plotters mortality which had been adopted so far in China, and adopt an open national policy towards India based on political and national ethics. The Iwakuro Organisation should not be a spy type plotters body. I wanted it to be some sort of ambassadorial organisation fit for representing Japan in Independent India. I request him to decline in case the authorities in Tokyo was intending to set up this organisation for just facilitating the operations of the Japanese army, or in other words a scheming body.

The colonel agreed with my viewpoint. I was extremely happy to find my viewpoint accepted by Col. Iwakuro, a capable officer of the Japanese army. I was very happy to find an enlightened officer like him due to take over the charge of the new organisation that was going to be set up for pushing through the India policy with great vigour. It was indeed very difficult to mobilise the positive support of the army and the government and the diet, where a proper understanding of such a project was almost totally lacking. Again, mobilising the support of the people in national scale was another important factor. In this respect the appointment of the colonel came as a great boon.

Around this time brisk propaganda activities beamed towards India started from the Saigon Radio. A team of a few members of INA headed by Capt. was engaged in this work with all out support from the Propaganda Division of the Japanese army. The propaganda from Saigon Radio was much more effective than that of the Tokyo Radio. Goho utilised this overnight stop over to make a broadcast to the people of India on the situation in Malaya and Singapore prevailing at that time.

At Saigon we had to board two planes due to some unavoidable reasons. It was decided that we seven, Col. Iwakuro, Capt. Mohan Singh, Lt. Col. Gill, Raghavan, Goho, Menon and myself would go straight to Tokyo from Saigon in a plane. The other team consisting of five members, Otakuro, Swami, Pritam Singh, Ayer and Capt. Akram, were to leave Saigon two days after us by plane. On 11th March we left Saigon by plane. But at Rainan Island our plane develope engine trouble detaining us in the island for two days. There was no facility worth mentioning where the delegation could be accommodated. I contacted the local naval command, but failed to elicit any cooperation. The naval commander there was unwilling to allow the foreigners inside the naval base. With great reluctance he allotted a dirty barrack to us close to the airport. This indifferent attitude of the naval commander indeed made the Indians very unhappy, and to make amends as much as possible, I ran about procuring fresh eggs and fruits. But the results fell far short of the efforts. The situation was so miserable that we were not provided with even the required number of cots. Even those provided were old and rickety ones. I had to sleep on the floor. It did not matter much to me as I was accustomed to such life in the front. But for the members of the delegation who were accustomed to luxurious living in Penang and Singapore, this was a memorable experience indeed. They felt more pity for me seeing that I was trying to do my best for their comforts. Finally our plane was repaired, and we reached Tokyo via Taipei and Shanghai, where we spent one night each.

As soon as we disembarked, the plane went back to Taipei to bring Swami and his party. Officials from the Imperial Headquarters were there at the airport to receive us and the delegation was comfortably lodged at the Sanno Hotel. Already Oskon and Khan were there as the delegates from Shanghai and Hongkong respectively. The weather was extremely cold for the visitors from the south. Especially elderly Menon was shivering with cold. In Tokyo the delegates were taken charge of by the officials of the Imperial Headquarters, which left me with a feeling of great dismay as I had planned all the time to show my friends round Tokyo.

The day following our arrival I went to the Imperial Headquarters together with Col. Iwakuro. There I got the opportunity to report on my work and the latest developments to the chief of staff and the concerned officials of the Imperial Headquarters. I took advantage of this to express my views and convictions on the policy that Japan should adopt towards India, which I had presented to the authorities whenever I got an opportunity. I concluded my briefing by emphasising the following four points : (a) That the Japanese government should immediately chalk out a concrete policy towards India on the basis of the declaration of Premier Tojo in the Diet on the 20th January and proclaim it to the world openly without any delay; (b) that this should be adopted as the committed policy of the Japanese nation as a whole; (c) that proclaiming the scope of the New Order in East Asia should be the precondition for justifying Japan's policy towards the occupied territories; and (d) that all possible support should be given to the movements arising from among the Indian people, and no undue moddling should be carried out. I also expressed the view that the Iwakuro Organisation which was going to be set up for taking over the works concerning India from the Fujiwara Organisation should be more of an ambassadorial organisation rather than an organisation for some specific objective. As far as possible it should have diplomatic status. I felt that all those present were deeply impressed with my speech. After finishing reporting, I met Lt. Col. - K and Maj. -O of the 8th section which was in charge of this work, and discussed with them on the plan prepared by the Imperial Headquarters. Col. Iwakuro also participated in the discussion over this draft plan. Here I came to know that the plan was drawn up on the basis of the plan which I had earlier submitted to the Imperial Headquarters. But the most disappointing thing was that this plan carried a title ' The Indian Stratagem (Draft). Moreover, the Imperial Headquarters kept the political affairs with respect to India within its direct control, assigning the miscellaneous works in the operational zone to the Iwakuro Organisation. With the approval of Col. Iwakuro, I strongly demanded a drastic modification of the whole conception on which the whole plan was prepared. It took full two days of argument to convince those people, and ultimately the title was changed from 'The Indian Stratagem (Draft)' into 'Indian Policy Plan', and the contents were also modified to eliminate all traces of stratagem. I was very happy to realise that this trip to Tokyo proved to be so significant. During this time, the delegates were going round Tokyo sightseeing according to schedules drawn up by the Imperial Headquarters. I devoted all my available time to accompany them round Tokyo and to fulfil their wish as far as possible. Here a very delicate issue cropped up. The delegates who came from the south alongwith me were unable to adjust mentally with the Indian representatives of Japan , who had been carrying on Indian Independence movement in Japan under the leadership of Rash Behari Bose, and who had the patronisation of the Imperial Headquarters. The allegation of the IIL delegates was that these people had lost their freedom of movement and speech as they had lived long in Japan and enjoyed Japanese hospitality, and hence they had a tendency to get degraded to the status concrete policy towards India on the basis of the declaration of Premier Tojo in the Diet on the 20th January and proclaim it to the world openly without any delay; (b) that this should be adopted as the committed policy of the Japanese nation as a whole; (c) that proclaiming the scope of the New Order in East Asia should be the precondition for justifying Japan's policy towards the occupied territories; and (d) that all possible support should be given to the movements arising from among the Indian people, and no undue moddling should be carried out. I also expressed the view that the Iwakuro Organisation which was going to be set up for taking over the works concerning India from the Fujiwara Organisation should be more of an ambassadorial organisation rather than an organisation for some specific objective. As far as possible it should have diplomatic status. I felt that all those present were deeply impressed with my speech. After finishing reporting, I met Lt. Col. - K and Maj. -O of the 8th section which was in charge of this work, and discussed with them on the plan prepared by the Imperial Headquarters. Col. Iwakuro also participated in the discussion over this draft plan. Here I came to know that the plan was drawn up on the basis of the plan which I had earlier submitted to the Imperial Headquarters. But the most disappointing thing was that this plan carried a title ' The Indian Stratagem (Draft). Moreover, the Imperial Headquarters kept the political affairs with respect to India within its direct control, assigning the miscellaneous works in the operational zone to the Iwakuro Organisation. With the approval of Col. Iwakuro, I strongly demanded a drastic modification of the whole conception on which the whole plan was prepared. It took full two days of argument to convince those people, and ultimately the title was changed from 'The Indian Stratagem (Draft)' into 'Indian Policy Plan', and the contents were also modified to eliminate all traces of stratagem. I was very happy to realise that this trip to Tokyo proved to be so significant. During this time, the delegates were going round Tokyo sightseeing according to schedules drawn up by the Imperial Headquarters. I devoted all my available time to accompany them round Tokyo and to fulfil their wish as far as possible. Here a very delicate issue cropped up. The delegates who came from the south alongwith me were unable to adjust mentally with the Indian representatives of Japan , who had been carrying on Indian Independence movement in Japan under the leadership of Rash Behari Bose, and who had the patronisation of the Imperial Headquarters. The allegation of the IIL delegates was that these people had lost their freedom of movement and speech as they had lived long in Japan and enjoyed Japanese hospitality, and hence they had a tendency to get degraded to the status of Japan's puppet. They were especially skeptic about Rash Behari Bose who had lived in Japan as exile for tens years marrying a Japanese lady, there, by loosing much of Indian character, on the other hand, the Indians of Japan asserted that the IIL representatives were, till the other day the loyal subjects of Britain without having any revolutionary background, and that for no rhyme or reason they bore grudge against the Indians of Japan. I tried to do my best in bringing about reconciliation between the two groups. The behaviour of one Mr. K who was appointed as the guide of the party by the Imperial Headquarters aggravated the complicated the situation all the more. The words and deeds of this gentleman displayed all the clumsiness of the Japanese people, like showing too much courtesy bearing upon infringement on privacy, deciding things on the basis of personal judgement without bothering for the views of the guests, posing as an authority on Indian affair, etc., which were not necessarily motivated by any ill will. Swami and his party was scheduled to reach Tokyo on the 19th of March, evening. Unfortunately strong wind started blowing since the morning of this day which gained in intensity as the day advanced. By afternoon, the visibility became poor with flying dust. Towards evening it started drizzling. I was sure that the arrival of the party would be postponed in view of the inclement weather. However, towards evening I came to know that the party had left Shanghi in the afternoon for Tokyo. I thought that the party would land at some airport in Kyushu or Osaka and would wait for the weather to improve. In the evening I got a telephone from the Haneda airport informing that wireless connection with the plane of the party had snapped around 15.00 hour when the plane was flying over the Ise Bay. Slowly it turned into a rain storm at night. I sent telegrams to the various airports enquiring about the plane. Inauspicious thoughts started contains my brain. The delegates also shared my anxiety. I earnestly hoped for the safe landing of the plan somewhere. That night I remained awake for the whole of the night waiting for replies from the airports, but there was no news. Towards dawn. I dreamt the faces of my dearest friends Pritam Singh, Capt. Agnam and Otaguro. By noon of the following day it became obvious that the plane had not landed at any airport in Central Japan.

Otaguro's wife had come to Tokyo to receiveher husband. I had to tell the IIL delegates and the wife of Otaguro to be prepared for the worst It was indeed a very sad and painful task. Towards evening I got a news that a plane had crushed in the hills beyond Nayoya the evening before. The worst had happened. The rescue teams all over central Japan were put on search duty. From all the available information it transpired that the plane permanently lost to the world alongwith the death of my five dear comrades. As I write these lines, my heart is filled with the sorrow for my departed dear friends and the irreparable loss of the precious document.

The conference of the Indian delegates of the East Asia was inaugurated at Sanno Hotel on the 20th of March in an atmosphere of gloom following the death of the four comrades. On the first day Col. Iwakuro and myself were permitted to be present as observers. Besides the four IIL and INA delegates from Malaya and Thailand, there were delegations from Hongkong, Shanghai, Philippines and Japan. The chairmanship of the conference was pressed on Rash Behari Bose. For some reason or other, one of the most influential leaders of the Indian community of Japan and a veteran freedom fighter, Sahai, was missing from the conference. Another notable absentee was Mohendra Pratap. I was very such intrigued by their absence. The wall facing the delegates was decorated with huge Indian and Japanese National flags. After first expressing condolence for the four dead delegates, the chairman welcomed the delegates for the various regions of East Asia. Next he explained the unique chance that had arrived at last following the declaration of Premier Tojo committing all possible support to the Indian Independence movement as well as the rapid success of the Japanese forces. Following this he thanked the delegation of IIL and INA from the south for their dedicated activities in Malaya and Thailand. He finally wound up by telling that the main objective of the meeting was to have a free and frank discussion on the political problems concerning the freedom movement of India besides free exchange of views among the delegates for evolving a concrete policy for mobilising politically the Indians in South Asia for the Liberation of Motherland. However, this eloquent speech of Bose apparently failed to make much impression on the delegates, especially the delegates of the IIL and the INA. Despite such apathy, all the delegates were determined to stick to their objective of working for the liberation of Motherland. The delegates individually and in groups, inside the conference hall and outside exchanged views and carried out discussions. Ultimately it was decided to save the IIL the status of the sole political organisation of the Indians of East Asia for carrying out the freedom struggle. And it was decided to convene a conference of the Indians of East Asia at Bangkok in May under the auspicies of the IIL to decide the future course of activity of the organisation.

It was decided that the regular activity of the IIL and the Iwakuro, organisation would start after that conference. The IIL delegates had a private meeting with Premier Tojo where they confirmed the Japanese

Government's intention to support the Indian independent movement.

When the search for the missing plane was on. I got another telegram which plunged me into fresh grief. It was from the chief of staff of the 27th Army informing the death of Harimau who was ailing in Singapore hospital. He was involved in all sorts of desparate criminal activities like looting gold bars from mail trains, and his reputation was so bad that mothers used to pacifying their troublesome children by threatening to call him. However, as war spread in Malaya, he suddenly changed his mind and as a true patriot started assisting the Japanese forces. He meticulously adhered to my strict order of not indulging in any anti-social activities, and his band did not including in any violent activity even once. His activities behind the British lines facilitated the Japanese advance greatly. Although he was only tv~nty eight years old, yet he had a very chequered career. It must be mentioned here that the reform and winning over of Harimau was achieved through the skilful persuation of Kamimoto and 2nd Lt. Yonemura. Especially Kamimoto was his constant companion eversince April 1941, persuading at every opportunity to give up the evil ways. Indeed it is very difficult to forget the noble dedication of Kamimoto who quite aften stood at the brink of death for fulfilling his duty. Immediately I took steps to get his name enrolled formally in the Ministry of Defence as a civilian attached to the army. The next day I was invited to the reporters club of the War Ministry to deliver a talk on the fascinating life and activities of Harimau before and after the war. The big newspapers devoted about a quarter of a page in reporting my talk. A memorial service was held for him in the Yasukuni Shrine at Kudan of Tokyo. Thus he ended his life as a loyal son of Japan. In the mean time Col. Iwakuro was busy preparing plans for successfully accomplishing his new assignment and was enthusiastically searching for people to staff his organisation. For this the colonel had to remain in Tokyo for some time. It was however, tentatively decided that the new organisation would take over the members of the F- Organisation excepting for myself and a few other civilian members. As for me, I was to go back to the Supreme Command of the Southern Force in Saigon. However, I was to carry on with my organisation for the time being till the Iwakuro Organisation took over the charge. Hence I had proceed to Singapore immediately ahead of the delegation. There I reinforced the F-Organisation by coopting, 2nd Lt. Hara, 2nd Lt. Kaneko, 2nd Lt. Matsushige and 2nd Lt. Tsukamoto and a few other NCOs to cope with the ever expanding scope of activity of the F-Organisation. I left Tokyo for Singapore on the last of April. Just before the departure I got the confirmation of the death of my five friends. Because of violent storm and rain the plane had lost its way and crushed in Japan Alps in Nagano Prefecture. On my way back I met the mother and older sister of Harimau in Fukuoka airport. As I tried to console them, in tears they said that they were happy that he had laid down his life for the cause of the country. They were very happy to hear the achievements of Harimau which I related to them. In Saigon I met the staff officer Lt. Col. -O at the Supreme command of the Southern Forces and reported the developments in Tokyo and requested him to make the necessary preparations for sponsoring the Bangkok Conference. During this talk it was decided that the Iwakuro organisation would take over the charges from the F-Organisation by the end of April. I returned to Singapore on the 5th of April. This trip of mine coincided with rapid developments in the war situation all over South East Asia. In Burma Rangoon fell to the Japanese forces on 8th March, following which the Japanese forces were regrouping for launching an offensive against Central and northern Burma. The 16th Army landed in Java on the 1st of March, and by 9th of the same month the Dutch East Indies army surrendered. The Konoe Division of the 25th Army landed in Sumatra on 13th March; and on the same day the Andaman group of Islands were captured.

In the Philippines, the final offensive against the Batan peninsula started on the 5th of April.

Appendix-IV

Interrogation Report of General Mohan Singh : Throws New Light on the Formation of the Indian National Army and his Views of the Japanese Policy (Extract)[1]

20. During November the clouds of war had been first looming and then seeming to recede. When the Bn moved back to Sungei Patani it had seemed that there was still hope, but H/1050 was ready for recall and on Sun 30 Nov. 41 had made special arrangements for any telegram arriving to reach him where he was staying. From 2 to 6 Dec. was spent in the well rehearsed Jitra position. By 0400 hrs on 8 Dec. however the bn lessone coy was at Alor Star railway station ready to move by train to Singora in Thailand. The remaining coy had been detached and had already set out by road to occupy positions on the Thai-Malaya border. But the Japanese had landed during the night of 7/8 Dec. at Singora and the railway was already cut. The bn therefore did not actually entrain and at dawn on 8 Dec heard the bombardment of a small railway station, and remained there all day. At 1700 hrs orders were lived to move back to Jitra and to take up the allotted position between the main Jitra position and the frontier. The previously moved to the frontier was by this time and contact with the enemy. Another coy was at once moved up also during the night 10/11 Dec. A Gurkhas Bn occupied the former bn position.

21. Between 1/14 Punjab and the Gurkhas there lay an extensive marsh which the road crossed by a mined causeway. The plan was that 1/14 Punjab, having fought a delaying action would retire behind the causeway which would then be blown. During these days of contact the Punjabis had gained considerable confidence and met with some success. They were however, retiring slowly, according to plan. On 11 Dec. they were to move behind the causeway but as this was being done, the Div

---

1. W.O. 208/833. Public Recent office London. Mohan Singh (H. 1050) was interrogated in 1945 by Col. Hugh Toye, the British Intelligence Officer.

Comd, encouraged by the successful delaying action fought, ordered 1/14 Punjab to hold on for another night. "You can do it", H/1050 heard him tell the CO, "they have no tanks." Five minutes later Japanese tanks attacked down the road while the bn was moving to the new position forward of the causeway ordered. Complete dissintegration ensued. Survivors were caught between the fire of the tanks and the deep waters of the marsh augmented by recent heavy rains. H/1050 and his Co found themselves together in the waters of the marsh East of the road. Together with 2 NCOs they remained in the water for about 24 hrs trying to find a way of escape to the South. Darkness fell almost immediately after the action and in attempts to skirt the marsh, the party became lost in the jungle. On the evening of 13 Dec, while enquiring the way in a village, the party fell in with Capt. Mohd Akram and about 10 Pathans of 1/14 Punjab. The 2 parties joined and on the morning of 14 Dec. found a footpath which they thought might lead to Alor Star. Other stragglers joined them. During the afternoon the party, now about 60 strong, emerged from the jungle at Kuala Narang and took up a position in a rubber clump. H/1050 then volunteered to reconnoitre for information on the general situation.

Reconnaissance and Surrender

22. H/1050 and an NCO went to the nearby Kuala Narang which they found full of confusion and rumours. After conversation with some local Indians they located a Malay officer who told them that the Japanese had now advanced far beyond Alor Star. H/1050 thereupon collected some food and drink which he took back to the position with the aid of several civilian Indians. When Lt. Col. Fitzpatrick[2] heard the news he said that he himself would go and see the Malay official. After doing so he conferred with Capt. Mohd. Akram and H/1050, and having considered all courses open decided to surrender. A message was accordingly sent by villagers to whatever Japanese Military Authorities might be in Alor Star that a party of men was at Kuala Narang and that it wished to surrender. The party thereopen moved from the rubber clump position to the police station in Kuala Karang. During the evening a reply came from Alor Star to the effect that there were Indians with the Japanese and that an Indian gentleman and a Japanese officer would come next morning to see the surrendering party.

23. At about 0900 hrs next morning Giani Pritam Singh arrived in a car which flew the Congress flag. He assured Lt. Col. Fitzpatrick that he, Giani

2. Lt. Colonel. Fitzpatrick was Commanding the battalion which surrendered to the Japanese. Mohah Singh was warking with him.

Pritam Singh, was responsible for the treatment of PW and that everything would be well. He also said that a Japanese officer was waiting nearby and would presently come to receive them. Lt. Col. Fitzpatrick then went with Giani Pritam Sigh to see Maj. Fujiwara who had halted his car some distance away. When they returned, H/1050 had assembled his men ready for the surrender which then took place. Lt. Col. Fitzpatrick was immediately separated from his men and H/1050 never saw him after that day.

24. The whole party of PW was then taken to barracks prepared for it at Alor Star. H/1050 and Capt Mohd Akram travelled in the car of Giani Pritam Singh and asked that gentleman what was the meaning of this mysterious protection which he seemed to have undertaken. Giani Pritam Singh, whose conversation and aspect was in religious terms tones and gestures, had replied that he had been for a whole year now working for the freedom of India. He thanked God that he had now with him two Indian officers who would be able to work to that end too. His dreams, he said, were at last being fulfilled. He had certain pacts with the Japanese and wished to raise an Indian Independence Army. H/1050 asked if he really did trust the Japanese, and Pritam Singh impressed both the newly taken PW with his blind faith.

25. At this point H/1050 recalls that during the early days of the battle for Malaya Bde HQ had sent men who could read certain Indian languages in order that they might translate some pamphlets which had mysteriously arrived in the front line. H/1050 was much too busy himself to take any notice at that time, but Habibur Rehman who had seen some told him afterwards that they contained a lot of nonsense and were subversive.

The Early Days

26. On arrival at Alor Star H/1050 was taken to the office of Maj Fujiwara who was extremely busy, H/1050 there met his battalion commander for the last time. In the office next door H/1050 found Giani Pritam Singh and with him from 7 to 10 Indians, mainly Sikhs. Pritam Singh once more expressed his great pleasure at meeting H/1050. Pritam Singh appeared to be on the best possible terms with Maj Fujiwara. When Fujiwara at last found time, he told H/1050 to rest for a while and have some food. Accordingly the rest of the day was spent in settling his men into their quarters, in collecting cooking utensils and food.

Late that evening when the PW were about to go to sleep, Maj Fujiwara sent for H/1050. Mohd Akram accompanied him to Fujiwara's office where they found also Giani Pritam Singh. This was the first of several interviews during which the project, mentioned by Giani Pritam

Singh in the car, was discussed. At these discussions Giani Pritam Singh was always a silent listener. The Japanese Atokuro invariably interpreted for Maj Fujiwara. Maj Fujiwara asked the two officers whether Giani Pritam Singh had explained everything to them. It had been quite evident to H/1050 from the very first that Giani Pritam Singh was an unintelligent dupe of the Japanese and he made this clear to Fujiwara many times. Giani Pritam Singh, he said, might be a sincere believer in the freedom of India, but he just did not understand the full implication of the things about which he was talking. He had no political background, and it was futile for a man with no political background to try to lead a movement which could only be political. H/1050 did then mention that there was a man, S.C. Bose, who would be a capable leader, but he was not to hand. As for Pritam Singh, H/1050 had not understood him at all. Maj. Fujiwara therefore proceeded to expound the matter in his own way. He did not particularly comment on the mention of Bose. He talked much of the "Co-prosperity Sphere", of "Asia for the Asiatics", and of the sincerity of the Japanese in their desire to help India to liberate herself. Much of his talk was extremely vague and H/1050 more than once asked for a written definition of this "Coprosperity Sphere" and "Greater East Asia", but Maj Fujiwara never committed himself to anything definite. He talked a great deal about Congress, about the high ideal of Freedom, and at last reached the point of his whole argument. Freedom, he said, could not be achieved by sitting on an arm chair, Gandhi was only a religious leader and could not cause any real political changes. To change the world there must be an army and soldiers fighting. It was soldiers, he said, who made history. Then he turned to H/1050 and told him in effect "And what are you going to do about it? It is for you to choose. If you want your freedom you must aspire to do something active, you must raise an Indian Independence Army."

28. H/1050's attitude on the Congress point was as follows :

He did not agree that non-violence was futile, and he strongly resisted Pritam singh's desire, expressed during the course of the talks, to keep the IIL, as it was already called by Pritam Singh, separate from Congress. Violence would of course come and H/1050 was all for it, but nothing must be done against Congress policy.

29. H/1050 reported to his officers and men next morning the conversation which had taken place on the previous night. He expressed his own feeling that extreme caution was necessary. In particular all should beware of private individual approaches both from Pritam Singh and from

the Japanese.

30. Maj Fujiwara reinforced his attempts to impress Indian officers with Japanese friendliness by taking them out to see Gen Yamashita, who gave them some tea, and uttered, though in less fluent form, some of Fujiwara's own slogans.

Mohan Singh's Depression and Major Fujiwara

31. The mental condition of H/1050 at the time when he felt the impact of these subversive attempts, deserves examination. It is explained in his own words in the document reproduced at appx "A"[3]. He was unusually cast down by the Jitra fiasco because his own bn had initially fought so well, and because at first hopes had been so high. The whole defeat was, in his view, and there was much in the immediate circumstances to make him think this, the result of the colossal blunder of the divisional commander in changing at the last minute a plan which had been rehearsed for months and which had so far worked extremely well. He saw great dumps of food, man and POL in the vast Jitra position, all abandoned and intact. The confusion that reigned, hunger, fatigue and the shock of defeat all combined to accentuate his mental depression. Nevertheless, H/1050 was only impressed by Maj Fujiwara's talk and was not convinced. From a purely nationalist point of view he felt that he would be ready to do something if India's benefit would really result, but he did not believe that the proposal of the specious Maj Fujiwara would achieve that end. Maj Fujiwara, he says, was an extremely clever man. His attitude was always one of great charm and friendliness. He was a man who, with a whisky bottle in front of him could talk all night and be fresh to start again at breakfast time. H/1050 did not, at these first interviews, accept Maj Fujiwara's offer of drink, well knowing that his sobriety at this time was of the greatest importance. The talks continued whenever Maj Fujiwara had leisure during 16 and 17 Dec.

Mohan Singh's Arguments

32. While the talks were going on, H/1050 heard that on 11 Dec a certain Puran Singh and another Gurkha Rfn had been captured. These men were at once instructed by the Japanese to move forward as a propaganda contact party. Under threats they did in fact go forward, but they returned without having attempted to carry out their instructions. They told H/1050 that there were some Gurkha PW at Alor Star aerodrome, and that when they were first captured a written document was read out to

3. All references to appendix in this report have not been printed here.

them on parade. This purported to be some kind of a pact between Giani Pritam Singh and the Japanese.

33. As soon as he heard this, H/1050 went angrily to Pritam Singh, wishing to enlist his support in accusing Fujiwara of exploitation and insincerity. Pritam Singh did not take the matter seriously and H/1050 therefore himself went to Fujiwara. "You are not taking the long view" he said. " This use of Indians as a Fifth Column is positive proof that you wish to exploit us. Do not think for a minute that if you defeat the British here you will shake more than the outermost branches of a vast tree whose roots you can only attack in India. Until you shake the British in India you will not have shaken them at all. If you go to India now, all India will join the British to turn you out. We are the only people who can defeat the British in India and we are willing to take up the cudgels if you give real proof of your sincerity. This frontline business must not recur."

34. By 18 Dec Fujiwara and Pritam Singh, who had been from the first hopeful that they could use H/1050, were sure of him. They had wanted some one with recent knowledge of India and a man with experience of and a name in the army. H/1050 was an active patriotic officer, facts which had made them all the more eager. Nevertheless, they had made no concrete proposals yet.

The First Step

35. On 18 Dec Maj Fujiwara and Pritam Singh went away. Kunizuka,[4] who had arrived a day or two before, remained, and ITO[5] joined him soon afterwards. By that time H/1050 had gone so far as to say that before he could be convinced to take any steps of his own, he must have the best possible proof and assurance of Japanese sincerity towards India. As an earnest of this he demanded complete control of all Indian PW so far captured. He felt in his heart that if he could do something for the prisoners, — the original 60 of his party had already increased to nearly 1,000 —that would be one clear gain from his dabbling with the Japanese. Maj Fujiwara had replied that of course he could do anything he liked; the Japanese, he said, were good, kind people, they were not out to stop anybody doing anything he wanted. Let H/1050 take the PW and do what he liked with them.

36. When Maj Fujiwara went away, therefore, H/1050 began to organise food, quarters and comfort for the 1,000 Indian PW with him, and

---

4. Lientenant Kazunon Kunizuka was an interpreter with F. Kikan.
5. Major Ito Keisaku, served as interpreter and Liasion officer with the Indian soldiers.

also to give them mild "spiritual" lectures in fulfillment of his side of the bargain. He continued to do this until 24 Dec. On the night of 23 Dec. Giani Pritam Singh returned to Alor Star. H/1050 found that Giani Pritam Singh had already organised Indian Leagures in Alor Star and Sungei Patani and that Maj Fujiwara used to address them. Pritam Singh painted a very rosy picture of Penang and said that there were other Indian PW in Sungei Patani. Many of these, he said, would be willing to co-operate, with the Japanese. H/1050 furious that he had not been told previously of these further PW, held a meeting on 23 Dec attended by Capt Mohd Akram, Capt Patnaik and about 10 VCOs, including Malik Fateh Khan and Sadhu Singh. He told his audience that this was the first step in their exploitation and a clear proof of Japanese insincerity. Giani Pritam Singh was quite incompetent to deal with people like the Japanese and he must be replaced as soon as possible by S.C. Bose. The meeting agreed with these sentiments.

37. On 24 Dec H/1050 went with Giani Pritam Singh to visit Fujiwara at Sungei Patani. He claimed that the Japanese had already provided sufficient proof of their sincerity, and after some vituperation he managed to persuade Maj Fujiwara to place in his charge the 400 new Indian PW at Sungei Patani. H/1050 also asked that Bose might be brought from Germany. He had from the first been corresponding secretly with Fujiwara regarding the possible removal of Pritam Singh. He had strongly objected to Pritam Singh's interference with PW and had on one occasion thrown out of a PW camp a civilian Sikh who had entered uninvited and called for volunteers. He put it to Fujiwara that either he should get some reliable Indian gentleman from Malaya to lead whatever movement he proposed, or else that he should call for Bose.

38. Fujiwara agreed that Pritam Singh would ultimately have to be discarded, but he insisted that he should remain leader of the movement in Malaya. As for Bose, his patriotism was undoubted, but, as an Asiatic, he should have entrusted himself to Japan and not to Germany. Fujiwara thought it would be impossible at present to bring Bose from Germany and was disinclined to ask for him. It was up to those present, he said, to build up the movement.

39. Having organised to some extent the PW in Sungei Patani, H/1050 returned to Alor Star on the same day. Pritam Singh and Fujiwara were about to leave Sungei Patani for Taiping which was the present front line, on 25 Dec. After this Pritam Singh never went to Sungei Patani or Alor Star in H/1050's knowledge. Up to this time H/1050 had had no contact whatever with the Indian Leagues, although he had occasionally met Indian civilians on their visits to Giani Pritam Singh.

The Plot Thickens

40. H/1050 now suffered a severe attack of malaria which put him out of action until 30 Dec 41. On 26 or 27 Dec he received a message from Fujiwara calling him to Taiping. H/1050 promised to go as soon as he was well enough.

The Conference at Alor Star

41. *Comment* : The story of 30 and 31 Dec can be reconstructed in its essentials from the letter reproduced as Annexure 2 to "S" Section CSDIC letter ST/17/4 of 23 Sep 45, and as Appendix A to this report. The carbon copy from which this was reproduced was found by M.Z. Kiani in May 42 in a drawer at H/1050's H.Q. Kiani is emphatic that it was written by H/1050 himself, and there can be little doubt that this is true (Note : The word "equipped" is spelt "equipped" a spelling mistake which H/1050 still makes). H/1050 cannot remember writing it nor can be remember discussing it at the conference which he held at Alor Star during the morning of 30 Dec. He says, however, that its contents represent the gist of his conversations with Fujiwara at Sungei Patani on 24 Dec and at Taiping on 31 Dec. We may safely assume that this letter was written either by Mohd Akram or by H/1050 at Taiping on 1 Jan 42 in reply to detailed written proposals from Fujiwara regarding the formation of an Indian National Army.

42. During the morning of 30 Dec H/1050 called a conference of officers and VCOs. He can remember the names of only 5 of those who attended :

1. Capt Patnaik
2. Mohd Akram
3. Sub Allah Ditta (H/876)
4. Sub Fateh Khan
5. Sabhu Singh

H/1050 told the meeting that he had decided to co-opetrate with the Japanese to the best of his ability, if they would hand over PW. Someone, he said, must take this risk as the possibilities were clearly worthy of exploration. Let no one else, for the moment, commit himself.

The Taiping Letter

43. The greater part of the letter reproduced at Appx "A" speaks for itself, but H/1050 makes a few comments in clarification of detail.[6]

(a) Ref. Para (1) The point in promising to denounce the Indian National Congress was this. The meeting wished the Indian National Army, as its

---

6. See Doc. No. 5.

name suggested, to work on the lines of the Indian National Congress. Pritam Singh wished to keep his movement separate. The meeting was not willing to follow the advice of Pritam Singh in this matter, but if S.C.Bose, having assumed the leadership, were to suggest the same thing, the meeting would be delighted to agree. (b) Ref. Para (2) Even now Fujiwara had not produced a clear definition of " the co-prosperity sphere". The meeting therefore gave up the idea of trying to obtain a definition and put the burden once more on S.C. Bose.

(c) Ref. Para (3) (e) The meeting appreciated that Malaya would be conquered very soon and that Burma would follow after no long interval. H/1050 felt that the organisation of an army out of material so dubious would take a considerable period.

(d) *Comment*: H/1050 cannot account for para 4. It may refer to one of two things. Fujiwara had evidently proposed a leader for the Indian National Army in Malaya. If, as is most likely, he proposed H/1050 , then this paragraph is an attempt to make his leadership substantive for all theatres and not merely temporary for Malaya. The alternative less probable in view of the discussions reported in paras 32 and 33, above, is that Fujiwara had proposed Pritam Singh.

H/1050 in Taiping

44. H/1050 reached Taiping late on 31 Dec 41. Pritam Singh met him, was very solicitous about his health, provided him with accommodation, dined him any during the evening told him about the League already organised in Taiping. He told him furthermore that he thought Fujiwara would now hand over all Indian prisoners captured.

45. (Note : Although H/1050 cannot remember it, it is considered probable that he handed over to Fujiwara the letter reproduced at Appendix "A" at an interview which took place on the morning of 1 Jan 42.).

46. H/1050 remembers the interview. Fujiwara was very gracious and said that PW would in future be handed over to him. H/1050 promised in return to do all in his power to secure the independence of his country. He would start patriotic education immediately, patriotic education which had been deliberately refused by the British in order that they might continue their exploitation of India. He would start preparing to raise the I.N.A. so that when the decision was taken the army would be ready to be raised. This, he said, would be a matter of time. He must see more of the Japanese, and he must consult the many civilian Indians with whose financial support alone the army could be raised. It was clearly understood that the I.N.A would be raised from Indians, directed by Indians, for the purposes of India and of India alone.

47. Next day H/1050 returned to Alor Star. He told his officers that he alone was committed, and that all others would take their time in deciding what they were to do. They approved, however, heartily of his action and praised him saying "We have a sincere man in you, that is evident. We pledge you our complete trust." On the same evening H/1050 addressed the IOR PW for 1½ to 2 hrs. He claims that he met with a rapturous reception, that the convinced all of his desire to work for India's benefit and that the men professed themselves united as one man behind him. Indeed they were readier than he; they wanted to become the "Indian National Army" at once while H/1050 could not see his way to organising it for some time. On 3 Jan 42 he similarly addressed officers and men at Sungei Patani, and was similarly received. All committed themselves to him. H/1050 emphasised to them that they were only committed to himself personally and that he alone was committed to the Japanese. H/1050 strongly denies the statement of Alah Ditta (H/876) that the Japanese asked him in Alor Star for a party to go and suborn Ind tps in the field at Kampar. H/1050 heard nothing about the Kampar fighting (in which) remnants of him own bn, it transpired, were involved, until he was in Ipoh. He points out that it is fundamentally unlikely that the Japanese would have admitted to him a setback of their own at this stage.

48. H/1050 then returned to Alor Star where he remained until 7 or 8 Jan 42. He spent his time in organisation of the PW camp, in the "partiotic education" which he had promised to commence, and in selecting for his future activities a personal staff. His future intentions were to move forward in order that he might be able to organise newly surrendered personnel as early as possible in their captivity. This he thought would both increase his personal prestige and prevent PW being exploited by the Japanese by unauthorised employment in the front line.

(*Comment* : H/1050 has admitted the above under interrogation. His aims at this point in his "public statement" are , however, not so definite).

Military Organisation of PW

76. From 15 Feb to 15 Mar 42 organisation of PW had proceeded. In addition to the central committee under Gill and the 2 committees under Bhonsle and Kiani respectively H/1050 had himself taken on as personal staff officers Maj Mehtab and Maj M.S. Dhillon (c25) By 22 Feb 42 the following officers had also been called from KUALA LUMPUR :

1. Capt. Habib Ur Rehman
2. Capt. I.J. Kiani (H/1159)
3. Capt. Patnaik.

Patnaik was made liaison officer between H/1050 and the medical organisation he had set up under Chatterji. The latter was assisted by Lt Cols Algappan and Loganadan. H/1050 at first paid a great deal of attention to the medical set up because of the large number of hospital cases among PW. There was no medical assistance available from the Japanese and medical supplies, hospital furniture and comforts were all obtained from Indian civilians of Singapore. By the end of the month things were working to H/1050 satisfaction.

77. Early in Mar 42 about 100 volunteers were supplied to work as a guard at Changi. H/1050 first of all put a VCO in charge of this party but after a few days he appointed Gurbaksh Singh Dhillon. The conduct of this officer at Changi caused him, when he heard of it, shame and sorrow, but he claims that he had no control over the actions of Dhillon or of any other member of the Changi Guard which was entirely Japanese controlled and Japanese armed. H/1050 tried repeatedly without success to establish control of this and other such detahments.

78. At the same time about 200 AA Gunners under a VCO were detailed to man their own guns, situated between Singapore railway station and Buonavista village on Singapore Island. Fatigue parties were also continually supplied to satisfy the extremely heavy demands of the Japanese. These were run by a separate working party office.

79. Towards the end of the month H/1050 collected officers at Bidadari, and then the ; officers and some VCO's at Neesoon. In a speech he gave a brief outline of his achievements and of his intention, without any political referene. He emphasised that when the I.N.A was raised it would be purely on a volunteer basis, no pressure would be used, and all ranks would be given at least a month in which to think over the proposal when it came, and to make up their minds freely. Lectures and propaganda would not, he said, be allowed at present. Now all ranks must set about overcoming the pressing administrative difficulties which faced them.

The Journey to Tokyo and the Aeroplane Accident

80. The mysterious circumstances which attended the death of 4 members of the Goodwill Mission while en route to Tokyo make necessary a detailed examination of the arrangements made for this journey, and the time table of events. The first point that is clear is that the 4 delegates were named by the Japanese at short notice for an air passage on 13 March to Saigon. The vacancies, said Fujiwara, had suddenly occurred and he suggested that those 4 could best be spared by Mohan Singh and Raghavan to leave early. Accordingly Nos. 4, 5, 6 and 9 of para 75 left by air on 13 Mar.

81. The main party left Singapore on 15 Mar and, passing the other party in Saigon where it had been delayed, arrived in Tokyo on 19 Mar via Hanoi. Formosa and Sanghai.

82. H/1050 thinks that Swami S.N. Puri's party must have left Saigon on 18 Mar. He afterwards verified that it spent 3 nights at Canton, its first stop. It must therefore have reached Shanghai on 21 Mar and, after a further halt of 3 nights, left for Tokyo on 24 Mar. The remaining members of the goodwill mission heard about the accident on 25 Mar from Fujiwara. He said that on 24 Mar the aircraft, having halted at Fukuoka soon after mid-day, had disappeared somewhere between there and Tokyo and had not yet been found. The pilot had been in radio touch with the ground until 1535 hrs.

83. H/1050 and his companions were extremely suspicious both because of the interval between the accident and their receiving information of it, and because 24 Mar had been a day of such bad flying weather that they rather doubted if any passenger.

86. At 1000 hrs next morning formal discussions opened. H/1050 and his companions from Malaya immediately voiced their opinion that the whole thing as far as they were concerned was a trap. Firstly a formal conference was taking place contrary to the understanding that had been given. Secondly the Malayan delegation had been fatally weakened by the loss of 4 members. Thirdly Bose had brought insufficient nominees from Tokyo to ensure him a majority. They insisted that their status as observers should be at once recorded in the minutes. Nevertheless, as the conference proceeded, it became evident that the Malayan party contained the only men of constructive ability at the conference. The rest of the set up as far as they could see was entirely dominated by Japanese influence, and the Japanese had not chosen their puppets well.

The Observers Draft the Resolutions

87. The Japanese had provided "for consideration of the conference" a draft constitution for the Indian Independence movement. This provided:

(a) Election of President

(b) A selection by the president of 2 Councils, firstly an Advisory Council of 8 members, secondly an Executive council of 11 members.

(c) Duties and responsibilities in detail of each member of the Executive Council.

(d) Power of the President to dismiss or replace any member or all the members of either council.

The draft constitution did not make any mention of the source of the funds necessary to run the movement.

88. The 5 from Malaya listened very carefully to what they came to consider an appalling document. They then rose in turn to express individually and collectively their utter revulsion and set about to destroy it item by item. The document was denounced in the very strongest possible terms. H/1050 said that no soldier serving under him would have anything to do with such a constitution and went on to demand that unless, in any future council or conference, his soldiers were represented by 50 of the total number of representatives he would have nothing to do with any further discussion at all. R.B. Bose, who had not expected such a storm, immediately agreed to drop the draft constitution, and appealed to the Malayans to do something, draft something, produce something, whatever it may betosave his credit with the Japanese. H/1050 and his companions, seeing clearly that none of the other delegates had the education or ability to draft anything at all sat to work on the following conditions :

(a) that no movement should be started until properly elected representatives could be provided from all parts of East Asia.

(b) That resolutions should be immediately drafted to be put before such a future conference.

89 Menon, Raghavan and Goho drafted the Tokyo resolutions on 30 and 31 Mar. The "conference" discussed, and adopted resolutions during 1 and 2 April. H/1050's demand for 50 military representation on any future conference was agreed. (Note : Proceedings of the Tokyo conference are at AppxV)

After several days spent in sightseeing in Japan the 5 delegates from Malaya left Japan via Fukuoka, and Shanghai where they spent 4-5 days. Singapore was reached on about 22 Apr. 42.

90. H/1050 summarises the achievements of the Tokyo mission as follows:

(a) It had a'ccomplished the end of any designs that Bose might have had for exploiting the Indian situation for the benefit of Japan by himself assuming a dictatorship.

(b) Preparations had been made for the establishment of the movement on a constitutional basis.

(c) The importance of the position of the I.N.A. had been recognised and the principle had been accepted of representation for the army in any future conference equal to the total civilian representation.

Raja Mohindra Parshad (Partap)

91. While he was in Tokyo H/1050 and other Singapore delegates

met Raja Mohindra Parshad.[6] H/1050 says that this man went to Germany through Afghanistan during the war 1914-18. While in Afghanistan he met Amanullah and Nadir Shah, and founded some futile movement in Germany. He returned to the East after the war, going to Japan through Russia and China. He has, says H/1050, a plan of his own for the successful govt of the world, and thinks that the centre should be in Afghanistan. At the outbreak of war with Japan he was publishing a newspaper in English and Japanese and was issuing pamphlets. On about 7 or 8 Dec 41 the Japanese High Command sent for him and asked him to head an Indian Movement. He told them that he was prepared to do this on condition that there would be no interference from the Japanese either in regard to propaganda or to personnel.

Any money supplied by the Japanese would be repaid when the movement was established. The Japanese decided that he was most unsuitable and sent for R.B. Bose. They placed Raja Mohindra Parshad under surveillance on the outskirts of Tokyo and told him he was not allowed to see the "Goodwill Mission" The Tokyo Indians would not say where he was. The Malayan delegates therefore found out for themselves and met him secretly. H/1050 considers him by far the ablest and sincerest Indian in Japan.

The Bidadari Resolutions

92. On his return to Singapore H/1050 found that the situation in camps had been complicated by the appearance of rifts, schisms and quarrels of various kinds. These had mostly arisen from one month's experience of the Japanese, without the saving influence of H/1050 . On 24 Apr there was a memorial ceremony for those killed in the aeroplane accident. On 25 Apr all senior officers and some captains, about 25 officers in all, assembled at Bidadari for a statement by Lt Col .Gill of what happened at Tokyo. During this explanation H/1050 for once, sat quiet. When Gill had gone, however, H/1050 indulged in a sentimental chat which led up to the drafting of the Bidadari resolutions. "I have done my duty" he said, "until now almost singlehanded. I have secured for you a draft agreement between the Indians of East Asia and the Japanese. Now my work is over and I place myself in your hands. There are many officers among you far senior to myself, and I have been feeling that I can no longer impose myself upon you without consultation. Gentlemen, I am in your hands". Lt Col Gill then spoke to the sincerity and worth of H/1050 whom he

---

7. This refers to Raja Mahender Partap, an old Indian revolutionary nationalist, who was not allowed by the Japanese to work with Rash Behari Bose. After the war, he was interned, because of his suspision of Japanese intentions.

admitted he had at first suspected. Now he had known him day and night for 5 weeks. There was no better leader; and in his view it was the duty of those present to follow him. All agreed that H/1050 should remain military leader of the movement with their full support. The Bidadari resolutions themselves, as is already well known, were vaguely worded and ambiguous. They pledged the full efforts of those who made them in accomplishing the good of India and made no promise of co-operation with Japan to any other end. Before the meeting broke up officers were asked to explain the Tokyo resolutions to the men under their authority. None were asked as yet to volunteer.

93. On 27 Apr H/1050 addressed a meeting of all officers at Bidadari, which had assembled to bid farewell to Fujiwara who was handing over to Iwakuru. Fujiwara made an ortatory speech in Japanese in which he referred to H/1050 as "GOC". H/1050 made the following points in his own speech :

(a) He was anxiou^ only for the good of India, and not working either for rank or for position.
(b) He would only recognise rank given him by his own fellow countrymen.
(c) The time for volunteering was not yet ripe. When the call came volunteers must be prepared to fight against the Japanese also if the interest of Indian so demanded.

Gill Goes to Bangkok

94. The Indian community in Bangkok generally did not believe in the death of S.N. Puri and his 3 companions. Moreover, much strife had arisen between rival factions who wished one individual or another to succeed to the Indian leadership. Furthermore, there was trouble in a working camp in Bangkok to which some Indian PW had been sent in the absence in Tokyo of H/1050. (Comment : See No. 2 Section Reports 952 and 934 from corroboration of this statement and No 2 Section Report 968 on Capt Jiwan Singh Bains for one account of the working camp in Bangkok). Fujiwara requested that Lt Col Gill should be sent to Bangkok to put an end to the quarrelling and trouble. H/1050 and Gill talked over the suspicion that was in both their minds that this might be a plot to separate them. United, they felt they were very strong, a fact of which the, Japanese must be aware. They talked this over also with Raghavan and Menon, and eventually decided that they could take the suggestion at its face value. The fact that it had already been agreed that the next conference would be in Bangkok, they thought, made a trick unlikely.

H/1050 Goes Up Country with Fujiwara

95. On about 1 May 42 H/1050 went with Fujiwara on his farewell tour

of league branches in Malaya. The programme was :

1. May - Meeting of civilians at Batu Pahat addressed by Fujiwara and H/1050. The two went on to another meeting at Muar where they addressed civilians. They also saw officers in the PW camp there. They reached Kulala Lumpur during the evening, and Fujiwara dined with the IIL. H/1050 did not attend the dinner, but was present for a few minutes towards the end of the party. The speeches were over, and he has no idea what was said.

   Immediately upon arrival H/1050 had gone to the house in which he had gone to the house in which he had previously stayed in Kuala Lumpur. A play was going on in an improvised theatre nearby, and it soon became bruited abroad among the Indian soldiers there that he had arrived. Many, therefore came to see him and all asked him to speak to the men. He did so for a few minutes from the stage on which the play was being acted.
2. May - H/1050 made a long speech to officers and IORs at Kuala Lumpur. He did not specifically ask for volunteers, but many men were volunteering continually none the less. The two went on to Ipoh and held meetings there on the same day.
3. May - They went on to Penang where they attended a dinner party given by the IIL.
4. May - Alor Star. After Lunch H/1050 addressed officers and IORs. Returned to Ipoh.
5. May - Returned to Kuala Lumpur, and spent the night there.
6. May - H/1050 addressed a miscellaneous audience in the Gurdwara.

H/1050 returned to Singapore with Fujiwara the same day.

Recruiting Begins

96. Two or three days after the return of H/1050 from this tour, camp comds were called together and informed that recruiting would now begin based on the Bidadari resolutions. There were still to be no lectures, because H/1050 had already found that suitable lecturing can make simple soldiers of the type with which he had to deal volunteer for almost anything. Camps comds returned next day with long lists of men they said had volunteered, and clearly expected to be congratulated on their individual success as recruiters. In some instances whole units were reported to have volunteered en masse. H/1050 refused to accept this sort of

volunteering and insisted that each individual volunteer should sign for himself, In every unit, he would say, there must be some sick, some weak, some unfit, and someone who is bound to object to volunteering. No unit is ever unanimous about anything unless there is good sound terrorism going on. H/1050 suspected that this was the case and accordingly demanded individual signatures. Lists poured in until 30 May. Then H/1050 decided to stop recruiting as the 25,000 names which had already been given were enough to begin with. Many complained that they had not beenincluded in lists of accepted volunteers.

97. Meanwhile H/1050 had come to the conclusion that the Bidadari Resolutions, sound as they were, could not be the basis for raising an army. He determined therefore to state his real purpose in a speech to all volunteers.The Bangkok Conference had already been fixed for 15Jun 42, and delegates were to leave on 5 or 6 Jun.

H/1050's Speech to Volunteers on 3 Jun 42

98. H/1050 addressed all volunteers who had been assembled near Alor Star Camp on 3 Jun 42. He spoke for about 1½ hrs. It was an all out propaganda speech and it worked up to a peroration which ran something like this :

> "Some of you have volunteered for this reason and some for that. Some with reservations in your heats, reservations based on those Bidadari Resolutions. I know those resolutions and what they have meant to us. But now I am going to plead the cause of the soldier before the Indian people of East Asia at Bangkok. I feel that I cannot go and be your fit, your whole hearted representative while I am bound by these reservations of yours. I must be free of them. I want you to cast all such reservations and clauses aside. I want you to have full confidence in me, that I may go, your plenipotentiary, to negotiate for you and to triumph with you."

The response was immediate, unanimous, and enthusiastic. The Bidadari Resolutions were no more. Propaganda was hence forward let loose and all encouragements were used to sharpen the faith of the volunteers.

Preparations For the Bangkok Conference

99. By the terms of the Tokyo Resolutions, H/1050 was entitled to take with him to the Bangkok conference a number of soldier delegates equal to the 90 civilians who had been delegated from the various IIL branches of East Asia. He had, however, by this time gained so much self confidence that he was sure that he alone could carry all opposition even without the presence of a single other army member. He took therefore

only 25 delegates. They were finally detailed on 4 Jun and the whole party left on 5 Jun by train.

100. H/1050summarises the period 22 Apr 5 Jun 42 as having included the following main events :

(a) The Bidadari Resolutions, a step preliminary to the raising of the INA.

(b) Departure of Gill to Bangkok.

(c) H/1050 tour up country with Fujiwara, and the departure Fujiwara, and the departure of Fujiwara.

(d) The beginning of volunteering, 25, 000 men signed on.

(e) Volunteers addressed for the first time. The scrapping of the Bidadari Resolutions.

(f) H/1050 is now fully prepared to raise the INA.

The Bangkok Conference

101. The Malayan delegates to the Bangkok conference arrived in Bangkok on 11 Jun and were accommodated at the Trocadero Hotel. On the same day H/1050 met Gill, Dhillon (C25) and Hussain (B919). On 12 and 13 Jun 42 preparatory committee meetings were held in the hotel. There was already a reception committee in existence under Ishar Singh or Sahay. On the night of 13 Jun there was a dinner party given by R.B. Bose at which H/1050 and other guests spoke. Next day H/1050, Raghavan, Menon called on the Italian and German embassies. On 15 Jun the conference opened with a plenary session at which representatives of the Axis powers spoke. Bose gave a presidential address in English. Many other delegates spoke including H/1050. The session closed at about 1300 hrs. The meeting was given full publicity and press reports.

102. During the evening there was a formal exchange, of views at a hotel on the banks of the Bangkok River, and next morning there took place the first business meeting at which there were no outsiders. The day was H/1050's. He made a full report on progress in the INA to an enthusiastic audience. As he spoke he felt that there were political undercurrents in the place which, if allowed to reach the surface, might wreck the conference on entirely irrelévant arguments. He saw in the congregation Dost Mohd Khan, the right hand man of Bose, who had even at Tokyo raised the Congress-League issue, and felt that the same issue would inevitably be raised again. He therefore made a great point in his speech of recognition of Congress leadership by the INA. In the view of the Army, he said Congress was alone the voice of India. Congress was the people of India. Supporters of other creeds, of Pakistan, Khalistan, and even Japanistan were the enemies of India as far as the INA was concerned. The Army

would only think of Hindustan. By this H/1050 roused the enthusiasm of Congress supporters to fever pitch, and left opponents and possible issue-raisers dumb founded on this matter for the rest of the conference. The first piece of business transacted was the election of the subject committee. This consisted of 12-15 members, including:

1. H/1050	5. Raghavan	9. Das B.K.
2. Gill	6. Menon K.P.K.	10. Ishar Singh
3. Gilani	7. Bashir Mallal	11. Member from Burma
4. Chatterji	8. Sahay	12. Member from Burma

103. The subject committee spent 17, 18 and 19 Jun debating resolutions which were put to the conference, discussed and adopted on 20 and 21 Jun. These are reproduced for convenience at appx D although they are already well known. One copy was forwarded to the Japanese for favour of reply and comment, and a reply was promised by Iwakuru who was in Bangkok for 28 Jun. The delegatcs therefore decided to remain in Bangkok until that date. But when 28 Jun arrived, the representative who went to receive the reply was told that it would not be ready for another week; the chiefs off delegations should therefore remain, and the rest of the representatives disperse. On 3 or 4 Jul the head delegates in their turn were told that the reply would be another week at least, and that there was no need for any but the members of the Council of Action to remain to receive it. The Council of Action was told on 12 Jul that such was the time necessary to translate this precious document, that it would not be possible to produce it for some time longer. The President therefore, said the Japanese, would alone wait to receive it. The Council of Action therefore dispersed. H/1050 heard in Bangkok for the first time of Gill's intelligence activities in that city before the war.

Exclusion of Gill from Council of Action

104. The Council of Action was formed on 21 Jun by open election, but H/1050 says that in fact it had already been nominated by the various groups meeting in secret before the meeting. Bose was president, H/1050's party agreed to that much because they felt, as they had done in Tokyo, that if the man had any influence at all with the Japanese, it could not but be valuable to the Council as a whole. For rest, he was not an impressive or even intelligent man, and would be a figure head, whom the Council of Action would rule. The members, H/1050 claims, were virtually nominated by him. As is already well known they were Raghavan, Menon, Gilani. and H/1050. Gill was not elected, and for this H/1050 gives several reasons. Firstly although liked by H/1050, he was generally distrusted. He had been an early supporter of H/1050, but nobody ever had a good word

to say for him. “He is ambitious, “one would say, “he is trying to oust H/1050.” - “Look at his weaknesses”, another would whisper, “how dependent he is on drink and women. Such a man cannot be a true supporter of a revolutionary movement. The influence of H/1050’s circle , most of whom spoke like this, had prevented H/1050 from carrying out what had one time been his idea, to hand over to Gill the leadership of the whole movement. It was again partly responsible for Gill’s exclusion from the Council of Action. H/1050 also considered that it would look bad and might arouse comment for both Army members of the Council to be Sikhs. The movement was already dubbed in some quarters a Sikh Movement . (Comment : See CSDIC(I) no Sec Report 958 on B 958 in which Mount Pleasant seemed to Capt Burhan Ud Din the HQ of a Sikh Raj. Furthermore Gillani, a Muslim, a State officer, and a plotter used to the intricate politics of Indian State Courts, was eminently suitable. H/1050 did at one time think of increasing the strength of the Council to seven, merely for the sake of including Gill. Gill was keenly disappointed, and when H/1050 saw this he genuinely regretted the decision he had taken. He attempted to make amends by a personal explanation, and by making it clear that whoever was on the Council of Action, Gill was 2IC of the INA, and by promising Gill redress, including the rank of General, in duc course. (H/1050’s attitude to Gill is best explained in his own words at Appx B, page 8)

H/1050’s Plan of the First Division INA

105. During the days of waiting after the conference, H/1050 put up to iwakuru, after obtaining the sanction of Bose who was so ignorant that he could not possibly do other than approve, his plan for the formation of the INA first Division, a body of 15,000 tps. This was to be an experimental formation, and future formations would depend on experience gained in raising this. The plan finally included 3,000 civilians, but H/1050 cannot remember whether this was his idea or whether it was added by Iwakuru. There were to be two main groups in the Division. Firstly, the Hind Field \Force consisting of 3 bns and attached services. Secondly, the Guerrilla Force, a formation of nine bns organised in three regts. There would also be the SS Group of 500 men for Intelligence duties. These would work not necessarily with the INA, but with the Japanese or alone as decided by H/1050. Iwakuru agreed to this plan, and emphasised the need for careful selection.

Ram Sarup Reports

106. When he was in Bangkok H/1050 met Ram Sarup (CSDIC (I) B 1000), who reported on progress in Burma. Over 2000 PW, he said, had been taken; of these many had been taken on road building fatigues

which few survived. Misra had joined him. H/1050 at this time gave Ram Sarup his intelligence role. He was instructed to report on topography, British dispositions and intentions, and the attitude of local tribes on the Burma border. During the months that followed H/1050 received some reports from Ram Sarup, but he cannot remember details. The last of these arrived during Nov 42. He regarded Ram Sarup, but he cannot remember details. The last of these arrived during Nov 42. He regarded RAM SARUP, as being an able rain and very good for his rank. He had himself planned to go to BURMA and carry out intelligence work on a rather larger scale.

First Meeting Council of Action

107. Several meetings took place at Bangkok. At the first, on 24 Jun, H/1050 was formally appointed to head the Army with the rank of full General. At subsequent meetings IIL HQ for the whole of East Asia was planned, personnel were selected, and propaganda lines laid down. Tours by R.B. Bose were mentioned, but H/1050 cannot remember whether it was then decided to move Bose's HQ to Syonan or not.

Gill's Party

108. Early in Jul 42 Iwakuru sounded Gill on his readiness for a special task, but was promptly referred to H/1050. H/1050 and Gill speculated on what the task might be and it crossed their minds that it might be another attempt on the part of the Japanese to separate them. Very respectfully and cautiously Iwakuru mentioned the matter to H/1050 next day, and H/1050 refused to consider parting with Gill at such an important time. No details had yet been given, and although he gathered the impression that Gill rather inclined towards accepting the offer whatever it might be, H/1050 does not think that it had been previously discussed by Gill and Iwakuru. H/1050 was not, however allowed to take Gill to Singapore with him as there was only one seat on the plane which took him, and it was only after forcing the issue with Iwakuru in Singapore that he finally had his way. Gill arrived on about 20 Jul by special plane.

109. Iwakuru broached the "special task" again in Singapore, but H/1050 again refused . About five days after this, however, Gill himself said, "Let us take this thing very seriously. If a secret service is to be organised, with tentacles all over fast Asia, with HQ in Bangkok or Rangoon, perhaps it would be as well for us to have the thing in our control. Perhaps we would be missing something if we refused any longer. H/1050 saw this point, and finally agreed to let Gill go if he so wished and if he really thought that there was danger of this thing falling into the hands of others, who might use it to the disadvantage of India. Gill was thereupon handed over to Iwakuru on the explicit condition that H/1050 could have

him back at any time when he called for him. Gill was allowed a free hand in the selection of personnel, and he selected about 15 officers and NCOs. (Comment : The full list can be found at Appx "A" to CSDIC (I) 2 Sec Report no 620) H/1050 thought that Gill had made a mistake in choosing so many Sikhs. M.S. Dhillon (c25) who was selected by Gill had been intended by H/1050 for the post of Military Secretary. (Comment : See S Sec CSDIC (I) ST/17 dated 23 Sept 45 Annexure 1 which refers to this fact.)

Planning Proceeds

110. H/1050 spent the period 20 Jul-31Jul in Planning in detail the rough outline he had presented to Iwakuru. He was assisted by about 20 of his officers whom he succeeded in keeping busy. The paper organisation was then submitted to the Japanese, who approved it in mid Aug 42.

The Personal Oath

111. Meanwhile H/1050 had approached the matter of collaboration with the Japanese purely as a soldier would, was beginning to have his own doubts of Japanese good faith. Either the IIL or the Japanese might one day try to dominate the Army, and then he would have to be very firm. In case of such an eventuality he decided to bind the Army to himself by a personal oath. He called together Gill, Gillani, Prakash Chand, Brar, both Kianis and told them that while he was not an ambitious man he felt that this oath was necessary in the interests of the Army as a whole. The draft was on the following lines :

> "I hereby volunteer unconditionally for the Indian National Army which is being raised under the command of Mohan Singh to fight for the freedom of my country."

This was to be signed by every volunteer and would cancel all previous undertakings. The "oath" was the subject of enquiry and recrimination by Raghavan on 2 Sep 42C See Appx E.)

112. When this was made public there were even more signatures than before, although H/1050 carefully abstained from lecturing until the signing had been done. When he did lecture to volunteers at each camp in turn, he inflamed, their enthusiasm to a white heat. When his propaganda was let loose, with songs, dramas and other devices, he was invited to visit non volunteers at Seletar. He claims that he created there a very good spirit, but that he did not ask for volunteers. (Note : Stracey was then Camp comd.)

Reaction to the Events in India

113. The August resolutions of the Indian National Congress became a main factor in propaganda as soon as they became known. The arrests

were of course regarded as proof of British insincerity to India, and of their fundamental unwillingness to grant independence. H/1050's feeling was that unless the British reached some definite agreement with Congress now, they would not do so late on.

They would just hang on to India as long as they could. Public indignation- both among volunteers, and as far as could be ascertained, among the Indian civilian community in Singapore, was high.

Raising of I.N.A.

114. About mid Aug 42, H/1050,s plans for organisation of the army had been approved. He therefore set about raising it. The Japs, in approving, had suggested a time table. I Div was to be complete by Dec, and was to be raised roughly as follows :

19 Aug. - Selection of HQ personnel : 15 days for organisation.
5 Sep. - Selection of Bde and major unit comds and staffs; 15 days to organise.
19 Sep. - Selection by Bde and unit comds of Bn comds. Bn comds then given 15 days to select staffs and choose coy comds.
19 Oct. - Selection of pl comds. These then given 15 days to organise pls and choose Sec comds.
5 Oct. - Selection of Coy comds. Coy comds then have 15 days to orgainse Coy HQS and choose pl comds.
5 Nov. - Selection of Sec comds. 15 days for selection of Sec personnel, issuing of equipt etc.
19 Nov. - Target date for completion of organisation from ex- military personnel.
5 Dec. - Selection of first batch of civilians (1500).
19 Dec. - Selection of second batch of civilians (1500).

Equipment and stores were collected from the Japanese dumps of captured, material, and complete in the central I.N.A. stores by the end of Aug. They were to be issued out to units as HQS were formed.

115. By the time this time table arrived, H/1050 had formed his own Supreme HQ I.N.A. had made a few plans himself, and had distributed a certain amount of work to the more capable of his staff officers. He also had worked out a programme in conjunction with his Chief of Staff M.Z. Kiani. He had decided not to include of civilains in 1 Div after all because of the delay involved and had made a time table by which the div would be formed within 10 days. H/1050 was to inspect the complete formation on the 10th day. This time table was submitted as a counter proposal to the Japanese, who replied through Ogawa that this was just another example of cantankerousness, that the way they had proposed was the proper way

to form a div, that the counter-proposal was all very well as a document, but that they would like to see how it worked. H/1050 thereupon carried it out from 1 to 10 Sep. On 8 and 9 Sep were held bn and then regt comds' inspections, and on 10 Sep H/1050 inspected the div. The Japanese were as much pleased as surprised. In the organisation, the AA gnrs lent to the Japanese in Mar 42 had been included as an arty unit, in fulfilments of H/1050's promise that they would be first members of his I.N.A. They were not present on the parade of 10 Sep as they were still under Japanese control. 1 Div strength was 17,000 instead of the 15,000 sanctioned by the Japanese. Offrs were gazetted 2/Lt on 1 Sep and thereafter were given promotion in accordance with their appointments.

H/1050 Asks for a Second Div

116. A week later H/1050 approached Iwakuru and very strongly pressed for the raising of 2 div. He said he had 25,000 surplus volunteers already and that provided the equipment was forthcoming, 2 div would be ready for parade on the 7th day after its foundation. He was by now extremely confident and went on to detail his Tokyo plans. He wished he said, to raise ultimately an army of half a million. He asked for immediate facilities to train 6,000 civilians instead of the 3,000 previously planned, and authority to recruit up to 100,000. His recruiting office had already gone out to various places in Malaya, to recruit the first 3,000, and had been overwhelmed with recruits. There had been quarrels at recruiting stations over selection by recruiting offrs. The 6,000 were ready. H/1050 further asked that an OTS should be established and opened by the end of Sept 42. This was only matter of equipment, the staff was already selected and standing by.

Crisis Begins

129. Bose arrived on 18 Nov, and on 19,20, and 21 Nov the Council of Action sat. H/1050 put before it all the points over which he had been pondering and which he had been preparing with K.P.K. Menon. Extracts from minutes of all these meetings are at Appx K,L, M, and N. The main points stated by H/1050 mainly on the morning of 19 Nov were :

(a) Army Matters

(i) The delay in raising a large INA. 3 months had passed and the Japanese had not committed themselves. They were delaying with diabolical cleverness, thought H/1050, until 1 Div was out of reach in Burma. The move to Burma of 1 Div would imede the formation of 2 Div, because cadres for new units would then have to be brought from Burma.

(ii) The delay in putting recruitment on a firm basis. It was now 3 months since H/1050 had put this matter up to Iwakuru first and there was still no definite answer.

(iii) Iwakuru had still not agreed to the formation of an CTS, in spite of continual promises.

(iv) The AA gnrs, lent to the Japanese in Mar 42, had not been returned in spite of frequent demands. Every demand was answered with a promise that they would be returned after just a little longer delay.

(v) Failure hitherto to secure the return from Burma of Lt Col Gill. This also had been frequently demanded by H/1050.

(vi) There had been instances of ill treatment of INA personnel by the Japanese, civilians and military. On one occasion 2 INA, offrs in a Singapore hotel had been abused by a Japanese civilian, assisted ably by Japanese offrs, and had been finally turned out of their places. H/1050 had made representations about this incident to Iwakuru several times, but without success.

(vii) About 400 volunteers had been lent to the Japanese by H/1050 in Oct 42 for one month only. These were to work as a transport coy in Sumatra. The Japanese had used them in fact as slave troops and had ordered them to remove their INA badges of rank.

(viii) In summary, H/1050 said that he felt the Japanese did not intend to make the INA a real army, but to maintain it as a puppet force, unable to enforce its own will.

(b) Civil Affairs

(i) The Bangkok resolutions had been unanswered. In the absence of a definite statement from the Japanese Govt of their intentions towards India and the Indian Independence Movement, of how far they agreed with the Bangkok resolutions, and of how far those resolutions could be taken as a basis of future policy, members of the Movement were living in a fool's paradise. There must be an immediate clarification.

(ii) H/1050, strongly supported by K.P.K Menon, suggested that the Council request a declaration from Tenno Heika himself. That, he said, would be the only sort of declaration which the Japanese were unlikely to repudiate later.

(iii) The Japanese were continually treating Indian property as enemy property. A representation received from Burma (to which reference is made in the minutes of 19 Nov) had indicated a similar state of affairs there.

(c) Other Points

(i) The Japanese had been sending Indians trained at Penang to India without the knowledge either of H/1050 or of the Council of Action. H/1050 had frequently tried to obtain from Iwakuru the truth about the Penang schools but had been so far completely unsuccessful. (Comments : H/1050 says that Gilani and Raghavan had both refused to tell him anything about what was going on in Penang except in the vaguest possible terms.)

(ii) H/1050 had secretly acquired 4 leaflets designed by the Japanese for dropping in India. In spite of the fact that the council of Action had long ago set up a committee for the preparation of leaflets for this purpose, and had with great care designed several, the Japanese had not shown their leaflets either to H/1050 or to the Council of Action. The Japanese leafletss were in any case extremely unsuitable in his view.

(iii) H/1050, with the support of K.P.K. Menon, closed by saying that he was certain that the Japanese had designs upon India and that any collaboration in the present circumstances could only be regarded by the people of India as rank treachery.

130. All this was not recorded in the minutes because members felt that if things turned out well in the end, the record would look bad.

(Comments : In any case the extracts from minutes which survive, were selected with a view to representing the crisis as an internal Council of Action quarrel and not the result of differences with the Japanese. Naturally, therefore, they would not include H/1050's outbursts.)

Movement of Troops

131. By the time the above meeting was held H/1050 had received news that a ship would be available on 4 Dec to take about 900 men to Burma. The council decided that pending the statement by the Japanese of outstanding questions, no further movement of troops would take place, and a note was sent to Kunizuka saying that no troops would be moved in future without the sanction of the Council of Action. This was intended to provoke a note, referring to the movement proposed on 4 Dec, to which the Council of Action would give a definite negative reply. The Japanese note of 21 Nov, however was on a scrap of paper and stated categorically: "The Movement of INA troops to Burma will be completed during Dec and Jan". This is referred to in the extracts from Council of Action minutes dated 21 Nov 42 reproduced at Appx M.

132. On 21 Nov Bose decided that a letter demanding general clarification should be drafted, but for the present he and Raghavan were

going to visit Medan. There had been no previous hint of such a visit and H/1050 thinks what it was simply a devise to delay action. The two left on 22 Nov.

Ogawa's Proposals for Expansion

133. As H/1050 reported the Council of Action on 21 Nov (see Appx M) he was approached, during the night of 20 Nov 42, with proposals for expansion. He realised that these had been produced thus suddenly because the Japanese had smelt trouble and were attempting to pacify him, and picked at once on their weak point -the date. He had been demanding expansion ever since Sep 42 (see para 132 above) and these "proposals" were no real step forward unless a date were given. The Japanese refused to do this.

Gill Returns Further Deliberations

134. Gill was met on arrival at the airfield on 25 or 26 Nov by a car which brought him at once to H/1050 for a conference. H/1050 detailed briefly the progress of the crisis to date, and Gill in his turn told H/1050 that Dhillon had deserted and gone to India. He did not say that he had sent him nor did he mention any letter either then or at any other time. H/1050 asked if the Japanese yet know about this, and on Gill's negative answer, old him to keep the whole matter secret. Dhillon's desertion was not disclosed to any Indian in Singapore until the Japanese did so when arresting Gill.

135. Bose and Raghavan returned on 26 Nov 42 and either men or on the following morning during a meeting of the C of A, Bose said that he was going to Bangkok on personal business. The other members of the Council told him that he was merely trying to avoid a crisis by running away, and was playing the delaying game of the Japanese. "What business", they asked sarcastically, "either personal or private could be more important than the crisis which had arisen ? you must stay." Bose eventually gave way.

136. Meetings of the Council of Action took place on 27 and 28 Nov. Appendix N represents, according to H/1050 what took place on 27 Nov. Minutes of the either meeting have not, unfortunately, been recovered H/1050 was instructed to present another note to Kunizuka on the subject of movement of troops to Burma. He said this.

Kagawa's Recruitment Proposals

137. During one of the 2 meetings Kagawa came in with a recruitment plan he said that it was H/1050's own plan (see para 116) with minor alterations,. H/1050, however, disagreed, as Kagawa's plan disposed of

the main points he had put up. Firstly he had said that the object of training Indian civilians was to make them soldiers of the I.N.A., while Kagawa's plan proposed to make them I.I.L. workers. Secondly, H/1050 had stated as his target figure for civilian recruitment an eventual 250,000 while Kagawa only mentioned the original 6,000 recruited in Sep 42 (see para 116 above). Kagawa's plan also said that the I.I.L. was to supply equipment and rations for the new recruits, and that no more arms would be provided by the Japanese.

138. This "Plan" made clarification an even more immediate necessity and ended any doubts remaining in the Council of Action. On 29 Nov, therefore, Bose took to Iwakuru the letter reproduced at appx O together with a copy of that presented and withdrawn in Sep 42 (appx H). Iwakuru received him very rudely and flatly refused to consider the matter. Accordingly the Council of Action drafted the following letter to Iwakuru for onward transmission to Tokyo.

Indian Independence League.
Syonan, 29 Nov 2602.

To,

Colonel H. Iwakuro,
Chief of the Iwakuro Kikan.
For Favour of Transmission to the Imperial
Government of Japan.

The Council of Action had a series of sittings recently when it took stock of the whole situation concerning the Indian Independence Movement in East Asia and the development of the revolutionary struggle in India. The enormous increase in the number of the members in the Indian Independence League, the wide network of League organisations throughout East Asia, the tremendous enthusiasm seen every where for the cause which we stand for and the spirit of sacrifice manifested by all classes of Indian in East Asia, have given us immense satisfaction in the progress of the Movement made possible by the help and co-operation of the Imperial Nipponese Government. The rapid march of revolutionary events in India resulting in the growing number of strikes, rebellions, sabotage and other mass actions have further raised our hopes and leave us in no doubt regarding the intentions and determination of our countrymen to overthrow British rule to regain our independence at any cost. We have new reached a stage at which we feel that before we take any further forward move it is necessary to clear matters, to understand our position perfectly and to cement Indo-Japanese friendship without which it is impossible for us to do any effective work for the attainment of our objective.

We are unfortunately so placed that we have not so far been able to contact with leaders in India and ascertain their views regarding our policy and own plans. This makes our responsibility all the more sacred and onerous. The time would not be distant when we shall have to deal with a provisional National Government in India and when that comes we must be in a position to convince them that we have taken every possible step to maintain the safety, dignity and integrity of our country when once our goal of independence has been reached.

We have, therefore, after very careful consideration, come to the conclusion that it will be advantageous and in the interests of our Movement to request the Imperial Government of Japan to favour us with a reply, at the earliest possible opportunity, clarifying the position on the following points :

1. A copy of the Bangkok Resolutions has been forwarded to the Imperial Government so long ago as the 22nd July (CSDIC (I) wrong, June) 2602. Though we have been working on the basis that such resolutions would be accepted by the Imperial Government we are not yet in a position to know exactly where we stand with regard to these resolutions. We do not want to conceal the fact that anxious enquiries are still being made by many leading members of our community regarding these resolutions and we find it difficult and even embarrassing to give them a satisfactory reply. It is therefore an urgent importance to us to request the Imperial Government to be good enough to inform us, formally and at the earliest possible opportunity, regarding the acceptance of the Bangkok Resolutions to which the Imperial Government cannot give their support, we shall be glad if they would kindly define their attitude towards the same.
2. Recognition of the Council of Action as the Supreme executive of the Indian Independence Movement in East Asia and the acceptance of their status as such is absolutely necessary in order that the Council of Action may function efficiently.
3. The Imperial Government must no doubt be aware of the propaganda that is being carried on the British Government in India regarding the intentions of Japan. Although we have had some declarations from His Excellency Premier General Tojo and other leading statesmen of Japan to the effect that Japan has no political or military ambitions in India, we would respectfully suggest that a full formal and solemn declaration binding on the present and future Government of Japan regarding the intentions of Japan to recognise and support the absolute independence

and full sovereignty of India immediately on the removal of British rule in India is found essential to instil complete confidence and to place the movement on an effective and proper footing.

4. As a corollary to the acceptance of the Bangkok Resolutions it is necessary that the formation and existance it is necessary that the formation and existence of the Indian National Army on the principles laid down in the said resolution will be formally and publicly recognised and all facilities offered for its expansion with a view to make the Army a strong and efficient one to carry out the great purpose for which it is intended.

We are conscious of and profoundly grateful to the Imperial. Government of Japan for, the great help they are rendering Indians in connection with this Movement and with further support, which we have no doubt will be forthcoming, we shall be able to attain our goal of Independence in the immediate future.

Dated This 29th Day of November, 2602.

Sgd. R.B. Bose,
President Council of Action
Indian Independence League.

139. On 30 Nov Iwakuru ordered all members of the Council of Action to meet him on the morning of 1 Dec.

The Storm Breaks

140. Bose and his Council presented themselves at about 1000 hrs. There were also present Mr. Senda 2 Japanese Diet members, and 2 or 3 senior Japanese officers besides Iwakuru. K.P.K. Menon was the Council of Action spokesman, Bose being far too dumb to cope with a situation like this. He spoke freely and boldly the mind of the Council in a speech which lasted for about 30 minutes. He said that the Japanese policy of continual delay had raised doubts in the minds of the Council of Action members and that while such doubts persisted the Council could not undertake to go on misleading the Indian public. Iwakuru replied in violent terms, accusing the Indians of having suspicious distrusting minds. He said that Indian Independence was as yet a babe unborn. It could only be seriously considered when the Japanese reached India. He, Iwakuru, was the representative of the Japanese Government, his view was the Government view, and he categorically refused to forward the letter. The meeting broke up at 1600 hrs after an excellent lunch.

141. H/1050 thinks that Iwakuru on that occasion acted in accordance with he instructions received from his C in C on the previous evening. Iwakuru himself would have liked to be less uncompromising.

142. H/1050 throughout the crisis had been in close daily touch with his INA senior officers, (majors and above), to whom he reported progress each evening. He had told them on the eve of Iwakuru's conference that he expected one of four things to happen. Iwakuru might refuse clarification point blank. He might be advised by other Japanese offrs to give way. He might compromise or he might begin another delaying action. H/1050 thought that either of the first two would be good, but that the third and fourth would be dangerous. He continued to inform his officers of every move and they knew exactly what was going on up to the end. H/1050 says that he was aware that Chatterji and Ehsan Qadir (B 978) reported all that went on at these conferences of officers to the Japanese. Both these officers were well in with Iwakuru and his underlings, and visited them frequently. B978 was carrying a whispering campaign against H/1050's position during this crisis. While H/1050 said that the Japanese were brutes, B 978 said "let us tame the brutes". He was suspected by all of secret dealings with the Japanese.

143. The Council of Action and the INA officers as a whole were rather relieved than sorry at the answer Iwakuru actually gave. The same day PW officers were summoned to a meeting in a PW camp, and were told by a Japanese officer that all Indian PW would be in future be treated as such, and that there would no longer be any chance for volunteering. H/1050 heard about this.

H/1050 Decides to Act

144. On the same evening H/1050 ordered that all surplus volunteers would revert to PW status. It was now quite clear to him that the Japanese only wanted a small INA of political and propaganda value : he also saw that they realised his own growing power and his real patriotism, and that they had decided they must check him. They must also know, he thought, that with such first class legal brains as Raghavan and Menon in the movement, they could only exploit Indians through a small army. They could trust, moreover their own tps with the available weapons better than Indians, and arms were in short supply. Finally, H/1050 felt that the Japanese had underestimated the Indian officers. They thought that they were men who had burned their boats, who would not now be received back into the British fold, and who would therefore finally submit to them.

145. From the INA point of view he considered the following things :

(a) Expansion was now clearly out of the question.

(b) The Burma offensive would certainly take place early in 1943.

(c) H/1050 would not be able to exercise effective control over his tps in Burma, scattered as they would be.

(d) Now the whole INA was concentrated, united in support of him, and any action he took would be thereby strengthened.

(e) If the Japanese later agreed to expansion, he would have great difficulty in carrying it out if committed to active service.

146. H/1050 therefore appreciated that the time had come for action. Menon entirely agreed, and all the points mentioned above had been discussed before and approved by INA senior officers. H/1050 knew of his own popularity with the Indian civilians, and decided that he must make some public demonstration of his feeling about Japanese insincerity. He told his officers that the movement could go on no longer. (*Comment* : At Appx B H/1050 alleges that it had been his intention from the first publicly to expose the Japanese if they proved insincere about India. It is considered that this claim should be treated with reserve.)

147. On 2 Dec 42 a further letter was sent to Iwakuru by Bose which said that he council of Action was seriously considering its own position. This is at Appx Q. A meeting of the Council of Action of which no minutes are available, discussed the present impossible situation. H/1050 and K.P.K. Menon suggested that the movement had played along with the Japanese for long enough, and that if any further collaboration was to take place it must be done after a conference of representatives and under a new Council of Action. H/1050 further said that it was now definite that not a soldier more of the INA could move from Malaya.

148. During 2 and 3 Dec great pressure was brought to bear on H/1050 by his Japanese friends and on 3 Dec Fujiwara arrived, having been summoned to bring H/1050 round. For 3 hrs Fujiwara tried to persuade H/1050 that this ship at least must go on 4 Dec, but H/1050 was adamant. H/1050 told the Council of Action about his stand in a session on the afternoon of 3 Dec. and his officers were informed during the same evening. By this time all INA senior officers had given H/1050 a pledge of their unconditional support, that they would resist all attempts by the Japanese to exploit them, and that should H/1050 be dismissed, or resign, they would under no circumstances continue the INA or raise another. This pledge was given at a meeting when Gill presided in H/1050's absence.

149. Fujiwara then approached individually each member of the C. of A. with some success, any H/1050 became a little annoyed with them for wavering. He put to the Council four demands (embodied in minutes of 5 Dec Appx R) without which he considered not movement should take place. Other questions, he said, could be settled at leisure. These must be conceded at once.

Resignations from Council of Action

150. On the morning of 4 Dec Raghavan resigned, and in his letter (Appx S(a)) excused himself by blaming H/1050 for the whole trouble. By the time the Council of Action met; however, Menon, Gilani and H/1050 had prevailed upon Raghavan to withdraw his letter for the sake of a collective resignation later. Raghavan was therefore present during the afternoon when the other three pur a draft letter of resignation for all to sign. Bose replied with a pathetic appeal for 2 months respite and promised to take up and solve all outstanding questions. (Minutes of this meeting are at Appx R) The draft resignation was withdrawn on Bose's promise.

151. Further consideration by Menon, Gilani and H/1050 only convinced them that Bose was playing Iwakuru's delaying game. Raghavan still vauered. On 5 Dec. therefore, they put up H/1050's four demands, and said they would resign if these were refused. These are embodied in the extracts from Council of Action minutes dated 5 Dec. reproduced at Appx R. If they were granted, the members concerned would consent to Bose's request for time. These points came to be known as "Mohan Singh's ultimatum". They were put to Iwakuru by Bose.

152. Iwakuru was even more outspoken than he had been on 1 Dec. and on 6 or 7 Dec categorically refused to consider this "ultimatum".

The Arrest of Gill

153. Before dawn on 8 Dec 42 the chief of the Kempei Tai[9] and 17 of his henchmen called upon H/1050 , and having wakened him, gave him a letter. The letter requested him to hand over Lt Col Gill who was wanted on charges "of a serious nature. The Kempei Tai chief had instructions to deal gently with H/1050 and if possible not to quarrel. The letter said that if Gill were handed over, no other member of the INA would ever be arrested. H/1050, however, refused to hand over Gill, knowing full well that his refusal would not make any difference. He was quite capable, he said, as Coc, of investigating any crime, and he must be told the charge. The Kemei Tai then proceeded to arrest Gill, H/1050 went with them to their office in order to ascertain the charges. A Japanese office took him aside and told him that Gill had sent a letter to the AG in India and that the Kempei Tai held a copy of it . H/1050 said that he did not believe this, but Gill was removed despite H/1050's violent protests, to the Kemei Tai lockup. The Japanese made further vain attempts to pacify the raging H/1050.

154. H/1050 told INA officers about the arrest of Gill on the same

9. Name of the Japanese Militery Police.

morning, saying that "the time" had come, that all ranks should now be ready for any sacrifice.

Resignations

155. The resignations of H/1050, Gilani and Menon had already been drafted when Gill was arrested. Raghavan sent in his resignation again during the morning, and when he was located by the other three towards evening he could not be persuaded to withdraw his letter once more and to resign jointly with them. He wished, says H/1050, to save both his face and his skin. Bose himself refused to resign, and the three therefore handed over their original joint lettrer, to which a paragraph referring to the arrest had been added. All resignations and Bose's replies are Appx S. Bose claimed that the only point of difference between himself and his resigning colleagues was whether or not to exercise "all patience" with the Japanese before deciding that the Movement had failed.

H/1050 Tells the INA

156. H/1050 spoke in Bidadari and Neesoon to all INA officers on 9 Dec. He told them the full story, already known to some of them. He appealed for unity and a spirit of sacrifice. He said that his duty was to fulfil the purpose for which the INA had been raised. He referred to the volunteers, oath and said he would take full responsibility. This was probably, he said, the end of the INA. Its continuance would only serve the designs of the Japanese and their puppet Bose who wanted to exploit PW for his own advantage. His audiences were profoundly moved and many, including H/1050 who says that nobody loved this army as he did, wept.

Further Correspondence 10-20 Dec

157. Bose, who was affecting to assume all power as the sole survivor of the Council of Action, now evidently realised that H/1050 was bent on dissolving the INA. He sent for all senior officers, with the notable exception of Gilani and H/1050, in an attempt to overpower H/1050's influence. The correspondence between H/1050 and Bose that followed this order is at Appx T. It ended in a crushing victory for H/1050 which probably decided his eventual fate.

158. On 15 Dec 42 H/1050 wrote to Iwakuru saying that all members of the INA would now revert to the status of PW, and that none of them and any confidence left in the Indian Independence Movement under the puppet Rash Behari Bose. Iwakuru's reply is given in H/1050's own words on page 8 of Appx B. He offered to let the INA work inside India, but this offer faded from his memory within 24 hours.

The Crisis Reported to India

159. On about 7 Dec H/1050, after discussion with Gill, felt that it was his duty to India by some means to convey there the news of what had happened so far. He knew that to help the British was now to help India, as it was quite evident that the Japanese were out only to exploit. At the same time he felt that he could not, because of his previous uncompromising attitude towards the British, and of the harsh things he had said about them, send intelligence to any British officer. He therefor selected 5 Sikh civilian recruits, of good education, who were natives of Kuala Lumpur and guaranteed reliable by Budh Singh, and old gentleman of Kuala Lumpur, who had been doing social work among PW there. (Comment : See CSDIC(I) report 978 para 6. This is the same man). These man were to proceed to Thailand, Burma and India in civilian guise. He made them learn their messages by heart and also gave them documents which they must absorb ad destroy before crossing the Malayan border. His instructions were to pass on the information to INA comds of PW camps, to Ram Sarup in Burma and to Congress leaders and Indian Officers of the Indian Army in India. The names of the 5 selected are :

1. Ajaib Singh
2. Kehar Singh
3. Dalip Singh
4. Ajit Singh
5. Mukham Singh

160. H/1050 says that between 7 Dec 42 ad 29 Dec 42 other men were detailed for similar duties by Gilani and Brar. Gilani agreed to pass information to India through Penang agents, if possible.

(Comments : The above information is confirmed generally by Gilani. Brar only knew of Nos 2 and 5 on the list above. He says they were commissioned to convey to various INA officers commanding PW Camps in Malaya, Thailand and Burma, news of what was happening, and to warn them not to let themselves be exploited by the Japanese. He knows of no order for these men go to India. Kehar Singh reached Bangkok, and having contacted the men whose names had been given to Brar by Gill, returned to report in Feb or Mar 43. Mukham Singh did not go further than the borders of Malaya. He did not join the 2nd INA and 6 months before the Japanese surrender he joined the Communist guerillas in Malaya because he was being pursued by the Kempei Tai.)

The Dissolution of the INA and the Arrest of H/1050

161. A warning order for the dissolution was issued on 21 Dec. It contained a full statement of the situation, and said that as the purpose for

which the INA was raised could not be served, duty to India demanded that it be dissolved. H/1050 also sent a secret letter to all units, which was marked "To be opened in the event of the removable, disappearance, assassination or arrest of the GOC". This contained final orders for the dissolution, for the removal of badges of ranks the burning of records, the absolution of all ranks from their personal pledge to H/1050, and their reversion to PW status. The purpose of this letter was not to make the dissolution conditional upon the arrest of H/1050, but to forestall and sudden attempt to take control of the INA before H/1050 was ready to dissolve it. (*Comment* : Gilani, who seems to have had a foot in each camp within the Council of Action, says that H/1050 delayed the dissolution because he still hoped to reach a separate understanding with the Japanese. Eshan Qadir (B978 (I) Report 978 (para 39 (I)) refers to Raghavan's anxiety to obtain control of the INA).

162. Although all this was now purely an army matter, K.P.M. Menon continued in the complete confidence of H/1050 and was informed of every move.

163. H/1050 may have held a few more meetings of officers between 21 and 29 Dec. On the morning of 29 Dec Iwakuru asked H/1050 to meet him at 1100 hours. Before he went H/1050 received a second message, that Iwakuru wished to see all INA officers of the rank of Major and above at INA HQ at 1200 hrs. H/1050 told his officers they he might not return from this interview, and ascertained that all his instructions were understood.

164. At Iwakuru's house there were also present Bose, Senda and four or five Japanese officers. When H/1050, arrived, Bose produced from his pocket a letter (H/1050 says not drafted by Bose) and handed it to H/1050. This was a dismissal and a statement of charges, clearly the sequel to the series of letters reproduced at Appx. T. It ended by saying that in consideration of his services H/1050 would be saved alive and provided with he necessities of life. H/1050 replied that this final injustice was not altogether unexpected, but that he understood how Bose wasn't really responsible for it. Iwakuru then read in Japanese, and para by para, Senda read in English, along statement setting out Japanese charges against H/1050 and answering H/1050's own accusations against the Japanese. H/1050 thinks that copies of this statement were subsequently distributed on a wide scale. H/1050's reply, although no reply to such a categorical document was strictly called for, was that he had done all in the interests of his country. H/1050 was then arrested and he never saw the INA again.

Remarks by H/1050

165. At this point H/1050 gives a summary of his intentions for and

views about the first INA. This follows the lines of his "public statement" at Appx "B".[10]

(a) He began it because he saw an opportunity of serving his country. He recognised the risks, but also realised that nothing worthwhile is ever accomplished without running risks.

(b) Had the Japanese remained sincere, there would today have been no distinction of volunteer and non-volunteer. All PW would have been united in the INA. Civilians too, -1942 was a time when every Indian worth the name was prepared to bear arms should a worthy purpose and a worthy leader appear : the INA would by now have been immense. The purpose of such an army was that it should go into action in Burma, and by suffering a very few casualties arouse such a storm of public feeling in India and in allied countries as would compel the British to come to terms with Congress. If this did not occur, the INA would fight to the last man. 1942 was the psychological moment, the INA might have achieved its purpose then, but the moment could not recur.

(c) Whatever concessions were after the dissolution wrong from the Japanese were —due to the brave stand made in 1942 by officers and men of the INA, and to a few brave and forthright civilians, one of whom was K.P.K. Menon. A second factor was, of course, the changing tide of war. The Japanese at no time honestly wished the freedom either of India or of any other country which they could subject by force.

(d) H/1050's decision in Dec. 42 was the result of mature and careful thought, and not of a sudden brainstorm. It was not easy for him to destroy that which he had created, but he was convinced that India's interests demanded its destruction.

(e) H/1050 categorically denies the suggestion made to "S" Section by Lt Col Gill that Lt. Col. Gill was in any way responsible, save as a supporter of H/1050, for the destruction of the INA. The matter had never been discussed by H/1050 and Gill before Dec. 42.

---

9. Appendix II.

Index

C

G

H

K

L

M

N

O

P

W

Y